The American Blockbuster

The American Blockbuster

Movies That Defined Their Generations

Benjamin Crace

BLOOMSBURY ACADEMIC
NEW YORK • LONDON • OXFORD • NEW DELHI • SYDNEY

BLOOMSBURY ACADEMIC
Bloomsbury Publishing Inc
1385 Broadway, New York, NY 10018, USA
50 Bedford Square, London, WC1B 3DP, UK
29 Earlsfort Terrace, Dublin 2, Ireland

BLOOMSBURY, BLOOMSBURY ACADEMIC and the Diana logo
are trademarks of Bloomsbury Publishing Plc

First published in the United States of America by ABC-CLIO 2022
Paperback edition published by Bloomsbury Academic 2025

Copyright © Bloomsbury Publishing Inc, 2025

Cover Photo: Star Wars: A New Hope. (ScreenProd/Photononstop/Alamy Stock Photo);
Black Pamther.(Photo 12/Alamy Stock Photo); Back to the Future. (Photo 12/Alamy
Stock Photo); Finding Nemo.(Pictorial Press Ltd/Alamy Stock Photo)

All rights reserved. No part of this publication may be reproduced or transmitted
in any form or by any means, electronic or mechanical, including photocopying,
recording, or any information storage or retrieval system, without prior
permission in writing from the publishers.

Bloomsbury Publishing Inc does not have any control over, or responsibility for,
any third-party websites referred to or in this book. All internet addresses given
in this book were correct at the time of going to press. The author and publisher
regret any inconvenience caused if addresses have changed or sites have
ceased to exist, but can accept no responsibility for any such changes.

Library of Congress Cataloging-in-Publication Data
Names: Crace, Benjamin, author.
Title: The American blockbuster : movies that defined their generations /
Benjamin Crace.
Description: Santa Barbara, California : Greenwood, an imprint of ABC-CLIO,
LLC, [2022] | Includes bibliographical references.
Identifiers: LCCN 2022007539 | ISBN 9781440877803 (hardcover) |
ISBN 9781440877810 (ebook)
Subjects: LCSH: Blockbusters (Motion pictures)—United States—History. |
National characteristics, American, in motion pictures. | Generations—United States. |
Motion pictures—Social aspects—United States. | BISAC: PERFORMING ARTS /
Film / General | PERFORMING ARTS / Film / Direction & Production
Classification: LCC PN1995.9.B598 C73 2022 | DDC 791.430973—dc23/eng/20220810
LC record available at https://lccn.loc.gov/2022007539

ISBN: HB: 978-1-4408-7780-3
PB: 979-8-7651-6704-5
ePDF: 978-1-4408-7781-0
eBook: 979-8-2161-8418-8

To find out more about our authors and books visit www.bloomsbury.com
and sign up for our newsletters.

Contents

List of Figures ix

Preface xi

Introduction xiii

Section 1: Thematic Essays

The Socialization Process: How Films Define Generational Consciousness 3

Capitalism and the Film Industry: Creating and Distributing Cinema in the Age of Television 15

The American Myth Machine: Film as a National Visual Literature 27

American Religiosity in the Age of Entertainment: Hollywood and American Values 39

Section 2: Boomers Make the Blockbuster (1975–1982)

Alien 53

Close Encounters of the Third Kind 57

E.T.: The Extra-Terrestrial 61

The Exorcist 65

Grease 69

Indiana Jones and the Raiders of the Lost Ark 73

Jaws 76

Kramer vs. Kramer 80

9 to 5 84

One Flew over the Cuckoo's Nest 88

Rocky 92

Star Wars: A New Hope 96

Superman 100

Tootsie 104

Section 3: Xers on a Quest for Identity and Belonging (1983–1998)

Back to the Future 109

Batman 113

Beauty and the Beast 117

Beverly Hills Cop 122

Forrest Gump 125

Ghostbusters 129

Home Alone 133

Independence Day 138

Jurassic Park 141

The Lion King 145

Star Wars: Return of the Jedi 148

Terminator 2: Judgment Day 153

Titanic 156

Top Gun 161

Toy Story 165

Section 4: Millennials and the American Myth Machine (1999–2009)

Avatar 169

The Dark Knight 173

The Fast and the Furious 177

Finding Nemo 181

Harry Potter and the Philosopher's Stone/Harry Potter and the Chamber of Secrets 185

Iron Man 190

The Lord of the Rings: The Fellowship of the Ring   194

The Matrix   198

Pirates of the Caribbean: The Curse of the Black Pearl   202

Shrek   205

Spider-Man   210

Star Wars: Episode 1—The Phantom Menace   213

Transformers   217

Twilight   221

X-Men   225

Section 5: Gen Z Finds Its Heroes (2010–)

The Avengers   231

Black Panther   236

The Dark Knight Rises   240

Despicable Me   245

Fast and Furious 7   250

Frozen   253

The Hunger Games   257

Inception   262

Joker   266

Skyfall   270

Star Wars: The Force Awakens   276

Wonder Woman   280

Zootopia   284

Bibliography   291

About the Editor and Contributors   309

Index   311

List of Figures

Figure 1: Brian Sturm's Storylistening Experience Model   9

Figure 2: Pew Religious Landscape Study   42

Figure 3: Pew Religious Landscape Study inset 1   43

Figure 4: Pew Religious Landscape Study inset 2   44

Figure 5: Six-in-ten Christians, "nones," hold at least one New Age belief   46

Figure 6: U.S. adults who say they are neither religious nor spiritual tend to reject New Age beliefs   47

Preface

Movie making and movie-going are perhaps two quintessential activities shared by Americans today. We love our audiovisual media, cannot get enough of it, carry it in our pockets, and stream it rather than sleep. We film ourselves, each other, our cats, our food, our travels, pretty sunsets, and leaves. In one sense, we have learned from Hollywood, that great metonym for filmmaking, that the real is not quite real until it has been filmed and watched. See the proud parents holding high their phones at concerts or sports matches: "I was there, I filmed it; see?" Some of us take filming to another level and perhaps attend one of the many film schools cropping up all over the country. Hoping to be the next Spielberg or Coppola, many quickly realize how difficult it is and opt for studying films instead of making them.

This is where a resource like this text comes in. It provides accessible summary and analysis of some of the greatest films of the last four decades. But unlike other reference works, it attempts to see these films with the twin lenses of "America" and "generation." How are these films products of their time and place? How do they transcend their particular cultural moment? How do they themselves become a part of what constitutes those moments and the ones that come "downstream," as it were? How do they help contest and construct American generational identity from one to the next? In short, what do they *mean* beyond their plots and sophisticated spectacles? Clearly, movies are more than an escape from the mundane world; they are art that reminds us and sometimes tells us who we are, where we have been, and where we are going.

Of course, a volume like this says as much about what it leaves out as what is included. The films included are blockbusters, that is, they are the highest-earning films within the years selected for each section. Such information is readily available on the internet. There are many beloved classics that did not break into the top 10 or even the top 20 in their respective time frames; their greatness was only discovered or rediscovered by later audiences. It is also true that "blockbuster" does not equate to quality. Just because a film earns a lot of money by cashing in on bored parents during summer vacation does not make it a master class in directing, acting, scriptwriting, or cinematography. But they are cultural artifacts that have flooded our collective unconscious, permeating it in ways too profound to fully articulate in many volumes much less a single one. To adapt one of Kurt Vonnegut's lines about his protagonist's mother in *Slaughterhouse Five*, "Like so many Americans, she was trying to construct a life that made sense from the things she found in gift shops," the underlying assumption of this volume is that we the people of the United States are trying to construct a life that makes sense from the things we find in our movies.

As the editor and primary contributor of this text, I must express my appreciation for my family: my wife Amy, and Isaiah, Isaac, and Lily, my three wonderful kids. They all endured hours of meticulous film screenings throughout the COVID pandemic. I had not intended to do a book like this during such an upheaval, but who does? Next, I owe a deep debt of gratitude to my contributors, of course: Dina, Angelica, Derek, Katherine, and Josh. I also appreciate Catherine Lafuente's early editorial assistance at the beginning of the project and then Erin Ryan's all the rest of the way. Special thanks to Matt Hill, who recommended ABC-CLIO in the first place and got the proverbial ball rolling. I hope reading this volume will be as enlightening and enjoyable as writing and editing it were.

Introduction

Films have occupied a central place in the American landscape. Although they were invented in Europe, it was American entrepreneurship and innovation that turned a novelty into an industry that has changed the course of history. Aside from affecting large-scale events and trends, films have helped shape a shared sense of identity, a way of being in the world. Not all films belong in this register of influence. The ones that do can be singled out by their popularity, signaled by their profitability. And while elitist notions of popular culture versus "high" culture often exclude the films that actually make a ton of money, these are, nonetheless, the movies that have the widest and perhaps longest impact—often to the befuddlement of critics who want less "fun" and more art than artifice.

AMERICAN

What does it mean to be "American"? Perhaps it consists of simply living within a shared geopolitical boundary. For some, it means a rather exclusive history that begins with European settlers, particularly English-speaking ones, who "founded" the nation on the rational values derived from the Enlightenment. Here a certain kind of politics, philosophy, and religion are often viewed as universal and transcendental rather than peculiar expressions of their time and place. Such views have, justifiably, been weighed and found wanting, leading to more inclusive dialogues and debates about whether there actually is a common identity that can be called "American." Increased multiculturalism and pluralism, due to increased immigration and high-speed forms of global communication and travel, have laid bare simplistic notions of "us" and "them." The hybridizing juggernaut of globalization itself has smoothed out, if not erased, the sharp demarcations of national identity that existed just 100 years ago. In response to these changes, some Americans have dug in, tapping into reservoirs of nationalism if not also white supremacy and conspiracy theory, such as the idea, among others, that the global elite are clearly arranging the end of national sovereignty.

Yet despite the polarization in the American landscape, non-Americans clearly see "American" as a type that can be identified, especially when Americans travel abroad. While only 42 percent of Americans own a passport (compared with 76 percent of Brits), those who do travel outside the spacious boundaries of the States have earned a reputation for being loud, obnoxious, demanding, insensitive, and generally ignorant of local customs and cultures. And while the novel *The Ugly American* is more than 60 years old, its fictional representation of this type seems as relevant today as it did during the Cold War. Any American expatriate who has lived for an extended time outside of the United States can tell numerous stories of unguarded moments when their non-American hosts have really expressed their true feelings for these "innocents abroad," as Mark Twain called American tourists in his 1869 novel of the same name. In one particularly telling and humorous scene, Twain depicts a group of American tourists in Genoa, Christopher Columbus's birthplace, being shown a letter written by the navigator himself by their local, Italian guide:

"Come wis me, genteelmen!—come! I show you ze letter writing by Christopher Colombo!—write it himself!—write it wis his own hand!—come!"

He took us to the municipal palace. After much impressive fumbling of keys and opening of locks, the stained and aged document was spread before us. The guide's eyes sparkled. He danced about us and tapped the parchment with his finger:

"What I tell you, genteelmen! Is it not so? See! Handwriting Christopher Colombo!—write it himself!"

We looked indifferent—unconcerned. The doctor examined the document very deliberately, during a painful pause.—Then he said, without any show of interest:

"Ah—Ferguson—what—what did you say was the name of the party who wrote this?"

"Christopher Colombo! Ze great Christopher Colombo!"

Another deliberate examination.

"Ah—did he write it himself; or—or how?"

"He write it himself!—Christopher Colombo! He's own hand-writing, write by himself!"

Then the doctor laid the document down and said:

"Why, I have seen boys in America only fourteen years old that could write better than that."

"But zis is ze great Christo—"

"I don't care who it is! It's the worst writing I ever saw. Now you mustn't think you can impose on us because we are strangers. We are not fools, by a good deal. If you have got any specimens of penmanship of real merit, trot them out!—and if you haven't, drive on!"[1]

In typical Twain fashion, he later demurs, "That joke was lost on the foreigner—guides cannot master the subtleties of the American joke." Yet the "joke" only works for a reader precisely because the tourists are playing (intentionally, apparently) into a type while riling up the local. But in another sense, Twain's closing comment could be seen ironically; the condescension involved in making one's guide the butt of a joke is exactly why non-Americans are easily frustrated and confounded by American tourists.

But perhaps foreign judgments on the 42 percent of Americans who do travel abroad are not indicative of the other 58 percent who stay home. Perhaps, too, when Americans leave the confines of the country, they change. As the Burmese journalist in *The Ugly American* says, "For some reason, the [American] people I meet in my country are not the same as the ones I knew in the United States. A mysterious change seems to come over Americans when they go to a foreign land. They isolate themselves socially. They live pretentiously. They are loud and ostentatious."[2]

Maybe travel reveals what was always there, simmering below the surface. But who are we when we are together, at home?

We are moviegoers. And it is in and through film we express and learn what it means to be "American." And films have taught us well. How prescient and germane is the speech on freedom by Edgar Friendly (Denis Leary), in the dystopic film *Demolition Man* (1993):

> I like to think, I like to read. I'm into freedom of speech and freedom of choice. I'm the kind of guy who wants to sit in a greasy spoon and think, "Gee, should I have the T-bone steak or the jumbo rack of barbecued ribs with the side order of gravy fries?" I want high cholesterol. I want to eat bacon, butter and buckets of cheese, okay? I want to smoke a Cuban cigar the size of Cincinnati in a non-smoking section. I wanna run through the streets naked with green Jell-o all over my body reading *Playboy* magazine. Why? Because I suddenly might feel the need to.[3]

Here uninhibited and unhealthy choices and antisocial behavior demarcate freedom. And it would seem this is exactly the kind of "freedom" many Americans have in mind when they hear the word. As a text of popular culture, Friendly's speech also reveals another key value that is perhaps the cornerstone of American culture and that recurs throughout cinema (and is shown in the films in this volume): individualism—or, more bluntly, that the individual is sacred; choice is sacred. The "world" out there is simply the arena where *my* desires are simultaneously frustrated and enacted. And there need not be a reason; "because I suddenly might feel the need to" is sufficient.

It is too facile and reductionistic to see moviegoing as an escape from the stress and anxieties of life. Beyond escapism, then, American blockbusters, in particular, are uniquely situated to certify the reality of "America" and source a shared, remembered mythology. In Walker Percy's novel *The Moviegoer* (1961), Binx Bolling is a stand-in for all Americans seeking existential enlightenment under our Bodhi tree, the silver screen. Percy, thinly veiled in the protagonist, speaks of "certification":

> Nowadays when a person lives somewhere, in a neighborhood, the place is not certified for him. More than likely he will live there sadly and the emptiness which is inside him will expand until it evacuates the entire neighborhood. But if he sees a movie which shows his very neighborhood, it becomes possible for him to live, for a time at least, as a person who is Somewhere and not Anywhere.[4]

Extending this concept beyond the neighborhood, when any place in America comes on the screen, we all become a person who is somewhere and not anywhere; we belong. New York is as much ours as Spider-Man's and Tony Stark's;

Chicago as much as Kevin's in *Home Alone*; and Los Angeles as much as all *The Fast and The Furious*'s. Recognizable American locations certify America for the moviegoer and become, for many, pilgrimage sites, made so on and by film (one wonders how many Instagram photos feature Times Square).

Films also source our collective memory and form our national mythology. Again, Percy's Binx Bolling waxes reflectively:

> The fact is I am quite happy in a movie, even a bad movie. Other people, so I have read, treasure memorable moments in their lives: the time one climbed the Parthenon at sunrise, the summer night one met a lonely girl in Central Park and achieved with her a sweet and natural relationship, as they say in books. I too once met a girl in Central Park, but it was not much to remember. What I remember is the time John Wayne killed three men with a carbine as he was falling to the dusty street in *Stagecoach*, and the time the kitten found Orson Welles in the doorway in the *Third Man*.

In an increasingly digital age of paradoxical fragmentation and connection, our shared cinematic memory is what unites us more than physical experiences do. Percy's audience of the '60s would have recognized the alluded-to films, sharing both Bolling's experience and its content. And while many Americans may be politically, racially, and religiously divided, "I am Iron Man" and "Life is like a box of chocolates" are literally scripts that run through all of our memories. Some of us have avoided the ocean for years because of *Jaws* and can never say "let it go" to anyone else without singing it.

In sum, moviegoing is the great American pastime, and to understand America, one has to consider its films—especially the ones that drew the largest crowds and made the most money: the blockbusters.

BLOCKBUSTER AND GENERATIONS

The movies in this volume represent just a slice of the films produced in a given period. The deciding criteria for which ones were included and which were not was relatively simple: money. Thus, the top-grossing films for the chosen time frame (discussed below) are featured. In some cases, a tie warranted including both. But here again, one must be cautious about falling into critical snobbery and the aforementioned notions of high and low culture. Simply because a film is a blockbuster and has earned significant profits does not mean that it is not significant as a cultural artifact through which America is refracted. America *is* its popular culture, for the people, by the people. As "the pursuit of happiness" is enshrined in our national documents, we can echo as a truism Bolling's self-disclosure: "I am quite happy in a movie, even a bad movie."

The other criterion for the selections in this volume is related to the concept of generations. While a contested term in and of itself, most sources divide Americans into four and sometimes five cohorts with the following birth years:

Greatest Generation: 1898–1927

Silent Generation: 1928–1945

Baby Boomers: 1946–1964

Generation X: 1965–1980
Millennials: 1981–1996
Generation Z: 1997–2012[5]

Again, for convenience, the entries and essays will sometimes conflate the Greatest Generation and the Silent Generation as simply the parents of the Boomers, in whose lifetimes the blockbuster first emerged.

For this volume, I have added the extra distinction that a person does not attend and remember a film as an infant. Consequentially, the date ranges are set from the first blockbuster (*Jaws*, 1975) to roughly the times when the next generation would have started moviegoing in earnest. Thus, the oldest Boomer would have seen *Jaws* at 39 and the youngest at 11. A Gen Xer is not as likely to remember watching *Jaws* in the theater (the oldest Gen Xer would have been but 10 at the time) but probably can recall *Back to the Future* (1985) at 20 and so on. As with most things, generational cohorts are not tidy boxes with sharp delineations, and movies are not made just for one generation. Some lean toward one generation more than others, of course—especially when that generation is at peak moviegoing habits and has cash.

Dividing and analyzing films in these ways show both the consistency of American values throughout generations and their constant renegotiation. Or as the saying goes, "The more things change, the more they stay the same." Yet there are things that are new under the sun, and the world of the Gen Zer is a radically different place than the earlier world of the Boomer—even if they spend holidays together. These differences are constantly in tension onscreen and off, as each generation vies for what truly constitutes the American Dream.

THEMATIC ESSAYS

This volume begins with a set of essays meant to situate the reader more specifically in the American film context. The first, "The Socialization Process: How Films Define Generational Consciousness," examines the mechanisms of how Americans are introduced and induced to consume films as a meaningful activity. Following a brief, autobiographical "thick description" in the cultural anthropological register, it explores how films entrance the individual and form a sense of social identity and cohesion.

The next essay, "Capitalism and the Film Industry: Creating and Distributing Cinema in the Age of Television," investigates the economic underpinnings of the entertainment industry at large and how television and streaming services have challenged Hollywood. Katherine Hennessey provocatively suggests that television and the proliferation of streaming services have "paved the way for greater diversity on film screens." Such a hopeful note, sounded for the further democratization of the entertainment industry, is much needed.

Eliding with some of the aforementioned observations and comments, Angelica DeAngelis's contribution, "The American Myth Machine: Film as a National Visual Literature," takes a deep dive into how film is, in fact, our new and most widely accessed national literature. After a brilliant historical overview of both the film industry and film studies, she more thoroughly contextualizes the relationships between the generations and American mythologizing.

The final essay, "American Religiosity in the Age of Entertainment: Hollywood and American Values," hits the exposed nerve of that ever-shifting landscape of American religion. Offering a reading through the lens of spirituality rather than "religion," it contends that cinema promotes a worldview that is roughly contiguous with a "faith" that rests on a blend of scientism and occultism rather than traditional Christianity and/or secularism. What is emerging, then, as evident in the blockbusters of the last two decades, is a new kind of postsecular mythology that is at once self-actualizing, spiritually aware, socially conscious, and, of course, patently American.

CONCLUSION

While many of the entries in this volume can standalone and be referenced individually, there is a unifying thread that runs throughout: "American" . . . "blockbuster" . . . "generation." Alternating between this triad and the contents of the films themselves, each contributor artfully offers more than just a simple reference entry for the curious or to save someone a trip to Wikipedia's page. In contrast, such heavily meditated-upon interpretations of the widely known blockbusters included here offer the opportunity for any member of any generation to see themselves reflected in their favorite texts and, perhaps, to get a glimpse of the other American.

NOTES

1. https://www.gutenberg.org/files/3176/3176-h/3176-h.htm.
2. William J. Lederer and Eugene Burdick, *The Ugly American* (1958).
3. https://www.imdb.com/title/tt0106697/characters/nm0001459.
4. https://www.goodreads.com/work/quotes/1209450-the-moviegoer?page=2.
5. https://www.pewresearch.org/fact-tank/2019/01/17/where-millennials-end-and-generation-z-begins. N.b.: This link does not include the span of years for the Greatest Generation; I extrapolated those myself.

I

Thematic Essays

The Socialization Process: How Films Define Generational Consciousness

It is difficult to recall my first experience going to the movies. I am sure that my parents took me as a child, before I could make conscious memories. I am also sure that some of these films were probably not appropriate for younger viewers; I distinctly recall them taking my infant sister to see *Predator* while on vacation. My brother and I were fine on our own at the hotel, but there was no one to watch her. So instead, her infant senses experienced Arnold Schwarzenegger killing an alien hunter. I have to admit, I was a bit jealous. But somewhere in those layered memories lies the first experience, one that was repeated over and over again all over the world.

Going to the movies, while different for everyone, is an American ritual and consists of similar movements and practices. Given the consistency of these practices across the cultural landscape, it is appropriate to attempt to provide a particular example as a potential representative type of the social phenomenon. Clifford Geertz, an American anthropologist, suggested that the qualitative study of cultural artifacts and rituals should involve a "thick description" of the activity in as detailed a narrative as possible. Out of this precritical narrative, various analyses can be applied. So before discussing how the experience socializes generations, let's detail the experience as thickly as possible—remembering, too, that the following narrative emerges from my own experience as a situated subject who is limited by his own cultural biases, perceptions, and so on.

My parents chose the film based on my interests as a young boy in the Appalachian foothills of East Tennessee. The film was *Star Wars: Return of the Jedi*. It was 1983. Undoubtedly, my father, a sci-fi fan, also wanted to see it. He and my mother knew it was playing that weekend from the shopping center's marquis that faced the main street in our small city of about 6,000 people. Perhaps they read the movie listings in the newspaper (literacy and print culture) or called the cinema to get the showtimes. Given the theater's limited capacity (two screens), only two films at a time were featured. I forget the name of the other film that was offered.

In hindsight as an adult, I realize that a matinee (economic and class consciousness) would have been cheaper, but nonetheless, we went on opening night.

The Capri Theatre was a unique building in the town. The British spelling of "theater" together with the name of an Italian island made it seem more exotic. (I, of course, did not know these things then.) It was square and squat, painted mostly white with red lettering. There was nothing ostentatious about the outer appearance except the dozens of rows of naked light bulbs slanted on the recessed front entrance. They appeared to be guiding you, like lights on a runway, toward the ticket office and then into the theater (most basic of attractions: bright lights). The four of us—my parents, my brother, and I—walked up to the ticket booth: "Two adults and two children for *Jedi*." My dad paid with cash out of his wallet.

Once inside, the place was decorated with red carpet, and the walls were covered with posters of previous and upcoming films. The refreshment counter was front and center, selling buttered popcorn, fountain drinks, chocolate, and candy. As per usual, these items were overpriced compared to what one could purchase outside of the cinema. Unlike other families, mine never sneaked in snacks. Again, as a child, I did not notice the price of the candy. Rather, I was too excited about the film, my small Coke, Reese's Peanut Butter Cups, and the size of the tub of popcorn my dad had purchased for us to share. I did plan on sitting next to him, so I would not have to get the popcorn secondhand.

After giving our tickets to the vested employee, who tore them and admitted us through the red velvet stanchion, we went to the entrance of Screen 1. My mother, knowing the size of our bladders and the size of our drinks, ordered my brother and me to use the conveniently located restroom before we got settled in our seats.

The theater itself was lit from high above in the dark gray ceiling, illuminating the seats and the curtained screen but not much more. Other dark, red curtains with luxurious folds hung from the ceilings down to the floors along each side. I quickly and furtively lifted one up to see what was behind it: a plain, concrete block wall. My dad chose four seats in a row of five in about the middle of the room but off to the side, close to the wall. With the empty seat and the wall on one side and my dad on the aisle seat, we were safely blocked in from strangers (security). Once settled to the left of my father, I noticed the glowing red exit signs on either side of the screen. Craning my neck behind and up, I could see the shadow of the projectionist preparing the film. Given this was opening night for a *Star Wars* film, the crowd that had been in the lobby with us buying refreshments now joined us, and the seats, arranged in their amphitheater fashion, filled up. The lights dimmed, my brother loudly slurped the last of his Coke from the paper cup, and the curtain rose.

All eyes were on the screen in front, the most brightly lit object that towered over us all, casting its reflected light on the eyes of everyone there. From the tiny tube in the booth behind us, the moving pictures were larger than life, captivating. After the perfunctory, theater-specific advertisements and codes of conduct (no smoking, location of emergency exits, stay quiet), there were a few previews and then the feature presentation. I was rocking in my thickly cushioned seat, enabled by the fact that it was the kind in which the bottom half would automatically fold up without weight. By displacing my weight on the shared armrests, I could get it to raise me up. My dad, annoyed by the squeaking and the movement, whispered in the darkness for me to stop. I had forgotten he was there, so absorbed was I by the film, the loud noise, and the effects of excessive amounts of salt, caffeine, and sugar.

At some point, I think it was during the scene where the Emperor is trying to recruit Luke to the Dark Side as he looks through a window at his friends being destroyed, I became aware of my full bladder. Moments like these are etched into one's memory; if you missed moments in a film in 1983, you either had to come back to the cinema to see it again or get someone else to tell you what happened. Freighted with this knowledge, I held it as long as I could, but then, bored by all the dialogue anyway, I asked my mom to take me to the restroom, saying, "I'll be quick!"

Stumbling out of the cinema partway through a film, back into the liminal reality of the cordoned-off zones to find the bathroom you just used an hour before is one of the essential parts of going to the movies—for children and adults. The cold, hard porcelain and fluorescent brightness, the sensation of release, and the wet water splashed on the hands to make mom happy are like defibrillator shocks to the imagination, the dream of the film losing its reality the longer one is absent. Upon nestling back into my seat, I knew better than to ask anyone what I had missed.

Throughout the film, as I recall, there was a sense of "us." "We," the theatergoers, the *Star Wars* fans (I owned dozens of the Kenner action figures as well as the hard-to-get ones, rare commodities you had to send UPC codes from cereal boxes to obtain) and the Rebels in the film were all in "this" together. When the Rebels, with the help of the Ewoks, beat back the Imperial Forces on the moon of Endor, we cheered with them. When Vader tossed the Emperor to his death, we cheered together. And when Williams's score swelled as we, with Luke, witnessed the Rebel Forces ghosts of Yoda, Obi-Wan Kenobi, and Anakin, many of us may have shed a tear or two. My mind was recording every moment, filling its cache with all the nuances and details I could capture. Returning to school on Monday having seen the film would greatly increase my social capital, and, when playing with my brother (who was always Han Solo), we could re-create and extend the cinematic experience for weeks and months at our house. Little did I know at the time that the images, narratives, and conversations from this viewing would last for decades. Even now I am talking about it.

One advantage of watching a film at night is that you avoid the unpleasant experience of going from a darkened theater to the bright sunshine. Thus you get to stay in the dream a little longer, going through the motions of collecting your detritus from what seems like ages ago and putting it in the trash can as another vested employee with the broom and dustpan waits nearby to purify the space for the next showing. There is always something final about leaving a building through a different door from which you came in. That heavy steel door with the stainless push bar spat each one of us back into reality, while that sense of "us" we had all attained inside was diffused all over the parking lot, as we all went our separate ways.

There are many things that could be said about this "thick description," which serves as the common grounding narrative for my own subsequent analysis and the readers' construction of meaning, eliding their own experiences with my own. I hope in this creative depiction of the experience, readers found themselves both in agreement at points ("Oh, I remember that!") and at odds ("That's never happened to me."). One of the tasks of sociology is to defamiliarize the familiar in order to see anew the occluded aspects of social experience. Here the experience is one of mass communication, of a "text" of popular culture. As a "text," both the film and the experience of watching it at the theater can be "read," that is, interpreted and interrogated. Multiple meanings arise from this inductive process, moving from the particular in the narrative to generalized abstractions that use interdisciplinary discourse (here mainly sociology and cultural studies). Unpacking these meanings demonstrates how a singular experience contributes to the socialization process into American culture.

My experience of viewing *Return of the Jedi* as a young Gen Xer is one that is shared with many in my generational cohort as well as with our Boomer parents. Yet there are aspects of this experience that flag American assumptions about the way social events are structured. The presence and availability of certain products and practices are rooted in historical and cultural processes that extend much deeper and further back than what is apparent in the surface. As an upper-middle-class family in a rural, Appalachian community, the act of "going to the movies" is charged with layers of significance. Given the price of and time commitment to performing such an activity, my family's presence at the Capri that night signaled our status among our peers. This status was carried over and reproduced in front of my school peers the next week, when I related to them my story of the experience; many of them came from families too poor to go to the movies. Another social layer involves the religiosity of the region. Going to the movies in my hometown, a home to many fundamentalist sects of Christianity, was seen by many as a form of sin against God. The actual content of the film did not matter. At this point, my parents did not see the mystical elements of the Jedi order in the film as pernicious to my spiritual development—that would come later. As church attendance was widely practiced and expected, some church members, upon learning of your attendance at the cinema, would be in doubt as to your commitment to Jesus. Thus going to the movies was not simply entertainment or something to do as a means of escape.

At another level, going to the movies was (and is) a form of participation in the American capitalist economy and in deeply rooted populist ideas. Money earned in a laissez-faire marketplace where hard work and effort are rewarded helps one obtain access to the goods and services that, in the past, would have been reserved for the aristocracy. Americans, who want to believe that we are a nation without social classes, hold strongly to this myth of egalitarianism obtained through expressed individualism: "I work to earn money to enact my choices out in a supposed-to-be fair world." Such an attitude hardly recognizes various and sundry forms of systemic injustice and how tastes and "free choices" are predetermined and prepackaged through social structures. What we think of as "our choice" is already, to some degree, a conditioned response to the ubiquitous and overwhelming presence of advertising. This is seen in the "choice" of the film (market-dependent availability) and the choice of refreshments (Coke or Diet Coke? Reese's Peanut

Butter Cups or Snickers?). We are culturally structured and awash in the white noise of consumerism; the cinema itself is part of a strip mall, near a grocery store, roller rink, and a fast-food restaurant. Additionally, the ability, based on that other American sense of how the world works, to choose one's seats at the theater on a first-come, first-served basis serves to strengthen that necessary sense of a free agent making decisions on a rational basis between various options. Americans, to quote the poem "Invictus," by William Henley, are "masters of our fate."

The enacting of personal choice extends beyond the individual; Americans choose where and when to come together as groups. Of the many places this choice occurs—sporting events, schools, public transport, religious gatherings, political rallies, restaurants, and so on—cinemas by their very structure are prime locations for socialization to occur (the mechanics of this will be discussed below). And while mass shootings have happened in various venues, real violence in the cushioned, dark sanctuary of the theater seems particularly transgressive and uncanny. But, to return to choice making, deciding to sit together under a similar code of conduct (direct and indirectly communicated: no smoking, male friends must leave a seat between them, loud conversations are forbidden, don't block another's view, don't stand in front of the screen, limit how many times you inconvenience someone in your row, etc.) taps into another American value. Freedom to assemble—for whatever reason—is such a deeply held value that we enshrined it in the First Amendment. Thus although I did not know it, going to see *Jedi* with a hundred of my fellow townspeople was a very American thing to do and a constitutionally protected one at that.

There are other historically produced conditions that structured my early experience of moviegoing. The patriarchal structure of the community determined my father's expected role as the proverbial breadwinner and "the one with the money" to decide the type and extent of our family's purchases. The established five-day workweek/school week/church attendance/workday/school day scheduling situated Friday night as the prime night for theater attendance for my family. Emerging from the Industrial Revolution, such time constraints geared toward worker productivity and value based on time spent, along with childcare and democratic indoctrination (public education), have become so commonplace as to be unquestioned until recently. With the rise of the Information Age and the COVID pandemic, physical presence in certain locations for prescribed periods of time seem to be less important than they previously were. Further, the design and decoration of the cinema itself recalls earlier movie houses, opera houses, vaudeville stages, playhouses, and so on—extending back as far as ancient Greek amphitheaters designed to maximize visual access and acoustic clarity. Excavating such cultural layers may begin with simply asking why popcorn and theatergoing are paired and can go as far as interrogating the function of mass entertainment in society (part of our concern here).

Aside, however, from these cultural functions or reductionistic explanations of the cinema as escapist fantasy, it is important to suggest various psychological models that can source an account for widespread theater attendance. Again, as intimated earlier, our main concern is film viewing in a public cinema, not so much streaming Netflix in the bathtub—although the psychological dimensions are broadly extrapolatable. One particular helpful model that includes cinema going but is more generally related to the experience of narrative is Brian Sturm's "storylistening trance experience" model (figure 1). In the figure, in the first stage, "realm of conversation," the T (Teller) and L (Listener) are aware of each other and that communication is occurring. In the second stage, "storyrealm," T becomes conscious of an S (Story) and comes to want to relate it to those present. This story consciousness is first known to T as the Ls turn their attention to and focus on T. Gradually, T's presence is preempted by the presence of the S in the consciousnesses of the Ls. The S eventually encloses T and Ls to produce what Strum identifies as an altered state of consciousness. This stage of the storylistening process can be seen as the "goal" of storytelling and will thus occupy our focus here.

Sturm (2000) identifies six key characteristics of this storylistening trance. These characteristics hearken back to the earlier narrative and to the claim that cinema is uniquely, if not superiorly, structured as a site of socialization. In short, cinema provides the most fertile conditions to expedite entrance into and maintenance of this altered state of consciousness. It should be noted that this altered state of consciousness seems to be so enjoyable, if not necessary, to human culture that there is not a single culture on earth that does not have narrative. The six characteristics of trance related to narrative are: "story and experience realism, lack of awareness of surroundings, engaged receptive channels. . . [,] lack or loss of control of the process, 'placeness,' and time distortion" (289). In terms of realism, Sturm explains, "Participants often experience a story 'as if' it were real, as if the story's plot and characters were the result of perception rather than imagination" (290). At the cinema, the overwhelming visual data presents itself as perception, that is, unless attention is broken (by a full bladder or a tall person who sits in front of you). Poor visual can also produce similar trance-smashing effects. For the lack of awareness of surroundings, Sturm adds, "Coupled with the sense of the pervasive reality of the story is a concomitant decreasing awareness of everything else" (290). This experience is expedited by the darkness, comfort, and meeting of basic needs in the cinema; you are not hungry and your body is situated and satiated so as to remove it as a factor that needs attention. For "engaged receptive channels," Sturm's respondents described visual, auditory, emotional, and kinesthetic responses. Again, these map onto the trance experience while watching a film—especially one in a public context (as will be explored shortly). The loss of control during a film, that is, that one is not creating the experience but perceiving it, is another obvious correspondence. Time distortion, too, due not only to the absence of time measurement technologies (clocks and windows) but also as a result of the trance state, notably occurs when one is watching an engrossing film. And, lastly, for Sturm, "placeness" does not so much describe the physical location of the experiencer as the description of their location "in" or being "there." Cinematographic and editing techniques have especially evolved to locate the viewer as a part of the scenes as they unfold, essentially turning the screen into a window or point of view rather than a flat representation. Such literal framing, in turn, constructs this sense of being inside the story itself in a quasi-ecstatic sense. Thus by limiting distractions and providing overwhelming stimuli, the theatergoing experience is capable

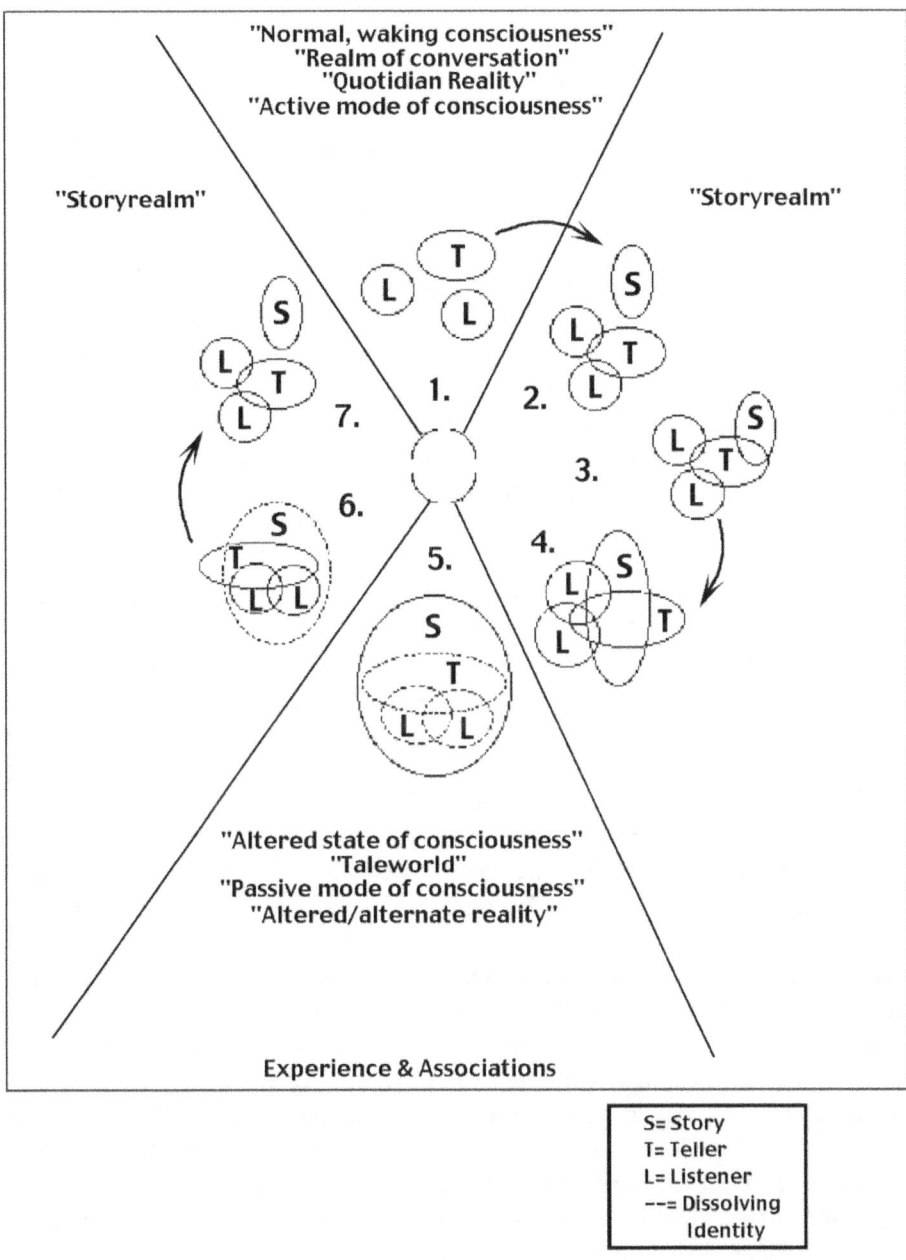

Figure 1. Brian Sturm's Storylistening Experience Model (2011) (Reprinted with permission [Sturm, 2000]).

of maximizing and maintaining the trance state longer than other forms of public participatory events. However, while Sturm's model is helpful in describing what happens to the individual watching the film and in touching upon a neurological motivation for watching films/listening to or reading stories, it does not scale up to the social aspects of film viewing.

In order to better understand the mechanics of the socialization process as it relates to the cinema experience, another model is necessary. Here, sociologist Randall Collins's (2004) interaction ritual model is especially germane. The model presupposes four main ingredients or initiating conditions, which in turn I will relate to the cinema experience. The first ingredient is that "two or more people are physically assembled in the same place, so that they affect each other by their bodily presence" (64). This is an obvious given in terms of a cinema space; there are other people present and, in my narrative, it was a packed house. The second ingredient is that there "are boundaries to outsiders so that participants have a sense of who is taking part and who is excluded." This condition is met in the theater through the ticketing process, the velvet ropes and stanchions, screens that show only designated films, the limitation of seating space and number of entrances/exits to a particular room. The third condition, for Collins, is that "people focus their attention upon a common object or activity, and by communicating this focus to each other become mutually aware of each other's focus of attention." Here the film is the common focus and the extended awareness that there are others in the room watching the film is reinforced through audience involvement (laughing, crying, breathing, chewing, moving, etc.). And, lastly, the fourth necessary condition is a shared mood or emotional experience. Clearly this is exactly what a movie is contrived to do: generate particular moods through lighting, visual effects, music, editing, and so on. Collins is clear: the object of mutual focus and the shared mood intensify in a feedback loop he calls entrainment, that is, the synchronization of emotions and even bodily functions (e.g., people laugh, cry, or clap simultaneously and collectively). The immediate effect of these conditions is what Collins, channeling Émile Durkheim, labels "collective effervescence"—which, in light of Sturm's model above, we could partly identify with a collective experience of the storylistening trance. While latent in his model—Sturm recognizes T and L's presence to each other—Collins's articulation adds more definition to this social aspect and necessary preconditions. Additionally, Collins goes further than Sturm to outline the outcomes of an interaction ritual.

For Collins, the experience of collective effervescence results in four basic outcomes that also relate to "reading" the cinema-going experience as a ritual of popular culture. It should be noted as well that rituals of all sorts are essential means by which cultures and societies socialize or acculturate their members. Deploying the interaction ritual model, then, is itself a recognition that moviegoing is, at heart, a socializing ritual for Americans. The content of the film and the makeup of the audience further delineate and differentiate in what ways attendees are socialized. Therefore—and this is part of the overall project of this book—the content and structure of each film, using these narrative and storytelling technologies, fashion generational consciousness dialectically. These outcomes, then, can be extended to each generation based on the degree to which a particular film communicates, affirms, or subverts the audience's already generationally determined consciousness. The first outcome Collins posits is "group solidarity, a feeling of membership" (66). This is that sense of "us" described in the narrative. But there are various levels to this as well: the general feeling of belonging to the same group of people who have just seen the same movie, *Star Wars* fans, young Gen X fans who will later want the toys, parents who don't get it, Boomers who remember the original, and so forth. The second result is "emotional energy in the individual: a feeling of confidence, elation, strength, enthusiasm, and initiative in taking action." This could be described as the empowerment of the witness, the one having seen something others have not and the resultant confidence in that experience. This result is perhaps most readily witnessed as the eagerness to converse about the film that people exhibit when they exit the theater. Further conversations energized with enthusiasm are themselves a form of "taking action." The third result is the generation of symbols that represent the group. Collins goes on: "Persons pumped up with feelings of group solidarity treat symbols with great respect and defend them against the disrespect of outsiders." While this particular result does not, at first, seem directly connected to cinema going, it is more particularly related to fandom and how a fan may defend a character or narrative or director's decision against someone who is not a fan of the franchise (e.g., *Star Wars* fans versus *Star Trek* fans). But there is a level at which cinema going itself generates this type of result; many people will keep ticket stubs for significant film-going experiences. Nonetheless, given the ubiquity of cinema attendance, there are fewer and fewer "outsiders" to ward off. One could, perhaps, identify various types of cinemas (downtown theaters versus cinema multiplexes) as "charged symbols" that need to be defended. And, lastly, Collins argues that there are "feelings of morality: the sense of rightness in adhering to the group, respecting its symbols, and defending both against transgressors." Again, this relates to fans and to cinephiles specifically who regard the aesthetics of a cinema as much as the content of the film. In my own particular narrative, there did exist the "Christians who go to the movies" who felt a sense of morality over and above "Christians who thought movies were from the devil." In sum, Collins's and Sturm's models taken together helpfully illustrate the essential mechanisms that cinema deploys to generate products such as American identity and generational consciousness.

CONCLUSION: ENTERTAINMENT BEYOND THE SHARED SCREEN

The telephone definitively displaced the telegraph, but radio did not die with television, and cinema going (prior to 2020) still remained a popular American pastime across all generational lines. As demonstrated above, *any* narrative has the potential to produce an addictive (perhaps constitutive) experience of an altered state of consciousness. For Collins, the physical presence of other people is a must (later on in his book he explores how our bodies attune to others through breathing, speech patterns, and heart rate). But what happens when Americans turn away from gigantic, shared screens in the dark recesses of cinemas to small, individual screens carried everywhere? In between the movie theatergoers and the commuter streaming Netflix on an iPad lies the family watching the gigantic home entertainment system, the replacement for the hearth.

Americans do indeed still watch a lot of television. By "television," I mean the actual technology and not so much the service that provides programming. And these TVs have grown in size and definition, occupying central wall space in living rooms. Further, with the advent of so-called binge watching, more and more Americans from all generations are spending more time in front of a screen of one sort or the other. Such sharp rises in screen usage (usually associated with the 2007 advent of the iPhone) have attracted many social critics' ire. Too much screen time has been connected to all manner of emotional and even physical conditions. Combined with multiplayer, online gaming platforms, people can spend most of their waking life consuming and interacting with content.

Yet the dire nature of these clarion calls need not be the only way we think of what communication theorist Mitchell Stephens (1998) calls "the rise of the image." He proposed a rule: "The more entertaining the medium, the more artistically and intellectually adventurous is has the potential to become" (228). Later, he carries this optimism even further: "I can't look at the magical devices we are coming up with for capturing, editing, and making available moving images without concluding that they will help us make additional progress" (230). Such prescient progressivism has turned out to be way more complex: think YouTube, TikTok, Facebook, and Instagram. Millions of consumers have become ersatz producers of moving images, a domain once limited to the Edisons, Warner Brothers, and Metro-Goldwyn-Mayers of the world. Not only that, these producers can capture the attention of millions as well—audiences the major studios of the past could not conceive of. And these devices and platforms have, to some extent, democratized the moving image and called into question the now-past facticity of photography. Images are not what they seem; editing and deep fakes abound.

Here's a little prediction of my own: inasmuch as our devices keep us from the shared physical experiences described by Collins, there will continue to be higher levels of fragmentation within our society. These lines of fragmentation will occur along generational boundaries but within niches so specific that microgenerations will proliferate, defined as much by their tastes within trending popular culture as by the time frame of their birth. With the absence of shared physicality, the sense of social solidarity will be ephemeral for most, lasting as long as the one with the most followers keeps posting.

So in a way, this text was outdated before it was finished. The consolidation of national identity and production of generational consciousnesses compete with other forms of slick socialization processes available cheaply and instantaneously. It is a curious thing that of all the technologies the modern West could have developed in the last 100 years, it has leaned most of its weight toward making computer technologies that can deliver better and more images. Moore's Law (processing power doubles every two years) seems like it was generated by the entertainment industry in order to keep pace with demand. The levels of identity construction and participation that are currently occurring because of the rise in technology and through the power of the image are unprecedented. And even if this text was outdated before it was finished, the need for deeper levels of critical thinking (such as are exemplified in this text) is as important as it ever has been.

Benjamin Crace

FURTHER READING

Collins, Randall. 2004. *Interaction Ritual Chains*. Princeton, NJ: Princeton University Press.

Geertz, Clifford. 1973. *The Interpretation of Cultures: Selected Essays*. New York: Basic Books.

Plant, Norman. 2011. "Carmike Capri 2." Cinema Treasures. http://cinematreasures.org/theaters/17602/photos/26368.

Stephens, Mitchell. 1998. *The Rise of the Image the Fall of the Word*. Oxford: Oxford University Press.

Sturm, Brian. 2000. "The 'Storylistening' Trance Experience." *Journal of American Folklore* 113 (449): 289–304.

Sturm, Brian. 2011. "Storytelling Models." Alison. https://alison.com/course/506/resource/file/storymodels.pdf.

Capitalism and the Film Industry: Creating and Distributing Cinema in the Age of Television

SHOW ME THE MONEY: CAPITAL AND THE HOLLYWOOD STUDIO SYSTEM

Making a film has always required an investment of capital. Even today—despite massive advances in smartphone camera technology, the proliferation of simple and user-friendly moviemaking software, and an abundance of online tutorials that promise to unlock the secrets of no-budget filmmaking—the overwhelming majority of filmmaking can't be done for free or even on a small budget. The cast, from principal actors to extras, need to be paid, as do directors; cinematographers; video editors; sound, lighting, set, costume, and makeup technicians; and/or graphic designers and animators. Factor in the cost of equipment, props and costumes, set construction, location fees, the rights to musical scores, and, where necessary, transportation, accommodation, and catering, and you'll start to see why a 2020 Investopedia article estimates that on average, major studio films cost around $65 million to produce and another $35 million to market (Mueller 2020).

"Low-budget" films can be made for much less than that, but even they require a significant financial investment. The low-budget category includes films such as *The Blair Witch Project* (1999), *Mad Max* (1979), and *Rocky* (1976), which cost an estimated $60,000, around $300,000, and $1.1 million to make, respectively. There's even a special category for "micro-budget" films, those that are the absolute least expensive to make; but while there is no exact consensus on where the dividing line falls between micro- and low-budget films, industry experts have suggested that films costing a quarter of a million dollars can still be considered "micro-budget," while up to $2 million would still count as "low-budget" (Follows 2014).

The sheer quantity and range of costs involved in making a film help explain the evolution of the Hollywood studio system in the United States. From the late

1920s through the late 1940s, the production of films was dominated by increasingly large and powerful studios, such as Paramount, 20th Century Fox, Warner Bros., RKO, and Loew's/MGM. The studios' economic aim was simple: control every aspect of film production and distribution. They controlled production by maintaining their own film lots, sets, equipment, personnel, and even their own stars, who would sign contracts that would require them to work exclusively for a single studio. They controlled distribution by owning their own movie theaters, so ticket sales generated revenue that went directly back to the studios, which could then manufacture more films to entice audiences back to their cinema seats.

The Hollywood studios cited above, often referred to as the Big Five, effectively divided the U.S. market into geographical territories, with Loew's/MGM, for example, prevalent on much of the East Coast, Paramount in the Midwest and the South, and Fox in the West. The Big Five mastered this economic model so thoroughly that in 1948, the U.S. Supreme Court ruled that their system was anti-competitive and monopolistic. Thus, over the subsequent decade, the studios' all-encompassing economic control was slowly broken up: parent companies split into separate entities for production and distribution, independent theaters and filmmakers grew in number, and stars began to demand nonexclusive contracts and a percentage of film revenues rather than a fixed salary.

In the midst of all of those crises, film studios also had to contend with a new competitor: television, which entered the American market in the late 1940s and swiftly became widespread in U.S. households. The experience of television was quite different, however, from that of cinema, particularly in those early years. Since videotape, the technology that allowed television to be recorded, was not widely available, almost all early TV was broadcast live, and it modeled itself after theater rather than film. Television screens were miniscule relative to the big screen of the cinema, of course, and television also lagged behind Hollywood in color technology. While the studios had slowly moved from black-and-white films to color from the late 1930s onward, television effectively shifted the cost of color from the producer to the consumer: buying a color television was significantly more expensive than buying a black-and-white one, and since the quality and reliability of color TVs remained inconsistent well into the 1970s, many households opted to forgo the expense, at least in the early decades.

Moreover, television utilized a completely different economic model from the vertical integration that Hollywood had pioneered: the consumer paid for the equipment—the TV set—but not for the programming, which was broadcast for free and supported by advertising revenue. So where a film spectator would see trailers for forthcoming studio films (and perhaps for the snacks sold by the movie theater) before the start of the feature film but could then enjoy the film itself uninterrupted, television viewers would find their programming broken at intervals by commercials for products and services of all types.

THE INTERPLAY OF FILM AND TELEVISION OVER TIME

Despite these obvious drawbacks to early television, the studios rightly saw television as a financial threat. They retrenched in response, producing fewer feature films. But as TV became near-universal in U.S. households, and then as video-recording technology took hold, the studios realized that they could make television too: sets could be constructed on their filmmaking lots and a cast booked and reused for dozens of episodes. So studios set up television divisions. They also began to rent their space and facilities to independent filmmakers and/or to invest in their work, which accounted for a larger and larger share of film industry production. Studios also began to create lower-budget films specifically intended for television broadcast and to prepare films that they had previously released in theaters to now be broadcast serially on television. A process of exchange developed between the two forms of media, allowing some writers, actors, and producers to move from the big screen to the small screen and vice versa.

Plotlines and characters also began to move from one medium to the other—not just through films serialized for television, as noted above, but also as new films that were inspired by popular television series. The crime drama *Dragnet*, for example, which ran on television from 1951 to 1959, was made into a feature film in 1954, starring Jack Webb and Ben Alexander, the same actors who played the main roles of the crime-fighting police detective duo on the TV series. The permeability of the two media continued in the 1960s with an upsurge in films that were made for TV, some of which were actually feature-film-length pilots for prospective television series.

Moreover, film's rivalry with television spurred technological innovations in filmmaking and distribution. Before television debuted, only the studios' most promising films were screened in color, but as television technology spread, the studios moved quickly to ensure that as much of their lineup as possible would screen in vibrant color rather than in black and white, to better distinguish themselves from TV. Innovations took place in cinematic sound and other types of visual technology as well, like CinemaScope anamorphic lenses, which allowed filmmakers to shoot widescreen features; stereophonic sound in movie theaters; and 3D visions. Nevertheless, in the 1960s, the film industry continued to lose ground to television. More and more American households bought color TVs, satellite technology made it possible to transmit programming across enormous geographies, and television began to showcase a remarkably diverse range of programming, from news to Westerns to sitcoms to game shows, with the occasional soap opera or animated series thrown in.

In response, the studios emphasized their unique strength: the epic, immersive qualities of the big screen. They made grand religious dramas such as *The Ten Commandments* (directed by Cecil B. DeMille in 1953, starring Charlton Heston and Yul Brynner) and *Ben-Hur* (1959, directed by William Wyler, with Heston in the title role). They explored the fates of larger-than-life protagonists from antiquity, such as *Spartacus* (played by Kirk Douglas in 1960, under Stanley Kubrick's direction) and *Cleopatra* (1963, directed by Joseph Mankiewicz, starring Elizabeth Taylor and Richard Burton). Disney emphasized family-friendly animated films with elements of magic and adventure, such as *Cinderella* (1950), *Peter Pan* (1953), *The Jungle Book* (1967), and *Robin Hood* (1973). But audiences also flocked to watch the sagas of men and their families corrupted by organized crime, as in Francis Ford Coppola's *The Godfather* (1972); or sweeping sci-fi epics, such as

George Lucas's Star Wars franchise (1977–2008); and vibrant action films such as Lucas's and Steven Spielberg's *Indiana Jones* series (1981–). Hollywood also continued a long-standing tradition of making combat films, a tradition that ran from director Lewis Milestone's reflection on the horrors of World War I, *All Quiet on the Western Front* (1930), through World War II films such as *They Were Expendable* (1945, directed by John Ford), *Sands of Iwo Jima* (1949, starring John Wayne), and *The Longest Day* (1962, directed by Darryl F. Zanuck). The late 1970s and 1980s witnessed a proliferation of gripping films about the Vietnam War, including Michael Cimino's *The Deer Hunter* (1978), Coppola's *Apocalypse Now* (1979), Oliver Stone's *Platoon* (1986), and Kubrick's *Full Metal Jacket* (1987).

Films like these were marketed to audiences as ones that must be seen on the big screen, of which the television screen was just a pale imitation. Moreover, revolutions in movie theater sound systems, including Dolby Laboratories' Stereo and Surround Sound, rendered the experience of watching a film in a cinema even more immediate and riveting.

To further distinguish themselves from television programming, films also began to reflect upon and comment on the negative aspects of TV and the shallow celebrity culture it promoted. As early as 1955, the film *All That Heaven Allows* shows a son buying his lonely mother a television set to keep her company and distract her from her sadness over a broken engagement. But while the experience of watching a film in a theater is a communal one, shared with other spectators, watching television alone simply renders the mother more isolated; it cannot replace the human interaction and companionship she craves. Similarly, in 1957, two other films spoofed television culture: the protagonist of the satire *Will Success Spoil Rock Hunter?* is a low-level TV ad writer who unexpectedly rockets to unwanted celebrity when he tries to convince a famous actress to endorse a new lipstick, while *A Face in the Crowd* illustrates its protagonist's meteoric rise from a marginal life as a drifter to that of an arrogant TV celebrity, followed by his hubris-inflicted fall from grace. This trio of films—a romance, a comedy, and a drama, respectively—set a pattern that the film industry continues to follow to this day of producing films that comment (usually negatively, if comedically) on television and those who make it. Such films include *Network* (1976), where an angry newscaster's announcement that he plans to commit suicide on live television causes a ratings spike that the network exploits by giving him his own television show, from which he delivers furious rants with the crowd-pleasing tagline "I'm mad as hell, and I'm not going to take it anymore!"; *The Truman Show* (1998), whose protagonist comes to realize that his entire life is actually the artificial construct of a reality TV show; The Hunger Games franchise (2012–2015), where teenagers fight each other to the death for the entertainment of mass television audiences; *Anchorman 2: The Legend Continues* (2013), with its satiric spoof of Fox News; and *Late Night* (2019), in which a female late-night talk show host must fight to retain her job when her network looks to replace her with a younger, crasser male comedian. By comparison, television programs that reflect upon the behind-the-scenes conflicts or the personal or social impact of filmmaking are fewer and farther between, with HBO's *Entourage* (2004–2011) being a notable exception.

The competition between film and television has thus had some positive results as well as negative ones for the film industry. It has impelled the film industry toward swift, new innovations in visual and sound technology, and it has encouraged many filmmakers to dream big, to envision stories and scenes that would fill the big screen. Television has provided content and inspiration for new films and additional avenues for screening films both old and new, allowing the films to reach even wider audiences.

THE IMPACT OF STREAMING SERVICES

In more recent decades, the technology through which we access both television and film has evolved by leaps and bounds. Cable TV technology, for example, significantly expanded the number of channels available to consumers from the mid-1970s through the '90s. Among the first U.S. cable companies was HBO, short for Home Box Office. True to its name, much of its early programming focused on films, which it usually screened uncut and without commercial interruptions, aiming to replicate as closely as possible the experience of going to the cinema but with all the comforts of home. Cable television offered consumers subscriptions to ad-free channels, providing an alternative economic model from traditional TV, a model that became increasingly popular. From the turn of the millennium onward, DVR technology has allowed subscribers to record programs digitally and then also to fast-forward through the ads that previously constituted the bulk of television revenue. Meanwhile, consumers' access to increasingly sophisticated screens and viewing platforms, via smartphones, laptops, or tablets, has shot up exponentially. Massive HDTVs and elaborate home sound systems now allow consumers to create the experience of the big screen in their own homes, enhancing individual viewing experience but also prompting concerns about the long-term emotional, social, and psychological effects of constant immersion in the alternative worlds that consumers can experience in their home theaters (Robbins 2010).

The potentially isolating effects of constant television watching are much more pronounced now than they were when *All That Heaven Allows* illustrated them back in 1955, particularly now that subscription-based streaming services such as Netflix both provide screen owners with immense quantities of film and television features on demand and mine their subscribers' viewing histories in order to suggest additional content that might attract them. The COVID-19 pandemic has further exacerbated these tendencies, with global lockdowns quite literally providing captive audiences for the content provided by over-the-top, subscription-based streaming services such as Netflix, Amazon Prime Video, HBO Max, and Disney+.

Moreover, such services no longer merely license and distribute film and television content for at-home consumption. They now produce their own films and television series, many of which, like HBO's *Game of Thrones* (2011–2019), have been wildly successful. Since HBO operates on a subscription basis that provides access to a variety of programming, it is difficult to pinpoint exactly how much subscription revenue *GoT* itself generated, but estimates range from $1.6 billion to

$2.2 billion. The series was staggeringly expensive to make, with budgets for its final season averaging an estimated $15 million per episode, but it seems to have provided HBO with at least a 100 percent return on its overall investment. Netflix reportedly spent over a quarter of a billion dollars to make *The Crown* (2016–2020), and though return on investment is even more difficult to calculate in that case, given the global popularity of Netflix's subscriptions, the publicity the series generated may well have allowed it to turn a profit for the platform. And certain streaming platforms generate revenue in other ways as well: Hulu, for example, sells subscriptions that still include ads and commercials as well as more costly, no-ad subscriptions.

Streaming services thus pose an obvious threat to the film industry, not just to the parts of the latter's economic model that still rely on selling movie theater tickets and filling seats but also to their production model. Streaming platforms have repeatedly demonstrated a willingness to fund independent, niche, or less commercially oriented films and to provide them with global distribution. They have also been able to bring to life projects that Hollywood studios, for one reason or another, have refused to fund. Martin Scorsese's film *The Irishman* (2019), for example, was an idea the celebrated director had pitched to studio executives for more than five years, only to have an initial deal with Paramount fall through; in 2017, Netflix secured the distribution rights and financed the film.

Streaming platforms' moves into production have sparked concern among the film industry establishment; some critics even suggest that films such as Netflix's *Roma*, *Okja*, and *The Meyerowitz Stories* were snubbed at awards ceremonies such as the Oscars and the Cannes Film Festival as a result of the mainstream industry closing ranks against the streaming service (see Seth 2019; Haridy 2019). Yet much like the earlier rivalry between film and television, the new realm of content streaming has also had certain benefits for the legacy studios, providing them with new opportunities to license their content and distribute it globally. In fact, in part as a response to the continuing pandemic, many films are now being released in movie theaters and on streaming platforms simultaneously (though this, too, has its pitfalls, as illustrated by the summer 2021 feud between *Black Widow* star Scarlett Johansson and Disney, which distributed the film on Disney+ and in theaters simultaneously, which Johansson argued cost her tens of millions of dollars in bonuses that she otherwise would have received for box office performance). The opportunity to license films for streaming distribution to global audiences who were locked down, or who feared congregating in crowded movie theaters, was indubitably a boon to Hollywood studios during the pandemic, and movie theaters have been experimenting with their own subscription services. MoviePass, an early attempt at offering movie tickets in exchange for monthly subscriptions, went bankrupt in 2019, but Regal, AMC, and Cinemark, the three largest movie theater chains in the United States, have all created subscription services. If in-theater audience numbers rebound postpandemic, as some analysts have predicted, then these new services will breathe new financial life into the movie theater chains by providing them with stabler revenue streams—and also, of course, by giving them the opportunity to track subscribers' viewing habits and suggest new content for consumption.

QUESTIONS OF REPRESENTATION, INCLUSION, AND PROPAGANDA

Another area in which streaming services are spurring long-overdue change in the film industry relates to questions of representation and diversity in terms of intersectional identity categories such as gender, race, class, sexual orientation, disability, and age. For example, all the films named thus far in this essay were directed by men. This tracks with recent Hollywood statistics showing that, out of the 100 most popular films in the United States in 2015, over 90 percent had male directors. Likewise, around 75 percent of the speaking characters were white. Male speaking characters outnumbered females by a two-to-one ratio, and female characters skewed much younger than their male counterparts did. Out of a total of over 4,000 speaking characters, only 32 were members of the LGBTQ community. And a mere 2.4 percent of speaking characters were depicted as differently abled (all statistics from Smith, Choueiti, and Pieper 2016), despite studies indicating that one in every four Americans lives with some type of disability.

Moreover, all of these issues are related to questions of social class and capital—questions like, Which members of our society have access to the financial resources necessary to create and distribute a film? By and large, women, people of color, and those marginalized by other aspects of their identity have less access to power, influence, and capital, which means they have fewer opportunities to create films or to contribute to their creation as directors, scriptwriters, composers, producers, and other such roles. This in turn limits both Hollywood's ability to showcase diverse perspectives and audiences' opportunities to view and learn from them.

This has been a serious problem for the film industry since its earliest years, not merely in terms of a dearth of diverse perspectives but also in terms of the medium's power to shape American society, for good or for ill. In the mid-1910s, for example, D. W. Griffith directed and produced *The Birth of a Nation*, a film that purported to show the last days of Abraham Lincoln and the interactions, after Lincoln's assassination, of two families who had taken opposing sides during the Civil War. The film pits its white protagonists against Black and mixed-raced characters, depicting the latter (played by white actors in blackface) as duplicitous, lazy louts who lust after white women, and the former as noble and heroic guardians of a moral order girded by notions of white supremacy, who mete out "justice" by lynching a transgressing Black character. Though a toxically racist film, it proved immensely popular in its day; it played to sold-out houses throughout the United States, and Griffith arranged special screenings for then-president Woodrow Wilson in the White House as well as for the entire U.S. Supreme Court. Its popularity seems to have stemmed in part from its epic battle scenes, which used 100s of extras, and its stirring, specially composed three-hour musical score, but the ideology it promulgated was deadly: the film is credited with revitalizing the white supremacist terrorist militias known collectively as the Ku Klux Klan. Furthermore, Harvard historian Desmond Ang has recently documented a direct correlation between screenings of *The Birth of a Nation* and an increase in violence against Black people: studying U.S. counties in which the film was screened, Ang found that lynchings in those counties increased by a factor of five in the month following the screening ("A Tarnished Silver Screen" 2021). He also found that in every state except Kansas, which banned the film, the counties that had a higher-than-average number of cinemas in the 1910s also had a higher-than-average number of Klan chapters by the 1930s. In other words, a film's ability to represent certain categories of "other" people on the screen, and thereby shape spectators' views and stereotypes of those people, is not just incredibly powerful—it is also potentially dangerous and destructive.

This problem has plagued the U.S. film industry (and, later, the television industry) for its entire history. The narrator of Viet Thanh Nguyen's award-winning 2015 novel *The Sympathizer* grapples with the same problematics of representation when he works as a consultant on a film that is set during the Vietnam War (though the film described in the novel is fictional, it is clearly intended as a satiric parody of Coppola's *Apocalypse Now*). The narrator is appalled to discover, upon reading the script, that the Vietnamese inhabitants of the village in which the film is set have no speaking parts (or at least no parts that are translated for the benefit of U.S. audiences) and are depicted as one-dimensional stereotypes: bloodthirsty Viet Cong soldiers and terrified and/or collaborating villagers. He attempts to convince the pompous director that a film about the Vietnam War should take into account the actual lived experiences of Vietnamese people and not just those of American soldiers, and the director eventually hires him as the "technical consultant in charge of authenticity" (Nguyen 2015, 163). But as filming progresses, the narrator comes to realize that his ability to impact the final product is very limited: "My task was to ensure that the people scuttling in the background of the film would be real Vietnamese people saying real Vietnamese things and dressed in real Vietnamese clothing, right before they died.... I was no more than the garment worker who made sure the stitching was correct in an outfit designed, produced, and consumed by the wealthy white people of the world. They owned the means of production and therefore the means of representation, and the best that we could ever hope for was to get a word in edgewise before our anonymous deaths" (Nguyen 2015, 163).

The narrator's disillusion is based in reality: Asian characters have been particularly underrepresented in the history of Hollywood films, as have Asian directors and writers. Smith, Choueiti, and Pieper (2016) found that of the 100 top films of 2015, only 6 were directed by Asians or Asian Americans; none featured Asian lead actors, and 49 had no Asian characters at all. Other minority groups have had to struggle against discrimination and misrepresentation as well: the casting of Black actors in negatively stereotyped roles, particularly those of criminals and thugs, was so prevalent in the 1970s that it gave rise to a new term, "blaxploitation," to describe the cinematic genre, while Hollywood has historically limited roles for characters of Arab or Middle Eastern descent, as Jack Shaheen has argued, to either terrorists or shaykhs. First Peoples, people of Hispanic or Latino heritage, and other minorities have also made comparatively few positive or complex appearances on the big screen even up to more recent, and supposedly more enlightened and inclusive, times.

Once again, television has in many ways paved the way for greater diversity on film screens. The small screen excelled, by necessity, at creating more intimate worlds, like that of the family sitcom—and each time a sitcom featured a nonwhite or nonhetero or nontraditional family, it helped broaden audiences' perceptions of and empathy for those previously perceived to be other. The film industry has moved slowly but surely in the same direction. And streaming services have created new opportunities for people from a variety of identities to bring their work to the attention of global audiences: Ava Du Vernay, director of *Selma* (2014), contrasts the meager international distribution of that film, via Paramount and 20th Century Fox, to Netflix's worldwide distribution of her film *13th* (2016), tweeting, "One of the things I value about Netflix is that it distributes black work far and wide" (quoted in Seth 2019). The major Hollywood distributors have yet to catch up with that model, but it has raised the bar.

One final point of note is that, while this essay has focused on the U.S. film industry, still the largest and most influential globally, there are other key hubs for filmmaking around the world. China has a hugely profitable domestic film industry, much of which is supported and regulated by the state. Bollywood, based in Mumbai, India, has the distinction of producing the largest number of films annually. The UK, France, Germany, and Italy all have their own film industries, each of which rakes in well over a billion dollars in annual revenue, as do Japan and South Korea. In fact, filmmaking and television making occurs everywhere around the world, from Argentina to Nigeria's Nollywood to Iran to Mongolia, and even productions designed with local audiences in mind can be picked up by streaming services and distributed globally. The current state of the film industry is, in fact, one where borders are increasingly blurred and where previously impassable boundaries are being crossed and redrawn on a daily basis. As film scholar Deborah Shaw points out, even the long-standing distinction between film and television is slowly eroding as television series stretch episodes to the length of a feature film and as more and more viewers access their content not just on the big screen of a cinema or on the midsize screen of a television but also on laptops, tablets, or the microscreen of a mobile phone. Money still talks, of course, in terms of both production and distribution—but the conversations have proliferated, and the quantity and diversity of speakers who can participate in those conversations have increased exponentially. All of that heralds an exciting, and mostly unpredictable, future for the entertainment industry as a whole.

Katherine Hennessey

FURTHER READING

American Cinema video series. 1995. Annenberg Learner/New York Center for Visual History in association with KCET/Los Angeles and the BBC. https://www.learner.org/series/american-cinema.

Aschieris, Jacob. 2020–. *The History of Film.* Apple Podcasts. https://podcasts.apple.com/us/podcast/the-history-of-film/id1519549773.

Boddy, William. 1985. "The Studios Move into Prime Time: Hollywood and the Television Industry in the 1950s." *Cinema Journal* 24, no. 4 (Summer): 23–37. https://www.jstor.org/stable/1224894.

Feldman, Dana. 2019, July 28. "How Netflix Is Changing the Future of Movie Theaters." *Forbes*. https://www.forbes.com/sites/danafeldman/2019/07/28/how-netflix-is-changing-the-future-of-movie-theaters/?sh=6f56bab45f46.

Fiduccia, Christopher. 2021, August 22. "Scarlett Johansson's Lawyer Slams Disney's Misogynistic Response to Lawsuit." ScreenRant. https://screenrant.com/black-widow-scarlett-johansson-lawsuit-misogynistic-disney-response.

Follows, Stephen. 2014, September 22. "What's the Average Budget of a Low or Micro-Budget Film?" Stephen Follows. https://stephenfollows.com/average-budget-low-micro-budget-film.

Hall, Stefan, and Silvia Pasquini. 2020, July 23. "Can There Be a Fairy-Tale Ending for Hollywood after COVID-19?" World Economic Forum. https://www.weforum.org/agenda/2020/07/impact-coronavirus-covid-19-hollywood-global-film-industry-movie-theatres.

Haridy, Rich. 2019, October 8. "Netflix vs. Cinema: How a Disruptive Streaming Service Declared War on Hollywood." New Atlas. https://newatlas.com/home-entertainment/netflix-disruptive-streaming-hollywood-cinema-exhibition-war.

Kushner, Jordan. 2016, February 24. "A Brief History of Sound in Cinema." *Popular Mechanics*. https://www.popularmechanics.com/culture/movies/a19566/a-brief-history-of-sound-in-cinema.

McKittrick, Christopher. 2019, June 21 (updated). "How Movies Went from Black and White to Color." Liveabout. https://www.liveabout.com/how-movies-went-from-black-white-to-color-4153390.

Mueller, Annie. 2020, March 28 (updated). "Why Movies Cost So Much to Make." Investopedia. https://www.investopedia.com/financial-edge/0611/why-movies-cost-so-much-to-make.aspx.

Nguyen, Viet Thanh. 2015. *The Sympathizer*. New York: Grove Atlantic. Kindle.

Richards, Sarah. 2020, December 17. "The Netflix Effect: The Movie Industry and New Data." University of Virginia-Darden, *Ideas to Action*. https://ideas.darden.virginia.edu/movie-industry-and-new-data.

Robbins, Jeff. 2010. "Missing the Big Picture: Studies of TV's Effects Should Consider How HDTV Is Different." *New Atlantis* (Spring): 118–122.

Sergi, Gianluca. 2020, December 17. "Streaming Wars: How Threatening Are They Really to the Film Industry?" The Conversation. https://theconversation.com/streaming-wars-how-threatening-are-they-really-to-the-film-industry-151649.

Seth, Par Radhika. 2019, March 25. "Netflix vs. Hollywood: The Fight to Define the Future of Film." *Vogue*. https://www.vogue.fr/fashion-culture/article/netflix-vs-hollywood-the-fight-to-define-the-future-of-film.

Shaheen, Jack. 2014. *Reel Bad Arabs: How Hollywood Vilifies a People*. Northampton, MA: Olive Branch Press.

Sharman, Russell Leigh. 2020. *Moving Pictures: An Introduction to Cinema*. Fayetteville: University of Arkansas.

Shaw, Deborah. 2019, August 29. "Can Cinema Survive in a Golden Age of Serial TV?" The Conversation. https://theconversation.com/can-cinema-survive-in-a-golden-age-of-serial-tv-122234.

Smith, Stacy L., Marc Choueiti, and Katherine Pieper, with assistance from Ariana Case and Justin Marsden. 2016. "Inequality in 800 Popular Films: Examining Portrayals of Gender, Race/Ethnicity, LGBT, and Disability from 2007–2015." *Media, Diversity, & Social Change Initiative* (September). https://annenberg.usc.edu/sites/default/files/2017/04/10/MDSCI_Inequality_in_800_Films_FINAL.pdf.

"A Tarnished Silver Screen." 2021, March 27. *The Economist*, 77.

Ugwu, Reggie. 2020, September 9 (updated). "The Hashtag That Changed the Oscars: An Oral History." *New York Times*. https://www.nytimes.com/2020/02/06/movies/oscarssowhite-history.html.

The Wiley-Blackwell History of American Film. 2011. 4 vols., edited by Cynthia Lucia, Roy Grundmann, and Art Simon. Hoboken, NJ: Wiley.

Zipin, Dina. 2021, June 30 (updated). "Movie vs. TV Industry: Which Is Most Profitable?" Investopedia. https://www.investopedia.com/articles/investing/091615/movie-vs-tv-industry-which-most-profitable.asp.

The American Myth Machine: Film as a National Visual Literature

Everything I learned I learned from the movies.
—Audrey Hepburn, actor

Because we all need to believe in movies, sometimes.
—pleasefindthis, I Wrote This *for* You, collection of prose and photography

Hollywood is the real American capital. Not Washington DC.
—Vachel Lindsay, American poet

Perhaps more than any other country, the United States is built on a foundation of national myths. In fact, the national myths of the United States stretch back to the pre-independence days, to the myths of discovery by Christopher Columbus and of the promised land of the Pilgrims and Puritans, of equality and democracy of the Founding Fathers, and of e pluribus unum and the melting pot of immigration. While the reality of these myths has been somewhat debunked in recent decades, they remain the myths that we tell ourselves as Americans and celebrate each year during one commercialized holiday or another.

More recent myths have been added onto the foundational myths named above (discovery, promised land, founding fathers, melting pot), many of which are wrapped up in the larger category of the American Dream, in which one's success in life depends not on birth or position but rather on hard work and ingenuity.

So America is the land of opportunity, of Yankee ingenuity, of rags-to-riches stories, and of the "self-made man." Of course, for each of these positives is a potential negative or dark side; the land of opportunity is not equally available to all, Yankee ingenuity has its limits, a life of hard work and privation doesn't always lead to riches, and the self-made person can easily morph into the con artist. And those are the "good" myths. We also have the myths of Manifest Destiny and American exceptionalism that have led to wars, imperialism, and genocide.

But at heart, Americans are an optimistic people who want everyone to get a fair shake, who believe hard work, not crime, pays, and who identify with and support the underdog, and this is reflected not only in the myths they tell themselves but also in the image they project to the world, in large part through Hollywood movies.

It is hard to overestimate the importance of these movies in the lives and the imaginations of an American and, to a large extent, a global audience. As the introduction to *America's Hollywood* notes, "Of all the products of popular culture, none is more sharply etched in our collective imagination than the movies" (Mintz, Roberts, and Welky 2016, 1). They allow for us to build, per Benedict Anderson's 2006 book-length study (originally published in 1983), "imagined communities" of groups of people who agree to create and share a sense of belonging and community, often on a national level. Anderson linked this with the rise of print capitalism, which allowed for a dramatically increased spread of information, often in the vernacular language of the region (rather than in Latin, a pan-Christian language at the time). Film technology functions in a similar way, allowing for imagined national and linguistic communities, sometimes described as "imagined spectatorships," as Helena Wu (2018) does in her discussion of cinema in post-handover Hong Kong. Films are data-rich environments for researchers in all three stages (production, distribution, and consumption), providing "insights into Americans' shifting ideals, fantasies, and preoccupations"—one of those being "ideological constructs that advance particular political or moral values or myths" (Mintz, Roberts, and Welky 2016, 3).

It is on their role in constructing, maintaining, and sometimes challenging national myths that the remainder of this essay will focus, thinking about ways in which Hollywood cinema, through its economic, technological, and often cultural dominance, has been a kind of "national myth machine" by rendering them into visual narratives that we can then consume as an imagined spectatorship. After explaining the concept of "visual culture" as a kind of literature or narrative, the essay will provide some historical background of key moments in American cinema and the mythology connected to these moments, focusing in the end on the era of blockbuster cinema and the stories these films told about America both to the country and to the world.

Rogoff (1998) defines "visual culture" as a multivalanced, cross-disciplinary study of images and how they produce meaning, establish and maintain aesthetic values, and depict power relations within a culture. This includes the production of a film, its distribution, and its consumption, which involves the "audio, spatial and psychic dynamics of spectatorship" (Rogoff 1998, 24) and allows us as consumers and critics to question "the ways in which we inhabit and thereby constantly make and remake our own culture" (31). While it is most often connected to architecture and artistic production (films, painting, photographs), it also includes advertising, graffiti, and fashion—anything that can visually express a belief, an ideology, or a mythology about a community or a culture. Film is perhaps the most complex form of visual culture, in part because of the number of steps required to bring a film from an idea pitched to producers to an art form enjoyed by a viewing audience. A single film cannot be created by one person (as can other forms of visual culture, such as a photo or painting); even in the case of auteur cinema, in which a single person (usually the director) exercises control of the project, it remains a collaborative endeavor. So while Sylvester Stallone wrote, directed, and starred in the film *Rocky* (1976), he still relied on a team of actors, technicians, and businesspeople to create and distribute the movie to its audience.

While cinema can be seen as belonging to the category of "visual culture" (anything our culture communicates within visual means), how does it participate in the related concepts of "visual literature" or "visual narrative"? While we generally think of literature as a written text (as opposed to a visual text), all films go through a written stage called a script, or more precisely, a screenplay. Many films today are adaptations of novels, thereby strengthening the connection to literature. And the dialogue, which forms an important part of most films, and certainly of all Hollywood cinema since the arrival of the talkies (although even silent films typically had important dialogue in subtitles on the screen), can be thought of aural delivery of the written script.

The further connection to film as a kind of literature emerged from the nouvelle vague or New Wave period of cinema, which originated in France and not only coincided historically with the New Hollywood period (see below) but was also in dialogue with it (for example, through film noir). One of its early directors and a theorist, Alexandre Astruc, proposed that the relationship of the director to a film should be similar to that of an author to a novel and that the director should wield not simply a camera but rather a *caméra-stylo* ("camera-pen") and, through the mise-en-scène (the stage design, props, and arrangement of actors), impart authorial presence over the film. This became one of the key precepts of the auteur, raising the status of the director-manager to that of author-artist, thus identifying another strand of connection between visual and literary narrative. American film critic Andrew Sarris popularized a theoretical approach to this genre of film in his article, "Notes on the Auteur Theory in 1962," in which he added to discussions occurring earlier in France by Astruc as well as André Bazin and François Truffaut, most often in the French film magazine *Cahiers du cinéma*.

While there were some (and sometimes originally categorized as B-rated) auteur directors practicing during the earlier French period of the nouvelle vague such as Alfred Hitchcock, John Ford, and Orson Welles, the heyday of auteurism in the United States came at a slightly later period, during the 1960s and 1970s, and continues even today, albeit to a somewhat lesser degree and prominence. Some of the key American auteur directors of the earlier period who have continued to be active today include Francis Ford Coppola, Oliver Stone, Steven Spielberg, James Cameron, and starting in slightly later periods, Spike Lee (1980s) and Quentin Tarantino (1990s). It will be interesting to explore in the discussion on blockbuster films specifically (see below) the clear overlap between auteur and blockbuster directors, which in part may be due to the notoriety of the auteur directors and their ability to raise enough money to film these big-budget "event" films, as the demise of studio system almost meant the demise of reliable funding for films.

Among more recent theorists, Roland Barthes has proposed the concept of *écriture* (or "writing") as a way to study cinema; another reads Sergei Eisenstein's use of montage in *October* (1927) as a kind of film writing (or *ciné-écriture*; Eisenstein himself, like other Russian formalist filmmakers, equated a cinematic shot with a word), and a recent book titled *Film Hieroglyphics* (so as not to confuse the reader with a manual on film writing, the more literal translation of the French term *écriture*) suggests that we can fruitfully study narrative film as a text that must be read and written by both the filmmaker and the spectator (Conley 2006, xxv). And finally, it must be noted that some of the most popular genres in film (comedy, Western, and melodrama) emerge out of literature (Cohen 2001, 11), as well as more niche genres such as noir, sci-fi, and fantasy, to name only a few.

The third term that needs defining (in addition to visual culture and visual literacy) is that of "visual narrative," which simply means telling a story primarily (but not necessarily entirely) through visual media, something in which most if not all Hollywood cinema participates. Sometimes called visual storytelling, this is used not only in movies but even in advertising, and the visual (whether still photography, illustrations, or video) can be enhanced by a variety of audio such as sound, voice, and music (Pimenta and Poovaiah 2010). While often used interchangeably, the words "story," "plot," and "narrative" are not exactly synonyms. The story is a sequence of events in chronological order, whereas the plot is the sequence of events as they relate to one another. The plot is related to sequence and structure and is sometimes diagrammed into Gustav Freytag's "Pyramid" (1963) into the following events: exposition—rising action—climax—falling action—dénouement. The narrative is concerned primarily with *how* the story is told, the best order and manner in which to explain and reveal the events to the audience. While it may not sound like there are huge differences among the terms, think of how different Orson Welles's *Citizen Kane* (1941) would be if we were told the meaning of Rosebud right at the start or if we had to wait until the very end of the film to be told that this held significance to the protagonist. The viewer would lose the excitement of discovering the mystery of the name. Or, for an example a bit closer to the present, imagine if Quentin Tarantino's *Pulp Fiction* (1994) had been told in chronological order—this would have been an entirely different viewing experience, as the viewer would lose the excitement of realizing the circularity and interconnectedness of the film's three primary storylines.

Now that the prevalent myths of American society have been introduced, and the concept of visual literature (and its related terms) have been explored within film history, the remainder of this essay will focus on how myths operate within Hollywood up until the period of Hollywood blockbuster cinema. Because films are, as noted earlier, "a mixture of art, business and popular entertainment" (Mintz, Roberts, and Welky 2016, 3), and because cinema, like any other kind of cultural production, both creates and reflects values and beliefs of a certain time and place, it will be important to discuss not only the way the story of the myth is incorporated into a film but also the way it circulates in the political, economic, and historical culture of the film and its reception.

While there are different ways to periodize Hollywood cinema, the following provides a clear and simple breakdown that will guide the discussion of its role as a "myth machine":

1. Silent era (approximately 1910–late 1920s)
2. Golden era, or classical period (approximately late 1920s–late 1940s)

3. New Hollywood or the post-studio period (1950s–1970s)
4. Contemporary period (after 1980)

Each of the four categories listed above can be divided into various subcategories and thematic and stylistic propensities that often connect to technological developments or cultural, political, and/or socioeconomic developments. For example, technological innovations in sound-on-film led to the ability to create feature-length "talkies" and marked the shift from the silent era to the classical period. Television was also an important technological development that at first was seen as a competitor but eventually became a partner in delivering movies to a larger audience. Similar trajectories and attitudes can be seen with the arrival of each new technological advancement connected to movies, such as Betamax, VHS, and DVD formats, which were often obtained from video rental shops such as Blockbuster Video, which itself was replaced by Netflix, first by its rental by mail of DVDs that did away with the dreaded late fee and fine for not rewinding and later by its streaming service, which has become the ubiquitous way in which films are consumed today. Similar anxieties and opportunities can be seen in movie theaters themselves having gone from single to multiplex venues, and home viewing today can range from large flat-screen televisions to palm-sized smartphone screens. Shifts in themes and genres are often influenced by historical or political events. For example, World War II and the Cold War led to the rise of patriotic and propaganda films; the dissolution of the studio system was based in large part on new antitrust rules that separated the production from the distribution of films, resulting in the production of fewer films each year but also giving rise to new phenomena in the industry such as film noir, auteur film, independent film, and the blockbuster.

The technology for motion pictures was invented in France by the Lumière Brothers, and the earliest films were short documentary pieces such as the 46-second La Sortie de l'usine Lumière à Lyon (*Workers Leaving the Lumière Factory*), which was screened in Paris in 1895. But as one critic points out in a fascinating study of the "American myth" in silent film, it was films produced in the United States and the rise of the Hollywood studios that mirrored the rise in global importance of the country itself in the early decades of the 20th century. There were several reasons why America came to dominate the film industry worldwide by 1920: the economic prosperity of the country in general, which allowed the masses to partake in the popularity of nickelodeons (storefront movie theaters); the influx of immigrants from Europe, who brought technical and creative expertise; the prescient decision to move the burgeoning industry to the then-inexpensive and climatically appealing Southern California; and the lack of competition, as much of the film industry in Europe had been destroyed during World War I (Cohen 2001, 5–6). But Cohen raises a critical question in her study that has relevance not only for this period of cinema history but for this essay as well: How do we account for "the profound symbiosis that has existed between America and the movies from the first decades of the twentieth-century onward" (Cohen 2001, 6)? According to her, this mutually deep and mutually dependent relationship relied on "film's ability to participate in the *myth of America*," which was at its core a founding myth of a naïve and virgin land unhindered by the restrictions and errors of the Old World and that needed, according to the poet Walt Whitman, a new cultural expression corresponding to the form of American life—and in many ways, the Hollywood film industry was ready to meet that need (Cohen 2001, 6). And like America in this period, film was seen as primitive and naïve and had a kind of rawness and realism that allowed it to speak directly to the masses. It was also democratic in nature; gone was the hand of the master creating a painting or sculpture, and in its place was the photograph or the film itself, presenting directly to the spectator, who has now been elevated to the role of critic.

Key myths dominated early narrative film. There was the self-made man, or the "American Adam," originally proposed for literature by R. W. B. Lewis, the founder of American studies as an academic field (cited in Cohen 2001, 14). And there was myth of untested talent via the studio star system, in which young actors were recruited, promoted, and often exploited by executives who were more interested in the glamorous image of these budding stars and starlets than in their acting abilities. Some have compared the way stars and films were produced by studios during this period to the way that Model-Ts were produced in Ford assembly-line factories.

Adding to the need to rely on untested talent was the fact that many professional theater actors were reluctant to become involved with early cinema, not only because they relied on their voice as one of their greatest tools on stage—a tool that would be useless, of course, in silent film—but also because they saw cinema as an inferior or low form of culture, aimed at the masses. But the studio star system fit well with both myths identified above; this reliance on the untested talent of American Adams and Eves allowed for an entirely new approach to acting, and these nascent stars were self (or studio) made personas. As Cohen (2001) notes,

> The great stars of the silent era were both self-made and audience-made in a combination that reconciled two opposing strands of the American myth: individualism and democracy. On the one hand, they extended concepts of physical self-reliance and resourcefulness associated with the American frontiersman and applied them to the material of personality. On the other hand, their ability to shape themselves to the needs of their audiences reflected a new kind of public, consensual process in the creation of the self that was in keeping with the democratic principles of the nation. This conjunction of individualism and democratic conformity was in turn adopted by the audiences themselves through the exercise of their consumer power. (12–13)

Of course, as noted early in this essay, there are limits to and stains on the mythology being produced and consumed in this early period of Hollywood cinema. While the actors often entered the studio with their ethnic name and identity, they exited into silver-screen fan magazines with nonethnic white and heterosexual personas. The central role of immigrants, often Jewish and/or from Eastern Europe, in the film industry should not be forgotten, but neither should their role in promoting a kind of "melting pot" of assimilation into a mainstream American society that, if it needed to identify its arrival to American shores, it would have been on the Mayflower to Plymouth Colony rather than by steerage to Ellis Island.

Many of these myths of American national identity continued into the next period of film history, the golden or classical period of Hollywood cinema, in part because the studio system dominated until the 1948 Supreme Court antitrust ruling, which prohibited the same person or organization from being in charge of the production, distribution, and exhibition of a film.

This early period of American cinema coincided with a period of reform in the country, and films, despite many having a comedic or melodramatic tone, often reflected or exposed serious social issues that the country was facing, such as "birth control, child labor, divorce, immigration, political corruption, poverty, prisons, prostitution and women's suffrage" (Mintz, Roberts, and Welky 2016, 14). The films also portrayed a kind of antiauthoritarian attitude combined with a desire for equality that has run deep in the psyche of America since its founding days.

Thus this first period of Hollywood cinema, the silent era, introduces many American myths to the newly created filmgoer. Some of these, such as the importance of democracy and individualism, dated back to the Founding Fathers and the country's creation in the 18th century. Others pointed to the country's strong connection to America as the land of opportunity, such as the self-made individual or the melting pot, the latter of which was especially potent given that many of those both making and consuming the films were immigrants to the country and could use film to create a place for themselves in their new homeland. Darker sides to national mythology could be seen in this earlier period, for example, the American Adam (sometimes called the Eternal Adam) had a clear connection to Manifest Destiny, the idea that God had ordained that the United States had the right to rule over the entire North American continent, spreading democracy and capitalism and eliminating obstacles (such as Native Americans) that obstructed this divinely mandated new Garden of Eden. Many of these myths would find their way into later periods of American cinema, where they would be at times revised, and at other times resisted, while being joined by new national narratives. The classical period of Hollywood cinema lasted at least 20 years, from the late '20s to the late '40s, although some prefer to combine this period with the New Hollywood period, which ended in 1979. Films of the studio period relied on proven formulas (such as the Western, the musical, the biographical film, the slapstick comedy, and the cartoon or animated film), and studios not only used the same actors but often the same creative personnel to create their films, adding to a sense of familiarity and shared experience. Studios kept large numbers of actors, writers, camera operators, and hundreds of others involved in the creative and technical aspects of filmmaking on salary, emphasizing the business and almost factorylike potential of this system.

This period can be seen negatively as one in which studios churned out formulaic and typically artistically inferior films, because the budgets were low and not every film needed to be a hit. But at the same time, studios could gamble on making films with unknown actors or directors that sometimes resulted in what are now considered masterpieces, such as *The Wizard of Oz* (1939) and Welles's *Citizen Kane* (1941), each of which was met by indifference from its contemporary audience and neither of which could be considered a financial success at the time.

Citizen Kane made $1.5 million on a budget of $884,000, and *The Wizard of Oz* barely covered its $2.7 million budget, earning only $3 million upon its release. Since then, they have both earned considerably more money through rereleases and sales, and also are considered masterpieces, with *Kane* frequently named as the best movie ever made. The year 1939 stands out with a stunning number of now classic films being produced in that year including but not limited to: *Gone with the Wind*, S*tagecoach*, *Mr. Smith Goes to Washington*, and *Only Angels Have Wings*.

While movies had earlier been seen as a form of mass (rather than high or cultured) entertainment, and movie houses in the first decades of the 20th century served audiences based on class and ethnic lines, the studio period resulted in regional and national ownership of previously individually owned venues. Not only were all audiences now seeing the same programs but they also saw them in the same space, creating a standardized and democratized experience (Mintz, Roberts, and Welky 2016, 16). The myth of democracy had played a key role in the silent film era, when so many of the filmmakers and audience were immigrants from countries in which they had been disenfranchised politically and economically. This sense of democratic equality and belonging was needed when the Depression hit the country and Hollywood cinema "played a valuable psychological and ideological role, providing reassurance and hope to a demoralized nation" (Mintz, Roberts, and Welky 2016, 17). While many films of this period could be classified as escapist, those especially of the early part of the Depression (1929–1933) continued to engage in social issues, providing their escape through dark or satirical jabs at violence (gangster films) or sexually provocative and irreverent comedies such as those made by the Marx Brothers. The New Deal (1933–1939) marked a more optimistic turn in film, in which the rugged individual or the beleaguered "little man" stands up to the corrupted powerful, reflecting American narratives of fairness and optimism. The next huge event to take hold in Hollywood was World War II, which provided an opportunity for movies to rebrand patriotism as a positive American attribute, sometimes in a jingoistic or propagandistic manner. According to Mintz, this shift to a pro-America attitude was encouraged by the Office of War Information, which recognized the power of film to narrate a vision of the nation and was unhappy with many films being produced by Hollywood at the time, which it saw as "escapist and delusive" (quoted in Mintz, Roberts, and Welky 2016, 21) and failing to promote an acceptable image of the country. This governmental interference continued through the postwar period and throughout much of the first Cold War, through censorship and blackballing, coinciding at its apogee with McCarthyism and the House Un-American Activities Committee. HUAC's investigation of the Hollywood film industry began in 1947, was nothing more than a Communist witch hunt, and remains a stain on American beliefs in free speech and democracy.

The cracks in the façade of the American Dream were caused by the Depression and a postwar prosperity that did not extend beyond the picket fence of the house in the "white" suburbs. They were exacerbated by Cold War tensions and communist witch hunts directed at Hollywood, and they resulted in genres of film such as Westerns, film noir, and other angst-filled dramas featuring method actors (those who follow the extreme approach of not simply portraying a character but becoming that character): Marlon Brando, James Dean, and Marilyn Monroe, among others. Westerns can be seen as the quintessential American film genre, incorporating John Wayne and the Marlboro Man. Yet the hero in many Westerns, when not an outright outlaw, is often a lawman driven by revenge and willing to step outside of the law to impose frontier justice, and the films themselves were often tainted by Manifest Destiny, racism, and genocide. Here we see an updated Manifest Destiny from the American Adam of the silent era, because the economic and political crises facing the United States (and the world) at the time required a darker hero that better reflected the struggles of filmgoers.

Other films of this period also display cracks in the American Dream through their aesthetic and thematic choices. Noir films are shadowy and grainy, and there is always the threat of corruption and violence lurking in the shadows. The protagonists want to participate in the American Dream, but despite their hard work and gumption, they fail. Other films, often featuring teenage or working-class protagonists, expose how consumerism can be an empty or unattainable utopia. Key films from the period include auteur filmmaker Hitchcock's *Rear Window* (1954), and method actors Marlon Brando's *On the Waterfront* (1954), James Dean's *Rebel Without a Cause* (1955), and Marilyn Monroe's *Some Like It Hot* (1959). The easy optimism of the earlier period of film in many instances seemed no longer possible. While some silent era films had been critical of social ills, and comedy masterpieces by Buster Keaton and Charlie Chaplin exposed humanity's vulnerabilities, those films did not create the same sense of darkness or hopelessness that some of the films of this later period did, showing especially the inaccessibility of myths of fairness and equality to certain marginalized communities. So while we begin this period full of postwar optimism and betting on the success of the "little man," global economic and political crises, as well as the introduction of a new category of citizen—the teenager—left filmgoers midcentury with conflicting versions of the nation flickering on the silver screen.

Although the studio system had been defunct for years, the 1960s began to experience a shift in the financial structure of filmmaking. Studios previously owned by individual moguls were now being assimilated into large conglomerations, changing the New Hollywood into the "Corporate Hollywood" (Markman 2005, 29). Hollywood filmmaking has always been a business, but there was a new emphasis on creating not only a hit but a megahit, a blockbuster film with financial tie-ins with other products (something Disney had begun decades ago but had not fully exploited until this period and included toys, collectibles, and fast-food franchises) that depended on star power, a massive budget, and relentless advertising to attract its audience. Gone are the failures and misfits of the earlier period, banished are the outlaws and mavericks who turn their back on society, and in their stead are the struggling heroes, often underdogs, whose desire to solve something or create something of value will not only benefit themselves but in many instances all of humankind. Thus Luke Skywalker battles the dark side, Indiana Jones fights Nazis, and Dr. Ian Malcolm (*Jurassic Park*) takes on dinosaurs.

The reign of the blockbuster began with the film *Jaws* in 1975 and, some would argue, continues today, with films being increasingly divided into the categories of independent and commercial cinema. This was an exciting period for audience members, when technological advances in sound and special effects made moviegoing "an event." Despite their financial and popular success, films of this period remain understudied and undertheorized to some extent because, as Julian Stringer notes in the introduction to his book *Movie Blockbusters*, although we are all "experts" to a certain degree on blockbusters (or event movies as he also calls them), we don't spend a lot of time thinking about them, in large part because "the Hollywood film industry makes the process of consuming such films both easy and pleasurable" (Stringer 2003, 14). He continues: "Critics, journalists, and scholars often claim an insidious superficiality and underlying awfulness for blockbusters, encouraging the worst extreme blanket dismissals of some of the most popular forms of commercial cinema. Films labeled as blockbuster are frequently positioned as examples of the culturally retrograde, beneath serious consideration or analysis" (Stringer 2003, 14).

Blockbuster films, like those of any other era, not only reflect the anxieties of their era but, because of their popularity with a mass audience of all ages, involve the American public in this cultural conversation in a way that is accessible to all. The period of the blockbuster, which has been marked by the release of *Jaws* in 1975, was one of intense cultural and economic change that shook American society to its foundations. The war in Vietnam, which tore society apart in a way no previous war had done since the Civil War, had just ended with the fall of Saigon in April 1975. Second-wave feminism was becoming a powerful cultural force, liberation movements for gay rights and Native American rights joined the voices of African Americans and other disenfranchised minority groups in demanding equal recognition as citizens. Blockbuster films participated in these conversations, expanding the ways in which contemporary concerns participated in previous national mythology, or demonstrating the ways in which new stories needed to be told to better reflect the period. *Jaws*, for example, while demonstrating the rugged individualism and independence of the protagonist, also revealed white male anxiety concerning his participation in wars and his general status in society. *Aliens* (1986), over a decade later, can also be seen as engaging in gender concerns, this time looking at female empowerment as well as anxieties about the place of motherhood in the changing role of women in American society. The film also engages with well-known myths of (westward) expansion and engagement with lawless frontiers, with critics acknowledging the thematic similarities between some sci-fi and Westerns.

The American Dream is often enacted through the character of the underdog and can be connected to the concept of American exceptionalism, the idea that the United States is endowed with unique qualities that are worthy of universal admiration. Underdogs, in fact, can be considered an archetype of American cinema, with *Rocky* (of the multifilm franchise) being one of the most beloved in film history. This "bum" and unexpected romantic lead did not even need to win his fight—he simply had to try his best and to go the distance. This underdog character becomes linked to a desire to find one's identity and belong, as seen in films from the 1990s through the early 2000s, through quests undergone by characters such as Simba (*Lion King*, 1994), Woody (*Toy Story*, 1995), Shrek (*Shrek*, 2001), or Nemo (*Finding Nemo*, 2003*)*.

As geopolitics became more complicated and the clear divide between good guys and bad buys less clear to many of the Millennials and Gen Zers, Hollywood blockbusters helped provide some guidance in navigating the mire. It can be argued that there was a kind of nostalgia present, too, which could be seen in the earlier period of blockbusters (for example, in the movie *Grease*, which romanticizes the "simpler" time of the 1950s). Harry Potter mania took over the world, first through the novels and later the film franchise. Superheroes began appearing everywhere in film franchises of the DC Extended Universe (DCEU) and the Marvel Cinematic Universe (MCU) of the 21st century—Spider-Man, X-Men, Batman, Avengers, Wonder Woman—at times flawed and cynical but always reflecting an underlying narrative of good versus evil and American exceptionalism. Cultural issues were also taken up during this time, with *Frozen* and *Zootopia* promoting an attitude of inclusivity, mirroring that of its generation.

The blockbuster era has not only expanded on or challenged previous mythologies of America but has done so in a way that has reflected the engagement of different generations with these myths. Boomers, for example, remain generally optimistic and continue to believe in the possibility of the American Dream. They remain in love with underdogs such as Danny Zuko (*Grease*) and Rocky Balboa. They cheer on both police chief Martin Brody (*Jaws*) and antisocial criminal Randle McMurphy (*One Flew over the Cuckoo's Nest*), who both exhibit the mythical characteristic of individualism, whether they are restoring order or challenging corrupt authority. Their almost religious devotion to capitalism can be seen in films throughout the 1980s (with two extreme visions being *Wall Street*, 1987 and *Scarface*, 1983). Despite criticisms of injustice and inequality, they still believe in the American Dream and American exceptionalism, as the films of their generation clearly show.

The Gen X generation (b. 1965–1980) is sandwiched between its two larger cohorts (Boomers, b. 1946–1964, and Millennials, b. 1981–1994) and is sometimes referred to as the lost (or lazy or late-blooming) generation. Often overeducated and underemployed, Gen Xers' cynicism with regard to the American Dream was reflected in much Hollywood cinema of the period, and films from *Reality Bites* (1994) to *Slackers* (2002) captured the zeitgeist of the generation. Millennials regained some of the optimism missing in the previous generation, with *Harry Potter* becoming *the* film of this generation. It was no longer individualism that would win the day but friendship and community that was needed to fight evil. The underdog character with the wonky hair, scar, and thick glasses could become the hero, democracy would vanquish tyranny, and the melting pot of assimilation gave way to the sorting hat of diversity. In its own way, Gen Z is just as nostalgic as the Boomer generation, not for a mythical 1950s America but for its mythical 1950s comic book characters, reinterpreted for the 21st century by MCU and DCEU. These superheroes are complex characters who challenge authority with their individualistic and independent attitudes while also belonging to a team of X-Men or Avengers or Justice Leaguers. They fight for the marginalized and oppressed, and while from diverse national, planetary, or even biological backgrounds, they seem to promote American democracy and its best impulses of fairness, equity, and possibility, as does the generation to which superhero films most appeal.

The imagined community of Hollywood filmgoers has expanded to a global audience, but many of the founding myths of the country and its cinema have remained and still help define the country's national character and current anxieties. At times, the cinema out of Hollywood can be jingoistic and reactionary, at others, it can be inspirational and visionary, but it has always retained its symbiotic relationship with the nation and continued to flex its economic, technological, and cultural role as America's national visual literature.

Angelica Maria DeAngelis

FURTHER READING

Anderson, Benedict. 2006. *Imagined Communities. Reflections on the Origins and Spread of Nationalism*. Rev. ed. London: Verso.

Cohen, Paula Marentz. 2001. *Silent Film and the Triumph of the American Myth*. Oxford: Oxford University Press.

Conley, Tom. 2006. *Film Hieroglyphics: Ruptures in Classical Cinema*. Minneapolis: University of Minnesota Press.

Markman, Ken. 2005. "Movies, Myths, and Messages: How Entertainment Is Creating a Global Brand Culture." *Licensing Journal* 25, no. 6 (June/July): 27–30.

Mintz, Steven, Randy Roberts, and David Welky, eds. 2016. *America's Hollywood, Hollywood's America: Understanding History through Film*. 5th ed. Hoboken, NJ: Wiley Blackwell.

Pimenta, Sherline, and Ravi Poovaiah. 2010. "On Defining Visual Narratives." *Design Thoughts* (August): 25–46. http://www.idc.iitb.ac.in/resources/dt-aug-2010/On%20Defining%20Visual%20Narratives.pdf.

Rogoff, Irit. 1998. "Studying Visual Culture." In *The Visual Culture Reader*, 2nd ed., edited by Nicholas Mirzoeff, 24–36. Milton Park, UK: Routledge.

Sarris, Andrew. 1962–1963. "Notes on the Auteur Theory in 1962." *Film Culture* 27 (Winter): 1–8.

Stringer, Julian. 2003. "Introduction." In *Movie Blockbusters*, edited by Julian Stringer, 14–29. Hoboken, NJ: Routledge.

Wu, Helena. 2018. "The Travelling of *Ten Years*: Imagined Spectatorships and Readerships of Hong Kong's Local." *International Journal of Postcolonial Studies* 20 (8): 1121–1136.

American Religiosity in the Age of Entertainment: Hollywood and American Values

INTRODUCTION

Long before *The Matrix*, the famous Greek philosopher Plato speculated about the nature of reality in his work, *The Republic*. In it appears the famous "Allegory of the Cave," where people are chained up underground and forced to watch shadows on the wall. The shadows are created by a fire in front of the prisoners, together with the movement and noise of unchained people behind them, whom they cannot see. The illusion thus has both a visual and aural component. Interestingly, the prisoners cannot move their heads around to see what is happening behind them; they can only look forward at the wall. Another element in this complex allegory is the fact that these prisoners have been in this position since childhood, so they take what they see and hear as reality itself.

But even further back in time, ancient humans climbed and clambered their way into deep caves intentionally, using crude torches in their descent underground. And after arriving to some of the least inaccessible areas, they stopped and drew pictures on the walls. Some of this art in Indonesia dates back to nearly 45,000 years ago. Perhaps the most famous, though, are the drawings in France's Lascaux caves. Dating roughly to 20,000 years ago, there are over 600 drawings covering the walls. While most of these are of identifiable animals (either extinct or living today), there are some therianthropes or animal-human hybrids. Together with a small number of abstract symbols, researchers have suggested that there is a great deal more significance to the art than merely commemorating a hunt; it has *spiritual* significance. Or, in older terms, there seems to have been a religious function to the art, its location, content, and materials. Speculatively, and given the fact that many of the scenes look to be in motion, it seems quite reasonable to assume that the artists intended to convey dynamism. Given, too, that this artwork was only visible to ancient people by flickering firelight, it would seem that the art was meant to be viewed in concert with that moving light. Moreover, since much of the art stretches over lengths of walls or on the ceiling horizontality, one can easily imagine the very torchbearer walking while lighting some parts and concealing others, perhaps adding some vocalizations in the mix. Representations of complex reality; a dark, cool room to watch in; a narrative; and "moving" images all sound rather like a cinematic experience.

For both our early ancestors and Plato, the human impulse toward understanding reality by creating dynamic representations of that reality—either by complex allegories and dialogues or cave drawings—included a metaphysical or spiritual element. For both the Greeks and prehistoric humans, the sensual apprehension of the so-called objective world was not adequate; there was a larger story, a different reality behind the scenes—a reality that was accessible through the imagination both of the individual and the community. The fact that the art at Lascaux is the work of multiple generations testifies to a type of tradition as each generation engaged with the traces of the manifest imaginings of its ancestors. One could speculate that there was a type of initiation into the grammar of decoding these images that developed and was passed down for centuries—a grammar we have now lost. But that creative impulse that sees a close connection between art, imagination, and spirituality remains.

Spirituality is a problematic category, so some clarification is necessary. There has been a recent rise in people who identify as "spiritual" but "not religious" in surveys and censuses across America. We have, then, a rise in spirituality and a decline in public religion, the former regarded as existing mainly in the private domain. Paul Heelas is helpful:

> Religion is . . . very much God-centered [and] especially since the 1960s, has increasingly come to be seen as that which is institutionalized. . . . For many, it has come to be associated with the formal, dogmatic, and hierarchical, if not the impersonal or patriarchal. "Spirituality" has to do with the personal; that which is interior or immanent; that which is one's experienced relationship with the sacred; and that wisdom or knowledge which derives from such experiences. At heart, spirituality has come to mean "life." Life, rather than what transcends life, becomes God (this contemporary spirituality may be more precisely termed "spirituality of life"). (Quoted in Main 2004, 145)

Roderick Main traces this slippage from religion to spirituality to the 1960s, just prior to the films that begin this text. Another scholar, Wouter Hanegraaff, offers five basic elements to this spirituality: "this-worldliness, holism, evolutionism, the psychologisation of religion and the secularization of psychology, and expectations of a coming new age" (quoted in Frisk, Gilhus, and Kraft 2016, 470). Thus when we speak of American religiosity, we are really speaking of American *spirituality*, which gives rise to the socially shaped values indicated above and outlined in greater detail below. This "new" spirituality and its attendant values are then encoded and transmitted through the most popular cave art in the world: Hollywood cinema.

It would be reductionistic simply to say that America is now spiritual and no longer religious. The shift from one to the other is differentiated across generations and exists on a spectrum. Broadly speaking, many Americans are fairly eclectic and uncritical about their beliefs and practices, often attempting to compartmentalize experiences and people. But taking Heelas's above rubric for religion as institutional, formal, dogmatic, impersonal, hierarchical, and patriarchal, together with American history, one can roughly sketch out the religious side of America—the side that sometimes uneasily exists with its spiritual and so-called secular counterparts.

RELIGIOUS AMERICA?

Americans are often portrayed as religious people. "In God We Trust" is on our coins. We are "one nation under God" in our pledge, and the president is expected to end speeches with "God bless America." These forms of civil religion are vacuous enough to leverage a wide variety of theological expressions into the gaps. Who or what is this "God" we trust, pledge our allegiance to, and expect to bless us? More often than not, this God has been and continues to be associated with the Judeo-Christian God of Western civilization. This is, of course, despite the persistent and insistent criticism surrounding Constitutional interpretation (the freedom *of* religion vs. freedom *from* religion), debates about the separation of church and state (even the debate is framed in Christian terms), and even opposition from some Christians themselves, who see any form of established religion as a deal with the devil. But how accurate is it to think of America as "Christian"? According to the Pew Research Center's 2014 survey of 35,000 Americans in all 50 states, Christianity is still the dominant religious affiliation, with 70.6 percent of respondents self-identifying as Christian (see figure 2).

And, as seen in figure 2, of that 70.6 percent, Evangelical Christians are the majority (25.4%), followed closely by Catholics, at 20.8 percent. But who are these Evangelical Protestants?

The beginnings of Evangelicalism are often traced to the 1730s. As it emerged from its European Reformation context, it manifested saliencies that David Bebbington labels "special marks of Evangelical religion" (1989, 1). He enumerates and defines these as: "*conversionism*, the belief that lives need to be changed; *activism*, the expression of the gospel in effort; *Biblicism*, a particular regard for the Bible; and what may be called a *crucicentrism*, a stress on the sacrifice of Christ on the cross" (3). Not only are these "special marks" indicative of 18th-century Evangelicalism but they have been continually reframed, differentiated, refined, and reaffirmed throughout Evangelical history and by the later movements it spawned. Bebbington's "special marks" help color in some of the spaces between Heelas's "religion" and American Evangelical religiosity. It also offers some explanation for the volume and urgency of some Evangelical leaders. For our purposes here, conversionism and Biblicism are most relevant.

The stress on changing individuals, conversionism, includes socializing them according to "what the Bible teaches" or Biblicism. Within the marketplace of American religion, Evangelicals have been highly successful at both of these—especially Evangelical Baptists who make up the majority of Evangelicals (see figure 3). Of note here, Jimmy Carter (president from 1977 to 1981) was the first president to identify as a born-again Christian (Evangelical) and was also Southern Baptist, a significant "win" in terms of gaining legitimacy and a platform.

Christian	70.6%	Non-Christian Faiths	5.9%
• Evangelical Protestant	25.4%	Jewish	1.9%
• Mainline Protestant	14.7%	Muslim	0.9%
• Historically Black Protestant	6.5%	Buddhist	0.7%
		Hindu	0.7%
Catholic	20.8%	**Other World Religions**	0.3%
• Mormon	1.6%	• Other Faiths	1.5%
• Orthodox Christian	0.5%	Unaffiliated (religious "nones")	22.8%
Jehovah's Witness	0.8%		3.1%
• **Other Christian**	0.4%	Atheist	4.0%
		Agnostic	
		• Nothing in particular	15.8%
		Don't know	0.6%

Figure 2. Pew Religious Landscape Study
(Source: Religious Landscape Study, "Religions." Pew Research Center, Washington, D.C. Survey conducted 2007 and 2014. https://www.pewresearch.org/religion/religious-landscape-study/)

The success noted above as well as success at training converts within a particularly constrained Protestant frame of interpreting the ancient texts has often set the Evangelical community at odds with other elements of American culture. Early in America's history, this included a form of physical separatism, the kind still practiced by the Amish and Mennonites of today. This not being that practical for the large number of converts, there was a shift of emphasis to an ethical separation; that is, real Christians do these things and don't do these others. Perhaps the most famous example of this at a national level was Prohibition (1920–1933), when there was a nationwide ban on selling alcohol. Many Protestants led the movement, learning the lesson that their Evangelical descendants would also attempt: converting a nation includes changing its laws through democratic processes. This ethical separatism, together with conversionism and activism, later evolved into a self-consciousness of being the moral conscience of America itself.

As the moral conscience of the nation, many activist Evangelicals seek to align the larger culture to biblical principles. This often means conflict with their fellow Americans—a conflict that has often been referred to as the "culture wars." In terms of the time frames and topics selected in this text (1970s–present day), the general trend has been to attack Hollywood on the grounds of influencing moral decay in society. These attacks have not solely been from Evangelicals but from many in American society who also believe that children especially should be guided away from adult content. Hollywood's response, in 1968, was to implement the now-familiar motion picture film-rating system: G, PG, PG-13 (introduced in 1984), R, and NC-17 (introduced in 1990 as a replacement to the previous rating of X). These ratings, their criteria, and their efficacy have long been debated; Evangelical pundits of today consistently bemoan what content still makes it past these ratings. While Americans have consistently bemoaned censorship of any kind in the news media, the entertainment industry has been treated differently

Evangelical Protestant	25.4%
Baptist Family (Evangelical Trad.)	9.2%
Southern Baptist Convention	5.3%
Independent Baptist (Evangelical Trad.)	2.5%
Missionary Baptist (Evangelical Trad.)	<0.3%
Conservative Baptist Association of America	<0.3%
Free Will Baptist	<0.3%
General Association of Regular Baptist Churches	<0.3%
Other Baptist (Evangelical Trad.)	1.0%
Methodist Family (Evangelical Trad.)	<0.3%

Figure 3. Pew Religious Landscape Study inset 1
(Source: Religious Landscape Study, "Religions." Pew Research Center, Washington, D.C. Survey conducted 2007 and 2014. https://www.pewresearch.org/religion/religious-landscape-study/)

partly out of deference to the Moral Majority and the Judeo-Christian ethic that underwrites nearly three-fourths of the American population.

COMPETING VALUES: SECULARISM, "NEW AGE" SPIRITUALITY, AND ENERGY FAITH

The largest blocks of the American population who do not identify as "Christian" are unaffiliated—religious "nones" (see figure 4). In perspective, there are more nones than there are Catholics in the United States. These nones, then, roughly form the primary target population for the conversionism of Evangelicals. However, it isn't just the size but the trending growth of the unaffiliated that creates worry among Christian groups (6.7 vs. −0.9 for Evangelicals). This movement has often been framed in terms of what scholars of religion have, in the past, called secularization theory.

From the beginnings of sociology itself, Auguste Comte, the French theorist and putative founding father of sociology, argued that as reason prevailed around the world (fueled and imposed upon by imperialism no less), religious superstition would fade away, replaced by science—especially the new "science" of sociology. This basic assumption that industrialization and modernization inevitably include the decline of religion was the modus operandi for much of the 20th century, with scholarly fingers pointing toward secularized Western Europe and its low church attendance and membership. Sociologist of religion Rodney Stark (among others), however, has (for this author) definitively shown that secularization theory is no longer a viable way of understanding religious change. In his landmark essay, "Secularization, R.I.P.," he sums up his position with a quotation from Peter Berger, another scholar who noticed the same thing: "I think what I and most other sociologists of religion wrote in the 1960s about secularization

Unaffiliated (religious "nones")	22.8%
Atheist	3.1%
Agnostic	4.0%
Nothing in particular	15.8%
Nothing in particular (religion not important)	8.8%
Nothing in particular (religion important)	6.9%
Don't know	0.6%

Figure 4. Pew Religious Landscape Study inset 2
(Source: Religious Landscape Study, "Religions." Pew Research Center, Washington, D.C. Survey conducted 2007 and 2014. https://www.pewresearch.org/religion/religious-landscape-study/)

was a mistake. Our underlying argument was that secularization and modernity go hand in hand. With more modernization comes more secularization. It wasn't a crazy theory. There was some evidence for it. But I think it's basically wrong. Most of the world today is certainly not secular. It's very religious" (2015, 259).

One doesn't have to look far to see the rise in radical forms of Islam and Hinduism as well as Christianity in the last ten years to see Berger and Stark's point. Given the statistics above, three-fourths of our country self-identify as recognizably and traditionally religious while the remaining population, the nones, do not. However, such categories are not that helpful when it comes to determining what these groups actually share; that is, what is the common "altar" around which the most Americans (religious and the nones) "worship"? In a word, Hollywood. But before moving to the ways in which entertainment functions religiously/spiritually in American society, it is necessary to briefly outline what could be called the larger zeitgeist or cultural spirit that permeates both groups and the entertainment industry.

Aside from the bedrock American cultural values—individualism, pragmatism, self-reliance, a generalized optimism, and the constellation of mores wrapped up in the problematic American Dream—a decentralized spirituality has diffused throughout American culture. For discussion purposes, I will call this shared, diffused spirituality Energy Faith for reasons that will become clearer below. As Wouter Hanegraaff, philosopher and historian of esotericism, notes, this shift from religious to spiritual includes "this-worldliness, holism, evolutionism, the psychologisation of religion and the secularization of psychology, and expectations of a coming new age" (quoted in Frisk, Gilhus, and Kraft 2016, 470). Broadly speaking, Energy Faith could be described, as Brian C. Wilson, a professor of comparative religion, writes, "as a hyperindividualistic evolution of [earlier] metaphysical and New Age movements" (Wilson 2018, xii). In more philosophical terms, at its base, Energy Faith is a movement toward a "monistic rather than dualistic cosmology, that is, one that posits that all is one, including God" (x). It is also characterized by an attempt to reconcile science with religion, both of which get expressed in terms of "energy": flow, positive, negative, power, "good vibes," quantum, atomic, nuclear, radiation, and so on. Again, as Wilson notes, this "new" zeitgeist is rooted both in the metaphysical tradition (think Ralph Waldo Emerson and the American transcendentalists) and New Age movements. For sake of space and scope, let's look briefly at the rise of the New Age movement and the influx of alternative spiritualities in the United States, specifically during the 1960s and '70s, where our film entries begin.

The rise of the New Age movement and other New Religious movements (NRMs) in America roughly corresponded to the shift from religion to spirituality that sociologist Paul Heelas and religious studies scholar Roderick Main noted: 1960s–1970s. Rebecca Moore, another religious studies scholar and writer, summarizes this context well, offering the repeal of the Asian Exclusion Act in 1965 as a major factor for the increase in "Eastern" spiritualities in the United States:

> The 1960s and 1970s saw the rise of many new religions in the United States. A major reason for this was the development of a counterculture that challenged the assumptions and values of society at large. Well-educated young adults, predominantly white and affluent, were drawn to New Religious Movements (NRMs) because of their readings in philosophy and their study of Zen Buddhism, because of their drug use, and because of their interest in alternative lifestyles. Drug use in particular created a desire for ecstatic experiences, either through chemicals or through religious ritual. An unpopular war and a militant civil rights movement also led many to question the values with which they had grown up. Another element that explains the rise of new religions was the repeal of the Asian Exclusion Act in 1965. Abolition of this act, promulgated in 1924 and aimed at limiting all immigration from Asia, enabled many religious leaders to come to the United States. These leaders brought with them a variety of new religions that attracted rebellious young adults who sought deeper meaning and a more involved spiritual practice than they had found in their parents' faith. All of these factors contributed to the willingness of young adults to try out new religions. (2009, Kindle location 291–305)

These currents were eclectically combined with perennial esotericism and forms of Spiritualism, a transatlantic 19th- and early 20th-century movement focused mainly on the afterlife and communication therewith, to generate what became known as the New Age movement.

Some of these elements have persisted and diffused throughout the broader American culture today. In fact, some of these beliefs—psychics, spiritual energy in objects, astrology, and reincarnation—were flagged in another Pew survey, this time in 2017 (see figure 5). As expected, the most resistant to such beliefs are Evangelical Christians, who report the lowest percentages across the board, but still, 60 percent of Christians in general hold to at least one New Age belief. And as shown below, despite the fact that some of the nones "tend to reject New Age beliefs," the emergent category of Spiritual but not Religious (SBNR in the sociological literature) generally does embrace at least one, as do the other two remaining identifications (see figure 6). From this discussion, then, it is clear that previously marginalized beliefs have gone viral, or in Michael Barkun's terminology, the fringe has been mainstreamed (2013). One can also see the operative monism underneath the above "beliefs" as well: energy and matter are essentially the same thing, thus spiritual energy is located in objects; the dead's energies or souls continue to exist in another form (thus enabling communication and reincarnation); and within a monistic cosmos, of course, distant planets and stars can have causal influence on a person (astrology). It is also clear that the widespread diffusion of these beliefs across both of the "Christian" and "Nones" categories indicates something else is going on—a new American movement is emerging:

Six-in-ten Christians, "nones," hold at least one New Age belief

	Believe spiritual energy can be located in physical things	Believe in physics	Believe in reincarnation	Believe in astrology	NET Believe in at least one
All U.S. adults	42%	41%	33%	29%	**62%**
Christian	37	40	29	26	**61**
Protestant	32	38	26	24	**57**
Evangelical	24	33	19	18	**47**
Mainline	43	44	33	30	**67**
Historically Black	41	43	38	34	**72**
Catholic	47	46	36	33	**70**
Unaffiliated	47	40	38	32	**62**
Atheist	13	10	7	3	**22**
Agnostic	40	31	28	18	**56**
Nothing in particular	61	52	51	47	**78**

Source: Survey conducted Dec. 4-18, 2017, among U.S. adults.
PEW RESEARCH CENTER

Figure 5. Six-in-ten Christians, "nones," hold at least one New Age belief (Source: "New Age" beliefs common among both religious and nonreligious Americans." Pew Research Center, Washington, D.C. October 1, 2018. https://www.pewresearch.org/fact-tank/2018/10/01/new-age-beliefs-common-among-both-religious-and-nonreligious-americans/)

Energy Faith. And to return to what was said before, the catalyst and medium of this movement is cinema.

THE NEW AMERICAN RELIGION AND ENERGY FAITH SPIRITUALITY OF CINEMA

A helpful text to this ongoing conversation, *The Altars Where We Worship* (Floyd-Thomas, Floyd-Thomas, and Toulouse 2016), seeks to demonstrate how Americans are fulfilling their religious impulses through popular culture apart from or in addition to traditional institutions. Nested within the shifting sociological landscape, the contestation of secularization, and the slide from "religious" to "spiritual," the authors broadly apply scholar of religion Ninian Smart's seven dimensions of religion from his *The Religious Experience of Mankind* (1969) to six areas of popular culture, which they call "altars." These seven dimensions are (1) myth, (2) doctrine, (3) ethics, (4) institutions, (5) rituals, (6) experience, and (7) materiality. The six different altars these dimensions are applied to are the body and sex, big business, entertainment, politics, sports, and science and technology. We will be focusing on their discussion of entertainment as an altar.

The intersection of these seven dimensions with entertainment generates a description of the industry that therefore can be labeled as religious. In terms of myth, the authors note, as I will below, how the superhero genre reenacts Joseph

U.S. adults who say they are neither religious nor spiritual tend to reject New Age beliefs

Among those who identify as ...	Believe spiritual energy can be located in physical things	Believe in psychics	Believe in reincarnation	Believe in astrology	NET Believe in at least one
... religious and spiritual	41%	43%	33%	29%	65%
... religious but not spiritual	35	27	27	29	58
... spiritual but not religious	60	54	45	39	77
...neither religious nor spiritual	28	27	22	19	45

Note: Respondents were asked two separate questions: "To what extent do you consider yourself a RELIGIOUS person? Are you very religious, somewhat religious, not too religious, not at all religious?" and "To what extent do you consider yourself a SPIRITUAL person? Are you very spiritual, somewhat spiritual, not too spiritual, not at all spiritual?" The table shows combined results from both questions. Respondents are categorized as "religious" if they describe themselves as "very religious" or "somewhat religious," and they are categorized as "spiritual" if they describe themselves as "very spiritual" or "somewhat spiritual."
Source: Survey conducted Dec. 4-18, 2017, among U.S. adults.
PEW RESEARCH CENTER

Figure 6. U.S. adults who say they are neither religious nor spiritual tend to reject New Age beliefs
(Source: "New Age" beliefs common among both religious and nonreligious Americans." Pew Research Center, Washington, D.C. October 1, 2018. https://www.pewresearch.org/fact-tank/2018/10/01/new-age-beliefs-common-among-both-religious-and-nonreligious-americans/)

Campbell's classic monomyth and parallels ancient mythologies (Floyd-Thomas, Floyd-Thomas, and Toulouse 2016, 73). They observe that "myths and entertainment generally reinforce existing cultural norms. . . . These characters are popular because they represent values connected to self-reliance and rugged individualism. They continue to reinforce specific cultural and mythical notions of the ideal person, the ideal life, and a better world, a world where evil is always defeated by good" (75). Doctrinally, they argue that "self-realization is all important to reaching the happy ending" (81). Ethically, entertainment offers models for how to live life. Here they have an extended discussion on comedy, offering, "Anyone seeking to understand more fully the true disposition of a culture and society really ought to take seriously what makes people laugh" (85). They explore ritual in terms of the celebration of celebrity, materiality by way of memorabilia and hall of fames, and institutions by means of business, economics, and time spent engaging with entertainment media. Relevant here is the authors' discussion of the dimension of experience. Here they focus mainly on music. They write, "Music is a divine experience to the extent that, within Western culture, it is omnipresent it exists everywhere, in the background of movies dictating emotions and moods on the elevator to fill the space of social awkwardness and ward off claustrophobia, in the operating and birthing rooms to provide pacing and comfort. Music sits with romantic diners and accompanies shoppers in malls. Like the Holy Spirit music is always there" (87).

Good sociologists and cultural critics defamiliarize the mundane and ubiquitous, and here we have that occurring. Music does indeed transport us to another place/space. Without it, our films and, specifically, the films covered in this text, would be much, much poorer.

To return briefly to the observation that many others have made regarding the mythological nature of the superhero genre and its centrality in today's cinescape, it is helpful to systematize things a bit and apply Smart's category of doctrine to what I am calling Energy Faith. Having already discussed *how*, to some extent, films function religiously, it is necessary to outline the beliefs of this emerging movement—beliefs that are especially salient in the superhero genre and link up to the other descriptions of spirituality given beforehand. These beliefs, I maintain, go beyond simply reinforcing cultural norms such as self-reliance and rugged individualism and even self-realization. These more fundamental beliefs of Energy Faith go as far as to provide a metanarrative that colonizes the space between traditional Christian theology and the worldviews of the nones.

Historian of religion Jeffrey Kripal (2015) has written extensively about this metanarrative (what he calls the "Super-Story") and, in particular, its emergence and diffusion through the superhero genre. Tracing the evolution of comic books back to earlier forms of proto–science fiction, theosophy, esotericism, and occult traditions, Kripal develops at set of what he coins as mythemes (or recurring archetypal tropes) that "lie at the base of a vast array of American popular culture." Notice well the religious overtones, evolutionary ideas, and monistic tendencies flagged earlier: "I also call it a Super-Story for spiritual reasons. I call it a Super-Story because the mythical themes and paranormal currents that give it life are commonly experienced by artists, writers, and readers as realities entirely above and beyond (super-) the material histories of plot design, character development, artistic layout, material production, distribution, marketing, even history and time itself" (Kindle locations 640–693).

"Mythical themes" and "paranormal currents" nest easily into the concepts of the metaphysical tradition and New Age spirituality. More helpful still are some of the mythemes themselves.

Kripal's mythemes offer a way of framing the "creed" of Energy Faith. For our purposes, there are five basic elements: divinization/demonization, orientation, alienation, radiation, and mutation. For the first, Kripal argues that there have always been "forms of intelligence that have appeared under the divine and demonic masks of local mythologies and religions." He continues, "Human beings have long sought communion with these superbeings and their transformative energies" (Kindle location 649). This communion, for Christian and none Americans alike, takes place in that ritual sphere of film viewing—either in the cinema or via other devices and means. And there, in the cinema or on the screen at home, we suspend our disbelief and watch Norse gods throw hammers at aliens. Kripal then moves to orientation, or the trope that "the sacred source of power and wisdom" was usually somewhere or somewhen else—often, literally, the Orient, or what is now called the East. In modern times, however, he maintains that scientific developments have relocated the sacred by means of the other remaining mythemes under discussion. Alienation, he observes, occurred as humanity realized that "the age, scope, and workings of the physical universe are not what our ancient stories claimed." So the sacred was shifted from the East or from some primordial past to outer space. And from there, the intelligences descend and "manipulate our religious beliefs and mythologies." Again, cue Thor, Thanos, and so on. Adding to this, science helps source the mythological imagination through radiation, the "stunning realization that matter itself is not material but energetic and potential." Recall the earlier observations regarding trends toward monism here. And, lastly, mutation: Kripal links it to evolution, and, in particular, humanity as "a transitional or temporary form, only one of countless possibilities that life can, has, and will take on this planet and, no doubt, on countless other planets." In short, life is not human, and it is constantly changing, constantly evolving. The paranormal has an existential and participatory aspect to it, the universe is much larger than expected (relativizing the importance of Earth), everything is just one thing (energy), and evolution changes what we think life and humanity are. These tropes or mythemes are what have to be accepted (however tentatively) for the metanarrative to work or at least be plausible enough to spend two hours and an afternoon on.

Overall, it seems Kripal is advocating a kind of ascended humanism, as clear in his assertion, "We can become our own authors. We can recognize that we are pulling our own strings, that the angels and aliens, gods and demons are us." For me, this moves past the descriptive nature of the other mythemes and takes an argumentative turn. I would suggest that such a move "alienates" a vast majority of Americans, who, as has been shown, still think of themselves as traditionally religious. It is a tough sell to argue that there are not ontologically distinct entities beyond ourselves. Thus in filling out the description and qualities of Energy Faith, I would draw the line with just the mythemes teased out above. They form, then, the via media and common ground where Christian and none both commune with each other in the cool darkness of the American theater.

CONCLUSION: BACK TO THE CAVE

As is clear by now, Americans are religious. And those who aren't also participate in worship around the altar of entertainment. We have entered into what could be called postsecularism.

According to theology professor John McClure, "Postsecularism [is] a mode of being and seeing that is at once critical of secular constructions of reality and of dogmatic religiosity" (2007, Kindle location 14). I would hasten to add that part of this mode of being and seeing is what theorists call an imaginary, or "the affectively laden patterns/images/forms, by means of which we experience the world, other people and ourselves." Further, "we cannot draw a sharp distinction between the imaginary and the symbolic, cognition and affect, between what is known and what is imagined" (Lennon 2015, 1).

Imaginaries are clearly social, creating discursive communities. Following philosopher Charles Taylor, they refer to "'how people imagine their social existence, how they integrate with others, and the deeper normative ideas that influence these expectations" (quoted in Kurlander 2017, Kindle location 295). They are largely "described by images and legends" as opposed to theoretical constructs

(Kindle location 302). Images and legends are carried most powerfully through narrative—especially audiovisual ones.

But it is not enough to simply posit that ours is a postsecular age that privileges narratives as a means of constructing social imaginaries. The space between the secular constructions and dogmatic religiosity is what historian Eric Kurlander calls the "supernatural imaginary" based on the "premise that the late nineteenth and early twentieth century witnessed a reframing and transposition of supernatural thinking from Christianity to occultism, border science, and alternative religion" (2017, Kindle location 306). Kurlander's "supernatural imaginary" scaled up to a cultural level within American society forms what I have designated as Energy Faith, held to some degree by both Christians and nones.

From these observations and definitions comes a simple proposition: *the imagination participates in the spiritual.* Here the imagination is that faculty within human consciousness that generates experiences that are not solely derived from sense data. Spiritual simply refers to a transpersonal realm, whatever that may be ontologically. And participation links back to what scholars of religion call "the participatory turn," described here by its best articulator, Jorge Ferrer: "Spiritual participatory events can engage the entire range of human epistemic faculties (e.g., rational, imaginal, somatic, vital, aesthetic) with both the creative unfolding of the mystery and the possible agency of subtle entities or energies in the enactment—or 'bringing forth'—of ontologically rich religious worlds. In other words, the participatory approach presents an enactive understanding of the sacred that conceives spiritual phenomena, experiences, and insights as cocreated events" (Ferrer and Sherman 2008, Kindle location 538).

Essential to the participatory model is the recognition that "religion" is neither reducible to cultural and linguistic elements nor only the realm of the supernatural ("the mystery and possible agency of subtle entities [gods or demons or angels perhaps?] or energies"); it is, more properly, the interaction—the participation—of both.

Films are, in fact, "spiritual participatory events" that allow large swaths of the American population to cocreate "rich religious worlds." The doctrine of one such world at this point in time in American history appears to be Energy Faith. Fused with some remaining American values that survive globalization's deconstructive power, Energy Faith may be the new religion of the next generation. Traces and trajectories of this amalgam of belief and practice are spread all throughout the films covered in this volume. One could even go as far as to say that part of the reason they became blockbusters is precisely because they mirror the cultural zeitgeist so well.

And now we have come full circle. The famous philosopher Alfred North Whitehead once quipped that Western philosophy is a series of footnotes to Plato. As suggested in the introduction to this essay, our religious, spiritual, and philosophical sensibilities are better manifested in our art and, in particular, our art of moving pictures in dark spaces. It is better said: human culture is a footnote to Lascaux.

Benjamin Crace

FURTHER READING

Barkun, Michael. 2013. *A Culture of Conspiracy: Apocalyptic Visions in Contemporary America*. Berkeley: University of California Press.

Bebbington, David W. 1989. *Evangelicalism in Modern Britain: A History from the 1730s to the 1980s*. London: Unwin Hyman.

"Changing U.S. Religious Landscape." 2015, May 7. Pew Research Center. https://www.pewforum.org/2015/05/12/americas-changing-religious-landscape/pf_15-05-05_rls2_1_310px.

Ferrer, Jorge, and Jacob Sherman. 2008. "Introduction: The Participatory Turn in Spirituality, Mysticism, and Religious Studies." In *The Participatory Turn: Spiritualty, Mysticism, Religious Studies*, edited by Jorge Ferrer and Jacob Sherman, 1–80. New York: SUNY.

Floyd-Thomas, Juan M., Stacey Floyd-Thomas, and Mark Toulouse. 2016. *The Altars Where We Worship: The Religious Significance of Popular Culture*. Louisville, KY: Westminster John Knox Press.

Frisk, Liselotte, Ingvild S. Gilhus, and Siv Ellen Kraft. 2016. "The New Age." In *The Oxford Handbook of New Religious Movements*, edited by James R. Lewis and Inga B. Tøllefsen, 469–481. Oxford: Oxford University Press.

Gecewicz, Claire. 2020, August 27. "'New Age' Beliefs Common among Both Religious and Nonreligious Americans." Pew Research Center. https://www.pewresearch.org/fact-tank/2018/10/01/new-age-beliefs-common-among-both-religious-and-nonreligious-americans.

Kripal, Jeffrey. 2015. *Mutants and Mystics: Science Fiction, Superhero Comics, and the Paranormal*. Chicago: University of Chicago Press.

Kurlander, Eric. 2017. *Hitler's Monsters: A Supernatural History of the Third Reich*. New Haven, CT: Yale University Press.

Lennon, Kathleen. 2015. *Imagination and the Imaginary*. Oxfordshire, UK: Taylor and Francis.

Main, Roderick. 2004. *The Rupture of Time: Synchronicity and Jung's Critique of Modern Culture*. New York: Routledge.

McClure, John A. 2007. *Partial Faiths: Postsecular Fiction in the Age of Pynchon and Morrison*. Athens: University of Georgia Press.

Moore, Rebecca. 2009. *Understanding Jonestown and Peoples Temple*. Westport, CT: Praeger.

"Religion in America: U.S. Religious Data, Demographics and Statistics." 2020, September 9. Pew Research Center. https://www.pewforum.org/religious-landscape-study.

Stark, Rodney. 2015. *Sociology of Religion: A Rodney Stark Reader*. Waco, TX: Baylor University Press.

Wilson, Brian C. 2018. *John E. Fetzer and the Quest for the New Age*. Detroit, MI: Wayne State University Press.

2

Boomers Make the Blockbuster (1975–1982)

Alien

Release Date:	1979
Director:	Ridley Scott
Box Office:	$149 million
Main Cast:	Ellen Ripley (warrant officer), played by Sigourney Weaver
	Dallas (captain), played by Tom Skerritt
	Kane (executive officer), played by John Hurt

Alien, written for the screen by Ronald Shusett and Dan O'Bannon, cost roughly $11 million dollars to make. Featuring 29-year-old Sigourney Weaver, a relatively unknown actor at the time, the film is set in the 22nd century and begins with a credit sequence, showing various planets, stars, and lights in the background. Soon thereafter, a large ship appears and the audience is informed that this is the *Nostromo*, returning from a mining venture and loaded with ore. Further, there are seven crew aboard. This ship, massive in size, is reminiscent of that of the opening sequence to *Star Wars*, which had been released just two years earlier—undoubtedly still fresh in the minds of the viewers. It should be remembered, too, at this point, video rentals were not widely available, so more care and attention were given by audiences to films in the theater. Thus Ridley's reworking of the massive spaceship recalls not only *Star Wars* but other space-faring television series's vessels Boomers would have been familiar with: *Buck Rogers* (1979–1981), *Battlestar Galactica* (1978–1979; 1980), and *Star Trek* (1966–1969). Yet the *Nostromo* is unique in that it is a primarily a working ship, extending capitalism and commercialism out into the galaxy. The ship's name is a reference to Joseph Conrad's 1904 novel, *Nostromo: A Tale of the Seaboard* (1904) and/or to Nostradamus, the 16th-century French "prophet." With regard to the former, Conrad includes elements that reappear in the film: a mining venture, a ship, class conflict, tragedy, and colonial expansion. Simultaneously, Ridley's film is "real" sci-fi, a vision of what space travel and exploitation of resources is likely to look like in the future rather than the hyperidealized or mythic visions of other productions.

As the credits continue, the scene shifts to the inside of ship, where the crew are being awakened from suspended animation. It is soon apparent that they have been awakened ten months early because a transmission has been received that they are obligated by law to respond to upon forfeiture of their pay for the ore. In the discussion about whether to respond, it becomes clear that the engineers onboard are in it for the money and want to ignore it. The engineers, Brett and Parker, insist that they should be getting equal pay. The higher-ranking members of the crew calm them down and indicate they will lose everything if they ignore the signal.

Ridley quickly moves toward the action, both following and establishing the basic tropes and themes that recur in later sci-fi and in his own filmography. Everything is wet, dark, and tight. Medium close-ups are dominant, suggestive of the claustrophobic nature of space travel. Extreme close-ups make the alien terror more real as the characters come face to face with the entity. Following the pattern of the blockbuster, *Alien* is less about the potential psychoses and broken interpersonal skills of the crew and more about the visceral, visual experience of the action itself. One hardly has time to ask why a character performs a certain action before another character does something else. In this manner, the film progresses rapidly to a planet's surface, where some of the members of the crew explore a wrecked alien ship. There are hints and suggestions in the wreckage that something bad has happened; there is a skeleton of a large, elephant-headed being with a hole in its chest. In many ways, Ridley's latest *Alien* film, *Prometheus*, is simply a reworking of these exact scenes.

As the team explores the crashed alien vessel, Kane finds an egg with an organism inside. The egg opens and a creature, breaking the spacesuit helmet, attaches to his face. The ship's science officer, Ash, breaches quarantine protocol to allow the victim back into the ship, against the protestations of Ripley that such action (foreshadowing) may doom them all. Once in the infirmary, Ash tries unsuccessfully to detach the horseshoe-crab-looking creature off Kane's face. In attempting to do so, it is revealed that the creature has acid for blood as it burns through multiple layers of the ship's compartments. The ship, having suffered some damage from the landing on the planet, undergoes repair and returns to space.

The creature mysteriously detaches and disappears. It is later found dead in the infirmary, while Kane appears to be back to normal. However, at a celebratory feast that precedes going into suspended animation, Kane falls on top of the table, and a small alien bursts out of his chest, runs across the table in a trail of blood, and disappears into the bowels of the ship. It was this scene in particular that almost earned *Alien* an R rating for gore.

Like previous disaster movies—*The Poseidon Adventure* (1972) and *The Towering Inferno* (1974)—the rest of *Alien* is a picking-off of the crew one by one or two by two, while different strategies are implemented but then fail. Ripley, the last remaining survivor, manages to set the ship to self-destruct and escape on a smaller shuttle. However, as it turns out, the alien is also on the shuttle. After sneaking her way into a space suit, Ripley manages to open the airlock, suck the creature most of the way out, shoot a grappling hook through it, and then burn it with the rockets as she blasts off back toward Earth. The film ends with Ripley recording a report just prior to reentering suspended animation.

Aspects of *Alien* are infused with its cultural and generational moments. The late '70s were a time of growing awareness about race issues, capitalistic exploitation, second-wave feminism, and societal anxieties about technology. Further, in the future setting of *Alien*, there are no Soviets, and everyone speaks with an American or British accent. This perhaps alleviated audiences' fears of the potential for the then-Cold War turning "hot." With a nuclear holocaust in the American mind, due to Carter's SALT II nuclear talks with the USSR and the beginning of the proxy war in Afghanistan, World War III loomed on the horizon for the Boomers in 1979. A vision of the future where blue-collared workers make their money in space assured audiences that the apocalypse would be adverted. Biological aliens from other worlds, not the Vietcong or the Soviet military that paraded on their news, would be the enemy of their great-great-grandchildren.

As with all art, the historical context of its production era has left its stamp. *Alien*'s female characters are seemingly devoid of romantic attachments, despite the intimate spaces of the ship, its mostly male crew, and lengthy voyage. The AI (artificial intelligence) that manages the *Nostromo* is referred to as "Mother" and is ultimately the one who calls the shots—even to the point of refusing to allow Ripley to reverse the self-destruct sequence. Here Ripley yells, "You bitch!" at the obstinate feminine computer as she smashes the video displays. With Ripley, too, there is a shift from the male captain who survives to the "strong" woman who outlasts all the male crew members. Yet despite the praise Ripley has received, pushing Sigourney Weaver's image as a feminist icon, her character is nonetheless ambiguous. Early in the film, she is at odds with Parker and Brett, the blue-collar workers on the ship. Later, she coldly refuses to break quarantine protocol. Her downturned, thin mouth is highly suggestive of what is now known as "resting bitch face," and this is how she comes off in the first half. When in a festive atmosphere of a meal, Parker makes crude suggestive remarks to the navigator, but none is directed toward Ripley by him or anyone else. Perhaps the closest she comes to the damsel-in-distress trope is when, frightened by the dying husk of the horseshoe-crab-like alien larva, she seeks shelter behind the captain. The most disturbing humiliation, however, of Ripley's character that firmly anchors *Alien* to its hypersexualized cultural moment is a scene in which Ash, revealed to be an android, tries to kill her by shoving a rolled-up porno down her throat while she lies helplessly on her back at his waist level. While this takes place, Ridley has more pornographic images of women taped up in the background, stereotypical clichés of the working-class tastes of Brett and Parker. The forced-porn-oral sex apparently takes place in one of their quarters. Parker ultimately rescues Ripley, and together they smash Ash, whose artificial blood strongly resembles seminal fluid/milk that sprays everywhere. In the penultimate closing sequence, Ripley strips to her barely there underwear and her midriff displaying, braless tank top, reminiscent of a burlesque. Seemingly self-conscious about the camera, she slowly prepares for sleep, reinforcing the voyeuristic nature of the sequence and contributing to an objectification of the female form that runs against her earlier agency. That the giant phallus-shaped alien head shifts around in response to her partly nude movements further underscores the sexualized and misogynistic aspects of the film while it supposedly breaks new ground with a strong heroine. Ultimately, the film, to modern viewers, comes off as a confused attempt to incorporate feminist concerns while titillating paying male viewers.

In terms of other societal concerns, *Alien* reflects a growing generational consciousness of workers' rights and diversity. Parker and Brett's focus on getting the job done, being paid equally, and exaggerated inefficiency-as-revolt against the white-collar stratum echoes the decade's preoccupation with labor unions and especially figures such as Jimmy Hoffa, who famously went missing four years prior to the film. Ridley's decision to include African American actor Yaphet Kotto (Parker) and Nigerian Bolaji Bodejo (the alien) demonstrates some sensitivity toward the inequities of Hollywood. Rather slyly and perhaps too quickly to be noticed, Ridley shows the audience a packet of cigarettes in one scene named Balaji Imperial. With what looks to be a maharaja as the brand icon, this suggests links to Bolaji's name, British imperialism, and even to the exploitation of minority world nations for the production of tobacco. Together with the working hierarchy on the ship and the nature of its commercial enterprise in general, Ridley offers the Boomer generation an opportunity to reflect on whether they want to participate in furthering such power inequalities, even into the 22nd century.

The last half of the 1970s included the first generation of personal computers and a growing uneasiness with the role technology was beginning to play in society. This anxiety about technology run amok appears most famously in the 1968 film *2001: A Space Odyssey*, which features HAL, a homicidal AI. Later films such as *War Games* (1983) and *Terminator* (1984) advance the idea that we are vulnerable to our own silicon creations. In *Alien*, too, that theme is partially developed in Mother, the ship's onboard AI and in Ash the android. Tied closely to these fears was that the government was involved in developing weaponized AI without proper oversight. In *Alien*, it turns out, the secret, military mission of the *Nostromo* was to bring the alien back to Earth at all costs—including the lives of the crew. Disillusioned Boomers' growing distrust of the government and the belief that it had a secret agenda had their roots in the Kennedy assassination, Vietnam, and overt government violence against protestors such as the Kent State Massacre (1970), and *Alien* reflects those sentiments.

Sandwiched between Voyager II's launch (1977) and the debut of NASA's space shuttle program (1981–2011), *Alien* also carries with it the softened hopefulness of a generation that saw the USSR's space attempts with *Sputnik* and Yuri Gagarin outmatched by the *Apollo* moon landing. Despite the horror and near invulnerability of the eponymous alien, American ingenuity ultimately wins again. Just before the havoc begins, the audience has a quick glance of another alien species—one that resembles the elephant-headed Hindu god Ganesh. This alien is seated and looking through what appears to be a telescope of some kind. This short shot telegraphs the perennial message of intrepid space exploring humanity: perhaps we are not alone and other curious species, to whom humanity is alien, are looking for us.

Benjamin Crace

See also: S*tar Wars: A New Hope*; *Terminator 2: Judgment Day*.

Further Reading

Erbland, Kate. 2017, May 16. "*Alien* Revisited: Nearly Four Decades Later, Ripley Is Still the Boundary-Busting Heroine We Deserve." IndieWire. https://www.indiewire.com/2017/05/alien-ripley-heroine-ridley-scott-sigourney-weaver-1201817775.

Holmlund, Chris. 2010. "Sigourney Weaver: Woman Warrior, Working Girl." In *The Star Decades: Acting for America: Movie Stars of the 1980s*, edited by Robert Eberwein, 139–159. New Brunswick, NJ: Rutgers University Press.

Nesbitt, Jennifer. 2016. "Deactivating Feminism: Sigourney Weaver, James Cameron, and *Avatar*." *Film & History* 46 (1): 21–32.

Rinzler, J. W. 2019. *The Making of* Alien. London: Titan Books.

Close Encounters of the Third Kind

Release Date:	1977
Director:	Steven Spielberg
Box Office:	$307 million
Main Cast:	Roy Neary, played by Richard Dreyfuss
	Jillian Guiler, played by Melinda Dillon
	Claude Lacombe, played by François Truffaut

Close Encounters, released just a few months after *Star Wars: A New Hope*, broke new ground in the sci-fi genre. Showcasing special effects then unavailable to television and some film studios, *Close Encounters* brought aliens back to Earth with all the spectacle and epic scope audiences had been expecting since Luke and Leia fought against the Empire. Spielberg, still in the wake of success from *Jaws*, decided to cast Richard Dreyfuss with all his manic energy as the male lead. *Close Encounters*, perhaps more than any other film, injected the UFO phenomenon into mainstream consciousness.

The film begins in a sandstorm in Mexico as an unidentified group of men wander about looking for their local contacts. Most of them are clearly U.S. military, but one emerges as a French scientist, Claude Lacombe. Through a translator in a mix of Spanish, French, and English, the men are led to a group of World War II–era planes that had suddenly disappeared in 1945, also known as Flight 19. Based on an actual account, Flight 19 was a squadron that had become victim to the Bermuda Triangle. In the film, they are perfectly intact, as if they had just disappeared the day before; the pilots, however, are all missing. An old, local, seemingly senile man tells the investigators that the sun came out at night and that is how the planes got there.

This first scene is rich with cultural artifacts. There is a prominent Coca-Cola sign in the window of the tiny hacienda where the investigators meet up with the Mexican military. American imperialism by capitalism parallels the use of Spanish and French among the various conversations. Mexico as a dusty and inchoate place is reinforced. Boomers climbing and investigating the planes as strange artifacts further underscores the distance attained from the Greatest Generation; they lost the planes, but Boomers will figure out where they went and how they were returned. The sense of purpose and march toward almost inevitable progress is palpable—especially in Roy and Lacombe. At the end of the film, this is brought full circle when the pilots are returned by the aliens; the first person they approach in their daze is Lacombe. While it may seem strange that one of the principal characters is French, it should be noted that Spielberg based Lacombe on the real-life UFOlogist Jacques Vallée.

The film shifts back and forth from the investigators trying to understand the phenomenon to Roy's private quest to follow his inner vision of Devils Tower in Wyoming, given to him in a blast of light from a passing UFO. Jillian's narrative to find her son, Barry, after he is abducted, intersects with Roy's journey at various points. Jillian's house is deliberately paralleled with Roy's; she is a single mother with only one child. Her house is full of delicate and feminine objects; Barry's father is not in the picture at all. Roy's house, as a father of two boys and one girl, is domestic, suburban chaos and cookie cutter, like the houses nearby. Jillian's house, also somewhere outside of Muncie, Indiana, stands alone in a large field, spacious and intentional, an incarnation of the American Dream. She is carefree, sleeping in short, cutoff jeans with only a diaphanous shirt that reveals more than it conceals. Here is the liberated feminist, living life on her own terms. There is the burdened family man waiting for a chance to escape. And how does he escape? In the typical American fashion: in a car to the West.

A transcendent cause here—the search for aliens—justifies all sorts of antisocial and secretive behavior. For Roy, the lone individualist unencumbered by family or respect for authority, drives through tollbooths, breaks into his neighbor's yard, and sneaks past military police into a restricted zone around Devils Tower, with Jillian at his side. They are both caught and questioned by the investigators who have put out a smoke screen that a nerve agent has gotten out and the 300 square miles around the Tower must be evacuated. Spielberg hits all the UFO-related conspiratorial notes: government cover-up, military black ops on U.S. soil, loss of private property, cattle mutilation, and, of course, the trope that "they" know much more than "they" tell the public. In a telling scene, Roy and Jillian are loaded into a Huey, the quintessential helicopter of Vietnam, along with other contactees who have made their way to the Tower. Many of them are much older, members of the Greatest Generation. All are wearing gas masks. Toward the end of the scene, Roy and Jillian defy their captivity and evacuation, taking off the masks in a symbolic death/resurrection move of identity making. Then Roy, Jillian, and a third Boomer leave the copter and run toward the monument. In the background, an elderly person intones, "If the army doesn't want us here, then it's none of our business." The distancing could not be clearer: Boomers, following a higher, personal vision, are pictured as distrustful and disdainful of the U.S. government that mired their generation in an unwinnable war and covered up the UFO narrative. The World War II generation may have trusted *its* government, but times have changed.

The film ends with a mother ship playing an upscaled version of Simon, a popular '70s/'80s kids' toy that combined lights and tones. The tones, a form of communication, lead to physical contact of the third kind, a reference to UFOlogist J. Allen Hynek's classification system of UFO experiences (Hynek was also a consultant on the set.). An exchange of sorts is made, abductees (including Jillian's son, Barry) from all over the world and from various time periods exit the craft, and then, after a spiny, thin alien gives a welcome sign, little "grays" appear, and astronauts wearing red jumpsuits come out and wait to board. Roy, who is among them, is the first one swarmed by the small grays. He then walks onboard, up a ramp, and out of the audience's vision.

Both the movie's poster and title credits minimize "of the Third Kind." In the title sequence, "Close Encounters" appears in large letters first, and then "of the Third Kind," appears briefly and disappears. This suggests that the film is only *partly* about alien contact and partly about human relationships. This is played out as Roy, obsessed with the aliens after his contact experience, distances his wife and children, ultimately bonding with Jillian. Roy eventually pushes even this relationship aside to go onboard the alien craft. In effect, through a synergistic process of alienation, Roy becomes an alien himself—to the degree that he has transcended the normal social bonds of home and hearth and even Earth's gravity.

Religion, too, is reworked in the film. At one point, the investigators travel to India, where large groups of religious Hindus are all chanting the five-tone sequence associated with the aliens. When asked where the tones came from, they all point up. Following the commercial success of Erich von Däniken's *Chariots of the Gods?* (1968) book and Academy Award nomination for Best Documentary (1970), it was already a well-known thesis that what appeared to modern people as "aliens" were "gods" to more primitive people (or, in this case, modern Hindus). Here, as in *E.T.* (1982) and in *Indiana Jones and the Kingdom of the Crystal Skull* (2008), Spielberg advocates von Däniken's ideas. The very name "Devils Tower" further suggests that the site has already been associated with a plurality of supernatural entities, extending back into Native American mythologies. Christianity is construed as a helpful ritual, willingly participating in the military-industrial complex. In the closing scenes, the departing astronauts are led in a corporate blessing for pilgrims by a putatively Catholic priest. Roy is not among them: he represents a particular form of religionless spirituality made up of ultimate subjectivity, wonder, and curiosity. His is a third way, sidestepping traditional religious institutions and scientism.

As with several films of the era, masculinity is reformulated away from the machismo of the '60s/'70s action hero or even the '50s father figure and toward the Everyman caught up in events larger than himself, larger than commitments to family and marriage. But despite this toning down of testosterone in one sense through Dreyfuss's adolescent-like performance, channeling his earlier role as a teenager in *American Graffiti* (1973), the film's symbolism is still very phallocentric; that is, it uses penis-shaped symbols of male dominance as grounding imagery for the narrative. Even Jillian's emancipated female role is subsumed beneath this symbolism. The major phallic symbol, or what could be called a lingam, a sacralized phallus of the Hindu god Shiva, is Devils Tower itself. It is this image that Roy, Jillian, and other contactees obsessively attempt to re-create through everyday objects and in art. In one telling scene, Roy and Jillian lay down on the ground as her son, Barry, molds a small Devils Tower–as-lingam out of mud. Together, with a look of purpose and transcendence, Roy and Jillian both stroke the object reverently. Roy remarks as he thoughtfully rubs it, "I know this. I know what this is. It means something. It is important." It is indeed important; it is the central motif of the film. In another scene, Roy builds a large model of the Tower in his living room that crowds out all other objects and concerns, except his TV. While watching TV and putting the finishing touches on the model, his wife calls and tells him she's not coming back; his phallus obsession has driven his family away. Ultimately, Roy and Jillian must make a pilgrimage to the natural lingam and ascend it before the "gods" descend in a light-ridden theophany that could be read as a reworking of Christ's transfiguration (Mark, chapter 9).

Close Encounters barely recognizes the diversity of American society and even the diversity within the UFO mythos. While some African American actors appear in the film, they do so only briefly with limited speaking roles. The most significant is a cameo by Carl Weathers, who, only a year out from playing Apollo Creed in the blockbuster *Rocky* (1976), has less than a minute as a military police officer who threatens Roy. And despite the fact that the premier filming location is in the backyard of several Native American tribes, the closest the film comes to recognizing the irony of the military confiscating the entire area and driving the inhabitants off is in the cryptic medical history questioning Roy receives before boarding the craft: "Have you been inoculated against smallpox, diphtheria?"—two of the main diseases that decimated Native American populations. Additionally, the UFO abduction phenomenon originally garnished the nation's attention when the story of Betty and Barney Hill, an interracial couple, was made known in a book (1966) and a TV film in 1975, just two years before *Close Encounters*.

Close Encounters ultimately domesticizes the UFO narrative's subversive power by affirming the then prevailing cultural norms, shaped by generational concerns and the American mythos. Boomer men (and others) should follow their inner vision, rooted in a primal masculinity-as-decisiveness and potency, above and beyond ties to family, dead-end jobs, God, and the government. Interpersonal relationships can be appreciated but may end up being a hindrance to that individualistic journey of self-actualization. A close encounter, in these terms, can be thought of in a sense of relief, as in "a close call" or "that was close"—the type of encounter or experience that almost but not quite derails the project of meaning making.

Benjamin Crace

See also: *E.T.: The Extra-Terrestrial*; *Indiana Jones and the Raiders of the Lost Ark*; *Jaws*; *Jurassic Park*; *Star Wars: A New Hope*.

Further Reading

"Close Encounters of the Third Kind (Movie)." 2018. *Cultural Studies: The UFO Encyclopedia*. Detroit, MI: Omnigraphics.

Kendrick, James. 2014. *Darkness in the Bliss-Out: A Reconsideration of the Films of Steven Spielberg*. New York: Bloomsbury Academic.

O'Connell, Mark. 2017. *The Close Encounters Man: How One Man Made the World Believe in UFOs*. New York: Dey St./William Morrow.

Torry, Robert. 1991. "Politics and Parousia in *Close Encounters of the Third Kind.*" *Literature Film Quarterly* 19 (3): 188.

E.T.: The Extra-Terrestrial

Release Date:	1982
Director:	Steven Spielberg
Box Office:	$793 million
Main Cast:	Elliott, played by Henry Thomas
	Gertie, played by Drew Barrymore
	Mary, played by Dee Wallace
	Michael, played by Robert MacNaughton

On the heels of both *Star Wars* and *Close Encounters of the Third Kind*, Lucasfilm worked closely with Spielberg to produce a more intimate kind of extraterrestrial encounter for audiences. Riddled with cross-references to *Star Wars* and *Star Trek*, *E.T.: The Extra-Terrestrial* (*E.T.*) managed to break new ground in the realm of science fiction films for families. Like *Close Encounters*, *E.T.* has conspicuous product placement; it also represents a distinct identification of Hollywood with the capitalist enterprise. It as much an endearing relationship story as it is a feature-length advertisement. Of note, too, is its female screenwriter, Melissa Mathison (*The Black Stallion*, 1979) and coproducer, Kathleen Kennedy (Jurassic Park franchise). Such a combination signals a breech in the male-dominated world of Hollywood. And as expected, the main female character is given more depth than the traditional male lead. In short, the mother's view is a more privileged view than the absent father's.

Despite a few brief scenes with children in both *Jaws* and *Close Encounters*, *E.T.* is arguably Spielberg's earliest attempt to work on what becomes his signature focus: the experience of children and teens in the world of adults. E.T. as alien to everything, separated from home, is largely a concretization of childhood/teen angst: alienation made visible. That E.T., the alien visitor, identifies most strongly with Elliott, the sensitive middle child who recruits his younger sister and older, teen brother, further reinforces the creature as symbol of a spectrum of preadulthood. Further, most of the adults' faces in the film are hidden for a good portion of the time, except, of course, the mother's. Much of the significant action, too, takes place in the bedrooms and closets of Elliott and Gertie.

The film begins with a large spacecraft in the woods, eerily reminiscent of both the ship in *Close Encounters* and of the drawings the Nazis supposedly made of their attempts at creating UFOs, called the Nazi bell. Several ETs are out and about, collecting plant samples to cultivate on their ship that already has a whole host of strange and alien fungi and plants. It is dark, and the lights from the outside of the ship illuminate the audience's vision in such way as to block most of the details of the creatures. Their scientific hunt for samples is interrupted when several cars and four-wheel drives show up nearby. E.T., now separated from his family by the investigators, ends up getting left behind as they close in on the ship. To elude capture, E.T. hides in a shed out behind Elliott's house.

In the house, Elliott is merely an observer to a game his older brother and friends are playing. They demand that he order pizza and then go out to collect it from the driver. While he is outside, the scene shifts briefly to show the mother, in her nightgown, coming happily into the kitchen full of teens. She bends over to get something in a cabinet while one of the friends pretends to touch her behind before Michael, the oldest son, wards him off. Such a scene early in the film, along with E.T.'s escape shot at a child's viewpoint, puts the audience into the position of being both in the action and a secret observer of this "alien" world of adolescence. The rules and culture of this world are as different as the rules and culture of another planet; they are transgressive of established norms, deceitful, playful, and they long to be taken seriously by the other dominant culture: full-grown adults. But Spielberg's choice of focus here is not so much a rendering of a nostalgic time for the enjoyment of Boomers. On the contrary, it is an educative project that offers Boomers, as parents of Gen Xers, a view into an unknown world existing right under their noses—a world they long to know and navigate well. Given, too, that Elliott's parents are separated and divorce is rising in general in American culture at the time, it is quite plausible *E.T.* allows Boomers to negotiate their own anxieties and concerns about the effects their relationships have on their children. And, as usual, it all works out in the end.

In line with the growing secularization of both America and Hollywood at the time, *E.T.* transmutes religious forms into the project of meaning making for oneself. Given its feminist underpinning, this meaning making occurs through emotional attachment with others instead of the then taken-for-granted masculine self-reliance. The upending of male domination occurs through the transformation of Christian imagery and E.T.'s gendering. The original artwork of *E.T.* featured two fingers, one Elliott's and the other E.T.'s, touching at the tips with a large full moon in the background. Perhaps signaling the female moon deity, Diana, the cover art reaches back to Michelangelo's *Creation of Adam* on the ceiling of the Sistine Chapel. But here, it is not Adam who is created but a promise of wonder to the audience, which gets to see how such two unlikely figures connect. Toward the end of the film, E.T. channels Jesus; he dies and then resurrects with a glowing heart, oddly similar to the burning heart of Jesus icon that decorates some Roman Catholic churches. After E.T.'s "resurrection," Michael and Elliott, silhouetted by the sun and standing in the doorway to his "tomb" (the operating room where he died), jump for joy while Elliott yells, "He's alive! He's alive!" Shortly thereafter, they escape with E.T. and along the way enlist others on their mission to get E.T. home. These "disciples" (other male teens from the neighborhood) are all present when the van Elliott, Michael, and E.T. are in arrives at a playground. The back doors open, and in a hooded, white robe, E.T., with a glowing heart, allows these teens to stare in wonder as thin fog rolls out behind him. He extends his neck to its maximum length, and the boys all gaze up. Here is the transfiguration and resurrection rolled together. Quickly, the boys then take him to a mountaintop so he can go home (the ascension), but before leaving Earth in the spaceship with his family, E.T. commissions the children. To the girl, he says, "Be good." To Michael (the name of an archangel), he simply says, "Thank you." As for Elliott, he tells him, "I will always be here," as he touches the middle of his forehead (the well-known sight of one's occultic, "third eye") with a burning finger (Pentecost). He then climbs aboard the spaceship and is taken out of sight. As the ship soars out of Earth's atmosphere, it leaves a rainbow chemtrail, again recalling the Noah's Ark narrative and other accounts in the Bible that associate God with rainbows. For those disciples left on the mountain, the single mother (Mary, with the obvious allusion to the Virgin Mary) and her children are now ready to form healthy emotional attachments, signified by the NASA scientist standing by the mother and the now-reconciled teens who were previously antagonistic to Michael and Elliott. It is a combination of Jesus's great commission, ascension, and Pentecost all rolled into one.

In a sense, the Boomer parent audience is commissioned as well. They are confirmed in their suspicions that teens and kids do things behind their backs, such as keeping an alien hidden. But they are also assured that, given the right and inevitable circumstances that accompany adolescence, such as alienation, their children will turn to them for help. This is brought home when Michael finally enlists his mother's help when both E.T. and Elliott are dying. She, as well as all the Boomer mothers in the audience, are finally brought into the circle. And again, when the older kids are planning to escape with E.T. and take him to the mountain, the youngest daughter reveals their plans to the mother, thus enabling her to stand with them as E.T. departs.

It is never quite clear whether E.T. is actually male or female, although it is fairly certain it is young. Elliott insists that he is male but at one point, the sister dresses him in a female costume. This fluidity of gender further underscores the upending of male domination. At various points, the audience sees E.T.'s entire body, and as is the case with actual reported ET encounters, genitalia of any kind are notably absent—almost as if the advanced races to which they belong have transcended such biological limitations. In terms of the audience, such gender fluidity and young age allows younger boys and girls in the audience to identify with the alien, perhaps as a site of projecting their own fears of separation from home/parents. This is underscored by E.T.'s famous quote: "E.T. phone home." In addition to his age and ambiguous gender, E.T. has a warm, glowing heart, perhaps stereotypically symbolic of the maternal and feminine attunement to emotions.

Coming out just one year before President Reagan's announcement of his Strategic Defense Initiative (SDI), *E.T.* represents one of the few, friendly narratives about space. With the launch, too, of the Space Shuttle program by NASA, beginning in 1981, space perhaps had begun to be seen as less about an arms race with the Soviets and more about a site of international cooperation and exploration. Reagan's plans to essentially weaponize space through the use of geosynchronous satellites in 1982 foregrounded both America's space supremacy and, strangely enough, its vulnerability to Intercontinental Ballistic Missiles (ICBMs). But such worries and fears seem downplayed in Spielberg's film; the only reference to the Cold War comes through a "No Nukes" T-shirt Michael wears. Given the teen/adolescent viewpoint of the movie as well as the general escapist tenor of Hollywood, the lack of engagement or commentary on the then contemporary political situation is not surprising. However, "space" and NASA are not simply sites of scientific inquiry and hopefulness. At a key moment in the film, a scientist dressed in a full astronaut suit breaks into Elliott's house. The bronze visor on the suit blocks facial recognition and the outstretched arms are quite ominous and foreboding. That the person makes little to no sound emphasizes the oddity and underscores the horror. Perhaps "science" and the government are not as benevolent as they may seem.

Boomer distrust of the government had already been well established by 1981. Disillusioned by the ambiguity involved in the Kennedy assassination, the Vietnam conflict, and poor handling of civil rights issues caused many Boomers to adopt somewhat of an ambivalent, even antagonistic, attitude toward the State. Throughout the film, the military invades personal privacy, requisitions property, sidesteps due process, and imprisons U.S. citizens—all in the name of national security. This is only tempered somewhat by the understanding scientist whom Spielberg projects as a type of grown-up Elliott.

E.T. is easily situated into the American context of consumption and the ongoing project to idealize the childhood of another era. Boomers were the first generation of Americans raised on television in the suburbs, distant from the rurality that defined their parents. Elliott's family lives in a rather large house in a tightly packed suburb (filmed in California, the quintessential West). His mother drives a late model Audi 5000. The TV is on constantly, showing *Sesame Street* in particular, and the living room is littered with high-priced educational toys such as Speak & Spell. Clearly this is an upper-middle-class family that, despite the father's departure, has maintained its signs of wealth and prestige. In one scene, the children (with E.T. dressed as a ghost in a sheet) go out to trick-or-treat for Halloween. They are shown to be wandering through the neighborhood with a host of other children in costumes. The depiction of such strong social ties within the "safe" boundaries of the suburbs rings true to and parallels the idealized Boomer childhood that continues to resonate to the present day.

Ultimately, *E.T.* is an old-fashioned, coming-of-age story. It is not a coincidence that *E*-l-l-i-o-t-*T*'s name fits within the title and that he is the protagonist who connects most deeply with the alien. In the film, he goes from little brother to leader, gets drunk for the first time (by proxy: E.T. actually drinks the beer, and the effects are telepathically transmitted to Elliott), and has his first kiss (again, partly telepathically influenced by the alien). He manages to assert both his masculinity and agency in the world of adults through deception and rebellion, adopting an uneasy form of teenage angst against the world. This sheds new light on the full title: *The Extra-Terrestrial*. By following one's own convictions over and against the perceived social order, one transcends earthly restrictions and has become a little more than human, that is, extra special.

Benjamin Crace

See also: *Close Encounters of the Third Kind*; *Indiana Jones and the Raiders of the Lost Ark*; *Jaws*; *Jurassic Park*; *Star Wars: A New Hope*.

Further Reading
Audissino, Emilio. 2017. "*Close Encounters of the Third Kind* and *E.T. The Extraterrestrial*: The Bonding Power of Music." In *Film/Music Analysis: A Film Studies Approach*, by Emilio Audissino, 191. Palgrave Macmillan.

D'Heurle, Adma. 1983. "The Image of the Child in Popular American Films." *ETC: A Review of General Semantics* 40 (1): 41–52.

Lyden, John C. 2003. *Film as Religion: Myths, Morals, and Rituals.* New York: New York University Press.

Newell, Jay, Charles T. Salmon, and Susan Chang. 2006. "The Hidden History of Product Placement." *Journal of Broadcasting & Electronic Media* 50 (4): 575–594.

Spielberg, Steven, and Melissa Mathison, 2002. *E.T.: The Extra-Terrestrial from Concept to Classic: The Illustrated Story.* New York: Newmarket Press.

The Exorcist

Release Date:	1973
Director:	William M. Friedkin
Box Office:	$441.3 million
Main Cast:	Chris MacNeil, played by Ellen Burstyn
	Father Merrin, played by Max von Sydow
	Father Damien Karras, played by Jason Miller
	Regan MacNeil, played by Linda Blair

What *Jaws* (1975) did for sharks, *The Exorcist* did for demons—and for priests, for that matter. As the film that brought supernatural horror into the realm of the blockbuster and critical acclaim (nominated for Best Picture), *The Exorcist* reflects a variety of the contextual and existential anxieties felt both by the aging Greatest Generation and young Boomers. In terms of the generational apparatus, films "do something" for the audiences that see them; entertainment is more than merely passing the time. *The Exorcist*, in this construal, as good overcomes evil through self-sacrifice, helps audience members "exorcize" those "demons" of anxiety.

The film begins with the title screen and the Islamic call to prayer in Arabic—an admittedly odd opening for a film about Christian exorcism rites. The title dissolves into a sunrise and then to an archaeological dig in Northern Iraq, where an aging archaeologist (Father Merrin, played by Max von Sydow) is asked to look more carefully at a discovery. Strangely enough, he finds a Catholic medallion of St. Joseph and an amulet of an Assyrian demon (called Pazuzu but not mentioned in the film itself). Merrin's facial reaction to the amulet and his squaring off with a larger statue of Pazuzu shortly afterward suggest that Merrin had had some experience with this entity before. As part of the exposition of the film, the audience also learns that this archaeologist is also a priest, has a heart condition, and plans to leave Iraq. Of note, generationally speaking, Von Sydow (b. 1929) is only 44 but made to look like he is much older, suggesting that the age gap that exists between him and Father Damien Karras (Jason Miller, b. 1939; appears to be his actual age in the film) is intentionally exaggerated to delineate the differences between the generations. Although not technically a Boomer, Karras's youthful appearance, clerical celibacy, and headful of hair easily places him within the same generational imaginary as the Boomer audience, while Merrin's heart condition, wrinkles, and conservatism clearly signal Boomers' parents.

The film then shifts to Georgetown, in Washington, DC. It is early morning, and a lady (Chris MacNeil, played by Ellen Burstyn, b. 1932) is laying on her bed reading over a screenplay for a role. She hears a noise in the attic and goes to investigate, but finding nothing, she goes into her daughter's room (that of Regan MacNeil, played by Linda Blair, b. 1959). Finding it cold in there (a foreshadowing of things to come), she closes the window and kisses Regan. She then heads downstairs for breakfast, where we meet her assistant Sharon, maid Willi, and general caretaker Karl—clearly, Chris is well off. She leaves for a shoot.

The film within the film is about student protests on campus. One protestor is proclaiming, "I've seen enough killing in my life. There's no reason for it anymore." Chris goes on set, takes the megaphone, and starts addressing the faux crowd. While she talks, the camera shows Father Karras watching and then walking away. The director stops the crowd scene; Chris is done for the day, and she walks home. Later, she describes her film/day of work: "It's like the Walt Disney version of the Ho Chi Minh story, but other than that it was terrific." Piling on several contextual intersections at once, the protest recalls the National Guard's killing of four protestors at Kent State University in Ohio in 1970, but in a Disney-fied version, it's just a simple protest where the students are encouraged to work within the system. Additionally, with the Vietnam War still going on, the reference to Ho Chi Minh (the main leader of North Vietnam up until 1969) further frames the prior depiction of the protest as an example of the typical whitewashing Hollywood often engages in. Ironically, this Disney-fication of uncomfortable narratives is precisely the opposite of what *The Exorcist* accomplishes, having narrowly avoided an X rating to become one of the most lucrative R-rated films of all time. Finally, Chris's use of Disney as a synonym for fake and unreal would have registered deeply with the television-nurtured Boomer raised on *The Mickey Mouse Club* (1955–1959). In essence, Disney created a fake world of fake innocence, an innocence lost with Vietnam and Kent State, and if not in those places, watching the horrible ways in which Pazuzu manipulates Regan on the big screen drives the point home: evil is real.

But so, perhaps, is good. At this point in the film, we know that Father Karras is struggling with his faith and role as a priest. The camera follows him as he takes the subway and goes to a run-down neighborhood where his elderly mother lives. While waiting at the station, a homeless man asks, "Hey, Father, can you help an old altar boy? I'm a Catholic." But Father Karras just looks disdainfully and boards the train. At his mother's, they eat a traditional Greek dinner (since they are a Greek family). They talk a bit, and he dresses a wound on her leg. The scene is fraught with tenderness and guilt. Father Karras wants to move her but cannot afford to do so even though, we learn later in the film, he has received the best education money can buy but cannot use it for profit. It also turns out that he has moved from New York to Georgetown and uprooted her. For this, he also feels guilt and shame. This guilt becomes a sore point the demon attacks later—especially after it is magnified by his mother's death in a psychiatric ward/ersatz elder home.

Although diegetically later, Father Karras's mother's death is a crucial part of the generational analysis. In the hospital, she asks him, "Why did you do this to me?"—a phrase the demon speaks to Father Karras again during the exorcism, when pretending to communicate with his dead mother's soul. Here the older Boomer vexed over his aged mother, mirrors Boomer anxieties about the economy (the Oil Crisis of 1973 had just begun) and about responsibility toward their parents. Would they haunt them from the grave? Could they pay for their care? Would their parents hold them responsible? Although clearly a concern for every generation, the early 1970s' turbulence and uncertainty magnified then extant anxieties.

At the MacNeils', Chris finds a Ouija board and talks to her daughter about it. Regan has been playing with it by herself. She talks about a "Captain Howdy" who plays with her but forbids Chris from playing. Although a short scene, it is weighed with contemporaneous significance. Throughout the late '60s and up to the early '80s, Satanism was thought to have been on the ascent in the United States by conservative Christians and even law enforcement. One of the common tropes of what came to be known as "Satanic panic" is that one can open doors to one's soul by toying with the supernatural. Here, the Ouija board, recalling the planchettes of the 19th century used for communicating with spirits, is somewhat ambiguously offered as the "door" Regan used that allowed Pazuzu to enter her. Such a suggestion both alleviated and heightened Boomer concerns about possible Satanism entering their homes: alleviated because all one had to do was avoid Ouija boards (easy enough) and heightened because Ouija boards were already ubiquitous (better get rid of them). This toy-as-door-for-possession motif becomes entrenched in the Boomer psyche and fuels Satanic panic for Gen X and so on. Interestingly, "Captain Howdy" recalls both *Captain Kangaroo* (1955–1984) and *The Howdy Doody Show* (1947–1960), two shows of Boomer childhood. The latter featured a ventriloquist dummy who "magically" talked on his own, a type of possession.

As the film progresses, things slowly begin to tense up. One scene inside a church shows a vandalized statue of Mary, with grossly pointed breasts and a huge penis. Viewers are left on their own to conclude that this is the work of the demon, using Regan's body as a physical agent. In the next scene, there is a dinner party at the MacNeils' home. During the party, Chris's Jewish director, Burke Dennings, accuses her employee, Karl, of being a Nazi sympathizer. Karl insists that he is Swiss (oddly enough, the actor was actually German). It gets to a point where Karl tries to strangle Dennings in the kitchen but is pulled off of him. Diegetically, this subplot makes Dennings's later murder seem to be the work of Karl—not by a child with demonic superstrength. It also suggests that the demon's presence in the house creates a sense of unease and conflict. The dinner party ends with Regan coming down and, after warning a visiting astronaut of impending doom, urinates all over the carpet. Clearly, something is wrong, and it is Regan.

Just as clearly, the conflict between Karl and Dennings gestures toward a generational complex. One dimension is the lingering guilt of World War II, of being in the Greatest Generation's shadow. But there is also the ever-present demon of anti-Semitism that haunts the corridors of American history and, germane to the film itself, the Catholic Church. Pope Pius XII (pope from 1939 to 1958) had allegedly collaborated with the Nazis (though solid evidence is still lacking), and the Second Vatican Council (1962–1965) explicitly rejected the long-held view that Jews were guilty of deicide, that is, killing God in Christ. A corollary to the appellation "Christ killer" meant that all Jews were cursed by God, and thus anti-Semitism had both theological and polit—al support. Undoubtedly, anti-Semitism in the Catholic Church continued despite the Council's schemas. However, the film artfully sidesteps possible *Catholic* anti-Semitism and redirects it toward the "neutral" Swiss caretaker, perhaps a metonym for the "neutral" World War II–era Vatican? There is also a slight intimation that Karl might be Catholic; Chris accuses him of giving Regan a crucifix. He denies it, but Karl's Catholicity and anti-Semitism have already found purchase in the audience's imagination.

At first, Chris attempts to treat Regan through medical means. This includes consulting with various doctors, who then send her to psychiatrists once all physical causes have been ruled out. In one poignant scene, she, one of the few women in the room, exasperatedly upbraids all the psychiatrists when they recommend finding a priest—not because there are actual spirits but because the power of suggestion may be helpful. She replies, "You're telling me that I should take my daughter to a witch doctor?"

Another subplot involves Dennings. While Chris's assistant steps out, Dennings offers to keep an eye on Regan. He is later found dead at the bottom of the stairs outside their house, his neck twisted all the way around. Lieutenant Kinderman (Lee J. Cobb) is called in to investigate à la *Columbo* (TV series, 1971–1978). At various points, he starts to piece together that maybe someone stopped by and threw Dennings out the window. But in terms of the film, his character serves as an objective release to the tension generated by the ongoing spiritual conflict. In short, without the detective investigating Dennings's death midway through, the film collapses into the classic "locked in a room or bottle episode" tropes so common on television.

Eventually, Chris ends up enlisting a reluctant Father Karras to help her. Given his lack of experience, his superiors summon Father Merrin to assist. Together they fight with the demon inside Regan. Their long and engaged exorcism is iconic in terms of special effects in film history: spinning heads and green vomit. Throughout Regan's possession, there are also strong sexual elements, hinting at the dark side of female liberation and the cultural revolution of the late 1960s. Freudian readings notwithstanding, Merrin's heart gives out, and Father Karras finds him dead on the floor of the room; Regan is still possessed. In anger, he attacks Regan, yelling, "Take me, take me!" She rips his St. Joseph medal off his neck (similar to the one Merrin found at the dig at the beginning of the film), and Pazuzu leaves Regan and enters him. Father Karras then jumps headfirst through the window, rolls down the staircase outside, and breathes his last as his friend, Father Dyer, administers last rites.

The film ends with Chris and Regan moving to California; she has no memory of the exorcism except a vague sense that people in priests' collars are good people (she kisses Father Dyer on the cheek). Before they drive off, Father Dyer gives Chris Father Karras's St. Joseph medal, and she accepts. This is significant, because Father Karras struggled with his faith until committing his self-sacrifice to save Regan. Chris had no faith until Regan was freed, and now it looks as though Chris might have started some faith journey of her own. This registers another element within the Boomer psyche: What do we do with religion? Does it have a place in the modern world? Does it have a place in the American Dream? How is faith passed from one generation to another? Perhaps, just perhaps, science does not have all the answers to all our problems.

Benjamin Crace

See also: *Ghostbusters*; *Jaws*.

Further Reading

Blatty, William Peter. 2019 (1976). "There Is Goodness in *The Exorcist*." *America* 220 (8): 38–41.

Bowles, Stephen E. 1976. "*The Exorcist* and *Jaws*." *Literature Film Quarterly* 4 (3): 196.

Hurwitz, Matt. 2017. "A Track from Hell: Vocal-Rich Sound Design for *The Exorcist*." *Mix* 41 (8): 28–30.

Kermode, Mark. 2020. *The Exorcist*. BFI Film Classics. London: British Film Institute.

Szumskyj, Benjamin. 2008. *American Exorcist: Critical Essays on William Peter Blatty*. Jefferson, NC: McFarland.

Grease

Release Date:	1978
Director:	Randal Kleiser
Box Office:	$132 million
Main Cast:	Danny Zuko, played by John Travolta
	Sandy Olsson, played by Olivia Newton-John
	Betty Rizzo, played by Stockard Channing

The romantic *musical* comedy film *Grease* was released in 1978 on the heels of John Travolta's sizzling screen performance in *Saturday Night Fever* (1977), which won him the Academy Award for Best Actor. *Grease* is based on the 1971 stage musical of the same name, and although the film is considerably less vulgar than the original version, it does retain some risqué elements, earning the film a PG rating. The film was commercially and critically successful, coming in second only to *Jaws* in 1978 box office receipts. Its soundtrack was the second highest selling album of the year, behind *Saturday Night Fever* (featuring the Bee Gees). Songwriter John Farrar earned an Oscar nomination for *Grease*'s "Hopelessly Devoted to You" at the 51st Academy Awards ceremony, and overall, five songs from the soundtrack were top five hits.

Travolta had been playing the role of teenage heartthrob and leader of the "Sweathogs" Vinnie Barbarino in the television series *Welcome Back, Kotter* (1975–1979), although the show takes place in the 1970s and so is not part of the 1950s nostalgia trend. However, his teenage angst and bravado in this show prepared him well for the character of Danny Zuko. Australian Olivia Newton-John, although a decade older than the teenage character she plays in the film, screen tested well with Travolta. In fact, they rewrote the backstory of her character so her accent would not sound out of place. She already had a well-established career as a singer in the United Kingdom, representing it in the 1974 Eurovision song contest, where she finished fourth. Her singing career had begun to take off in the States too, primarily in the adult contemporary and country categories, although her role as Sandy, and her transformation from virgin to vamp, actually helped her update and sharpen her subsequent singing career.

Grease was part of the nostalgic 1950s revival that was present in television and cinematic entertainment throughout the decade of the 1970s, launched by George Lucas's *American Graffiti* (1973), which featured several future movie and TV stars such as Harrison Ford, Richard Dreyfuss, Ron Howard, and Cindy Williams. Howard, now known for his directing work, had been a child actor, but his career as an adult was revigorated in the '50s-revival sitcom *Happy Days* (1974–1984), which also starred Henry Winkler (the Fonz), who had originally been up for the starring role in *Grease*. Older Boomers had grown up in the '50s, and it was a period of hope and clarity for them, especially if they were white and middle class. The Nazis had been defeated, the Cold War had peaked, and rock and roll was here to stay. They looked back on the period with nostalgia, especially when confronted with the turbulent world of the '70s, with its "women's libbers," anti–Vietnam War protests, and Euro-inspired disco music.

Grease at its heart is a love story, telling the tale of the bad boy with a heart of gold, Danny Zuko, and the Australian ingenue, Sandy Olsson. Following their summer romance, they unexpectedly reunite at Rydell High School at the start of their senior year. Sandy's family has decided not to return Down Under, and much to her dismay, she must enroll in an American high school. The film credits open with a cartoon montage of the main characters and some stereotypical pastimes of the era—hula hoops, phone booth stuffing, and cruising the strip in a modified car. The title of the film refers to what was put on or in the hairstyles, food, and cars favored by many teenagers during the 1950s.

The opening scenes of the film show Sandy and Danny at the beach in a clear reference to the famous beach scene in the wartime romance *From Here to Eternity* (1953). The film then cuts to members of the T-Birds, the male greaser gang clowning around in front of the school. Kenickie is a gang leader extraordinaire, with a slicked-back duck's tail hairdo, leather jacket, and cigarette behind his ear. They spot the other alpha male in their gang, Danny Zuko, engaged in his favorite activity, chatting up some girls. Danny struts over to join his friends, and they soon engage in their favorite activity, bragging about their romantic exploits.

The bell rings, and as they exit the scene, enter Sandy and Frenchie (known by that name for her ability to inhale cigarettes French-style or, perhaps, to French kiss), the latter a member of the Pink Ladies, a female gang. Sandy mentions her homesickness and recent heartbreak. The rest of the Pink Ladies arrive and strut inside in an echo of the T-Birds, proclaiming their readiness as seniors to "rule the school." During the morning announcement by the principal (one of several 1950s TV stars to have a role in this film), the students and the audience are told that the school has been chosen to be the site of a live television broadcast of *National Bandstand*, recalling *American Bandstand*, a real TV music performance and dance show that aired from 1952 to 1986. This TV broadcast is one of several climactic moments in the film and also provides a great venue for Travolta to show off his dancing skills, something an audience familiar with his demonstrated talent in *Saturday Night Fever* would have been expecting.

Just before Sandy is introduced to the other girls, we learn that Danny and Rizzo have a romantic history, which will prompt Rizzo's animosity toward Sandy, one of the conflicts in the film. It is also at this time that the audience is presented with the first musical number of the film, "Summer Loving," in which Danny and Sandy relate their summer romantic adventures to their male and female friends in separate yet juxtaposed scenes. For Danny, it was a summer fling, while for Sandy, it was true romantic love. Yet at the end of the song, in the split-screen close-up, the audience is given the sense that for Danny, too, this was more than a fling, as they both wonder what the other is doing now.

The scene has now been set for their reintroduction and the problems this will cause, as the sweet Danny of the summer now has his reputation as a T-Bird to uphold. Their meeting is a disaster, but eventually they reconnect, although it is clear that he is still torn between his love for Sandy and his desire to maintain his reputation as a greaser. We catch up with the T-Birds and Pink Ladies at the drive-in, where they have begun to form couples in advance of the big dance. We also learn that Frenchie has not been a success in beauty school when Frankie Avalon makes his cameo appearance as the character Teen Angel singing "Beauty School Drop-Out." Now a new generation is introduced to this actor, singer, and former teen heartthrob from the 1950s who had appeared with former Mouseketeer (in an early Disney television series, *The Mickey Mouse Club*) and actress Annette Funicello (mentioned in Rizzo's earlier song) in a number of beach party movies.

The Kenickie-Rizzo subplot thickens (and parallels the rocky romance of Sandy and Danny) as they break up and then both bring a member of the Scorpion gang as a date to the dance. Danny shows up with Sandy, who is dressed from head to toe in virginal white with a cape that suggests angel wings. This outfit will provide a strong contrast to Sandy's metamorphosis at the end of the film. It also provides a clear juxtaposition to Cha Cha, a St. Bernadette's Catholic school "bad girl" (the best dancer with the worst reputation). Danny ditches Sandy to take on Cha Cha as his dance partner, and they win the dance contest. This scene serves as a climax that spurs Sandy, we find out until later, into changing into the kind of girl that she thinks Danny really wants, while he has ironically been earning his letterman's sweater so he can become the kind of guy he thinks Sandy desires.

The dance contest also provides another moment for a Boomer stroll down memory lane, featuring a cover band—the rock and doowop band Sha Na Na, actually an established and respected band that in 1969 had opened for their friend Jimi Hendrix at Woodstock, whose appearances in the stage and movie versions of *Grease* as well as the film *American Graffiti* and the TV show *Happy Days* led to a TV show of their own (called by the band's name, from 1977 to 1982) They are also credited with having a driving role in the '50s music revival of the '70s, which included the introduction of oldies stations on the radio. In addition to the songs of the '50s, popular dances of the '50s were reintroduced, such as the jitterbug, the stroll, and eventually the hand jive, which led to Danny and Cha Cha winning the dance contest.

When the guys' big drag race occurs, an accident knocks Kenickie unconscious, and Danny must take over driving for him. To anyone familiar with the 1950s, this will recall the famous "Chickie Run" scene in James Dean's 1955 *Rebel without a Cause*, the quintessential teenage drama also starring Natalie Wood and Sal Mineo. Danny wins, and Sandy watches the race, coming to a decision in a reprise of the song "Sandra Dee." We don't learn about her decision until her appearance as a greaser girl, when she and Travolta perform the famous duet, "You're the One That I Want" at the graduation carnival. He shows up in his letterman's sweater, which he had earned in track, while she is decked out in leather from head to toe. The film ends with the two lovebirds driving into the sky, a strangely magical and anachronistic moment in an otherwise realistic (or as realistic as musicals can be) film, referencing the children's film about a flying car that had been released in 1968 and so would have been familiar to Boomer audiences who might have seen it themselves as children.

Keeping this film a musical (like the original play) can also be seen as a nostalgic gesture, for audiences in the 1970s preferred music soundtracks to be performed by the original artists rather than the actors within a scene in the film (known as a diegetic number). This kind of performance was seen by many younger Gen Xers as old fashioned, which of course was ideal for a film trying to create just that feeling. Despite the genre's decrease in popularity during this decade, there were several musical hits during the 1970s, including *Fiddler on the Roof* (1971), *Cabaret* (1972), and the even more provocative *Jesus Christ, Superstar* (1973) and *Rocky Horror Picture Show* (1975), although the latter was not a success until its midnight screenings in the 1980s made it a cult classic.

Embraced and romanticized by the Boomers, many of whom had been young during this period, the '50s revival can be seen as a commentary on the uncertainty of the present decades as nostalgia for the past. Not only were the '50s seen (idealistically) as a simpler time but they were also a period of great financial growth, as the GDP went from $200 million to more than $550 million dollars, much of it in government spending. It was the period of the Baby Boom (hence the name for the generation born at that time, Boomers) and a mostly white exodus (known as white flight) to the suburbs. Of course, the period was less than ideal for women desiring more than the role of wife and mother or for those from ethnic, racial, or sexual minority communities. It marked the start of the Cold War, which would last for decades, as well as the rise of the teenager, often signaled through the arrival of rock and roll.

The troubling political and cultural landscape of the 1970s (oil embargo, the Vietnam War, radical and countercultural movements, Watergate) led many (and especially white working- or middle-class) Americans to yearn for a time when they felt confident in their role in their country and their country's role in the world. The uncertainties of the period (inflation, rising crime, political and foreign policy turmoil) had left many exhausted, and this exhaustion expressed itself not only in nostalgia for a largely imagined past but also a growing conservatism that was to bloom in the 1980s along with the election of Ronald Reagan (himself a Hollywood B-movie actor) and the rise of the Moral Majority and the Christian Right.

Grease has remained an audience favorite, with retrospective rereleases enjoying critical and financial success. Generations of high school and college students have performed the play (often a G-rated version), with parents and grandparents who remember the original release of the film singing along. A sequel was released in 1982, but by then, '50s nostalgia was waning, and the film was a disappointment, although it was Michelle Pfeiffer's first starring role. However, the United States is experiencing another period of turmoil and anxiety and a new (often troubling) nostalgia for the past, and in the works (at this writing) is an HBO Max web television series *Grease: Rise of the Pink Ladies* that will help launch '50s nostalgia into the 21st century.

Angelica Maria DeAngelis

See also: Zootopia.

Further Reading

Callahan, Michael. 2016, January 26. "How *Grease* Beat the Odds and Became the Biggest Movie Musical of the 20th Century." *Vanity Fair.* https://www.vanityfair.com/hollywood/2016/01/grease-movie-musical-john-travolta-olivia-newton-john.

Canby, Vincent. 1978, June 16. "Screen: A Slick Version of 'Grease': Fantasy of the 50's." *New York Times.* https://www.nytimes.com/1978/06/16/archives/screen-a-slick-version-of-greasefantasy-of-the-50s.html.

Dwyer, Michael D. 2015. *Back to the Fifties: Nostalgia, Hollywood Film and Popular Music of the Seventies and Eighties.* Oxford: Oxford University Press.

Indiana Jones and the Raiders of the Lost Ark

Release Date:	1981
Director:	Steven Spielberg
Box Office:	$389.9 million
Main Cast:	Indiana Jones, played by Harrison Ford
	Marion Ravenwood, played by Karen Allen
	René Belloq, played by Paul Freeman
	Sallah, played by John Rhys-Davies
	Marcus Brody, played by Denholm Elliott

The first in the Indiana Jones saga, *Raiders of the Lost Ark* reaches back to the adventure serials of the 1930s and '40s. And yet *Raiders* isn't simply a neoserial, cliffhanger, adventure movie trying to recapture some golden age of cinema. Like other films of its generation, it serves as a means of negotiating war guilt accrued between the Greatest Generation and Boomers. It does so by using the serial form to accent its Western-like packaging while leveraging its setting, characters, and plot to revise a what-if aspect of pre–World War II history. And yet it doesn't leave its Americanism behind: the film is *Indiana Jones and the Raiders of the Lost Ark*; it is about Jones and what he represents—the ark is just a prop.

At the center of the film is Indiana Jones, played by Harrison Ford, b. 1942 (just on the edge of the Boomer range). He is an adventurer, treasure-seeking (for museums, not really profit), archaeologist-professor who, after narrowly avoiding getting killed in South America trying to recover an ancient bronze idol, is enlisted by the U.S. government in 1936 to find the ark of the covenant before the Nazis do.

As it turns out, the Nazis have already found Tanis (in Egypt), an ancient city thought to be where the ark is, so time is of the essence. He agrees, goes home to prepare, and flies to Nepal to talk to his mentor's daughter about her father, an expert on the ark who had a medallion that could help locate it in Tanis. After successfully defeating some Nazis who want the same medallion for the same reason, Jones and Marion Ravenwood (Karen Allen) partner up and depart Nepal for Egypt. However, in a bit of a convoluted plot twist, one of the Nazis, upon trying to get the medallion out of a fire, has its surface and markings branded onto his hand. This brand, as shown later, is used by the Nazis to dig for the ark—but in the wrong place, because it is only one side of the medallion and not both. But as they depart for Egypt, neither Jones nor Marion knows this.

Upon arriving to Egypt, Jones meets up with an Egyptian friend, a fixer named Sallah. Sallah tells him that one of Jones's nemeses, René Belloq, the same French archaeologist that nearly kills him at the beginning of the film, is involved in the excavation. They make plans to take the medallion to someone who can decode it, and they leave Sallah's house. However, they are followed by a one-eyed Arab man who, accompanied by his pet monkey, has been spying on them for the Nazis. As Jones and Marion look around the souk area, more Nazi henchmen—hired Arabs with swords and knives—attack them, and in the course of the fight, Jones believes Marion is killed. During this extended scene, however, is the classic shot where a large Arab man with a huge sword stands Jones down to kill him. He deftly does some swordplay, demonstrating his prowess, and Jones casually and dismissively shoots him with the gun on his hip—in classic, "this is beneath me" fashion of the Old West gunslinger. Here the cowboy (with a fedora instead of a 10-gallon hat) shoots down the bad guys (the main swordsman is wearing all black) and attempts to rescue the damsel in distress, apparently unsuccessfully.

After seeing Marion "die," Jones does what all cowboys do and heads to a place he can drink his pain away. As he finishes off a bottle, he is taken into the restaurant area to face Belloq. After a brief conversation, where Jones nearly draws to shoot him, Sallah's kids come in and save him. Together, he and Sallah go to have the medallion interpreted, and Sallah saves Jones from eating some poisoned dates. Realizing now that the Nazis are digging in the wrong place, they plan to go to Tanis and do what is necessary with the medallion to find the final resting place of the ark.

At the Nazi dig site, Jones and Sallah make their way to the map room, the place where the medallion can be used to locate the ark. Jones drops in, locates the ark, and climbs out. As he and Sallah run through the camp, Jones ducks into a tent to hide from some Nazi soldiers. Inside, he finds Marion tied to the tent pole. Although elated to see she is alive, he nonetheless leaves her captive so he can find the ark without being discovered. He promises that he will come back for her. He meets up with Sallah and some diggers to start excavation.

There is a telling shot of the excavation that underscores the various power structures and generational sensibilities that constitute the film. In the shot, the workers, Sallah, and Jones are silhouetted by a setting sun. Jones, closer to the camera and not bent over digging, removes his turban disguise and dons his fedora. Not that dissimilar to the Nazis digging a few hundred yards away, here is another white, capitalist imperialist overseeing Arab manual laborers. Once they hit the stone capstone that covers the entrance to where the ark is, Jones jumps back in to help lever the stone out of place to properly claim the discovery, thereby displacing (as usually happens) local recognition for great archaeological discoveries. This display models the ideal arrangement proper to American males and, with the Nazis as the main enemy, displaces the Greatest Generation's actual efforts with a fictionalized Boomer, who, by jumping the timeline to 1936, delimits Nazi ambition for the ultimate weapon. The suggestion here is that the Nazis would have been far more successful and harder to beat had it not been for Jones. Again, the function of such fictive revisionism is not to actually replace real history but to conflate it with the Boomer historical imagination so as to assuage their present anxieties about standing in the Greatest Generation's shadow. Thus, entertainment is never "just" entertainment but a process of generational sublimation.

After discovering the ark and packing it up, they are discovered by the Nazis and Belloq. They take the ark but not before dropping Marion into the snake-laden cavern where Jones is. They then seal the capstone, and Jones and Marion get to planning their escape. Jones figures out a way to use one of the Egyptian statues to break through a wall. After escaping and destroying one of the Nazi planes, Jones takes off to chase down the ark, which has been loaded onto a truck. After an extended adventure sequence of Jones fighting the bad guys off and taking control of the truck, Jones and Marion end up on a freighter with the ark on the way to England. En route, the Nazis intercept them via submarine, taking the ark and Marion with them. Jones manages to swim to the sub and stow away just in time.

Just before the Nazis depart from the freighter, there is an interesting scene with the African captain, Simon Katanga (George Harris). He tells the lead Nazi, Dietrich, that he has killed Jones and wants to sell Marion, trying to save them both. Belloq, however, having some affection for Marion, manages to talk Dietrich into giving her to him. While a key scene, the African as slave dealer and Marion as trophy are not contested enough by simply turning the whole exchange into a ruse. In other words, their roles seem a little too fitting and stereotypical. As it turns out, the real savior-hero is the white American cowboy. A cowboy, as shown in an earlier scene when he chased down the truck with the ark, rides a white horse.

The sub arrives at an island base, and preparations are made to open it. In the planning, Dietrich expresses his disapproval of a Jewish ritual. Belloq counters that he wouldn't want to deliver an empty product to Hitler; Dietrich concedes. On the way to the place set up for the ritual, Jones threatens to blow up the ark in exchange for Marion, but its value stops him from doing so. The Nazis, with Belloq reenacting the role of the Jewish high priest, opens the ark. In one of the classic scenes in film history, ghastly, ghostly figures fly out of the ark and melt all the bad guys. Jones and Marion are saved by keeping their eyes shut while tied to a post nearby. After the ordeal, the lid (the mercy seat) falls back out of the sky solidly onto the ark.

Back in the United States, Jones, once assured by government men that the ark is safe, goes out to meet Marion. The closing scene is of a workman in a gigantic warehouse crating up the ark and rolling it off into the vast network of other crates. Such an ironic ending for such an important artifact links up well with the Boomer sensibility that the U.S. government is not a trustworthy and transparent entity but survives on lies and obfuscation. Boomer audience members, disillusioned from Vietnam, would have clearly identified with Jones's frustration at the empty reassurances that the ark was being studied by "top" men.

Raiders also signals a growing awareness of both the effacement and, paradoxically, maintenance of the Judeo-Christian cultural element within American society of the 1980s. To what extent America has ever been "Christian" is beside the point; that a film about a biblical relic found so much popular purchase strongly suggests that the previous generation's entanglement of patriotism and faith (President Eisenhower, 1953–1961, put "In God We Trust" on the money) carried over into the consciousness of the next, the Boomers. This ethos is directly manifested in one scene where Jones explains the ark and its power, questioning the government men, "Didn't you guys ever go to Sunday School?" They uncomfortably shift in their seats and hem and haw. Jones's question and character arc thus model the "cool" position: educated in religion but still agnostic, calling the ark's power "hocus pocus" to his older friend, Brody, in the following scene. Perhaps it isn't surprising that Jones still remains a secularist even after the ark destroys all the bad guys—and, as *The Last Crusade* (1989) shows, the Holy Grail has miraculous healing powers. On the contrary, Jones trusts more on his wit and whip than on transcendence.

Benjamin Crace

See also: *Close Encounters of the Third Kind*; *E.T.: The Extra-Terrestrial*; *Jaws*; *Jurassic Park*; *Star Wars: A New Hope*; *Star Wars: Return of the Jedi*.

Further Reading

Audissino, Emilio. 2014. "10. *Raiders of the Lost Ark* Analysis: The Return of Max Steiner." In *John Williams's Film Music: Jaws, Star Wars, Raiders of the Lost Ark, and the Return of the Classical Hollywood Music Style*. Madison: University of Wisconsin Press.

Knee, Adam. 2010. "Harrison Ford: A Well-Tempered Machismo." In *The Star Decades: Acting for America: Movie Stars of the 1980s*, edited by Robert T. Eberwein, 160–179. New Brunswick, NJ: Rutgers University Press.

Laist, Randy. 2020. *Excavating Indiana Jones: Essays on the Films and Franchise*. Jefferson, NC: McFarland.

Laist, Randy. 2020. "Heads A-Poppin': The Ambiguous Drama of Seeing in *Raiders of the Lost Ark*." *Journal of Popular Film & Television* 48 (3): 155–162.

Jaws

Release Date:	1975
Director:	Steven Spielberg
Box Office:	$470 million
Main Cast:	Martin Brody, played by Roy Scheider
	Matt Hooper, played by Richard Dreyfuss
	Quint, played by Robert Shaw

Based on the novel *Jaws*, by Peter Benchley, the film adaptation cost $7 million to make. Although he already had several films under his belt, it was *Jaws* that truly launched Spielberg's career and established his reputation as a director. Not only did the film catapult Spielberg but it also paved the way to successful careers for both Scheider (1932–2008) and Dreyfuss (1947–). Having previously starred in George Lucas's *American Graffiti* (1973) Dreyfuss went on to play the iconic lead in Spielberg's next blockbuster, *Close Encounters of the Third Kind* (1977). Scheider reappears in *Jaws 2* (1978) and in Stanley Kubrick's masterpiece, *2001: A Space Odyssey* (1984). While Spielberg, Scheider, and Dreyfuss were launching their careers, Robert Shaw's was in its twilight. Just three years after *Jaws*'s release, Shaw passed away, leaving behind a long filmography that included the James Bond film *From Russia with Love* (1963). The career of the main female lead, Lorraine Gary (1937–) career did not fare so well. She starred in *Jaws 2* and in *Jaws: The Revenge* (1987) but did not appear in any other films with *Jaws*'s impact. Many of the other supporting actors as well as the main cast were involved in television and cinema, reflecting the post–World War II reality of the dichotomy between the small and large screen. By the 1970s, however, managing a career in both was fairly common.

As the name suggests, *Jaws* is essentially a monster movie, one of the few horror films that cut across the genres into popular consciousness. It is the film for which the word "blockbuster" is really first used as a designation. A blockbuster, as noted in the introduction, draws such large crowds that it "busts" the space around the block, with a line of people waiting to buy tickets to see it over and over again. This phenomenon would be repeated in the next few years, especially with *Star Wars: A New Hope* (1977). But perhaps more than any other film of its era, *Jaws* instilled a terror of the water into the Boomers' children who were taken to see it. In fact, Universal even marketed the film with the tagline "You'll never want to go back into the water again!" By today's standards, the film would never earn the PG rating it received when it was released, with its strong language, barely hidden nudity, and graphic, bloody violence.

The film begins on the island of Amity ("Friendship"), which is located somewhere off the coast of New York. It is a sleepy town for most of the year that gets a substantial amount of income from fishing and summer tourism. The appearance of a man-eating shark has serious economic and safety consequences. The audience has its first encounter with the monster at the very beginning of the film, although Spielberg is careful not to actually show the shark in the beginning sequence. Instead, he begins with a beach party of what might be called hippies. One girl, off to the side, catches the eye of one of the young men in attendance and invites him to chase her to the water. Along the way, she strips naked to skinny-dip in the sea while her pursuer is too drunk to get his clothes off. The scene takes place near dawn while it is still fairly dark, so it is impossible to see more than the light allows. Nonetheless, it is highly suggestive and as the lady swims in the water, the camera moves to the low, menacing angle of the shark's view, looking up between her legs. The drunk man on the beach, like the audience member, is incapable of catching up with the woman and saving her from what is about to happen as the intensely voyeuristic moment of potential summertime sex is ravaged by the sick, rhythmic twisting and jerking of the shark eating her. It simply begins with the woman's neck and head floating in the water, a small tug and hint of distress, and then moves to a bloody, frenzied boiling of the water. All the while, the now iconic *Jaws* theme plays, and then the water smooths out, the camera pans back, and the audience sees the young man mumbling drunkenly on the beach, completely unaware.

From this inciting incident, Spielberg wastes no time at all getting the action and the tension built up. He often overlays the narrative with overlapping dialogue and yelling, creating a sense of conflict and confusion. At first, no one wants to believe that such a thing has happened. Brody, a New York City cop transplant who is now chief of police in Amity, has an array of small-town problems to deal with when the girl's mutilated and mauled body surfaces on the beach. Right away, Brody, who already, we find out, has had a fear of water since childhood, wants to close the beaches. He is confronted by the mayor, who does not want people afraid, because of the upcoming tourist season; sharks are bad for business. Overriding Brody, the beaches remain open, even though, at first, no one wants to go into the water. With the urging of the mayor, however, people begin entering the water until it looks like a normal beach scene. Predictably, the shark finds its next victim: a small boy.

With the boy's death, the shark problem becomes real. Outsiders and locals all go on the hunt. An oceanographer, Hooper, comes into town for the opportunity for research. As the town reels from the deaths and the influx of tourists and incompetent shark hunters, an old seaman named Quint emerges from the mélange with irrefutable confidence and offers to kill the shark by himself. Spielberg takes the action on a brief detour as a large shark is found and is presumably the killer. However, as the audience knows but the citizens of Amity do not, this is not the shark. The real monster comes back and devours a boater only feet away from Brody's own child. Afterward, both Brody and the mayor agree to hire Quint to hunt and kill the animal for $10,000.

Brody then joins Quint and Hooper on the appropriately named *Orca* (or killer whale, one of the few predators in the ocean that kill sharks) at roughly 01:12:00 into the film's total 02:02:00. In other words, the rest of, if not most of, the film takes place on the boat with these three characters. From here, *Jaws* takes on a spiraling rhythm with waves of intense action, reminiscent of the way sharks hunt. There is waiting, punctuated by various attempts at tagging and catching the shark. One way the characters and the audience can measure the passing of time on the quest is how many empty barrels they end up attaching to the beast: one, two, three. Throughout the process of the attack-wait-attack cycle, both the audience and boat's crew learn the size and strength of their foe, prompting the famous line from Brody: "We're going to need a bigger boat."

After a night of drinking, storytelling, and scar showing, things begin to get worse, as the shark hits the boat hard enough to cause leaks and even a small fire. As the action increases over the next few screen hours, Quint, apparently in an act of either mental illness, anger, rank individualism, or fatalism, destroys the radio. From that point on, it is the three men, the boat, and the monster Great White.

Eventually, the shark and unforeseen circumstances do enough damage to the boat that it begins to sink. In the process, Quint is eaten, and Hooper manages to escape a damaged shark cage to hide in the coral. Meanwhile, Brody remains on the sinking vessel as the Great White seems to be after him personally. As the mast slowly dips closer into the water, Brody manages to shoot a SCUBA tank that had gotten lodged into the shark's mouth, causing it to explode in a spray of chunky flesh and water. It is a rich payoff from all the tension, and the amity of Amity closes the narrative, with Brody and Hooper using bits of the wreckage to swim back to shore, away from the camera.

As with any text, *Jaws* reflects its cultural moment. Middle-aged and middle-class, white men are in charge of everything. As with many portrayals of women in the '70s, they are either supportive, sexually interested sidekicks (At one point, Brody's wife asks, "Do you want to get drunk and fool around?") or scared and grieving mothers. Quint is the quintessential, sailor-misogynist, spewing clichés and innuendos about women as they leave the harbor. Later, he sardonically dismisses Mrs. Brody's fears about her husband over the radio. Racial diversity is lacking in Amity as well; New England white culture is dominant, as are its economic concerns. Nothing should ruin summer vacation—not even a shark with the taste of flesh. The vast majority of beachgoers are white, again reflecting stereotypes of African American leisure activities and economic empowerment in a capitalistic society.

In addition to its expected outdated sensibilities, *Jaws* takes up the issues of its generation. Given the oil embargo of 1973–1974, the future of vacations and the future—period—was uncertain. *Jaws* offered an audience suffering from lines at the gas stations to turn its attention to lines at the box office. The film gave them a chance to see a tangible, primal enemy nearly as old as the sea itself instead of focusing on the extremely complex historical and socioeconomic factors affecting everyday life.

Perhaps somewhat surprisingly, *Jaws* also allowed its Boomer audience to come to grips with its World War II ancestry and ambivalence toward Vietnam. In a crucial scene, a drunken Quint (Shaw was apparently actually drunk) recounts his time in the navy. Upon being asked about a scar on his arm, he replies that it was where he used to have a tattoo. This opens the conversation about his time on the U.S.S. *Indianapolis*, the ship responsible for carrying parts for the nuclear bomb used on Hiroshima. Quint relates how, after delivering the parts, the ship was attacked and sunk (factually true). The survivors remained in the water for days, but sharks picked them off (also true). During his monologue, Hooper and Brody, two Boomers, listen to this member of the Greatest Generation downplay the glory and glamor of war—even to the point that he has removed his tattoo. It was not, for Quint, an honor to go to war but, rather, a deeply traumatic experience that shattered his psyche. The horror the bomb unleashed and the presence of the sharks relativized all notions of patriotic grandeur. He ends his speech with "I'll never wear a life vest again." As the last U.S. troops were pulled out of Vietnam the very year *Jaws* was released, such a scene allowed the guilt of not living up to the generation that stopped Hirohito and Hitler to be reframed as historically and situationally relative and contingent as the present. Simultaneously, the scene helpfully draws audience sympathy toward those who have gone to war, that beneath their bluster lies deep pain. This sympathy for the broken soldier as a type of hero potentially sensitized audience members to those returning from Vietnam. In the end, however, Quint is ironically eaten by a shark, a fate he had managed to avoid for nearly 30 years. On a more symbolic level, the World War II survivor fades away and the Boomer, taking up his World War II–era rifle, saves the day.

Jaws, however, as a contemporary viewing will reveal, is not confined to its cultural moment. It runs on perennial conflicts that are recognizably and universally human. There is the conflict between the locals and the outsiders, the ones who know and those who do not. There is the fight over life and death, and there is youth and the experience that comes with age. There are the classic themes of shame, guilt, responsibility, authority, expediency over safety. Masculinities are asserted and fears overcome. But there is also an essentially American ideal on full display, linking *Jaws* to other great works of American literature like *Moby Dick* and Stephen Crane's "The Open Boat": Yankee ingenuity can overcome that primal chaos of the sea and even man-eating sharks, but it always comes with sacrifice.

Benjamin Crace

See also: Close Encounters of the Third Kind; E.T.: The Extra-Terrestrial; Indiana Jones and the Raiders of the Lost Ark; Jurassic Park.

Further Reading

Clasen, Mathias. 2017. *Never Go Swimming Again: Jaws (1975)*. In *Why Horror Seduces*, 104–112. Oxford: Oxford University Press.

Gottlieb, Carl. 2005. *The Jaws Log*. New York: Newmarket.

Jankiewicz, Patrick. 2015. *Just When You Thought It Was Safe: A Jaws Companion*. Albany, GA: BearManor Media.

Quirk, Antonia. 2002. *Jaws* (BFI Modern Classics). London: British Film Institute.

Kramer vs. Kramer

Release Date:	1979
Director:	Robert Benton
Box Office:	$173 million
Main Cast:	Ted Kramer, played by Dustin Hoffman
	Joanna Kramer, played by Meryl Streep
	Billy Kramer, played by Justin Henry

Based on Avery Corman's 1977 novel of the same name, *Kramer vs. Kramer* is an American legal drama written and directed by Robert Benton, as well known for his screenwriting as his directorial abilities, having already been nominated twice for an Oscar for Best Original Screenplay (*Bonnie and Clyde*, 1967, and *The Late Show*, 1977) before he began his work adapting *Kramer vs. Kramer* from Corman's novel. Dustin Hoffman was already a celebrated actor by the time he was cast in the lead of this film as Ted Kramer, which had earlier been offered to James Caan and Al Pacino. Hoffman's breakthrough role had come a decade earlier as Benjamin Braddock in Mike Nichols's critically acclaimed film *The Graduate* (1967), and in the decade since then, Hoffman had acted in films such as *Midnight Cowboy* (1969), *Papillon* (1973), *Lenny* (1975), and *All the President's Men* (1976), demonstrating astounding versatility and talent. The role of Joanna Kramer was offered to some of the top actresses of the time such as Kate Jackson, Faye Dunaway, Jane Fonda, and Ali MacGraw. Meryl Streep, better known at the time for her work in theater but coming off a powerful performance in *The Deer Hunter* (1978), had been cast originally in the part of neighbor Phyllis but nailed the role of Joanna through her powerful audition. The main cast was rounded out by casting the eight-year-old Justin Henry in his first film role as Billy Kramer, a role for which he became the youngest person ever to be nominated for an Oscar.

Kramer vs. Kramer tells the story of the aftermath of the breakup of a marriage and its impact on the couple's young child, Billy. Ted Kramer is a workaholic ad executive, expected and seemingly willing to put his climb up the corporate ladder, including whatever it takes to get an anticipated promotion, ahead of his wife and child. Less than five minutes into the film, we see the result of years of his marital neglect, as Joanna packs her suitcase to leave not only her husband but also her son. Ill prepared to pick up the reins of parenthood, we see Ted's failed attempts to care for his son through breakfast fiascos, bungled trips to the supermarket, and nearly forgotten school pickups. An early climactic scene sends the father-son duo on a different trajectory, which is then developed in the first half of the film. Ted loses his temper with a misbehaving Billy, which results not only in him telling his son, "I hate you right back, you little s—," but also in acknowledging his own responsibility in his failed marriage (for trying to make Joanna into the kind of wife he wanted and for thinking his happiness equaled her happiness). At the end of the scene, he assures Billy that he will never leave. Here the film repeats the opening scene Billy had shared with his mother, only this time, it is his father, Ted, who has assumed the role of caregiver for the now seven-year-old child.

Now that the father-son relationship has been strongly established, a new conflict arises, and this comes in the form of a newly returned Joanna who wants her son back. The film shifts from a domestic comedy to a legal drama, where Ted's capabilities as a father and as a man are put on trial. A playground injury becomes evidence of his negligence and his inferior salary evidence of failure as a provider. The audience has watched the father-son bond blossom and knows that Ted refused to leave Billy's side while he got stiches for his injury and that Ted now earns less than Joanna because he prioritized his son over everything else—to the point where he was let go from the ad firm and had to accept a different job for lesser pay. The audience is finally able to hear Joanna's side of the story, which is much more sympathetic in the final cut than it had been in the novel and original screenplay. While on the stand, she states that just because she wanted "a creative or emotional outlet other than my child" does not make her unfit as a parent. She also tells the judge, and the audience, that she has "worked very, very hard to become a whole human being." Ted has his turn on the stand, too, and is shown to have learned not only how to be a better parent but also a better man. He asks, "Why can't a woman have the same ambitions as a man?" but "By the same token, what law says a woman is a better parent simply by virtue of her sex?" Both common belief and even legislation favor the mother as a better parent. Granting Joanna custody of the child seems to have been sealed with Joanna's repetition of the phrase "I'm his mother."

The film, however, has one final twist in store for the audience, which is perhaps signaled by the restaging of the original breakfast fiasco, which has now become a successful example of father-son teamwork. Joanna has an epiphany at the end of the film, stating, "I came here to take my son home [but] I realized he already is home." She then allows the elevator doors to close on her and the film after being reassured by Ted that she looks "terrific."

Kramer vs. Kramer was extremely well received by critics and audiences alike. It was nominated for nine Oscars and won five of them, including Best Director, Best Actor, Best Supporting Actress, Best Screenplay, and Best Film. While this was Hoffman's fourth best-actor nomination, it was his first win. Both Streep and Benton had also been nominated (Benton for screenwriting) earlier, and this was also the first win for them both. Audiences loved the film, not only for the superior acting and directing but also because it reflected issues that were becoming key to American society and gender relations in the late 1970s. These included gender roles, single parenting, father's rights, and life-work balance. Ted Kramer exudes male Boomer values; he is goal-centered, self-assured, and resourceful. When we meet him, he is laser focused on his job and sure that he will soon be getting the promotion that he knows he deserves. When he loses his job and any chance at custody of his son, he forces a job interview during a Christmas party, and his gumption lands him a new job. Even after he shifts his focus in the film from work to parenting, he is still exhibiting an important Boomer value: the importance of family relations.

Female Boomers had grown up with somewhat different messages than their male counterparts. Sure, they could go to college and go to work but only until they got married and had children. Then they would return to their rightful place, supporting their hard-working and successful Boomer husbands. But the zeitgeist of the 1970s, the decade of movements, blew that traditional family model apart. Women like Joanna wanted more to life than being a wife and mother, and if they could not get that in their marriage, then they would leave it.

Second-wave feminism (1950s–1980s) shifted its focus to women's experiences (including politics, family, work, and sexuality) and to raising women's consciousness about these issues. Like Ted's conversations with neighbor Margaret (who had gone through a divorce of her own), Joanna's monologue from the witness stand reveals her dissatisfaction with a life reduced to wife and mother, one in which she was "scared" and "unhappy" and from which she felt she had "no other choice but to leave." It is this monologue, as critics have noted, that saves the film from presenting Joanna as a one-dimensional character. It is also a monologue that was not included in the original screenplay (which was built on the less sympathetic character in the novel) but was rather improvised by Streep during the filming. While not the worst cinematic depiction of mothers who leave a marriage to "find themselves," even Streep's monologue does not save Joanna from sexist stereotypes of the time that sadly linger today. She describes herself as what can be understood as mentally ill ("I felt that there was something terribly wrong with me"), but after getting therapy, she was able to realize her son was not really better off without her, that she was not bad or ill, and that she wanted some kind of emotional or creative outlet and an identity outside of a traditional, patriarchal role—a result of her time in therapy and presumably consciousness raising in the more progressive California.

Early in the film, we see Ted ask his neighbor Margaret, who is trying to help him understand why Joanna left, "How much courage does it take to walk out on your kid?"—a truthful yet brutal way of framing her actions. We see him struggle to balance his work and parenting obligations yet eventually make the "right" decision to miss the closing meeting for a big account in order to attend to his child's needs. He chooses to forfeit his career for his child, a choice that is never really an option to a woman. How can you forfeit a career if you don't have one or are not afforded the opportunity to have one in the first place? During his time on the stand, Ted first states, "My wife, my ex-wife, says that she loves Billy, and I believe she does, but I don't think that's the issue here," but he concludes with "We [he and Billy] built a life together and we love each other. If you destroy that, it may be irreparable. Joanna, don't do that, please. Don't do it twice to him." Joanna's love for her child is not the issue, but Ted's love for his son is. Not only that, but this love is also presented as something that is intentional and reciprocated, while Joanna's is one-way and something that relies on Ted's belief rather than being a given or fact. While the sacrifice demanded of Ted is to be a father to his child, the one exacted in the end on Joanna is to give up being a mother to her child.

Kramer vs. Kramer in all its messiness about gender relations accurately reflects changing values in American society. While Joanna is allowed to express her dissatisfaction with traditional female roles of the previous generation, the film seems unsure what to do with this "liberated" woman and in the end must write her out of the story. While Ted's career takes a hit, he remains employed in his field and presumably will be awarded custody of his child after Joanna abandons Billy for a second time.

The film's unbalanced treatment of the parents, including the unfair court ruling in the woman's favor, which is felt sharply by an audience not given screen time with Joanna to develop any sympathy for her, detract at times from the film's achievements, as does the no-win situation in which the mother is left at the end of the film (either destroy her son's life again by taking him from his father or walk away and abandon him again). While often mentioned in the same breath as the 2019 *Marriage Story*, that comparison does not do justice to the cinematically brilliant and powerfully acted *Kramer vs. Kramer*, which despite its flaws remains a masterpiece to this day.

Angelica Maria DeAngelis

See also: Tootsie.

Further Reading

Asimow, Michael. 2000. "Divorce in the Movies: From the Hays Code to *Kramer vs. Kramer.*" *Legal Studies Forum* 14 (221): 1–77.

Canby, Vincent. 1979, December 19. "East Side Story: Review/*Kramer vs. Kramer.*" *New York Times*. https://www.nytimes.com/1979/12/19/archives/screen-kramer-vs-kramereast-side-story.html.

McMullen, Wayne. 1996. "Gender and the American Dream in *Kramer vs. Kramer.*" *Women's Studies Communication* 19 (1): 29–54.

Schulman, Michael. 2016, March 29. "How Meryl Streep Battled Dustin Hoffman, Retooled Her Role, and Won Her First Oscar." *Vanity Fair*. https://www.vanityfair.com/hollywood/2016/03/meryl-streep-kramer-vs-kramer-oscar.

9 to 5

Release Date:	1980
Director:	Colin Higgins
Box Office:	$103.9 million
Main Cast:	Judy Bernly, played by Jane Fonda
	Violet Newstead, played by Lily Tomlin
	Doralee Rhodes, played by Dolly Parton
	Franklin Hart Jr., played by Dabney Coleman

Tapping out the sound of the typewriter on her acrylic nails, Dolly Parton's theme song "9 to 5" set the tone and laid out the themes of the comedy hit by the same name. Released in 1980, the film *9 to 5* starred veteran actress Jane Fonda, celebrated comedian Lily Tomlin, and iconic country singer Parton in her debut acting role. The cast was rounded out by Dabney Coleman, whose portrayal of the sexist boss in the film established his character actor bona fides as the comic-relief villain for the rest of his career. Although originally written as a dark comedy by screenwriter Patricia Resnick, it was reworked by the director into what some have called the cult comedy that we know today. A great success with audiences, the film received somewhat mixed reviews from critics who called it such things as "pleasant," "an amusing romp," and even "inane." They all had to admit, sometimes in what seemed almost like disbelief, that the film was a definite "audience pleaser" and that the jokes never failed to land. Even Ronald and Nancy Reagan gave the film two thumbs-up, except for the pot-smoking scene—although the film did predate Nancy's failed "Just Say No" campaign by a few years. One thing critics all agreed upon, however, was the breakthrough performance of Dolly Parton as someone with a future on the silver screen.

A sometimes-silly comedy that addressed serious social issues and spoke to the concerns of working women then and now, this female buddy movie tells the story of three dissimilar women who develop camaraderie over shared misery and near murder. Violet Newstead is the brains of the trio—and of the entire department, we learn, as she is able to keep it running during the time their boss is incapacitated. Violet has worked for the firm for years, and although she has trained most of the men who have been hired, she is never promoted beyond the glass ceiling that separates the men in private offices from the girls in the typing pool. Her manager, Franklin Hart Jr., is one of the men she trained and also one of the many who have used her as a stepping-stone as they climb up the male ladder of success in very patriarchal, corporate America. Hart's private secretary (these were the days before the term "administrative assistant" was used) is the buxom Doralee Rhodes, who spends as much time brushing off his adolescent attempts to peak down her blouse as she does performing actual secretarial work. The trio is rounded out by the newly employed Judy Bernly, whose husband has just run off with his own sexy secretary.

Each of the women (or rather "girls," as their boss prefers to call them) faces her own personal and professional struggles at Consolidated. The professional and innovative Violet sees her ideas being passed off to upper management by Hart as his own, and the promotion she deserved given to yet another man she had trained. Judith struggles to perform basic office tasks such as photocopying, providing Hart a chance to berate her in front of another office frat boy. Doralee, unbeknown to her, is the subject of office gossip that even Violet and the recently discarded-by-her-husband Judith perpetuate. Everyone assumes Doralee is having an affair with Hart, a rumor we find out later in the film that he started himself. Like secretaries of the time, she was expected to function more as a personal assistant, picking up his dry cleaning, buying gifts for his wife, and fetching him endless cups of coffee with the artificial sweetener "Skinny and Sweet."

Individual unpleasant interactions with Hart drive each of the women to leave the office for a local bar, where they meet up and realize they have more in common than they realized. Their initial bonding over alcohol is cemented over a marijuana cigarette Violet's son had rolled for her the day before, and the most amazing "Maui Wowie" high ensues, during which each imagines a scenario (and in the case of Violet, a live-action/animated scenario) of revenge against their misogynistic boss. Judith wants to hunt him like big game, Doralee lassoes him and roasts him on a spit, and Violet imagines herself as Snow White (replete with cartoon animals circling around her) as she turns the poisoning tables and serves up Hart a cup of doctored coffee. The problem is that this happens in her real life: distracted by getting passed up again for a promotion given to someone she had mentored and annoyed that she has yet again been asked by Hart to fetch him a coffee, she accidentally grabs the box of rat poison from her lunchtime grocery run. The boxes look remarkably similar (except for the skull on the front), and although unintentional (or at least consciously so) the damage has already been done—or so the three friends believe. In fact, Hart had spilled the coffee when he leaned back in his broken office chair and, at the same time, knocked himself out cold. He's taken to the hospital emergency room and can leave on his own accord. Meanwhile, the police have brought in a real poisoning victim, who dies on the table. Unaware of this, Violet steals the body, and a madcap car chase occurs, but after discovering the truth, they manage to return the body to the hospital. Unfortunately, their concern that they'd poisoned him had been overheard by the office snitch Roz, and Hart uses this information to his advantage to try to blackmail Doralee into sleeping with him. The women leap into action, kidnapping Hart and holding him captive in his house until they can get hold of some financial reports that will prove he has been embezzling money from the company, thus ensuring his silence about the poisoning fiasco. During this time, Violet institutes many progressive changes in the office such as split shifts, friendlier décor, and even an on-site daycare center. All of these are a big success with the big boss—such a success, in fact, that Hart, who is the presumed architect of these changes, is sent to open a new business venture in Brazil, and Violet finally gets the promotion that she, and by extension, all qualified working women, deserve.

A twist on the female buddy movie, which has been dated in recent cinematic history to the French film Céline and Julie Go Boating (1974) and features two characters, *9 to 5* showcases the talents of all three stars. While this type of movie, sometimes known as a "womance" to counter the better-known term "bromance," came into its own after the culturally significant *Thelma and Louise* (1991), ground had already been broken on the small screen by TV shows such as *Laverne and Shirley* (1976–1983), the *Happy Days* (1974–1984) spin-off that featured the daily and, often, individual romantic struggles of two factory workers in Milwaukee. *The Mary Tyler Moore Show* (1970–1977) had earlier broken ground by highlighting the struggles of single women, particularly Mary, in the working world and included several other single women in a similar situation, such as Sue Anne, Phyllis, and Rhoda, the latter two of whom were given their own spin-off TV shows, named after them. It was important for society to see that women could exist not only as props for male stars, or as adversaries fighting over a male star, but as independent beings who were strong and smart enough to succeed in a male-dominated society and to help other women along the way.

The stars of the movie were all powerful and successful women in their own rights. Dolly Parton, while not a traditional "feminist" figure at the time, was a respected singer and songwriter in the male-dominated country music universe. In more recent times, now that the image of a feminist has become less rigid for most, she herself has accepted that title. In a 2020 interview with *Time* magazine, she stated, "I suppose I am a feminist if I believe that women should be able to do anything they want to." She continued, "And when I say a feminist, I just mean I don't have to, for myself, get out and carry signs. . . . I just really feel I can live my femininity and actually show that you can be a woman and you can still do whatever you want to do." Lily Tomlin was more the sign-carrying type of feminist, never shying away (as Dolly had) from the label, which she wore quietly but confidently, the same way she did her sexuality. Jane Fonda has claimed that she was a "late bloomer" when it came to feminism, which she didn't fully understand until she was in her sixties. But her radical anti-war political activism and her marriage to Tom Hayden, as well as her strong female characters dating back to *Cat Ballou* (1965) and reaching into her current Netflix hit with Lily Tomlin, *Grace and Frankie* (2015–), make her a clear supporter. She has become openly engaged with feminist issues in the NGO she founded in 2005, Women's Media Center, and was one of the women featured in Netflix's recent documentary about second-wave feminism, *Feminists: What Were They Thinking?* (2018), which also featured Tomlin.

In many ways Jane Fonda was a lightning rod for right-wing hatred of leftist/progressive political activism. For Fonda, this role was codified in the infamous "Hanoi Jane" picture taken in 1972, during a visit to North Vietnam as part of a publicity campaign to end the war. While she has apologized profusely for the optics and unintentional hurt the photo caused, many vets and some Boomers in general have refused to forget what they see as treasonous acts—even though many of these acts have since been proven to be lies or rumors. The Vietnam War was the national trauma for the Boomer generation, and in some ways her acceptance by Hollywood and by audiences is a testament to the resilience of Fonda as well as the nation. This is especially powerful given that rumors of being a communist sympathizer effectively "blacklisted" entertainers and barred them from working in Hollywood studios during the McCarthy era only a few decades earlier, during the 1940s and 1950s.

Older Boomers came of age in the height of Vietnam-era protests and the woman's liberation movement, with about half of American women in the workforce by 1980. Although the majority of the legal and social struggles of second-wave feminism had peaked in the 1970s (such as the Equal Rights Amendment and Titles IX and X, to name only a few), inequality was still a reality for most women in the workplace. The United States was (and remains) a patriarchal society, and the atmosphere in some companies was closer to that of a frat house than a corporate office. Men such as Hart, the "sexist, egotistical, lying, hypocritical bigot," as the three women liked to call him, can count on the other men in the office to laugh at his misogynistic jokes and follow his lead in stepping over Violet and any other woman who has the audacity to think she deserves a place at the table. But patriarchy cannot survive without the participation of women, and early in the movie, we see that women are willing to spy on others for Hart and are willing to believe the worst about one another, as the gossip about Doralee demonstrated. While not yet sporting the woman's power suit whose excessive shoulder pads gave them the more masculine silhouettes of linebackers (as can be seen in the 1988 romantic comedy *Working Girl* or in any fashion magazine in the latter part of the decade), one of the paths open to women in corporate America was through mimicry of male corporate behavior. Yet this is *not* what we see happen in this film when a woman is in charge, for Violet institutes changes that benefit women and that are squarely in line with feminist demands of the time. These changes include split shifts that allow women to take care of family responsibilities at home and/or on-site daycare for when they have to bring those family responsibilities to work with them. Not only do these kinds of changes make happy employees but they also make more productive employees, which results, as we see in the film, in measurable financial gains for the company.

9 to 5 packed a deceptively powerful message as a feminist text, one that still resonates with young women today. As a 2020 article notes, "Though it's a timeless comedy, its themes of sexual harassment, misogyny and gender discrimination still resonate with us four decades later." Although decried by one *Guardian* critic as a faux-feminist film (along with other feminist classics such as *The First Wives Club*, 1996; *Fried Green Tomatoes*, 1991; and even *Thelma and Louise*, 1991), other recent reviews call it a "quietly radical revenge satire" ahead of its time that "did not feel the need to balance the female characters with an emollient male romantic lead." And that, in addition to its snapshot of office gender politics of its era, may be part of what makes the film still relevant. That and the pot-induced revenge fantasies.

Angelica Maria DeAngelis

See also: Wonder Woman.

Further Reading

Bradshaw, Peter. 2018, November 15. "*9 to 5* Review- Dolly Parton's Quietly Radical Office Revenge Satire." *The Guardian*. https://www.theguardian.com/film/2018/nov/15/9-to-5-review-dolly-parton.

Buchanan, Kyle. 2013, June 28. "There Are Even Fewer Female Buddy Comedies Than You Thought." *Vulture Magazine*. https://www.vulture.com/2013/06/female-buddy-comedies-very-rare.html.

Demetrakas, Johanna, dir. 2018. *Feminists: What Were They Thinking?* Los Gatos, CA: Netflix.

Mulvey, Laura. 2018. "Introduction: 1970s Feminist Film Theory and the Obsolescent Object." In *Feminisms: Diversity, Difference and Multiplicity in Contemporary Film Cultures*, edited by Anna Backman Rogers and Laura Mulvey, 17–26. Amsterdam, Netherlands: Amsterdam University Press.

Murtha, Tara. 2015, December 18. "Why *9 to 5* Is Still Radical Today." *Rolling Stone*.

Ryu, Jenna. 2020, December 19. "*9 to 5* Turns 40: The Feel-Good 1980 Comedy Covers a Depressing Reality Even in 2020," *Knox News*. https://www.knoxnews.com/story/entertainment/2020/12/19/9-to-5-turns-40-themes-sexism-misogyny-more-relatable-than-ever/3972607001.

One Flew over the Cuckoo's Nest

Release Date:	1975
Director:	Miloš Forman
Box Office:	$163.3 million
Main Cast:	Randle McMurphy, played by Jack Nicholson
	Nurse (Mildred) Ratched, played by Louise Fletcher
	Martini, played by Danny DeVito
	Chief Bromden, played by Will Sampson
	Billy Bibbit, played by Brad Dourif

Miloš Forman's 1975 film *One Flew over the Cuckoo's Nest* is based on the 1963 Broadway adaptation of Merry Prankster Ken Kesey's novel *One Flew over the Cuckoo's Nest*, published the previous year (1962). Kirk Douglas had played the lead in the Broadway production and, for years after purchasing the rights to the novel from Kesey, struggled to find financial backing for the film project, eventually passing it over to his son, Michael Douglas, already an established television actor from the series *The Streets of San Francisco* (1972–1976). When the film was released in 1975, Kirk was deemed too old to play the lead, so instead, an up-and-coming Jack Nicholson was chosen for the role, after it was rejected by actors such as Gene Hackman, James Caan, Marlon Brando, and Burt Reynolds.

Forman claims that he felt an immediate affinity with the story and that for him, his birthplace of Czechoslovakia, where he had lived for over 30 years of his life under communist rule, was his Nurse Ratched. Forman was initially interested in Shelley Duvall for the role (who later starred with Nicholson in the classic horror film, *The Shining*, in 1980), but while pursuing her, he was introduced to the work of Louise Fletcher, who was finally offered the role—but only after it had been turned down by actors such as Jeanne Moreau, Colleen Dewhurst, Ellen Burstyn, Angela Lansbury, Anne Bancroft, and Geraldine Page. The film was nominated for nine Academy Awards and remains to this day (at this writing) one of only three films to win all "Big Five" Awards (Best Picture, Director, Actor, Actress, and Screenplay), the first being *It Happened One Night* (1934) and the last, so far, being *Silence of the Lambs* (1991).

The opening song, performed on a musical saw, creates a sound that suggests to the audience that something is not quite right. We are almost immediately brought from the expansive landscape outside to inside the psychiatric hospital, where most of the drama takes place. Filmed in the mental health building of the Oregon State Hospital, patients and staff were actively involved in many aspects of the making of the film, from providing real-life training to the actors to being involved in technical aspects and in some cases having bit parts in the film itself. The physical freedom of the open landscape is juxtaposed with the claustrophobic indoors of the hospital, just as the unpredictable sounds of the opening song are juxtaposed with the diegetic classical music that is played at an uncomfortably loud volume and orchestrates the actions of the patients. We see them line up in an orderly fashion to the sounds of the music during the "medicine time" ritual, and we see that their conversations and interactions with one another are limited by the music's volume. All staff and patient movements are regimented by Nurse Ratched (rhymes with "hatchet")—at least until the arrival of a new patient, Randle McMurphy.

McMurphy has feigned insanity in order to shirk the hard labor at the work farm prison where he is serving time for the statutory rape of a 15-year-old girl. Having an energetic and rebellious nature, McMurphy tries to liven up the atmosphere through basketball games against the orderlies or blackjack with the other patients. Not only does he challenge Nurse Ratched's authority at every turn but he also encourages the other men to do so too. This cannot be tolerated by Ratched, who is used to being able to control the patients through medication and passive-aggressive bullying and, when necessary, trips to the locked ward, where electroshock therapy is only one of the treatments available. She initially tries to control McMurphy the same way as she controls the others, through punishments such as confiscating cigarettes, through verbal humiliation during group therapy sessions, and by refusing to allow them to change the work schedule so they can watch the World Series on television. She and McMurphy are engaged in a deadly game, but the problem is that McMurphy is not aware that the rules are stacked against him. McMurphy, and the audience, get the first inkling of this when the orderly tells him, "You still don't know where you're at, do you? With us baby, you're with us. And you're gonna stay with us until we let you go." But McMurphy has still not experienced his epiphany and continues antagonizing Ratched.

Everything that McMurphy does leading up to stealing a bus full of men and taking them on a fishing trip installs in them a sense of confidence and self-worth that many had not experienced for years, if ever. They begin to express themselves more freely and to resist the arbitrary regulations of Ratched's regimented system. McMurphy has been enjoying his struggles against Ratched, which he saw as a temporary distraction until he finished serving his term at the hospital. But as the orderly told us earlier, he's wrong. It is during one of the group therapy sessions, when one of the men demands the return of his cigarettes, that it is revealed to McMurphy that most of the other men are in the hospital voluntarily and are free to leave at any time, unlike him. And worse, they all were aware of this but allowed him to continue antagonizing Ratched and thus prolong his stay in the hospital. In a meeting about McMurphy's return to the work farm, she convinced the panel of experts to leave him in the hospital so he could be helped. While waiting to receive electroshock therapy for riling up the others, he and the Chief (who, it is revealed, is neither deaf nor dumb) plan an escape to Canada.

But McMurphy wants to throw one last hurrah for the boys, and unfortunately, they all fall asleep and are awakened by Ratched's return in the morning. She humiliates Billy to the point where he kills himself, and McMurphy throws himself on Ratched and attempts to strangle her with his bare hands. He disappears from the ward for some time, and when he is returned in the middle of the night, Chief discovers that he has been given a lobotomy. Chief suffocates him with a pillow and breaks through a window, disappearing into the night.

Cuckoo's Nest is both a commercial success and cinematic masterpiece. It also engages in commentary on a number of social ills and issues, especially concerning psychiatric care and attitudes toward people with mental illnesses. In the decades prior to the making of the film (including the 1960s, when the novel was published), many believed that what we now call mental illness was a private and family matter, something to be hidden away as it was somehow shameful or scandalous. The treatment of Rosemary Kennedy, JFK's oldest sister, was a perfect example. At the age of 23, her father chose to have her lobotomized because she was having convulsions and behaving in ways the nuns at her convent boarding school thought might lead to promiscuous behavior with men. The lobotomy left her unable to walk and talk properly and diminished her to the mental capacity of a two-year-old. The film is set in 1963, as we learn from overheard snippets of television news, but filmed in the mid-'70s in Oregon, just north of California, where the up-and-coming B-actor-turned-politician Ronald Reagan was beginning his defunding of mental health care, first as governor of the state and later as president of the nation,

In the film, funding does not seem to be a key concern, perhaps because most of the patients (with the exception of Native American Bromden) seem to be white, middle-class men who can afford their own care or are financed by the state, as McMurphy is. Although never openly discussed in the film (but perhaps pointed to by a television news report of the infamous church bombings in Alabama in 1963), racial discrimination is on display. The doctors (with the exception of one who appears to be Southeast Asian) are white males, the nurses are white females, and the orderlies are Black men. Society was highly segmented, and everyone knew their place in the hierarchy. And if you did not, like McMurphy, there were ways to compel you to learn it quickly. McMurphy has a history of problems with authority, starting with his dismissal from the military during the Korean War for insubordination (which we learn about in the novel). Murphy's antiauthoritarian stance would have resonated with many audience members, as the draft for the Vietnam War had just ended three years earlier (in 1972), as would have his plan with Bromden to escape to Canada, which thousands of young American men had done to avoid being sent to fight a war they did not believe in. This was only one of several dystopian films, such as *The Stepford Wives* (1975), or even revenge films, such as *Dirty Harry* (1972) or *Death Wish* (1974), that showed how Hollywood adapted its messages to the zeitgeist of the decade and Boomer tendencies to resist or challenge authority.

The Native American issue was also relevant to Boomer audiences. While Bromden does not play the central role of narrator (or protagonist) in the film as he does in the novel, he still holds a vital narrative function, as McMurphy's partner during key moments, and symbolic function, as representative of the mistreatment and silencing of Native Americans. The '70s were the decade of movements, and the American Indian movement (AIM) took inspiration from the civil rights movement (which was at its height in the early '60s and referenced in the film by the Alabama church bombings seen on TV). The institutionalization of Native Americans, whether in Indian residential schools, in prisons, on reservations, or as seen here, in psychiatric hospitals, was a way to try to hide away this national "stain." Hollywood elites in the audience of the 1973 Oscars and the 85 million viewers at home had been forced to face the industry's racist and stereotypical depiction of Native Americans when Marlon Brando sent Sacheen Littlefeather in his place to refuse his Oscar for *The Godfather*. Boomer audiences would have had these current events in mind when viewing Bromden's stoicism throughout the film and his eventual escape into the open landscape as he puts McMurphy's plan into place and allows him to die with dignity—a key component to Native American struggles.

Although justified critiques of misogyny have been raised about the film, even that cannot diminish the force of this cinematic masterpiece. The doll-faced Ratched is the villain of our worst nightmares, able to drive grown men to suicide without ever raising her voice or her hand. She personifies, as the director himself suggested, the social control of the state that must mold us into useful citizen automatons in order to guarantee its smooth functioning. And like a good villain, she never really dies (see, e.g., the 2020 Netflix prequel series *Ratched*). McMurphy's manic rebellion is energizing but without hope, leaving us with the option of either conforming or, like the Chief, slipping off quietly into the dark night.

Angelica Maria DeAngelis

See also: *Batman; Joker.*

Further Reading

Butler, Tina. 2005, April 2. "The Methods of Madness: *One Flew over the Cuckoo's Nest* and *Awakenings*." Mongabay. https://news.mongabay.com/2005/04/the-methods-of-madness-one-flew-over-the-cuckoos-nest-and-awakenings.

Hoad, Phil. 2017, April 11. "Interview Michael Douglas: How We Made *One Flew over the Cuckoo's Nest*." *The Guardian*. https://www.theguardian.com/film/2017/apr/11/michael-douglas-and-louise-fletcher-how-we-made-one-flew-over-the-cuckoos-nest-interview.

Lambe, Jennifer. 2019. "Memory Politics: Psychiatric Critique, Cultural Protest and *One lk, Flew over the Cuckoo's Nest*." *Literature and Medicine* 37, no. 2 (Fall 2019): 298–324.

McCreadie, Marsha. 1977. "*One Flew over the Cuckoo's Nest*: Some Reasons for One Happy Adaptation." *Literature Film Quarterly* 5, no. 2 (Spring 1977): 125–131.

Rocky

Release Date:	1976
Director:	John G. Avildsen
Box Office:	$156.2 million
Main Cast:	Robert "Rocky" Balboa, played by Sylvester Stallone
	Adrianna "Adrian" Pennino, played by Talia Shire
	Paulie Pennino, played by Burt Young
	Apollo Creed, played by Carl Weathers
	Mickey Goldmill, played by Burgess Meredith

There have been several great boxing movies in Hollywood cinema. Martin Scorcese's 1980 *Raging Bull*, starring Robert De Niro was one, and Clint Eastwood's 2004 *Million Dollar Baby*, starring Hilary Swank, was another. However, John Avildsen's 1976 Rocky, which the then relatively unknown Sylvester Stallone both wrote and starred in, is for many a boxing film like no other. It not only tells the story of the uneducated struggling amateur boxer, Italian American Rocky Balboa, who works as a collector for a loan shark to pay his bills, but it is also the quintessential "rags-to-riches" story of the underdog who through hard work and guts became a contender and had his shot at the American Dream.

The *Rocky* films (comprised of six *Rocky* films and two *Creed* films) can be understood as an American auteur film cycle equivalent in some ways to French New Wave filmmaker François Truffaut's Antoine Doinel cycle: roughly autobiographical films that allow for character development across the films. For Rocky, this does not involve romantic entanglements with women (as his love interest Adrian remains constant throughout the cycle until the character is killed off in *Rocky VI*) but rather revolves around an inner turmoil and his desire to prove that he is not a "bum" but rather a "contender" willing to go the distance, even if that means, initially, he does not actually win the fight.

Stallone was a relatively unknown actor prior to *Rocky*. He had just gotten a break costarring in the 1974 *Lords of Flatbush* (as had Henry Winkler, famous as the Fonz in TV's *Happy Days*, one of the 1950s revival shows of the 1970s). Although many important players in the film industry recognized the storyline's potential, it was difficult to find anyone willing to take a chance on Stallone's main requirement: that he star as the character Rocky in the film instead of casting an already established Hollywood star that would be considered less of a risk by the big studios. The film was eventually made on a small budget of just over $1 million. *Rocky* was the sleeper hit of 1976, becoming the highest-grossing film of the year. Beloved by fans and acclaimed by critics, the film earned ten Academy Award nominations and won three, including Best Picture. In 2006, the film was chosen to be preserved by the Library of Congress in the U.S. National Film Registry as something deemed "culturally, historically or aesthetically significant." The film launched Stallone into stardom, and the film cycle remains a popular global phenomenon into the 21st century.

The film opens to the trumpet strains of the now iconic theme song, Bill Conti's "Gonna Fly Now," and by intertitle the action is located: November 25, 1975, Philadelphia. The next shot is a close-up of a Catholic mural that pans out to reveal the interior space of a run-down boxing club where a fight is going on. Although Rocky wins the fight, he is portrayed as slow, out of shape, and, as one spectator screams at him as he leaves the ring, a bum. He earns a mere $40 for the fight after all the fees and taxes are taken out of the already paltry prize money, and his next fight will not occur until at least two weeks later. As he heads home, we see through the exterior shots that this is an impoverished inner-city neighborhood, the likes of which could have been seen in any large American city during this period of national economic hardship. We are also slowly introduced to the main character. He is seen as a sympathetic and simple, even simplistic man, who has a kind word for the puppy in the window of the pet store and for the neighborhood teenagers singing a cappella on the corner. In his meager and dilapidated one room apartment, we find further evidence of what at this point we assume is his love of animals, as he spends time caring for his pet turtles and fish. He seems lonely and sad, with his pets and his family photos his only company.

The next morning, we learn that it was not only the animals that drew him to the pet shop but also the awkward and introverted Adrian Pennino (sister of the abusive Paulie, Rocky's only friend), who is a part-time employee there. Rocky's next stop is the docks, where he begins his workday as a collector for a loan shark, but despite being a boxer, he does not demonstrate the necessary violent proclivity for collecting money. His low educational level and possibly low IQ are shown through his inability to spell a simple name or confidently remember his gym locker combination. We see him constantly beaten down by life and disrespected by others, whether it is a local teenage girl, who answers his fatherly advice with an obscene gesture, or the gym manager (played by Burgess Meredith, who later becomes his trainer and surrogate father), who strips him of his status and locker of six years by giving it to another fighter and has Rocky's gear hung in a dirty gym bag on a "skid row" hook.

Despite all this, Rocky is by nature a quintessentially American character—one who exudes optimism and believes in hard work and pulling oneself up by the bootstraps—or at least that is the public face that he strives to present to others. Yet it is in his interactions with Adrian that we see other sides of his personality: his determination and especially his vulnerability. He never stops pursuing her, despite no encouragement on her part (today his behavior might border on stalking), and later he confesses to Adrian his doubts in his ability to face Creed in the ring. In one of the film's many iconic moments, he removes his sweater, leaving him looking vulnerable in his sleeveless undershirt, despite his muscular boxer's physique. His relationship with Adrian is a true romance that lasts the cycle of the *Rocky* films.

But this romance is only part of the storyline in the film; the other, of course, is his exhibition match with the world heavyweight champion, Apollo Creed, a brash and theatrical character loosely based on Muhammad Ali. In fact, Stallone was inspired to write the screenplay after watching the 1975 championship match between Ali and Chuck Wepner. Creed must find someone to replace an injured opponent and, exploiting the idea of America as the land of opportunity, he decides to open the fight to a local underdog, which he knows will appeal to the fans. Creed chooses Rocky based almost entirely on his fighting name, the Italian Stallion. Much of the middle of the film focuses on Rocky's training for the fight (including drinking raw eggs and running up the Philadelphia Museum of Art steps, now thought of by many as the "Rocky steps"), which is juxtaposed with his deepening relationship with Adrian.

The climax of the film takes place in the last 20 minutes, where shots of Rocky with a now more glamorous Adrian are crosscut with those of Apollo as the boxers prepare for the fight, in a series of close-ups, extreme close-ups, and even Italian close-ups (where only the eyes can be seen) to suggest the intensity and inner emotions of the characters. The fight is described by announcers as "the cave man against the cavalier," and that of the "underdog" living a "Cinderella story"—all sports clichés but also tropes that are familiar and comforting to an American audience. They also express doubt that he has the skill and stamina to last three rounds in the ring with Creed. Entering the ring a full 20 pounds lighter than the reigning champ, it is uncertain that Rocky will be able to last long in the ring. An easy ending, one that could even be called a "Hollywood" ending, would have had Rocky beat the champ, whether by a knockout or through points. But this film, although a blockbuster hit and an enduring classic, provides a deeper message to its audience by having the underdog lose the match.

Scholars have begun to pay modest attention to the boxing film as a subgenre, with its own set of characters, values, symbols, and ideology that connects to specific political and material concerns over increased industrialization in the late 20th century. The '70s were a decade of cultural restlessness, in some ways a continuation of social justice activism of the 1960s in the areas such as women's rights, gay rights, and Latinx and Native American rights. But it was also a period of great political and economic upheaval, with the oil embargo of 1973–1974, Watergate and Nixon's resignation in August 1973, and the end of the grueling Vietnam War in April 1975. The challenges and anxieties of the mid-1970s can clearly be seen in *Rocky*, even if the film does not address them explicitly.

The nation was facing economic crisis that not only impacted Americans' wallets but also their psyches. There was this sudden realization that the United States was not all powerful but actually vulnerable to the "whims" of foreigners, which not only produced a genuine anxiety but also made some jingoistic. The "white flight" from cities to suburbs during the 1950s and 1960s by those with sufficient financial means increased racial and economic segregation, leaving behind the populations of working-class immigrants and people of color in general. Cities were neglected, and there was a generalized feeling that they had become significantly less safe than just a decade earlier. This neglect can be seen in exterior shots of Rocky's neighborhood, as well as interior shots of his apartment and the gym. The move from patriotism, a rallying cry for a depressed nation (which includes situating the film in Philadelphia, which played a key role in colonial and revolutionary history), to jingoism can be seen in the spectacle of the fight itself, in which Creed and his retinue donned hyperpatriotic costumes of the Statue of Liberty, Uncle Sam, and George Washington. While this film and its lead character are clearly of the Boomer generation, it is a working-class or even underclass Boomer seen here. In this film, no amount of hard work or gumption is going to get him a house in the suburbs and all the other Boomer material trimmings, and if Boomer identity is tied closely to career, the Rocky we meet early in the film will have "loser" and "petty criminal" written on his AARP (American Association of Retired Persons) card. While many (at least white) Americans did make it into the middle class, Rocky's lack of education, entrepreneurial spirit, and ethnic identity bar him from professional neighborhoods. But what he does still share with others of his generation is a firm belief in the American Dream. *Rocky* is a celebration of foundational national myths such as the melting pot and the land of opportunity, all part of that dream. The inner-city Italian (American) Stallion, Rocky Balboa has a chance at the brass ring in this multicultural nation, one so democratic that the character who takes on the iconic patriotic roles is an African American. *Rocky* thus engages with the racialized political climate of the post–civil rights period in American history.

The film also describes an identifiable American ethos (of the underdog having a shot at the American Dream) and recognizes the advances that have been made by women and African Americans (Creed himself; the African American reporter) without ignoring the struggles the country was facing at the time (inner-city poverty; post-Watergate and post-Vietnam loss of innocence). It has been argued by some, however, that the inclusion of women in power dynamics is tentative at best, and the success of the African American male is linked to his willingness to continue to be tied to the success of the white male.

In the end it is not winning that matters, as southpaw and underdog Rocky Balboa, the Italian Stallion, does not win his exhibition match with Apollo Creed. In fact, at the end of the film, he is more concerned with finding his girlfriend Adrian, whose name he keeps bellowing, than with hearing about the split decision that finally declares Creed the victor. What matters to Rocky and to all of us is having the guts to try to go the distance. He would know for the first time in his life that he was not just another bum from the neighborhood. And in this, Rocky and the entire country are victorious, for at the end of the movie he can proudly proclaim, "Yo, Adrian. I did it."

Angelica Maria DeAngelis

See also: *Independence Day*; *Terminator 2: Judgment Day*.

Further Reading

Elmwood, Victoria A. 2005. "'Just Some Bum from the Neighborhood': The Resolution of Post–Civil Rights Tension and Heavyweight Public Sphere Discourse in *Rocky* (1976)." *Film and History* 35 (2): 49–59.

Grindon, Leger. 1996. "Body and Soul: The Structure of Meaning in the Boxing Film Genre." *Cinema Journal* 35 (4): 54–69.

Kleinfield, N. R. 1983, September 26. "American Way of Life Altered by Fuel Crisis." *New York Times*.

Star Wars: A New Hope

Release Date:	1977
Director:	George Lucas
Box Office:	$775.5 million
Main Cast:	Luke Skywalker, played by Mark Hamill
	Han Solo, played by Harrison Ford
	Princess Leia, played by Carrie Fisher
	Obi-Wan Kenobi, played by Alec Guinness

Envisioned as a new myth for a new era and as a way to sell toys, *Star Wars* consciously borrows fairy tale conventions that would have resonated with its coming-of-adulthood Boomer audience. In addition to fairy tale conventions, Lucas synthesized universal mythological tropes and repackaged them as science fiction. Yet beneath or perhaps between these layers, *Star Wars* is, at a very basic level, a Western.

Young adult male Boomers were raised on a steady diet of Westerns as television became widely available in the post–World War II boom that lent them their name. This was the so-called golden era of television, dominated by the Western: *Gunsmoke*, *Bonanza*, *The Rifleman*, *Wagon Train*, *Rawhide*, *The Roy Rogers Show*, and *Have Gun—Will Travel*, among others. As a genre, Westerns emerged early on in American cinema, *The Great Train Robbery* (1903) being one of the first films and a Western in its own right. By the 1950s, as the above attests, the Western had successfully survived the end of the studio era and migrated to television, where it "raised" a generation of Boomers. Thus, Han Solo (Harrison Ford) a black vested, hip holster–wearing smuggler (read: cowboy) who nonchalantly shoots an enemy in a bar before swaggering out, firmly grounds *Star Wars* as a sci-fi Western. Additionally, his partner, a Wookie (Bigfoot-like creature) named Chewbacca, like all hero cowboy partners, barely gets a voice. He just growls and moans in a language few understand while wearing a minimal amount of clothing. His preferred weapon is a bowcaster, or basically a crossbow that shoots lasers. For all intents and purposes, Chewbacca is Tonto to Han's Lone Ranger.

But in the post-Apollo program/pre-shuttle world of *Voyager* spacecrafts, it would seem that the Western had been edged out by the newly emergent genre of science fiction. *Star Trek*, already 11 years old when *New Hope* debuted, had already widely established space travel and alien races as weekly possibilities. Before *Star Trek*, there were *Space Patrol*, *Flash Gordon*, and the like to balance out the young Boomer television diet. *Star Wars*, perfectly timed, dropped as a synthesis of the two defining genres of Boomer memory. Space, however, as Boomers were becoming aware, was not an uncontested region full of possibilities but, rather, a gaping hole in the nation's defense from ICBMs (intercontinental ballistic missiles). A deep-rooted fear of Soviet aggression (firmly established by the Cuban Missile Crisis of 1962 and the recently ended "communist containment" war in Vietnam) foregrounds *Star Wars* as a fight against tyranny where the freedom-loving good guys win against the bad guys despite the bad guys' best efforts.

The interplay between myth, fairy tale, and sci-fi Western is telegraphed in the famous, opening title: "A long time ago, in a galaxy far, far away. . . ." Both myths and fairy tales are "once upon a time" or "a long time ago." All Westerns happen on the frontier, away from the centers of established power and ways of knowing: "In a galaxy far, far away." The repetition of "far" here contributes to the lyricism of the line; John Williams's blasting score that immediately follows the opening line recalls the fact that even the most ancient mythological stories required musical accompaniment.

Following the *Star Wars* logo, the title crawl, operating like a chorus in ancient Greek drama, gives just enough exposition to the audience to jump into the narrative in medias res without being too confused. Briefly, we're told that the Galactic Empire has a space station that can destroy planets (the Death Star). However, "Rebel spies" have stolen plans for the station Princess Leia can use to "save her people and restore freedom to the galaxy." As the words scroll out of view, a smaller ship chased by a massive Imperial Cruiser appears and is overtaken.

As they are being boarded, Leia (Carrie Fisher) manages to download the stolen blueprints and a message into R2-D2, a small robot that is shaped like a thick bullet with wheeled legs as shoulders. His (R2 is presumably male, manned, as it were, by little person Kenny Baker) constant companion is C-3PO, a golden, metallic humanoid protocol droid played by Anthony Daniels. Oddly enough, both C-3PO and R2-D2 look surprisingly like a Cyberman and a Dalek, which were introduced on the British series *Doctor Who*, in 1966 and 1963, respectively. This American appropriation of British culture flags another layer of meaning in the film in terms of the Boomer generational apparatus.

The sci-fi Western formatting of *Star Wars* partly obscures its generational function. An ongoing theme in this text is that film allows each generation to psychologically process in a collective fashion (sitting together in a cinema) the historical and cultural legacy of the prior generation, or "reckon" with their parents' past. Part of that past was dominated by World War II, which left a severe mark on the psyche of the Greatest Generation. In order to come to terms with this, Boomers produced and consumed media that allowed them to witness the conflict in a secondhand fashion (war films). *Star Wars*, on the other hand, mythologizes war and distances it in such a way as to make such a generational reckoning more accessible by not ostensibly being another World War II movie. And yet traces of the war are interspersed throughout the film. The Empire with its legions of all-white (Aryan?) Stormtroopers is a thinly veiled allusion to Nazi Germany. The Dark Side is embodied in Darth Vader, a cyborg that uses the Force (the energy force that surrounds all living things) for evil, including choking people at a distance. The occultic nature of the Dark Side links back to Hitler's own fascination with esotericism. The Rebels are fighting for "freedom" against a genocidal Death Star, commanded by Governor Tarkin. Tarkin's uniform, as well as those of other officers, is nearly identical in design and color to that of the Third Reich. Along with the aforementioned appropriation of British culture as a sign of shared historical memory, Lucas's casting underscores the film's function as generational anxiety management, as will be demonstrated shortly.

Once the plans are safely transferred to R2-D2, the droids escape, but Leia is taken by the Empire. The droids land on Tatooine, a desert planet, where they eventually wind up in the care of Luke Skywalker, a young man who lives and works a farm with his aunt and uncle. Luke, an impatient teenager who is tired of waiting to go out on his own is a manifestation of younger Boomers' desires to make an identity separate from their parents and family. He and the droids make it to the home of Obi-Wan (Ben) Kenobi (Sir Alec Guinness), where Leia's message is replayed. Obi-Wan determines that he and Luke should take Leia's mission seriously and get R2-D2 to the Rebel Alliance command. Obi-Wan also tells Luke (and the audience) about the death of his father, the Clone Wars, the Jedi Knights, and the Force, and introduces him to a lightsaber (a laser sword). (Of note here is that Guinness is actually a British World War II veteran, adding an additional layer of gravitas to this scene.) Luke's father, a fellow veteran, died, leaving a vacancy for Obi-Wan's tutelage (which will be short lived). Obi-Wan's giving Luke his father's lightsaber, a glowing laser flame, is at once Obi-Wan literally passing the "torch" to Luke *and* the Greatest Generation passing the future to Boomers. Shortly after this moment, Luke realizes that the Empire is probably looking for the droids and returns home, only to find his aunt and uncle incinerated, their house in smoke. Free of all attachments, Luke, Obi-Wan, and the droids charter Han's *Millennium Falcon* to fulfill their mission, that is, take R2-D2 and the Death Star plans to Alderaan, home planet of Princess Leia.

However, by the time they arrive to Alderaan out of hyperspace, the Death Star, with Leia onboard as a prisoner, has already destroyed the planet. All that is left is a debris field. As the group deals with this setback, they are pulled into the Death Star itself by a "tractor beam." Once on board, they realize that they cannot escape unless they disable the tractor beam. They also figure out that the princess is onboard. Chewy, Han, and Luke go to rescue Leia; the droids hide in a command center; and Obi-Wan goes off to extinguish the tractor beam. All accomplish their respective missions and, upon returning to the *Falcon*, under fire, they see Obi-Wan fighting Darth Vader with lightsabers. Obi-Wan fights up to a point and then says, "You can't win, Vader. If you strike me down, I shall become more powerful than you can possibly imagine." Vader then takes a lateral swipe at Obi-Wan, who disappears—absorbed, as it were, into the Force. His robe falls to the ground, and Vader stands over it, perplexed. In the typical cinematic ghost voice, Obi-Wan then tells Luke to run, which he does, and they all escape.

Again, remembering the Greatest Generation/Jedi master role that Obi-Wan holds, his physical departure from the narrative opens the space for Han, Luke, Leia (all Boomers) to carry on the mission against tyranny and evil. His spiritual presence and self-sacrifice echo Christ himself, who, through the church continues his "mission" on a grander scale than he could do individually against Satan ("I shall become more powerful than you can possibly imagine"). Thus *Star Wars*, in a single scene, incorporates and reconfigures the Christian story as a new, alternative mythology that offers its Boomer audience the chance to honor and then move past their parents' cultural faith and history while attending to a deeply seated intuitive need for supernaturalism, that is, the Force as god. (That several attempts in recent years to make Jediism an official religion demonstrates how effective, if belated, this remythologizing has been.)

The *Falcon* and its crew (now with Leia) make it to the rebel base on a moon of the planet Yavin in time to give the plans to the command there. The Death Star is not far behind and starts preparing to destroy the moon. The Rebels figure out a weak spot, a two-meter-wide shaft that leads to the heart of the station. A successful shot into the shaft would set off a chain reaction that could destroy it. Luke and others prepare for battle while Han and Chewy (ostensibly) collect their reward for the return of the princess and the droid and, after saying goodbye, make plans to leave. Luke, in an X-Wing Fighter, a type of single pilot plus droid fighter jet/spaceship, takes off with the rest of the fleet to attack the Death Star. During (or after) various dogfights (another hat tip to World War II and other aerial military conflicts; this is *Star* Wars, after all), Luke flies down a narrow valley, is almost shot down but is covered by Han, and accurately shoots the torpedoes down the shaft. The station explodes in what looks a lot like a nuclear blast (a symbol of Cold War anxieties briefly relieved). Darth Vader's ship, which had been in pursuit of Luke but damaged in combat, is shown flying off into deep space, obviously an opening for the sequel that would come out three years later. The film ends with Luke, Han, and Chewy receiving military honors in a huge, formal ceremony back at the Rebel base, with Leia as officiant.

Unlike the typical Western, however, where the female lead has to be constantly saved or managed by the male hero, Leia is shown as strong and capable, holding her own against Vader, Tarkin, and Han. Although Han and Luke both think of making a play for her, her romantic attachments remain minimal. Here is no fairy tale Disney princess such as *Snow White* (1937) or *Cinderella* (1950) but a liberated and responsible woman of second-wave feminism. She makes her own choices and has her own agency. Although at various points, she is depicted as the damsel in distress, her stubbornness and spunk through sarcasm ("You're a little short for a Stormtrooper," "Get this walking carpet out of my way," "I knew you'd be holding Vader's leash," "Some rescue this is," etc.) shows that she is not beholden to the whims of the patriarchy. Although she isn't overtly sexualized for the male gaze as she is in *Return of the Jedi* (1983), she is noticeably missing a bra for the majority of the film (her nipples were purportedly covered by electrical tape). Ambiguously a sign of female independence and Lucas's sexualization ("No underwear in space," he reportedly told Fisher), her bralessness is not significant enough to counterbalance the gains of feminism attained through her character and performance.

Problematically as a new mythology for Boomers, however, *Star Wars* fails to be inclusive enough to serve as a cultural touchstone for minority Boomers. There are simply no people of color involved in any visible and important way in *A New Hope*. The closest acknowledgment comes in the form of Darth Vader's voice: the indomitable African American James Earl Jones. Surely the same cultural moment that produced *Roots* (1977, TV series; 1976, book) would have been more attentive to Black Boomer consciousness as well. But the color, often a cipher for ethnicity and further reinforced through Jones's narration, is associated with Darth Vader, the epitome of evil, who, as it turns out, answers to older white men. With his black, melted plastic bad guy cowboy hat, Vader serves as a clear contrast to goodness and hence "whiteness." It wouldn't be until the next film, *The Empire Strikes Back*, that a Black actor is incorporated visibly into the franchise. Nevertheless, given that most of the Empire's foot soldiers are masked and helmeted, they are meant to be dehumanized beyond ethnicity, fodder as it were, for a Boomer catharsis and purging of the past: "A long time ago. . . ."

Benjamin Crace

See also: Indiana Jones and the Raiders of the Lost Ark; Star Wars: The Force Awakens; Star Wars: Episode 1—The Phantom Menace; Star Wars: The Return of the Jedi.

Further Reading

Atkinson, Joshua, and Kristina Drumheller. 2003. "Taking the American Dream to a Theatre Near You: The Mythology of *Star Wars* as a Product of the Culture Industry." *Conference Papers—International Communication Association*, May 1–29.

Ellis, Kathleen. 2002. "New World, Old Habits: Pa-Triarchal Ideology in *Star Wars: A New Hope*." *Australian Screen Education*, no. 30 (Spring): 135.

Erlandson, Karen Thea. 2012. "Teaching Intercultural Awareness with *Star Wars: A New Hope*." *Communication Teacher* 26 (1): 17–21.

Gordon, Andrew. 1978. "Star Wars: A Myth for Our Time." *Literature Film Quarterly* 6 (4): 314.

Gutiérrez, Peter. 2016. "The Cultural Ubiquity of *Star Wars*." *Screen Education*, no. 82 (Winter): 58–65.

Superman

Release Date:	1978
Director:	Richard Donner
Box Office:	$134 million
Main Cast:	Superman/Clark Kent, played by Christopher Reeve
	Lois Lane, played by Margot Kidder
	Lex Luthor, played by Gene Hackman

What Boomer is not familiar with the catch phrase, "It's a bird! It's a plane! It's Superman!"? Based on the DC comic character who debuted in 1938, this 1978 film not only introduced a new generation to the character but was the start of the superhero film franchises that have taken America and the world by storm and continue today, well into the 21st century. Once doubly marginalized as a subject best left to juvenile comic books or science fiction pulp magazines, Superman has become the archetypical superhero and the subject of scores of scholarly books, essays, and dissertations. While he can seem somewhat "quaint" when compared to the angst-ridden Batman, the half-breed *dhampir* (half human and half vampire) Blade, or any of the characters in the X-Men series, Superman continues to be reimagined on the large and small screen to new generations of fans. *Superman* was not only the most expensive film made up to that point ($55 million) but it edged out *Grease* to have the highest-grossing domestic (but not worldwide) box office receipts. It was nominated for four Academy Awards—Editing, Original Score, Sound, and Visual Effects (Special Achievement)—and won in the last category. It propelled Christopher Reeve into stardom and won the hearts of critics, filmgoers, and comic book afficionados.

This 1978 film (originally meant to be the first of a two-part release) tells the origin story of the superhero, from his infancy on the planet Krypton to his exile to Earth, early life in Smallville, and eventual move to Metropolis, where he works under the persona of his alter ego Clark Kent at the *Daily Planet*, alongside photojournalist Jimmy Olsen and love interest Lois Lane. The film opens on the futuristic planet of Krypton, whose warnings of impending doom foretold by Superman's father and high council member Jor-El (played by Marlon Brando) are ignored. The infant Kal-El (as he was then known) was placed on a rocket ship large enough only to hold the infant and sent alone toward Earth while his parents and the others on Krypton died when the planet was destroyed. The child is found by a farming couple in Smallville; they adopt the boy and raise him as their own. Although aware of his superior strength and other superpowers, they choose to ignore them, as does Clark (as he is renamed by the Kents)—until after his adopted father's death, when Clark discovers a glowing green crystal that compels him to journey to the Arctic Fortress of Solitude. There his biological father reveals to him his true identity and the reasons he was sent to Earth: not only for survival but also to fight for "truth, justice and the American way" by becoming the hero that the planet needed.

Clark moves to Metropolis and becomes a reporter for the *Daily Planet*, and here he meets the characters who have become ubiquitous in any telling of the story: the young photographer Jimmy Olsen and the beautiful Lois Lane, both of whom work on the paper alongside Clark. Although Clark quickly falls for the quirky Lois Lane, it is Superman whose crime fighting exploits cause her to interview him for an article and who steals her heart. In perhaps the most uncomfortable scenes in the film (for the viewer at least), Lois and Superman flirt over things such as the color of her underwear (pink). We also learn that he is not able to see through lead and that he is vulnerable to kryptonite; these are facts published in her article that are used by the villain who becomes his archenemy, Lex Luthor, played brilliantly by Gene Hackman. Superman is captured by Luthor and his gang, who plan on simultaneously destroying the East and West Coasts of the United States by redirecting missiles fired by the military. Superman saves the East Coast but does not make it back to the West Coast in time and arrives to find a dying Lois. He disobeys one of the core tenets taught to him by his father—never to interfere with human history—and reverses time so that he is able to divert the second missile, repair the San Andreas Fault, save his beloved Lois, and deliver the villains to prison.

Like many high-budget Hollywood films, there were twists and turns in the casting of *Superman*. The producers tried to entice many big-name actors to play the lead, including Robert Redford, Paul Newman, Muhammad Ali, Al Pacino, James Caan, Steve McQueen, Clint Eastwood, and even Dustin Hoffman, to name only some of those considered. Reportedly, Sylvester Stallone and even Neil Diamond expressed interest in playing the role at some point during the casting process. Eventually they settled on the relatively unknown Christopher Reeve, who was originally turned down because he was seen as too scrawny for the part. But several months of intensive physical training under the tutelage of British bodybuilder David Charles Prowse, who himself had been turned down for the role because he was not American and who is famous for his portrayal of Darth Vader in the original *Star Wars* trilogy, Reeve's unimpressive frame was 25 pounds of muscle heavier, and he clinched the role. Similarly impressive names were considered for the role of director (George Lucas, Steven Spielberg, Francis Ford Coppola, Sam Peckinpah), with Richard Donner, fresh off his success with *The Omen* (1976), eventually being chosen for the role. Donner went on to even greater blockbuster and franchise fame, directing films such as the Lethal Weapon franchise and several films in the X-Men franchise.

Superman not only set the standard for taking the superhero seriously but he also was a fashion trendsetter, as his cape, tights, and underwear worn on the outside became the generic "superhero" costume, whether onscreen or for trick-or-treating. Peter Coogan's essay in the edited volume *What Is a Superhero?* argues that we can consider Superman the "prototypical superhero" who established the key conventions of the archetype: "A selfless, prosocial mission; extraordinary, perhaps superhuman, abilities; a secret identity and codename; and a colorful costume that expresses his nature." Swiss psychologist Carl Jung proposed a theory of character archetypes, with the hero as the ideal masculine type, arising mythologically from man's unconscious, the sum or culmination of all twelve archetypes. But Umberto Eco's essay "The Myth of Superman" (originally published in 1962) argues that Superman (and by extension, the superhero) is quite different from the mythological and archetypal figure of the classical hero discussed by Jung. That character was from a known (if imagined or mythological) past, whereas the superhero was located in the potentiality of the future. What was important for an audience was not what the superhero had done but what he might do, as the story is simultaneously unfolding with its telling, whether in comic books or onscreen. This fits in well with the science fiction aspect of Superman's backstory as well as with his ability to disrupt chronological time, as we see him do to save Lois in the film.

The character does resonate with certain historical aspects of American history and culture, such as the anti-Nazi "How Superman Would End the War" episode that appeared in *Look* magazine in 1940, two years before the United States even entered the war, and his personal motto of fighting for "truth, justice and the American way" throughout the Cold War period. The creators of Superman, the scenarist Jerry Siegel and the draftsman Joe Shuster, were children of Jewish immigrants, as were the creators of Hulk, Captain America, and the X-Men series: Jack Kirby and Stan Lee. Superman himself was an immigrant, and although he did not suffer from persecution for his "difference" (as do the mutant characters of the X-Men series), he did struggle to find his true identity and his sense of belonging in American society. He can be seen (despite his superhero powers) as the personification of the American Dream, someone who came from a humble background as an adopted farm boy but who, through hard work and perseverance, became not only a successful reporter (as Clark Kent) but also a superhero (as Superman). Several critics have discussed, in fact, which is his true identity: Clark Kent, Superman, or the original Kal-El from Krypton. Yet like any immigrant, Superman has multiple identities that he must assume, sometimes for his own sake or sometimes for the comfort of others. Clark Kent, for example, represents the "assimilated" personality, the one that fits in with society and poses no threat, sexual or otherwise. Superman, whose costume and superhero attributes Clark is always wearing beneath the mild-mannered and bespectacled journalist outfit, is his authentic yet foreign (or alien) self—or is it? For beneath that is another identity, that of the orphaned Kal-El, who is not just an immigrant but an exile from a planet that no longer exists.

Superman also symbolized a simpler and also simplistic way of conceiving the world: into the absolute opposites of good and evil. That is why he is able to utter his motto, "Truth, justice and the American way," without the slightest hint of irony and without any shadow of doubt that we see in many other superheroes, from Batman to Spider-Man, the Hulk, and Wolverine, to name only a few. It is because of Superman's connection to absolute good that he has been seen in religious or biblical terms. He is at once the baby Moses set adrift for his own safety and (as the rewriter of the screenplay Mankiewicz himself admits) an allegory for Jesus, who is sent on a messianic mission by his father (Marlon Brando's disembodied voice of God) to lead humanity into a brighter future in a spaceship that has been noted to resemble a Star of David. Linguistic connections of the Krypton names to Hebrew have been noted by some, although dismissed as coincidence by the comic's creators. The Nazis, apparently, did not dismiss this so readily and were convinced that Superman was "a Jew." While Zack Snyder's 2013 Superman film, *Man of Steel*, lends itself more easily to a discussion of morality and the concept of the Übermensch (or the superman) developed by Fredrich Nietzsche and found influential by Nazis and American eugenicists alike, the superman persona always embodies a kind of moral superiority. Lois Lane laughs at Reeve's Superman when he tells her he has come to fight for "truth, justice and the American way," but for the audience, it rings true to the belief in American exceptionalism they had been taught since childhood.

While the Greatest Generation had proven the Nazis were not superior beings in World War II, the Boomers faced a new enemy during the Cold War (1946–1991): the "commies." The rise of the military-industrial complex is on display in the film, and while President Eisenhower famously warned Americans in his 1961 farewell speech of the dangers of allowing capitalism and militarism to unite, these warnings, while oft repeated, have gone mainly unheeded. In this film, it is the missiles developed to ward off communist attacks and launched by the competing branches of the U.S. military that are hijacked by the villains and almost lead to the simultaneous destruction of both coasts. It takes a "superman" to save the day: a morally and physically superior being, this Christlike figure who is sent to an America-centric Earth to save their way of life from their nihilistic enemies, who had morphed from the Greater Generation's Nazis to the Boomer's "commies."

While espousing conservative values, at best, and more vulnerable to reactionary appropriation than any other superhero, at worst, Superman the character, and *Superman* the film continue to hold a special place in the hearts of Baby Boomers, who grew up on the comics and TV shows; Gen Xers and Millennials, who grew up on the movies; and more recent generations, who are most definitely in need of a brighter future. Without *Superman* (and its sequels), there might have been no X-Men franchise, no *Joker*, no *Wonder Woman*, and no *Black Panther*. And so moviegoers remain forever grateful to Christopher Reeve for his interpretation of the Man of Steel that paved the way for the explosion of superhero movies that continue to entertain and inspire us well into the 21st century.

Angelica Maria DeAngelis

See also: *Batman*; *The Dark Knight*; *The Dark Knight Rises*; *Wonder Woman*.

Further Reading

Bettinson, Gary. 2018. *Superman: The Movie: The 40th Anniversary Interviews*. Bristol, UK: Intellect Books.

Darowski, John. 2021. *Adapting Superman: Essays on the Transmedia Man of Steel*. Jefferson, NC: McFarland.

Tye, Larry. 2012. *Superman: The High-Flying History of America's Most Enduring Hero*. New York: Random House.

White, Mark D. 2013. *Superman and Philosophy: What Would the Man of Steel Do?* Malden, MA: Wiley-Blackwell.

Tootsie

Release Date:	1982
Director:	Sydney Pollack
Box Office:	$177 million
Main Cast:	Michael Dorsey/Dorothy Michaels, played by Dustin Hoffman
	Julie Nichols, played by Jessica Lange
	Sandy Lester, played by Teri Garr
	Jeff Slater, played by Bill Murray

Tootsie represents a significant dramatization of the conflict between the Greatest Generation's mores and the rising power and authority of Boomers. Originally given an R for language, it was released with a PG rating—language and sexuality still intact. Depicted normalization of taboo topics, such as the fluidity of sexuality and gender and "crass" language, stands in sharp contrast to similar films of the previous generation, such as *Some Like It Hot* (1959), which also featured cross-dressing men but without the self-awareness and running commentary on what is now called LBGTQ+ issues.

Dustin Hoffman, a hot commodity after an Academy Award–winning performance for *Kramer vs. Kramer* (1979), plays Michael Dorsey, a clichéd struggling actor in New York City. Although he coaches other actors and actresses who want to make it big, he himself is unable to "land a gig" because of his continual antagonism with directors. He claims he is a "character actor" and his approach often conflicts with what the directors want. He is told relatively early in the film by an agent/friend (George Fields, played by the director, Sydney Pollack) that no one will cast him—either in New York or in Los Angeles. This forces him to do something radical: become someone else offstage to get a job onstage. Initially, then, it is his unemployed status as a true-to-oneself-only bohemian that drives him to become the female character Dorothy Michaels.

As Dorothy, a conservatively dressing southern belle, Michael manages to procure a continuing role on a locally produced soap opera called *Southwest General*, an obvious satire of the television series *General Hospital* (1963–). He does so by standing up to the chauvinistic director of the soap, Ron Carlisle, played by Dabney Coleman. Thus, perceived as a strong, independently minded woman, Michael-as-Dorothy is cast as Emily Kimberly, a hospital administrator in the series. The parallels and irony between Dorothy's role as Emily the hospital administrator, an uncommon position for a woman even today, and the fact that she is really an empowered male beneath the makeup is not lost on the audience. Both personas, Emily and Dorothy, become feminist icons for American women. In one particularly telling montage, Dorothy appears on the cover of various magazines: *Woman's Day*, *Time*, and even the feminist magazine *Ms.*, which in real life was cofounded by feminist Gloria Steinem. Disturbingly, the whole reason Michael auditioned for the part is that his female friend and acting mentee, Sandy, had been turned down for not being strong enough.

What ensues is a behind-the-scenes look at the misogynistic and patriarchal television industry. Ron Carlisle, the director, condescendingly refers to the actresses as "toots" or "baby" or "honey." Even the title, *Tootsie*, refers to a sexually available young woman and is endeared to the audience through the honeyed voice of Stephen Bishop, who sings such lyrics as "We're gonna go far/Go, Tootsie, go/Roll, baby, roll. . . . I dare you not to smile/Every time she struts her stuff. . . . Could you ever get enough?/Tootsie, you've got it all." In one telling scene, Julie, who plays a nurse, is on the set and kneels down to attend to a patient who has fallen to the ground. Ron comes from behind the camera to help coordinate the scene, telling the male patient that her kneeling close "inflames your desire" and then adds, "It always inflames my desire," and follows up with a pat on Julie's behind. Later, it is shown that he and Julie are in a relationship, albeit one of convenience and inequality. Additionally, another one of the series actors, John van Horn (read: Horn-y), who plays Dr. Brewster, tries to kiss every actress—so much so that his nickname is "The Tongue." Thus despite the fact that the coproducer of the fictional series is a woman who maternally refers to everyone as "children," the set of *Southwest General* is a #metoo movement nightmare. Sexual harassment is tolerated for gainful employment and potential advancement.

The narrative advances as Dorothy's friendship with the actress Julie develops. Michael starts to fall in love with her, while Julie believes that it is simply a rich friendship between women. Their friendship grows to a point where Julie invites Dorothy to come away with her to visit her father on his farm. Julie's father, Les, played by Charles Durning, has, by this point, already made romantic overtures toward Dorothy while on a visit to the city, but this weekend seems like a prime opportunity for him to romance "her." During the visit, Dorothy and Les are left alone and he misreads her rebuffs of his advances as a kind of coyness. Somewhat confused and bewildered, he nonetheless ends up proposing to her later on. While on the visit to the farm, Dorothy and Julie share a bed in a sexual frustration–filled comedic fashion. Still, Dorothy ends up stroking Julie's hair in a maternal way as she falls asleep. Michael, supposedly, is getting in touch with his feminine side.

In another scene, Michael approaches Julie as himself, without the Dorothy makeup. At first, it seems as though they are going to hit it off. Unfortunately, when Michael tries to use knowledge that he learned as Dorothy for sexual ends, Julie rejects him, throwing her drink in his face. Michael still seems stuck within a type of masculinity that uses whatever means available to bed the object of desire. This objectification and instrumentalizing of women are not limited to Michael's relationship with Dorothy.

In contrast to Les's strict patriarchy structured around the traditional nuclear family, Michael's understanding of the relationship between the sexes is one of manipulation and utility. Les longs for a bygone era of marital commitment, a previous state of affairs pre-"liberators," as he calls second-wave feminists. He claims, "I'm all for this equal business. Women ought to be entitled to have everything. . . . Except sometimes what I think they really want is to be entitled to be men." This patinaed but open chauvinism is in contrast to Michael, who consistently deceives people such as Sandy, a high-strung, struggling actress who is one of Michael's acting understudies/friends. In one particularly dehumanizing moment, Michael is rummaging through her closet, looking for clothes for Dorothy. When Sandy comes out of the shower and sees him in his underwear, rather than telling the truth, Michael claims he has undressed because he wants to have sex with her. Thus the resulting, consensual, physical intimacy with Sandy becomes a means of deceiving her, so she won't know that he has the part she didn't get. Such subterfuge plays into the "casual sex" practices associated with the era. However, the amount of agency on the part of the female is greatly attenuated.

Later on, Dorothy offers to watch Amy, Julie's daughter, as she goes out one last time with the director. As can be imagined, Dorothy is completely inept at mothering a child. Again, comedically, Dorothy uses Michael's voice to try to calm the child down. When Julie returns home, in a vulnerable state after breaking it off with Ron, Michael sees it as his chance to come out to her about Dorothy. Misperceiving his motives, Julie thinks Dorothy is inviting her into a lesbian relationship, apologizing that she's "just not well-adjusted enough" and claiming, "I'm sure I've got the same impulses." Completely frustrated, Michael returns home to find Van Horn outside.

Reluctantly, Dorothy invites Van Horn inside his apartment to keep him from singing in the streets. Once in, Van Horn attempts to rape Dorothy, as Michael, ever the character actor, does all he can to avoid exposing his secret. In the nick of time, Jeff comes in, and Van Horn, thinking that he is Dorothy's partner, apologetically speeds out. By this point, Michael has determined to reveal his secret.

Michael chooses a live broadcast of the soap to reveal that Dorothy is actually a man. He does so by making up a speech about the character Emily and her brother that mirrors the silly complexity of the genre. Of course, as he strips off the wig and makeup, the other actors and production crew are completely taken aback. Ultimately, in the upside-down world of art, the entire Dorothy ruse turns out to make Michael more of a commodity. It does not, however, help him with Julie, and it deeply disappoints Les.

In a rather tender and vulnerable scene, Michael approaches Les in a stereotypical bar (with boxing on the TV) to return the engagement ring. At first, Les is very cold but eventually warms up to Michael, seeing in him a potential friend—regardless of gender. They end up drinking together, and this settles for the Boomer audience the anxieties of how to relate to the previous generation and still be "true to oneself."

The film ends with an extended conversation between Michael and Julie. Like her dad, at first, she doesn't want anything to do with him, still wincing from the deception. But he persistently pleads with her and ends up convincing her to consider him. He claims that the hard part of the relationship is over: "We already were good friends." As they walk down the street, they discuss dresses of Dorothy's that Julie would like to borrow as Michael teases her about spilling wine on them.

The film itself is self-consciously aware that it exists in tension between generational understandings of the "battle of the sexes" (Les vs. Michael) and within the context of second-wave feminism. Second-wave feminism refers to the generation of feminists that followed the first wave, which fought for the right to vote. Second-wave feminists sought social as well as political equality with men. This self-consciousness comes through particularly strong in one of Sandy's speeches when she, trying to show her feminist credentials, exclaims, "I read *The Second Sex*. I read *The Cinderella Complex*. I'm responsible for my own orgasm!" Both texts she alludes to are key books within second-wave feminism, and yet, as it turns out, it isn't Sandy who is the liberated woman but Julie, who is tutored to quasi-equality by a man dressed as a woman.

Tootsie concentrates considerably more on issues surrounding gender, but it is modern sexuality, femininity and masculinity, that is still interlaced with the Boomer generation and Americanism. In one telling montage, Dorothy, wearing a red sequin gown, marches in front of a large American flag. Such a scene recalls the opening to *Patton* (1970), a World War II movie based on the life of General George Patton, played by George C. Scott. This new form of "war hero" emerges out of the battle of the sexes and struts in front of the flag, equally comfortable in a dress or pants. With a hat tip to the Greatest Generation yet in an act of defiance as well, Boomer identity is created not on the foreign battlefield but in self-actualizing relationships in the pursuit of happiness.

Benjamin Crace

See also: *Ghostbusters*; *Kramer vs. Kramer*.

Further Reading

Abbott, Martin L. 1989. "*Tootsie*." *Teaching Sociology* 17 (1): 135–136.

Abbott, Traci B. 2013. "The Trans/Romance Dilemma in *Transamerica* and Other Films." *Journal of American Culture* 36 (1): 32.

"Dustin Hoffman." 2020. *Columbia Electronic Encyclopedia*. 6th ed. New York: Columbia University Press.

Higgins, Bill. 2019. "Hoffman Cross-Dressed for Success in 1982's *Tootsie*." *Hollywood Reporter* 425 (14): 64.

McIntosh, William D., John D. Murray, Rebecca M. Murray, and Sunita Manian. 2006. "Sexual Humor in Hollywood Films: Influences of Social and Economic Threat on the Desirability of Male and Female Characters." *Mass Communication & Society* 9 (2): 239–254.

3

Xers on a Quest for Identity and Belonging (1983–1998)

Back to the Future

Release Date:	1985
Director:	Robert Zemeckis
Box Office:	$388.8 million
Main Cast:	Dr. Emmett Brown, played by Christopher Lloyd
	Marty McFly, played by Michael J. Fox
	Lorraine Baines, played by Lea Thompson
	George McFly, played by Crispin Glover
	Biff Tannen, played by Thomas F. Wilson

Zemeckis's *Back to the Future* is a radical departure from the typical '80s coming-of-age, rebellious teenager films that take place somewhere outside and offstage of the adult world (e.g., *Footloose* (1984); John Hughes's oeuvre, *The Breakfast Club* (1985); etc.). As a time-travel film, it interrogates the nature of personal, family, and communal history across the generations through the indefatigable yet diminutive Marty McFly.

There is, too, a sense that the film's very title is a site of resistance that must be overcome for real change to occur; one must not have one's "back" to the future but must face it head on. This isn't just important for the average moviegoer but goes for America collectively. Released six years before the end of the Cold War and at the beginning of Soviet leader Mikhail Gorbachev's perestroika initiatives (Russian for "restructuring"; a reform movement within the USSR), the anxieties that shadow other '80s films (e.g., *Red Dawn*, 1984; *Rocky IV*, 1985) are presciently shifted away from the Soviet bugaboo toward Middle Eastern terrorism. In order for Doc Brown (Christopher Lloyd) to power the DeLorean time machine, he uses plutonium. This plutonium was stolen from the Pacific Nuclear Research Facility by Libyan terrorists, for whom he promised to build a bomb. But instead of a bomb, he uses it for his time machine experiment. As Doc and Marty (and Doc's dog, Einstein) run an initial experiment that actually works, the terrorists drive up, kill Doc, and chase Marty, who escapes by taking the time machine back to the day when Doc had first thought of how to time travel: November 5, 1955.

What is interesting in this scene, filmed in the parking lot of Twin Pines Mall—the quintessential symbol of American materialism—is how the Arab characters are portrayed. They yell at each other in Arabic and are fairly inept and just angry. One wears a traditional, checked keffiyeh, which is more apt for the Arabian Peninsula, Syria, Jordan, and Palestine than for Libya. Given the high profile of keffiyeh-wearing Palestinian leader Yasser Arafat at the time, this particular "Libyan" terrorist thus serves as a cipher for the various Middle Eastern regimes and terrorist organizations operating against U.S. interests in the region. A volatile region throughout the 20th century, the Hezbollah bombing of U.S. Marine barracks in Beirut in 1983 would have still been fresh in the minds of the original audience, especially when the terrorist takes out a rocket launcher: a familiar image. In addition, growing tensions between President Reagan and Libya's Muammar Gaddafi culminated in a U.S. strike against the nation just one year after Marty "escapes" to the past.

In 1955, Marty hides the DeLorean, realizing that he is stuck there without more plutonium. He then heads into the 1955 version of Hill Valley. There are several stark differences in this earlier version of Hill Valley. The life of the city revolves around the square, which is clean and bright. The Texaco gas station operates a full-service crew, vinyl records are for sale, and instead of the XXX-rated *Orgy American Style* that is playing at the theater in 1985, *Cattle Queen of Montana* with B. Stanwyck and R. Reagan is advertised. After picking up a discarded newspaper with the date on it, Marty heads to a diner to think about his next move.

In the diner, he looks up Doc Brown in a phone book, recalling that he came back to this date because that was the date Brown invented time travel. After ripping the page out of the book for the number and address, he tries to order a Tab and then a Pepsi Free, two examples of conspicuous attempts of the film's copious use of product placement. Eventually, he ends up with a coffee and sits down next to a guy who turns out to be his dad but obviously a younger version. In what follows, Biff, the town bully, harasses George, Marty's father, in much the same way with almost the same dialogue as the audience saw in a scene before Marty went back in time. Here history rhymes: Marty's dad is the same spineless ne'er-do-well in both the past and the present/future. George leaves the diner, hops on his bike, and speeds away. Marty follows.

When he catches up to him, he sees him in a tree using binoculars to spy on Lorraine Baines, Marty's (future) mother, as she dresses in a window. Realizing that his dad is a "peeping Tom," Marty startles George, who falls off the limb where he is perched into the street below. Just before a car hits him, Marty shoves him out of the way and is himself hit by the car driven by Lorraine's dad, Marty's grandfather. The dramatic irony here is that the audience knows that this is the moment (from a scene in 1985) that Lorraine begins to be enamored with George, as he convalesced after the accident in her house. However, Marty's intervention means that he has replaced George and his mother develops an incestuous crush on him instead.

After leaving the Baines home, Marty looks up Doc, who initially disbelieves but assents to helping him after Marty relates the significance of the date. After brief despair about being able to generate sufficient power to send the car back to the future, they develop a plan to harness the famous lightning strike that is about to take out the clock tower on the square. Marty knows about this because of a flyer stuck in his pocket from 1985 made by a group that was trying to restore the clock. In the meantime, Marty and Doc also discover that Marty's family picture of him and his two siblings is beginning to fade. Doc theorizes that it is because Marty has disrupted the course of events that led to his parents' marriage and his birth. So they hatch a plot to get George and Lorraine together before the storm takes out the clock.

At first, Marty tries to get Lorraine to like George by encouraging him and then by scaring him as a visitor from outer space, calling himself Darth Vader (from *Star Wars*) and playing '80s rock band Van Halen through headphones as torture. It only works because Marty still had the radiation suit he had been wearing in the mall parking lot. Scared to death, George tries to approach Lorraine in the diner to ask her to the Enchantment under the Sea dance (where, historically, they had first kissed) but is disrupted by Biff. Marty punches Biff and is chased by him and his cronies, while Lorraine and friends look on, commenting on how great he is.

Back at Doc's house, Lorraine stops in and asks Marty to the dance instead. He decides to go but then comes up with a plan to get her to accept George instead of him once they're at the dance. Marty's plan is to pretend to take advantage of her in a parked car while George comes up and saves her. As it so happens, Biff gets to Marty and Lorraine first and, after stuffing Marty into the band's trunk, begins to rape her. George arrives, thinks at first that it is Marty, and then realizes it is Biff. Biff twists George's arm as he writhes in pain, and Lorraine screams for Biff to stop. As George's anger increases, he balls his fist up and lays Biff out with one punch. Meanwhile, one of the band members gets the trunk open, freeing Marty. However, in the process, the band member injuries his hand so Marty has to play the guitar. On stage now, he anxiously watches as George brings Lorraine into the dance and finally sees them kiss. Marty now knows the future is secured—except that he has to get back to it as quickly as possible.

Racing from the dance, Marty makes it to the DeLorean and just in the nick of time, Doc connects two cables that send the electricity down to the car, sending it into the future. Marty, knowing that Doc is gunned down by the terrorists, had written a letter to Doc telling him to take precautions. But just before leaving, he saw Doc tear it up. Defeated but not down, Marty reset the time machine to arrive just moments before Doc is shot. Once back in 1985, however, he is at the square, not the mall, which is some distance away. He runs to the mall just in time to see Doc being shot (again) and himself being chased. When he gets to Doc's body, it is revealed that Doc had been wearing a bulletproof vest. He smiles and pulls out a taped-up, yellow version of the warning letter. The scene ends with Doc driving off into the future.

The next morning, Marty awakes at home, thinking it has all been a dream, but many things have changed. Biff is subservient to his dad. His once-derelict house is now a nice, '80s-style modern dream. A 4x4 truck he dreamed of in the other 1985 is now his. His brother and sister even get along and are successful. Just before the film ends, Doc reappears in the DeLorean and tells Marty and his girlfriend, Jennifer, that they need to come to the future with him to save their children. All three pile into the DeLorean, which can now fly, and they zip off to 2015.

Throughout the film, there are many points of contact between Boomer generational consciousness and emergent Gen X sensibility. Yet this is a transitional film: the Boomer American Dream is still tenuously alive and cautiously explored. Success means rampant consumerism and purchasing power; Marty dreams of owning a new Toyota, the time machine is a DeLorean, and so on. But that dream is also contingent on successfully navigating the project of the self through assertiveness and self-determination—that is, you cannot allow yourself to be bullied by others. And although there are contemporaneous historical/pop cultural referents scattered throughout the film, the main tension that generates the film's overarching meaning is that which exists between how one generation represents the past to the next versus how it actually was. Marty does what everyone of any generation has dreamed of—witnessed the truth of his own genesis, but it is not what he thinks.

Historical misrepresentation, ironically enough for a film that stages and fictionally represents the '50s, layers *Future* with the dual sense that only change is constant and the past is always a fiction unto disillusionment. For Marty, this is brought home when his mom is sexually aggressive, smokes, and sneaks alcohol—all in contradistinction to her insistence that she was a well-behaved, good girl. Marty then finds himself in this odd position of being the conservative adult as a teenager. Additionally, the only cognizant character link between 1985 and 1955 other than Marty is Doc Brown. It isn't clear in the film how Marty and he became friends but, intriguingly, Doc functions as a symbol of the old past that led to the 1985 Marty changes. His "fake" death and resurrection through Marty's intervention suggests that the re-presentation of the historical revisionism that occurs through the metanarrative of the film has profound changes on the present. Historiography, be it personal or national, is always an exercise in misrepresentation, but some misrepresentations change things for the "better": here, a reduced vision of the American Dream and teenage independence. Doc's new life in 1985 is a manifestation of the ongoing need Boomers have for Gen X to help them make sense of their own past.

Benjamin Crace

See also: Forrest Gump; Star Wars: A New Hope; Star Wars: Return of the Jedi.

Further Reading

Bartlett, Myke. 2015. "The Future Is Now." *Screen Education*, no. 79 (Spring): 16–25.

Gilmore, Brad. 2020. *Back from the Future: A Celebration of the Greatest Time Travel Story Ever Told (*Back to the Future *Time Travel Facts and Trivia)*. Miami, FL: Mango.

Ní Fhlainn, Sorcha. 2010. *The Worlds of* Back to the Future*: Critical Essays on the Films*. Jefferson, NC: McFarland.

Ruud, Jay. 1991. "*Back to the Future* as Quintessential Comedy." *Literature Film Quarterly* 19 (2): 127.

Wittenberg, David. 2008. "Oedipus Multiplex, or, the Subject as a Time Travel Film: Two Readings of *Back to the Future*." *Discourse: Journal for Theoretical Studies in Media & Culture* 28 (2–3): 51–77.

Batman

Release Date:	1989
Director:	Tim Burton
Box Office:	$411.5 million
Main Cast:	Bruce Wayne/Batman, played by Michael Keaton
	Jack Napier/The Joker, played by Jack Nicholson
	Vicky Vale, played by Kim Basinger
	Alexander Knox, played by Robert Wuhl
	Dent, played by Billy Dee Williams

Tim Burton's *Batman*, screenplay by Sam Hamm and Warren Skaaren, was the first of several reboots within the DC Comics Universe, significantly preceding Marvel Comics' adaptations. With the success of the Superman franchise (1978, 1980, 1983, and 1987), it naturally followed that the Caped Crusader would see the silver screen. It was also the first *Batman* film since 1966 and departed from the earlier Batman incarnation serialized on television from 1966 to 1968. Burton capitalized on Keaton's success throughout the '80s (*Clean and Sober, Gung-Ho, Mr. Mom,* and *Beetlejuice*) as well as Nicholson's well-known ability to play psychotic characters (*One Flew Over the Cuckoo's Nest* and *The Shining*). It also features a short performance by Jack Palance, Hollywood royalty as it were, known for his numerous roles in older horror films. Kim Basinger, who had starred earlier in the erotic drama *9½ Weeks* (1986), alternates between a strong female character with significant agency and a powerless princess in need of a (dark) knight.

The opening credits take the viewer on a confusing journey in and around an unknown, gray, stone shape, full of turns and curves. As the credits come to a close, the camera moves out to reveal the familiar but edgier and darker Batman logo. The rebranding is clear: this is not the campy Batman of the '60s with a sidekick and patriotic blue costume. This Batman is dark and operates in the shadows, as the next scene shows.

Gotham, a thinly disguised version of New York with undertones of Chicago, is mired in crime and corruption. This corruption is manifested for the viewer as a wholesome couple and their child make their way down a crowded city street, where a prostitute propositions the preteen. Fleeing from this encroachment on innocence, they turn into an alley and are promptly accosted by thugs. Echoing the origin story for Batman himself that appears later in the movie, Batman catches the criminals, scaring one into what appears to be a psychotic break. Throughout this opening sequence, Burton careful draws out a continuing motif of the film. This Batman is closer to Dracula than an unambiguous moral crusader.

While the film seemingly centers on Batman, Jack Nicholson's performance as the Joker tilts the narrative in a way that sets the precedent for later Batman/Joker films. In short, the colorful, insane, and unexpectedly violent Joker is more interesting when onscreen than either Bruce Wayne or Batman, however morally fraught. This Joker, formerly Jack Napier, falls into acid, ends up with a permanent smile on his face, dances around in clownishly colorful suits, randomly shoots people, plans to poison the whole city through cosmetics, and then lands on killing everyone. First as one of the city's organized crime bosses' main henchmen, then as the rebellious protégé who is sleeping with the big boss's wife, Jack gets sold out while on a mission to stage a phony crime. Once trapped in a chemical plant aptly named Axis (the "bad guys" in World War II) Chemical, Batman appears on the scene and seemingly attempts to save Jack as he hangs over a vat of chemicals. Again, it is not clear if Batman lets him go or cannot hold on any longer, but Jack ends up in the vat. After a basement quack, German plastic surgeon attempts to fix his face, Jack, now Joker, returns to his old boss and shoots him several times with no remorse at all. He then, through a series of maneuvers that resemble the gangster films of the 1950s, kills his competitors or brings them on to his side.

Concurrently with the rise of the Joker and the nightly forays of Batman, Vicky arrives at the city's newspaper looking to do a story on the Batman phenomenon. The audience is first introduced to her in an objectified way while one of the newspaper correspondents, Alexander Knox, spies her legs, commenting, "Hello, legs." Following his gaze upward, the audience is then shown a bespectacled, Marilyn Monroe blonde who, as the cover of the *Time* magazine on the table demonstrates, is a war photographer and not just a pretty face. She has, apparently, left the frontlines of the Corto Maltese Revolution to take pictures of Batman. This fictional revolution is an Easter egg for DC comic fans familiar with Frank Miller's graphic novel *The Dark Knight Returns*, which had appeared three years prior to the film. In one of the few cross-references to the real-world context of the late Cold War, the fictional revolution involved the Soviets.

As expected, Vicky ends up at Wayne Manor at a dinner party, where she meets the mysterious host without knowing it. Together with her sidekick, Knox, they find themselves in a room full of armor from various countries. Here it is revealed that the man she had met earlier really was Bruce Wayne, the host and owner of the mansion. Knox jokingly asks for a grant and, at the end of the conversation, Wayne directs his butler, Alfred, to give him one, with the now-clichéd Xer nonchalance preoccupied with some inner turmoil that fuels a certain type of anxiety and action.

Later, Vicky is invited to Wayne's house for a private dinner. This dinner is eaten at a table so large that, seated on either end, neither can really carry on a conversation. At one point, Wayne jokes he has never been in that room before. Moving into the more intimate space of the kitchen, social walls are torn down as

Alfred regales Vicky with stories of Wayne's youth over multiple glasses of wine at the smaller kitchen table. In this scene, it is clear why Burton cast Keaton, as he embodies the vulnerable yet darkly mysterious character of the conflicted Wayne who exorcizes his demons at night on the streets of Gotham. Shortly after the kitchen scene, Wayne, operating in the same morally ambiguous areas as Batman, takes advantage of Vicky's drunkenness by sleeping with her—he clearly being the more sober one at the time.

Meanwhile, the Joker sets his plan into action of turning all of Gotham into permanently smiling head cases. After more deaths from the Joker's plan, Gotham City's district attorney, Harvey Dent, played by African American Billy Dee Williams of the *Star Wars* films, is under even more pressure to find out how the Joker is delivering his deadly mix. Wayne, using his intelligence and technology, cracks the Joker's scheme, uncovering that it is a combination of cosmetics that cumulatively poisons people. This incites the Joker to target Batman specifically.

The first confrontation Batman has with the Joker takes place in an art museum. Phoning in earlier as Bruce Wayne, the Joker lures Vicky to have dinner with him. After delivering a gas mask to Vicky at the table, the Joker and his gang gas all the other visitors. Then, accompanied to Prince's soundtrack playing over a boom box, the Joker and his crew use bright spray paint to deface the art—most of it a random collection of famous pieces of European art. Some of the crew are oddly dressed in Roman Catholic priest collars. This scene is strangely textured. The name of the museum is clearly a play on the Guggenheim, a Jewish family. The way the patrons are all gassed instead of shot or tied up seems closer to the Zyklon-B used during the Holocaust. Vicky, a blond-haired, light-eyed Caucasian survives the gas. Given the perpetrators wear the Roman Catholic collar, it seems as though Burton is suggesting that the Catholic Church's complicity with the Nazis is to blame for the Holocaust and the ruining of a culture heritage. Yet the Joker's charisma adds a disturbing layer to the whole sequence.

This type of religious appropriation, the popular Prince soundtrack, and the disrespectful graffitiing of art with fluorescent colors solidly resonate with the Xer embrace of the MTV aesthetic and ethos. This is perhaps the clearest dissolve between the film as art and as a social commentary. In contradistinction to their Boomer parents, who may have held at least a nominal respect for American civil religion, Xers have attempted to distance themselves from those traditional forms of authority through sacrilege. In addition, the defacing of the art itself as well as his acid artistry on the face of his former lover telegraph a disgust toward the idol of image so prevalent in Hollywood. The Joker, with a peculiarly strong Xer variety of irony, manages to skewer high culture, implicate the Catholic Church in anti-Semitic violence, and critique popular culture's obsession with looks, all in a single effort to twistedly romance a reporter. This depth of cultural mutuality is another instance of how the Joker steals the narrative away by diverting the audience's attention from lesser developed and somewhat passive characters who are mired at this point in the plot in their own inaction.

Another important scene occurs shortly afterward when, at the prompting of Alfred, Wayne decides to tell Vicky that he is Batman. He goes to her apartment, which is decorated with expensive and genderless furniture and art that is unlike most of the background décor of the other sets but perfectly in line with what constituted fashionable in the late '80s/ early '90s. Wayne remarks that it has a lot of space as well (the Joker makes the exact same comment when he enters later in the scene). Her place, then, serves as the epitome of what middle-class Xers would have considered to be material success at the time. It is odd, however, that within this space, she is disempowered. At one point, when trying to tell her his secret through her angry rant, Wayne forces Vicky to sit down on the sofa while he remains standing, telling her, "Shut up." As she is seated submissively at waist level, looking up, Wayne begins in typical, halting Keaton style to tell her he's the vigilante. But the doorbell rings, and the Joker arrives with a present for her. Wayne steals back to her bedroom and slides a silver tray up his shirt, a gentle nod back toward an older Western film where Clint Eastwood's character does the same thing. He comes out of the bedroom and the Joker, though initially caught off guard, begins a monologue. As he does so, he moves to the mantle of the fireplace, and just above it, there is a piece of art that is shown only briefly. In it, an African figure, bare to the waist, is seated with his back toward the viewer. The angle of the painting suggests the artist was standing looking down on the seated subject. This faceless African in a position of subjugation juxtaposed with the Joker's white face gestures toward an absence within the film industry itself of minority actors. Burton, with some sensitivity, decided to use both Prince and Billy Dee Williams's talents in the film's production. Further, in keeping with the birth and then-growing cultural domination of MTV, such a silent and subtle inclusion parallels the Xers' tentative movement beyond mere tolerance to active appreciation of African American culture. But such moves toward social justice in the film are belied by the misogynistic elements that, as this scene ends, come to the fore.

After supposedly "killing" Wayne, the Joker leaves his box and walks out into the hallway, where ever-so-briefly the audience sees a Gaugin-like nude of a female, not a celebration of the female form but an object open for the male gaze in the same way the Joker views women instrumentally. The closing shot shows the box popping open, with an abstract hand holding dead roses that frighten Vicky so much she collapses like a Victorian housewife, completely disempowered and objectified on her own floor since all those with real agency, Wayne and the Joker, have now left.

The film ends with a Gotham-situated play on *The Hunchback of Notre Dame*, as Batman chases the Joker up the tower of Gotham Cathedral. Vicky, at this point, has been reduced to passive bait. The Joker, again sacrilegiously and unpatriotically, tries to stop Batman by dropping the church's Liberty Bell–looking bronze bells down on him. Eventually, after fighting his way through some henchmen, Batman signals to Vicky to distract the Joker while he is dancing with her rather limp-with-terror body at the top of the tower. Vicky suddenly begins to pretend to be sexually interested in the Joker and starts working her way down toward his waist off camera as if to perform oral sex on him. Batman, seizing the opportunity afforded by this dehumanizing act, jumps in to confront the Joker. Ultimately, the Joker falls to his death, partly due to his own actions.

In the last scene Vicky, who now knows Wayne is Batman, walks away from a press conference and gets into the back seat of Wayne's limo as Alfred offers her champagne. Un-ironically, she has become the very ideal the Boomer generation tried so hard to deconstruct: the kept woman, always waiting for the male provider to come home after work. But it is paradoxically precisely in this failure to break free from the Greatest Generation's dominating hierarchy that the film ultimately succeeds as an Xer text. It does so by the detached and ironic dark humor so elegantly captured by the Joker, the real "hero."

Benjamin Crace

See also: *The Dark Knight*; *The Dark Knight Rises*; *Joker*; *One Flew over the Cuckoo's Nest*.

Further Reading

Brody, Michael. 2012. "Holy Franchise! Batman, Psychic Trauma, and Clinical Cases." In *Seductive Screens: Children's Media—Past, Present, and Future*, by Michael Brody, 33–49. Newcastle upon Tyne, UK: Cambridge Scholars Publishing.

Durand, Kevin K. J., and Mary K. Leigh. 2011. *Riddle Me This, Batman! Essays on the Universe of the Dark Knight*. Jefferson, NC: McFarland.

Wojtas, Paweł. 2019. "Taking a Leap in the Dark: The Ethics of Batman." *European Journal of American Culture* 38 (2): 169–184.

Yockey, Matt. 2014. *Batman*. Detroit, MI: Wayne State University Press.

Beauty and the Beast

Release Date:	1991
Directors:	Gary Trousdale, Kirk Wise
Box Office:	$440.1 million
Main Cast (Voices):	Beast/Prince, played by Robby Benson
	Belle, played by Paige O'Hara
	Gaston, played by Richard White
	Lumiere, played by Jerry Orbach
	Cogsworth, played by David Ogden Stiers
	Mrs. Potts, played by Angela Lansbury

The 1990s saw Disney produce 10 of the top-grossing animated films. *Beauty and Beast* became the first animated film to win a Golden Globe for Musical or Comedy. Nonetheless, even though it is hard to directly categorize it as a musical or a comedy, it is thoroughly Disney. In propping up Disney as a type of genre, it is important to note that it has remained remarkably consistent and relevant across generations. For the Boomers, Disney produced and maintained some of its most classic characters: Mickey, Minnie, Goofy, Donald, and so on. Yet at the same time, beyond the animated cell, Disney built its theme parks (Disneyland, California, 1955; Disney World, Florida, 1965) and launched the careers of actors such as Kurt Russell, Annette Funicello, Dean Jones, and others through various film and television productions, among them, *The Mouseketeers*. In 1983, as Xers were beginning to tune in to cable television, Disney began the Disney Channel and continued its cultural dominance as a youth-oriented, "wholesome" entertainment company. This relative "wholesomeness" along with the promise of a happy ending with a touch of nostalgia kept Disney stock high, as Boomers continually reinitiated their children, Gen X, into the wonderful world of Disney.

Following its normal 12- to 18-month release pattern, *Beauty and the Beast* came on the heels of *The Little Mermaid* (1989) and *The Rescuers Down Under* (1990) but a year before *Aladdin* (1992). *Beauty and the Beast* added yet another heroine to the Disney "princess" pantheon: Snow White (1937), Cinderella (1950), Aurora (1959), Ariel (1989), and now Belle, the "beauty" of the title. Like her predecessors, Belle is a young, thin, symmetrical, Western European/Caucasian from a nonnuclear family (her mother is dead). It would be another year before Disney would add a person of color, Jasmine, to this elite group.

From the very beginning of the film, Belle ("beautiful" in the language of France, where the story takes place) is presented as atypical of the local village girls. Her father is an eccentric inventor, she spurns the romantic overtures of the most eligible bachelor, and she reads all the time—even to the exclusion of what is taking place around her. As a young adult with long brunette hair, she hovers on the blurred border between teenager and woman. Initially, she wears conservative blue and white clothing, reminiscent of various depictions of the Virgin Mary. Meanwhile, other townswomen literally have their cleavage spilling out of their bodices. Three of these women, all blondes, hang on every word of the alpha male, Gaston, suggesting a type of polyamorous relationship that Belle must avoid to remain pure. Further, playing to its Boomer/Gen X market, Belle is both loyal to her father but strongly independent against a parodied version of patriarchy and masculinity portrayed by Gaston and his followers.

The story, like most Disney fairy tales, is framed by a larger myth. As part of the dramatic irony, the audience knows that there is a castle nearby that is in a state of cursed disrepair because the prince who lived there was unable to appreciate people for who they were rather than what they looked like. Thus, in order to teach him the lesson that beauty was more than skin deep, a witch transformed him into a monster and all those in his household into various objects until he could get someone to love him for who he was on the inside. He was then given a magical rose as a kind of timer of how long he had to accomplish this feat. The rose would lose a petal, and once all petals were gone, the "beast" and all his house would be forever condemned to live in their transformed states. The rose was also synched to his (Prince Adam/Beast) age; he had until he was 21.

This frame story and its countdown not only adds urgency to the narrative but taps deeply into the American mythos, itself an admixture of the European cultural legacy, modern psychology, and generational, consumeristic moral philosophy. Not only are fairy tales embedded in the Euro-American collective psyche, brought over to the continent through waves of European immigration, the disrepair and chaotic condition of the kingdom as a reflection of the cursed status of its ruler has its roots even further back, back to the Grail legend of the late Middle Ages. In the film, Prince Adam's immediate domain, the castle and surrounding forest, are overrun by vines, weeds, and wolves, and whole wings of the castle are in utter ruin. The messaging is clear: the prosperity of the land and its people is only as good as its ruler. Given the United States at this time was embroiled in a war with Iraq and hunting down Saddam Hussein, such ruinous and dark imagery of a reign in tatters would have aligned with the nightly news as well. Here, too, are other common tropes. The magical rose is basically a "she loves me, she loves me not" game, playing itself out. The rather random age of 21 as the time limit seems like a rather obvious allusion to the legal drinking age of Americans, suggesting real love is "intoxicating" and belongs to the mature. The rose, too, as the flower of the Virgin Mary, connects to the virginal imagery around Belle. The sexual overtones of "deflowering" come into play as the petals fall off, and, later, when Belle finds and reaches for the magical plant, only to be warded off by Beast; she is not ready. Psychologically speaking, the literal transformation of the house staff into household objects reflects the objectification of people (especially women) that Prince Adam is cursed for. Perhaps like the supreme capitalist who commodifies everything, he thought of people as objects, so they became objects (in line with their duties and jobs, for example, the kitchen staff were turned into plates, forks, knives, cups, etc.). But at its heart, the frame story gears the rest of the narrative toward the same basic conclusions about life that Boomers learned and yearned to pass on to their children: the good life consists of material wealth, authenticity, and marriage. It is hard to think of a company more invested in maintaining the middle-class American Dream more than Disney has been.

The film proceeds in a fairly predictable way, albeit a bit more complex due to its medium and length. Belle's father, Maurice, a blue-collar inventor who, with Belle's help, finally gets an invention to work, takes off to the fair to sell it (good, old American entrepreneurship here; think of Edison, Ford, Jobs, and others) but gets lost in the dark forest along the way. He stumbles into the ruined castle of Beast, who then holds him prisoner for trespassing. Meanwhile, Gaston attempts to propose to Belle, but she eludes his advances and ends up tricking him into falling outside into a pigsty (where chauvinist, male "pigs" must land). Soon after, Belle spies her dad's horse returning without her dad or his wagon. She knows something is wrong and takes off after her dad. Such concern for the absent-minded, older father seeds the young, female Gen X viewer's mind with notions that female heroism is tied into taking care of one's aging, Boomer parents—no matter the cost. For immediately after finding her dad in Beast's dungeon, Belle offers her life for his—a deal Beast readily accepts. Her dad is released, and Beast tries to make her feel at home in her new prison.

A significant amount of the film at this point seeks to develop the relationship between Belle and Beast. Beast confers with his staff about the possibilities of breaking the spell; they give advice. His two main confidants are a candle, Lumiere, who unlike everyone else in the film speaks with a French accent, and a clock, Cogsworth, who has a British accent. Obviously, this is where Americans see themselves situated in the world, as citizens of the main superpower who receives advice from smaller, subservient European friends. This advice is akin to the services provided by their respective shapes: a candle and a clock. A candle may help one see and a clock tells the time, but real decisions must be made individually, authentically, by the powerful and influential, here the Beast with the heart of a young, white, upper-class American male with the primordial name of humankind's foremost progenitor: Adam.

In light of female Gen X dysmorphic anxieties, Belle and Beast's relationship initially conflicts over food. Beast orders her to eat; the staff tries to coax her to eat. At one point, the angry Beast proclaims, "If she doesn't eat with me, she doesn't eat at all." Later that night, Belle sneaks down to the kitchen to eat and, with a little convincing, gets the staff to disobey Beast and feed her. Recalling that it was within the childhood of Gen Xers that disorders like bulimia were first officially recognized, such hesitancy around eating, eating in secret, and so on suggest more than just Belle's displeasure with Beast's attitude and behavior. A fairy tale princess with an impossible waistline who prefers to eat alone is hardly a model for developing young women.

Shortly after a *Fantasia*-inspired musical number in the kitchen, Belle makes her way to the forbidden part of the castle, the west wing (incidentally, also the name of the location of the Oval Office for the U.S. president). In the west wing, Belle finds the magical rose and Beast's magic mirror, which signals both his narcissism and voyeurism, for it can "see" anyone anywhere. Learning his secret, Beast becomes angry at Belle's intrusion into what amounts to his libido and ego and goes into a rage, at which point, Belle breaks their deal and leaves, signaling to teenage Gen X girls that leaving is always an option in an unhealthy relationship.

In her flight, she is attacked by wolves in the forest. Beast, interestingly, comes to her defense but is not solely responsible for her rescue. She manages to fight off many on her own and ultimately helps Beast after he suffers many wounds on her behalf. Here the Virgin Mary/Jesus imagery is fairly strong, as Belle, in blue and white, attends a wounded Beast pietà-like, after which he "resurrects." Again, Disney adroitly walks the generational tightrope: Belle has a significant part to play but still needs a strong male who loves sacrificially. Boomer parents' values are ratified and Gen X's intuited desire for "real" love beyond sexual gratification is realized. This Gen X desire for transcendental love, beyond perceived Boomer procreative sex without real love, will continually be woven throughout the film industry's adjustments to its new market.

After thanking Beast for saving her life, Belle and Beast's relationship flowers through a series of montages—many of which depict elaborate dinners, suggesting again that a strong, loving patriarchy can balance a young woman's anxieties about her body and eating. These scenes culminate with a dance and a walk back to the west wing. There, Beast asks her if she is happy. As proscribed for Gen Xers by Boomer desire, she admits that she wants to see her father again. Beast shows Maurice to her via the magic mirror, and she sees him struggling and dying in the snow on the way to her rescue. Beast tells her that she is no longer his prisoner, and she runs out with the mirror to find her father. Left behind, Beast and confidants lament that it is probably too late for the spell to be broken.

Parallel to this action, Gaston has hatched a plan to get Maurice admitted to an insane asylum in order to marry Belle. His plan is to get the head physician of the asylum to hear Maurice talk about the "imaginary" Beast to show that he is insane. When Belle returns with her father to recover, Gaston and company go to their house in order to commit Maurice to a mental institution. Initially, it looks as though Gaston will succeed, but Belle uses the mirror to prove that Beast is actually real. At that point, Gaston pivots and leads a mob to hunt him down, but not before imprisoning Belle and her father in their own basement so they cannot warn Beast.

At the castle, Beast despairs as his staff fights off the mob. These scenes have some rather overt sexuality that would not have been missed by Boomer audiences. Consistently, the French candlestick character, Lumiere, is depicted as sexually promiscuous with the feather duster (clearly a French maid). Here European, particularly French, stereotypes of sexual libertinism are on full display to indoctrinate the next American generation. Later, one member of Gaston's mob holds the feather duster upside down and pulls her feathers out of her bottom as the penis-shaped candlestick gets hot and angry, burns the rapist, and saves his mistress. Knowing the feather duster is, in fact, when the spell is broken, a French maid in typical sexualized costume, makes this scene particularly disturbing and out of place for the supposed Disney image of wholesomeness. But this is precisely another element of the Disney genre: an underlying sexuality that titillates adult viewers while prematurely sexualizing younger ones, grooming them for further media consumption based on the most basic of human drives. At the end of the film, the maid, with bare shoulders, huge cleavage, and a "take me now" look in her eye, literally rubs her feather duster into Lumiere's lascivious face. He excitedly rubs his hands and chases after her. Such a sequence of shots aptly captures exactly what Disney hopes its viewers will do, follow after its repeatedly sexualized female characters.

As expected, the mob is beaten back but not before Gaston finds and wounds Beast. Beast fights back but does not kill Gaston. When Beast returns to Belle, Gaston comes behind him and stabs him in the back before falling to his own death. Again, in the classic American construal of a hero, Beast cannot kill the villain; Gaston must be the cause of his own death to keep Beast innocent. Subsequently, Beast dies from the wound but is resurrected when Belle says, "I love you," in a reversal of the Sleeping Beauty myth, as the last petal falls and the spell is broken. Oddly again, Beast levitates from the ground and is transfigured, Jesus-fashion, back into the handsome prince he always was. All the staff are transformed back to their respective states, and the film ends with a crowded room where Belle and Adam dance as everyone watches.

The final shot of the film encapsulates the dominant, Boomer version of the American Dream, with few subversive accents. The middle-class, white, female nonconformist has been married off to a white male of higher class. All the people in attendance are white and well dressed. The couple's success at love and life is evident to all, as they are both the center of attention and occupy/possess physical space as home/landowners, symbolized by the vast room and wide berth given to the dance. Yet the film does not simply end with a wholehearted affirmation of Boomer values; it also, though more subtly, appeals to its Gen X market. The couple, as could be interpreted, are part of a community of people who are more than just staff but are friends, extending the role of friendship beyond the small groups Boomers allowed for. There is also an equality nestled within the patriarchy of the setting. Belle gets what she wants, not what her father wants for her. She has much more agency and is the one mainly responsible for the favorable outcome in the film and the relationship. She truly deserves first billing the title gives her.

Benjamin Crace

See also: *Finding Nemo*; *The Lion King*; *Toy Story*; *Zootopia*.

Further Reading

Cummins, June. 1995. "Romancing the Plot: The Real Beast of Disney's *Beauty and the Beast*." *Children's Literature Association Quarterly* 20 (1): 22–28.

Dick, Jeff T. 2003. "Beauty and the Beast (Film)." *Library Journal* 128 (9): 143.

Ilinskaya, Svetlana, and Douglas Robinson. 2018. "#MeToo and the Estrangement of Beauty-and-the-Beast Narratives." *Social Research* 85 (2): 375–405.

Pauly, Rebecca M. 1989. "Beauty and the Beast: From Fable to Film." *Literature Film Quarterly* 17 (2): 84.

Ross, Deborah. 2004. "Escape from Wonderland: Disney and the Female Imagination." *Marvels & Tales* 18 (1): 53–66.

Beverly Hills Cop

Release Date:	1984
Director:	Martin Brest
Box Office:	$316 million
Main Cast:	Axel Foley, played by Eddie Murphy
	Det. Billy Rosewood, played by Judge Reinhold
	Sgt. Taggart, played by John Ashton

Beverly Hills Cop, in the Black-led cop drama tradition of *Shaft* (1971), reworks and, in some ways, undermines the preceding era's narratives of the violent and angst-ridden loner bent on revenge. Directed by Martin Brest in his first major breakthrough film, *Beverly Hills Cop* went on to earn nominations for Golden Globe and the Academy Awards. The film, too, marked Eddie Murphy's first solo lead, a departure from his previous work on TV's *Saturday Night Live*, his previous buddy/cop film with a white partner, *48 Hours* (1982), and the comedy *Trading Places* (1983, with Dan Aykroyd). Part of its popularity is due to the then newly emerging Generation X consciousness that sought to expand, extend, and even refute Boomer views on race, the working class, and masculinity, while complicating the cop drama genre.

The film begins in Detroit, Michigan. Foley is shown working as an undercover agent trying to buy a truck full of cigarettes from two mobster-looking men. The transaction is interrupted by two uniformed police officers, one of which thinks he knows (Detective) Foley. The scene quickly erupts into an extended chase scene through the city, as Foley hangs on for his life in the back of the open trailer. In classic '70s–'80s style, the damage is widespread as the semi plows through parked cars, red lights, and residential areas. Filmed before the advent of CGI, the impacts and crashes are real and visceral in ways special effects are just now beginning to capture without actually junking numerous cars. As expected, the chase ends, and Foley gets chewed out by his supervisor for his tactics and off-the-books, ad hoc approach to detective work.

The real inciting incident, however, is the death of Foley's childhood friend, Mikey—a ne'er-do-well, always scheming white friend. Mikey has apparently found a way to make it rich with German bearer bonds that he had stolen. This theft leads to Mikey's death and, consequently, Foley's unsanctioned investigation in California.

Once he arrives in Beverly Hills, Foley follows up with another childhood friend, Jenny. Jenny, a blonde woman who works in an art gallery, directs Foley to her employer, Victor Maitland. Mikey had been working for Maitland before he was killed in Detroit. Foley's visit to Maitland, however, ends with him being tossed out of a plate-glass window at the hands of Maitland's security. In an ironic and racial twist, Foley is arrested by two, white uniformed police officers who simply assume he is the one who is at fault since he is Black. Foley repeatedly points out this prejudiced logic, observing he was the one who was thrown out of a window, the true victim.

After the standard confrontation with the local police, Foley is discovered to be a fellow cop and two local policemen, Rosewood and Taggart, are assigned to make sure he does not cause any more trouble. After evading them while they're staked out in front of his hotel, Foley conducts his own investigation into the death of his friend, along with some assistance from Jenny. Eventually, however, he wins over both Rosewood and Taggart to his side through the demonstration of his professional abilities and through his repeated attempts at developing a form of masculine camaraderie. In a rather ironic twist, characteristic of R-rated films of the era, masculinity depends on female exploitation; here, they all visit a strip club. The stripper, whose naked torso is clearly seen, barely registers as a human being while Foley hands Rosewood, a kind of naïve innocent, money to slip into her underwear saying, "She'll like that." Foley then goes on a rather long rant about penises and erections. In the course of this solidification of male friendship/strip club as a rite of manhood, Foley figures out that two patrons of the establishment are on the verge of robbing the place. After enlisting Taggart, the older of the two local cops, to help him take down one of the perpetrators, Foley bravely confronts the other and disarms him without even using his own gun. From this point on, both Rosewood and Taggart view Foley differently, though Rosewood is the first one to fully support him.

Both Foley and Jenny end up captured by Maitland's thugs. After a confrontation with Mikey's killer, Foley is left to be beaten and killed in the warehouse, but Rosewood saves him. Jenny, however, is taken to Maitland's mansion, and this sets the scene for the final showdown of the film. Interestingly, depending more on friendship and loyalty and less on a romantic connection, Foley mounts a rescue operation to save her and nail Maitland for his dirty business dealings. Rosewood and then Taggart jump in to help Foley break into the heavily guarded property. Comedically, Rosewood and Taggart are shown to be rather inept at climbing walls and sneaking around, while Foley moves gracefully with all the art of a dancer-athlete. Here, as in other places in the film, Foley exudes a level of confidence, despite his surroundings, that is attractive to other characters and the audience. As expected, Foley ends up shooting both Mikey's killer and Maitland himself but not before getting himself "winged" by a poorly aimed shot.

The film ends with the traditional police cleanup at the mansion and then shifts to Foley checking out of his hotel. The Beverly Hills Police Department pays for his stay, and he makes an elaborate gesture of giving Rosewood one of the expensive hotel robes, on the police department's tab, of course. Again, following the archetypal motif of the trickster, common throughout many culture's mythologies, Foley manipulates people and situations through deceptive and confusing language, bravura, and sheer charisma lined with self-confidence.

As already noted, race is at the forefront of the film's consciousness. The quasi-integrated Detroit Police Force (Foley's supervisor is also African American) is sharply contrasted with the gentrified and mainly white Beverly Hills Police Department. The one Black detective on the force is, at one point, singled out by Foley for ridicule because of his white-sounding voice—a voice apparently without African American dialect markers. In another scene, Foley manages to acquire a room in an upscale hotel by loudly insinuating that they will not rent him the space because he is Black. The maître d' acquiesces to keep him quiet, insisting that is not the case. Ultimately, Foley gets a suite with a deep discount. In another scene, he breaks into a warehouse to find clues and, when caught, poses as an official from the customs agency. As he castigates the night watchman for being derelict in his duties, he says, "How can a Black man come in and walk around?" These direct references to race perform the double function of making characters in the narrative aware of (possible) latent prejudices while at the same time forcing the audience to do the same. The film invites viewers to see Foley more as a brave, concerned friend and a good cop by comedically highlighting Black stereotypes against his actual character and abilities. When Foley draws explicit attention to his race, he does so mainly to unsettle and deconstruct the stereotypes except when it allows him to gain an advantage in a given situation. Clearly, Foley is an empowered agent who transgresses boundaries of race and privilege.

Interestingly, the antagonists of the film are led by the wealthy German businessman, Victor Maitland, who illegally cheats the customs system while running drugs and bearer bonds. Maitland is an amalgam of racial, generational, and class-conscious concerns. His white hair, ice-cold blue eyes, German accent, and penchant for violence telegraphs to the '80s audience both Nazis and the East German Stasi, the brutal secret police of the communist era. Maitland's villainy thus draws attention to the defeated enemies of the Greatest Generation while at the same time foregrounding the much closer, in-your-backyard threat. But Maitland is not simply a stand-in symbol for real-world bad guys but also a member of the upper class of Beverly Hills, confirming for the blue-collar moviegoer that wealth goes hand in hand with crime. Further, rich white crime is as violent and malevolent as inner city, Detroit crime. This amalgam in the character of Maitland sets up the sharply contrasting hero, Foley.

Foley represents one of the first Gen X heroes who eschews expectations and unwanted responsibilities handed to him from institutions and prior generations. He defies authority to pursue his personal vision of justice on the basis of friendship. He defies the expectations of the Beverly Hills Police Department by winning them over to his real-world approach to police work instead of their stuffy, by-the-book program. And perhaps most surprising: for the most part, Foley's masculinity is not predetermined by romantic attachments. In fact, the only two people he professes love for are males: Mikey and Rosewood. Here is a masculinity constructed through the admiration of peers rather than sexual domination.

Accompanying this gender construction, however, is the very American view that bravery and maleness cohere in the willingness to use violence if necessary. This violence, of course, as with most police movies, involves the central icons of Americanism: the car and the gun. The film is replete with the requisite car chases and car scenes. Foley's dilapidated clunker is contrasted with Jenny's Mercedes convertible, Detroit's police cars from the 1960s are contrasted with Beverly Hills's modern cruisers, and on and on. Additionally, the movie poster for the film features Murphy sitting on the hood of the convertible holding a large, .45 Magnum, positioned in such a way as to suggest it is an extension of Murphy's anatomy. Like the American Western, the gun makes the man, and the character's choice of caliber embodies his physical traits and dispositions.

Benjamin Crace

See also: Black Panther; Independence Day.

Further Reading

Brown, Jeffrey A. 1993. "Bullets, Buddies, and Bad Guys." *Journal of Popular Film & Television* 21 (2): 79.

De Semlyen, Nick. 2019. *Wild and Crazy Guys: How the Comedy Mavericks of the '80s Changed Hollywood Forever.* New York: Broadway Books.

Freeman, Hadley. 2016. *Life Moves Pretty Fast: The Lessons We Learned from Eighties Movies (and Why We Don't Learn Them from Movies Anymore).* New York: Simon & Schuster.

Gates, Philippa. 2004. "Always a Partner in Crime." *Journal of Popular Film & Television* 32 (1): 20–29.

Whalley, Jim. 2010. *Saturday Night Live, Hollywood Comedy, and American Culture: From Chevy Chase to Tina Fey.* New York: Palgrave Macmillan.

Forrest Gump

Release Date:	1994
Director:	Robert Zemeckis
Box Office:	$683.1 million
Main Cast:	Forrest Gump, played by Tom Hanks
	Jenny Curran, played by Robin Wright
	Mrs. Gump, played by Sally Field
	Lieutenant Dan, played by Gary Sinise
	Benjamin Blue (Bubba), played by Mykelti Williamson

Forrest Gump, like Zemeckis's other films, *Back to the Future I, II,* and *III* (1985, 1989, and 1991), was a cultural touchstone and phenomenon. Unlike the Back to the Future franchise, it also received critical acclaim, winning six Academy Awards: Best Picture, Actor, Directing, Editing, Visual Effects, and Writing. Based on a 1986 novel by Winston Groom, *Gump* follows the ups and downs of the life of a mentally handicapped man, Forrest Gump (Tom Hanks, 1956–), as it intersects with some of the most turbulent times in American history (1950s–1980s). As with other films examined through the generational apparatus, *Gump* plays out generational anxieties about the nature of history, thereby offering its largely Gen X audience momentary alleviation of those tensions.

The plot has three basic levels or frames. The widest frame that persists through most of the film is an older Gump sitting on a bench, waiting for a bus in Savannah, Georgia. He has a single suitcase and a box of chocolates. As he waits, he tells various strangers who come and go his fantastic life story. The second frame, then, consists of all these flashbacks that begin chronologically and, interspersed with voice-overs and short shots of Gump talking to someone, move forward up to the exact time when Gump is narrating. The third and final frame is the standard film's present as audience's present and follows Gump as he leaves the bench to reunite with Jenny and meet his son. Still within this frame or time, Jenny, his lifelong love but only lately his wife, dies from AIDS, and Gump is left with the responsibility of raising Gump Jr. (Haley Joel Osmont). The film ends with Gump Sr. helping Gump Jr. get on the school bus (with the same driver Forrest had as a child) in front of the drive to his ancestral house in Greenbow, Alabama. Parallel but opposite to the opening scene, a feather falls out of a book and blows away from Gump instead of toward him, suggesting that life itself, like the film, consists of the mysterious interplay between randomness and meaning. The majority of the film, however, takes place in the past.

The establishing flashback is of Forrest as a child in Alabama. In a series of shots, the audience learns that Forrest is named after the founder of the Ku Klux Klan, an ancestor, because his mom wanted his name to be a reminder that "sometimes we all do things that, well, just don't make no sense." This flashback is briefly interrupted by short, sepia-colored, archival-like footage of Hanks as Nathan Bedford Forrest riding on horseback with other robed Klan members. This type of irony is lost on the titular character, since, as the audience also learns, his IQ is only 75, far below average. His narration, in a peculiar southern but hesitating inflection mixed with odd grammatical constructions, also betrays the fact that he really does not understand the nature of southern white supremacy, a theme that returns later in the film as Gump fails to distinguish between people according to their color. The audience also learns that Gump has a crooked spine, which, in the 1950s, was treated by putting metal braces on the child's legs. Gump was already an outcast because of his intelligence, and the braces further marginalize him from all his peers—all except Jenny.

Jenny sees something valuable in Forrest, allowing him to sit next to her on the bus after being denied by the other children. They soon become good friends ("like peas and carrots"). At one point, some cruel kids are bullying Forrest and throwing rocks at him. Jenny tells him, "Run, Forrest, run!" As he does so, his braces fall off and he leaves his assailants in the dust. Later, within the time frame of him and Jenny as children, they both run and hide in a cornfield while Jenny's incestuous, abusive father searches for her.

Within the childhood flashback, *Gump*'s constant real-world, pop culture origin story narrative is launched. There really was a Nathan Bedford Forrest, and he did start the Klan. But in another scene, boarders are renting out rooms at the Gump estate, and one of these individuals happens to be Elvis. He is singing for Forrest, who is dancing awkwardly because of his leg braces. There is a brief flash forward to Forrest and his mother walking past some TVs in a storefront. The actual Elvis is doing his trademark, now Gump-inspired, pelvis gyration on the real *Ed Sullivan Show*, marking the year as 1956. The older Forrest on the bench, gives the rest of the story in a voice over: "Some years later, that handsome young man they called the King, well, he sung too many songs. Had himself a heart attack or something." Again, Gump's gloss and misunderstanding about what happened to Elvis and why, is at once a symptom of his low IQ and a metonym of the ephemeral nature of fame. It also functions, in terms of the Gen X audience, to acknowledge a cultural debt to such a figure but then lay that debt aside.

At other points in the film, Gump is shown to be the originator of other things that make up pop culture. Oddly enough, the film itself then becomes part of pop culture, mirroring the same historical processes it seeks to fictionalize. Gump innocently inspires John Lennon to write "Imagine" and the creation of the ubiquitous bumper sticker, "S— Happens." In each case, as with Elvis, Gump narrates what became of the people who were inspired by him. For Lennon, specifically, he simply says that he was shot "for no particular reason," providing cathartic closure for some and biographical information for other audience members but distancing both from the emotional tragedy.

These mythological origins of real-world artifacts tied into the fictional character of Gump accomplish something very important for members of Generation X. Perhaps unlike other generations, X constantly negotiates and renegotiates its own identity, in turns against Boomers and toward the new, the transgressive, and the unique. The film itself thus becomes a generational artifact that subsumes and thereby replaces all of Boomer history from the 1950s to the early 1980s. Gump's absurd presence in so many different situations and places within that timeline (the White House three times, Vietnam, China, New York, Washington, DC, peace rally, and then *all* of America as he runs coast to coast over three years) means that the character itself serves to encapsulate, repackage, and embody the totality of Boomer consciousness. That he is clueless about the events he lives in and through is simply a reflection of Gen X's own perspective about the bathetic way the previous generation dealt with its own history. Jenny's ongoing search for identity and struggle with drugs and suicide is Forrest's generational counterpart, that lost segment of Boomers captivated by causes but inattentive to their own brokenness. In her death and Forrest's passing of his legacy to Forrest Jr., Gen X viewers stand as witnesses to the end of Boomers' hegemonic influence on America.

Further, *Forrest Gump*'s soundtrack, a "greatest hits" of all four decades, licensed Gen X to consume their parents' music. Detached from the real history that produced it, the songs were reattached in Gen X's consciousness to moments in the film. Elvis's "Hound Dog" becomes Gump teaching Elvis to dance. Creedence Clearwater Revival's "Fortunate Son" is transfigured from anti-Vietnam, anti-American materialism to the soundtrack of Bubba and Forrest's friendship, which is ironically extended posthumously through entrepreneurship. Bob Seger's "Against the Wind" is diminished in its scope from the bittersweet reflection on the mutability of life and love to a scoring of Forrest literally running "against the wind." That is not to say that the film robs all the songs it samples of their deeper content, but in generational terms, it audiovisually reconfigures the music, forcing it into the ethos of the 1990s.

Another arresting technique Zemeckis uses to weave his tale is to blend Hanks-as-Gump image into actual new footage of key historical events. Undoubtedly, the reason for winning Best Visual Effects and Editing, this mixing of footage and film looks artificial to 21st-century audiences but left '90s' audiences in much the same awe as did James Cameron's groundbreaking *Terminator 2* (1991). We see Gump help Vivian Malone with her notebook as she walks into the University of Alabama during the early days of racial integration. Gump meets Presidents Kennedy, Nixon, and Johnson in the White House. He sits alongside John Lennon, one of the Beatles, on the *Dick Cavett Show* in 1971. Functioning mythologically, the Gen X audience thus witnesses Gump as a witness who, due to his IQ, is unable to understand the full weight of each moment's significance.

Further, Gump's naïvely sincere dismissal of pain, "That's all I have to say about that," empowers viewers to realize that Gump's approach to life and history is uniquely his and, despite his worldly success, is remarkably free from attachments. Gump may embody the attenuated Boomer historical consciousness, but he also anchors the Gen X value for authenticity disconnected from Boomer materialism. Following his value for friendship and loyalty, Gump starts Bubba Gump Shrimp Company as a way of keeping his promise to his dead friend, Bubba, a Black soldier with a similar IQ who was killed in Vietnam. Following up on his promise, Lieutenant Dan, now missing both legs from the battle where Gump saved him, becomes partners with Gump in the shrimping industry. At first, they don't have much luck, but after a hurricane destroys all the other shrimping boats, they hit it big. After Gump goes home to take care of his dying mother, he receives a letter from Dan that he has invested in a "fruit company" (Apple Computers) and that he, Gump, needn't worry about money anymore, "Well, that's one less thing," he narrates. Yet despite being on the cover of *Fortune* magazine and being wealthy, Gump is happy living at his ancestral home and mowing the grass at the high school. Again, this type of modest detachment from success appealed to Gen Xers precisely because they witnessed their own parents' striving to attain the American Dream that was as much about luck as hard work. Holding loosely to one's efforts, as Gump does, seems to be exalted in the film over and above digging in deeper at the cost of one's self.

Lieutenant Dan and his mangled body constitute the site through which the Gen X reckoning with the Boomer psychic wound of Vietnam achieves resolution. Unlike Gump, who gets the million-dollar wound (a bullet in the butt cheek), Dan loses both legs. Although not a paraplegic in real life, Sinise's leglessness on the screen also played a part in *Gump*'s Oscar for Visual Effects. Dan begins as the loyal and committed soldier who, after his wound, becomes disgruntled and angry—especially at Gump, whom he blames for denying him his destiny to die with honor. Sinise's performance recalls Tom Cruise's earlier role as a disgruntled, paraplegic Vietnam vet in *Born on the Fourth of July* (1989). Yet *Gump* extends the angry, handicapped vet trope to include a redemptive element achieved through a type of religious conversion linked to Gump's loyalty and brave action. During the hurricane that destroys all the other boats (which is tenuously connected to Gump's church attendance and prayers for shrimp), Dan lashes himself to the mast of their boat and curses God throughout the night. Later, on a peaceful day, he maneuvers himself to the rail of the boat and tells Gump, "Forrest, I never thanked you for saving my life." He then drops off the rail into the water and starts to backstroke toward an endless horizon and setting sun. Gump's narration: "He never actually said so, but I think he made his peace with God." Taken together, this quick scene resonates with baptismal accents; Dan's staring into heaven as he swims, and tranquil, soft music affirms Gump's observation. For the audience, Dan's salvation unto spiritual and relational wholeness operates symbolically to heal the vicarious pain Gen X felt about Vietnam, a pain inherited but not experienced. Dan's later appearance, wearing prosthetic legs and accompanied by his Asian American fiancée, at Gump and Jenny's wedding reinforces this symbolic healing of national and intergenerational pain toward the war. It also equipped Gen X with a type of reconfigured empathy not only for vets of their parents' generation but Gulf War (1990–1991) veterans too.

Benjamin Crace

See also: Back to the Future; Toy Story.

Further Reading

Hoerl, Kristen. 2018. "Good Citizens, Ambivalent Activists, and Macho Militants in *Forrest Gump* and the '60s." In *The Bad Sixties: Hollywood Memories of the Counterculture, Antiwar, and Black Power Movements*, by Kristen Hoerl, 93–122. Jackson: University Press of Mississippi.

Nathan, Judith Raizy. 2017. "Disrupting the *Forrest Gump* Effect: Countering Suggestibility in the Social Studies Classroom through the Use of Actual Footage." EdD diss., Hofstra University.

Pautz, Michelle C., and Jennifer Lumpkin. 2020. "The Influence of Film on Attitudes about the American Dream: Audiences and *Forrest Gump* and Idiocracy." *Public Voices* 16 (2): 42–65.

Scott, Steven D. 2001. "'Like a Box of Chocolates': *Forrest Gump* and Postmodernism." *Literature Film Quarterly* 29 (1): 23.

Wang, Jennifer Hyland. 2000. "'A Struggle of Contending Stories': Race, Gender, and Political Memory in *Forrest Gump*." *Cinema Journal* 39 (3): 92–115.

Ghostbusters

Release Date:	1984
Director:	Ivan Reitman
Box Office:	$229 million
Main Cast:	Peter Venkman, played by Bill Murray
	Ray Stantz, played by Dan Aykroyd
	Winston Zeddemore, played by Ernie Hudson
	Egon Spengler, played by Harold Ramis

Ghostbusters, written by two of the main actors in the film, Dan Aykroyd and Harold Ramis, utilized some of the most spectacular special effects in the 1980s, especially for a comedy. Directed by Ivan Reitman (*Stripes*, 1981, which also featured Murray) *Ghostbusters* became a cultural phenomenon, entrenching the American underdog, male-dominated team approach to overwhelming problems (seen primarily in sports) while also proving that the supernatural need not be limited to the horror genre. *Ghostbusters*, too, stands as a transitional text that extends Boomer concerns and anxieties but also begins to shape the Gen Xer narrative.

Shot and based mainly in New York City, *Ghostbusters* further cements that city as a microcosm of the American experiment—the new Rome of the American Empire. As the New Rome, New York City's Central Park area features a building with supernatural qualities, a temple to the Sumerian god Gozer. It is this god's desire to reenter the everyday dimension of New Yorkers that plays a decisive role in the narrative of the film.

After losing their university funding and positions and forced into the private sector, where the powers that be "expect results," three parapsychologists—Venkman, Stantz, and Spengler—launch their own business of ghostbusting, that is, helping people deal with supernatural disturbances. Taking the mantle away from the traditional role of the exorcist priest, the ghostbusters use science, in particular *nuclear* science, to create weapons that turn the metaphysical into the physical, reducing the spiritual to "slime" (ectoplasm, a mucus-like substance left after physical contact with a ghost). Once word gets out about their business, the demand goes through the roof as does the ghostbusters' place in the film world's version of media. The ghostbusters, in a clever montage that intertwines real-world media outlets with the film's fantasy narrative, make the cover of *USA Today*, the *New York Post*, *Time*, *Omni*, *The Atlantic*, and *Globe*, and they even merit radio commentary by Casey Kasem and Larry King, popular radio and TV talk-show hosts of the time. The montage also features iconic New York City landmarks such as Rockefeller Center and Chinatown. Also, throughout the montage, the ghostbusters, whose headquarters is in an old firehouse, behave very much like firefighters: sleeping when they can, responding to a fire alarm, and driving a car with flashing lights. Their business needs prompt them to hire a fourth ghostbuster, an African American named Winston Zeddemore.

Just before the montage ends, however, there is an interesting and short scene that serves as representative of the way sexuality is handled in the film. In the scene, a dream sequence, Stantz is lying on a bed in what looks like an 18th-century military outfit, complete with tasseled epaulets. As he lies there, a wispy but still definably attractive spirit woman floats above him. She visually disappears but then her invisible force unbuckles Stantz's belt, unbuttons his pants, and begins performing oral sex on him—as evident from Stantz's comedically crossed-eyes. The messaging is clear: women are just as eager for sex as men are, even, apparently, from beyond the grave. Such lustfulness in women occurs again and again, and not just in *Ghostbusters*; it has become a standard trope in Hollywood across the generations.

A parallel narrative features Sigourney Weaver's character, Dana Barrett. In a departure from her heroine role in *Alien*, Dana is a cellist that lives in an expensive Central Park–area high-rise. In fact, her apartment takes up nearly a quarter of the floor near the top. Her neighbor, Louis Tully (Rick Moranis), is a nerdy accountant who embodies all of the cliché yuppie (young, urban professional) stereotypes of the early '80s. He is into fitness and diet fads, dresses in sports outfits, and hosts parties for people he does not even know in order to get more business. Obviously attracted to Dana, he begs her to come down to his apartment for the party. She rebuffs him numerous times. But later, once she is possessed by Zuul, an ancient Sumerian entity also known as the Gatekeeper, Tully, likewise possessed, by an entity called the Keymaster, becomes her sexual partner. Although their coupling is not explicitly depicted, both are shown to awaken on top of what looks like an altar in a postcoital haze that bares and objectifies much more of Weaver's body than it does Moranis's; she is obviously the dominant one. In an ironic twist, while Venkman has tried unsuccessfully to woo Barrett throughout the film, the "nerd" sexually engages the main female lead *before* Venkman does. Such inversions in the social order of things or what the audience may understand as a consensus narrative underscores the apocalyptic nature of the film's plot. Things are upside down and the end of days has arrived, characterized by, as Venkman tells the mayor of the city, "Human sacrifice, dogs and cats living together, mass hysteria!"

The popularity of their business, of course, attracts government interference. This comes in the form of a visit from the EPA. A rather condescending and insistent officer demands to see the containment unit where they have been depositing all the ghosts. Although Venkman and others try to stop him, eventually the EPA officer gets his way, and the containment unit is shut down. This, then, releases all the ghosts back into the city and expedites the coming of Gozer for the final showdown in the film. The conflict and tension depicted initially between the EPA agent, Walter Peck (William Atherton), and Venkman spills over to all the other ghostbusters and, later, includes City Hall. This tension between an upstart business and a self-important government agency telegraphs a variety of Boomer conservatism and distrust of bureaucracy—especially when it stands in the way of the capitalistic enterprise. It is also noteworthy that the ghostbusters' headquarters is in a neighborhood that, according to Egon, is "like a demilitarized zone." The ghostbusters' business enterprise, funded by a triple mortgage on Stantz's ancestral home and located in an economically deprived area of New York, strongly links into the self-reliance, can-do ethos necessary for the American Dream. The success of their business endeavor, of course, depends on the foundational conflict between socioeconomic classes.

Throughout the film, the ghostbusters are depicted as the down-and-out, misunderstood keepers of fringe knowledge and champions of lower- to middle-class values. Theirs is a world of popular culture and populism. It is no mistake that a significant amount of ghostbusting seen by the audience occurs in the materially wealthy areas of the city. In a Robin Hood–like fashion, at one point, Venkman overcharges the manager of a high-class hotel, threatening to put the ghost back if he doesn't want to pay—even though they have significantly destroyed hotel property. The centerpiece of the entire conflict is in an upscale high-rise full of accountants and fine arts people such as Dana; clearly, the rich need the working class. *Ghostbusters* darkly underscores the suspicion not frequently articulated that the rich have achieved their wealth by selling their souls to the devil. The rich are the ones who are easily possessed (Tully and Dana) because they are already possessed by their greed; freedom comes from cooperating with struggling businesses outside of the closed world of their usual networks.

The reductionistic and ironic qualities of the ghostbusters' approach to the afterlife are writ large by making an ancient god/ghost become a Macy's parade blimp-like figure of the Stay Puft Marshmallow Man (a created logo), which strongly suggests that materialism and science have ultimately displaced the transcendence offered through religion. For Gen Xers, this practical use of science over and against spiritualism and religion resonates strongly with their ethos of continual deconstruction and suspicion of inherited values. Yet this deconstruction is not total; at one point, just before the giant marshmallow man steps on a neighboring church, Murray's character, Venkman, exclaims, "Nobody steps on a church in my town!" Further traditional religious signaling occurs at the end of the film, when the Ghostbusters exit the building after the battle. As they each come out to adoring crowds, there is a line of Catholic priests blessing them and Ecto-1, their hearse-ambulance-turned-ghostbuster vehicle. At best, then, traditional religion comes off as innocuous and harmless, a feature of society; whereas ancient religions and the modern cults that revive them retain a potency that has long since disappeared out of the church, temple, and mosque.

A deep Americanism runs throughout the film. Aside from issues of race, class, and sex, the core value of nearly uninhibited personal freedom is displayed through movement and space. The ghostbusters, with little to no concern about belonging to a single stratum of society, fluidly move from Midtown to Downtown to Uptown. And they do so in that great American totem of freedom: the automobile Ecto-1. The other marker of personal freedom is deeply interconnected with the concept of space: the more you have, the better. Thus, despite their headquarters being in a state of total disrepair when they lease it, it has a great deal of space, is cavernous even. Upon entering Dana's apartment, Venkman remarks, "A lot of space. Just you?" It is reflexive, simply something one says when one enters a person's home for the first time, yet it registers that association between physical space and personal freedom.

The opposite, of course, is imprisonment, or, in terms of the film, possession and containment. Ironically, the ghostbusters increase their ability to self-actualize insofar as they imprison spirits within their containment system. Ghostbusting is, in fact, a form of enslavement. Here, in true American form, the rights and legacies of the dead/past are impediments to present progress. In order to downplay this obvious parallel, the ghosts are dehumanized as scary, rotting corpses, gluttonous blobs, or malevolent deities; communication and understanding are not possible. The only remaining solution is a type of nuclear violence through an electrified and penis-looking "gun" that, when held and operated at waist level by men, unleashes a crackling stream of pure energy.

Despite the then amazing special effects, wisecracks, and irony, *Ghostbusters* is, in essence, a reworked Western, the most American of all film genres. The showdown at the end is a type of gunfight at the OK Corral. The city, indeed, the whole world, is in peril, and the local law and order are powerless to fight it. The four "gunslingers" are called upon to save the day and, of course, rescue the pretty maiden. In this framework, Boomers, raised on serialized Westerns on television and John Ford movies, could deeply relate to the underlying generic structure. And yet, it is and it is not a vamped-up Western. *Ghostbusters* is also a parody, if not a near sacrilege, of the genre. In this way, it stands out as a transitional text that both affirms Boomer sensibilities while cultivating Gen Xers' identity over and above their parents. By casting mainly comedic actors and turning the black hat "bad guys" into marshmallows and an androgynous punk rocker, Reitman deflates the seriousness with which many Westerns took themselves as carriers of the American mythology.

Benjamin Crace

See also: *The Exorcist*; *Tootsie*.

Further Reading

Blodgett, Bridget, and Anastasia Salter. 2018. "*Ghostbusters* Is for Boys: Understanding Geek Masculinity's Role in the Alt-Right." *Communication, Culture & Critique* 11 (1): 133–146.

Labrecque, Jeff. 2014. "1984 *Ghostbusters*. (Cover Story)." *Entertainment Weekly*, no. 1337–1338 (November): 50.

McAllister, Matt. 2020. Ghostbusters*: The Inside Story.* New York: Hero Collector.

Shay, Don. 1985. *Making* Ghostbusters. New York: Zoetrope.

Wallace, Daniel. 2015. Ghostbusters*: The Ultimate Visual History.* Los Angeles: Insight Editions.

Home Alone

Release Date:	1990
Director:	Chris Columbus
Box Office:	$476.7 million
Main Cast:	Kevin McCallister, played by Macaulay Culkin
	Harry Lime, played by Joe Pesci
	Marv Merchants, played by Daniel Stern
	Kate McCallister, played by Catherine O'Hara
	Peter McCallister, played by John Heard
	Gus Polinski, played by John Candy

As one of Chris Columbus's landmark films (before going on to direct *Harry Potter*), *Home Alone* has reached iconic status as a perennial, family Christmas film. Produced by John Hughes, *Home Alone* initiated the younger end of the Gen X spectrum into the midwestern, middle-class, white suburban drama so artfully subverted in films such as *Sixteen Candles* (1984), *The Breakfast Club* (1985), and that other Hughes's Christmas film, *National Lampoon's Christmas Vacation* (1989). In this film, however, the protagonist is not an angsty teen, misunderstood by a clueless parent or authority figure, but, rather, a precocious eight-year-old child of a large (presumably Catholic?) family on the outskirts of Chicago.

As the youngest of five, Kevin McCallister receives the brunt of the family's criticism and neglect, pushing him to wish them all away and leaving him home alone for a few days over the Christmas season. The film begins with the extended McCallister family (cousins, aunt, and uncle) preparing to leave Chicago for Paris, where they will all spend Christmas with other family members who live there. In the course of their preparations, Kevin is told to pack his own suitcase. Feeling overwhelmed at the prospect, Kevin asks his siblings for help, and each one refuses with an insult. To add further insult to injury, Kevin has been assigned to sleep with a cousin who routinely wets the bed. Already overwhelmed and angry, Kevin goes to the kitchen where the entire family is feasting on pizza. Buzz, his antagonistic older brother, has already devoured the cheese pizza that Kevin likes. After provoking him even more, Kevin attacks Buzz, pushing him backward and setting off a chain of accidents around the table and kitchen, which results in Kevin getting dragged up to the attic by his mother. On the way up the stairs, Kevin says, "Everyone in this family hates me. Family sucks. I don't want to see you again for the rest of my whole life." After his mother tells him that he does not mean it, he retorts with "I hope that I never see any of your jerks again," and stomps up to the attic bed.

During the course of the evening's events, Harry (one of the future burglars of the McCallister house) has come inside dressed as a policeman to case the place and determine when they will all be gone. Just before he is sent packing, Kevin notices Harry's gold tooth, which will play a key part later in the film.

During the night, a strong wind blows down a branch on an electric line and cuts off the power to the house, disabling their alarm clocks. There is some ambiguity as to whether the chain of events is the fulfillment of Kevin's wish or just bad luck, but such ambiguity is part of what adds mystery to the story. The next morning, the taxi service has arrived to take them all to the airport, but they're not ready since the alarms did not go off in time. In a mad rush, they load up, miscount kids (a neighbor kid is counted as Kevin), run through the airport, board, and take off—all the while, Kevin is still sleeping upstairs in the attic space. On the plane, in first class, Kevin's parents talk about the trip and his mother has a nagging feeling of having left something behind. It is not until they are quite a distance into the trip that she realizes they have left Kevin.

It is every mother's nightmare to leave a child behind, especially if going to another country. It is especially nightmarish to leave that child alone after having exchanged some fairly harsh words with the child. The comedic element of all this hinges on it being a real possibility but only simulated, since it is just a movie after all. Yet the underlying anxiety of Kevin's "successful" parents echoes the unease

Boomers felt about raising children in a more globalized world than the one they were born in. At one point, Peter, the father, assures the mother that the kids are fine in coach because they are on a plane to Paris and all the flying he ever did as a kid was in a station wagon. This contrast between Boomer childhood and Gen X childhood mirrors the constant need of each generation to top the former in terms of providing experiences for its offspring. And yet—and here is where Boomer anxiety is triggered—it is precisely in the rush of providing a better childhood that one child is forgotten.

Kevin, upon awakening, realizes his family is gone and is at first trepidatious but then gleeful as he associates his wish with the reality before him: "I made my family disappear." He proceeds to do things that he knows are off-limits: he goes through Buzz's private chest, eats junk food, and watches gangster movies. From time to time, he calls out to see if anyone is going to stop him. In many ways, Kevin's initial, hedonistic behavior is in line with the growing secularism and atheism of Gen X. Suspicious of the institutional and organized religion of their parents and grandparents, or perhaps falling in line with the nonconformity of the earlier hippie movement, Gen Xers sought out visceral experiences and popular culture to replace the loss of transcendence. And yet the yearning for the metaphysical remained buried. With Kevin, calling out to others to catch him doing bad things and finding no one there resonates with the Gen Xers' sense that they are truly home alone on the physical and spiritual planes. This isolated loneliness thus required a self-reliance that earlier generations did not need, nestled as they were in their contained worlds. It is here that the film depicts another generational technology; in rebelling against its immediate predecessor, each generation manifests characteristics of its grandparent.

Kevin's surprising independence and identification with members of the Silent Generation expands his potential as a type of life cipher for a younger Gen X audience. Scenes that show Kevin sleeping in his parents' bed, showering in their shower, and even using his father's comb and aftershave show how he is literally displacing their presence in his life through routine by becoming them. Yet he goes even further, becoming his own grandparent in a sense by doing what older people than his parents would do: narrating his day to himself, asking nitpicky questions about toothbrushes, and even telling one cashier that his purchase of already antiquated plastic, toy soldiers was "for the kids." He even prefers film noir, black-and-white gangster movies. The famous line "Keep the change, ya filthy animal" is mouthed by Kevin as he uses the faux film to scare off a pizza guy. Why an eight-year-old enjoys and memorizes old films is never really explained. Falling asleep in the chair as he watches them, makes one wonder if he is not really 80 at heart. Beyond the ease with which Kevin strikes up conversations with total strangers (another trait of the elderly), cashiers, a woman dressed as an elf at a Santa display, and with the Boomer dressed as Santa, Kevin's relationship to the street's marginal old outsider, Marley, further underscores his peer-like nature with the Silent Generation.

The first few times the audience sees Marley, he is framed as a serial killer who haunts the neighborhood, having escaped capture by the police because there was not enough evidence to convict. He is a thin, old man with even thinner hair and a full, gray beard. He is typically shown wearing dark colors and using or carrying a snow shovel, presumably his murder weapon of choice. Each time Kevin encounters him, Marley is literally silent, and Kevin interprets his gaze as sizing him up for killing him later. It is not until the ending of the film, when Kevin encounters Marley in a church, that they communicate as peers. Kevin even dispenses advice on how he can repair the relationship with his son. Marley offers Kevin something no one else in his family does: nonjudgmental friendship with no strings attached. They recognize in each other a common wisdom shared by the old and young but absent in the worldly pursuits of middle age, a wisdom birthed of the vulnerability that bookends life. Both Kevin's parents and the robbers, Harry and Marv, are the quintessential foils to this wisdom, as the former pursues experiences and chases after the "perfect" Christmas and the latter, the best house to rob, the so-called silver tuna. It is probably not coincidental (nothing in films ever is) that Marley is also the name of the ghost in Charles Dickens's *A Christmas Carol* who launches Scrooge into his transformative journey.

There are two basic plot lines to *Home Alone* after the initial explication. Kevin's mother, Kate, goes on an adventure of sorts to get back home to her son. Peter stays with the other kids and family trying to get back a different way. The other basic plot is Kevin's defense of his home against Harry and Marv, Boomer blue-collar criminals who want to steal suburbia's Christmas treasures. Both Joe Pesci and Daniel Stern have symbolic linkages to the Boomer parents in the audience. Part of the comedy in the film relies on Pesci's persona as the accessory to the not-so-perfect crime. His role in *Goodfellas* (1990), released just two months before *Home Alone*, saw him as a violent mobster, thereby shading in the threatening undertones in his character Harry—especially in the scene where they have caught Kevin and are telling him all the torturous things they will do to him in retaliation. During that period, Stern was the narrator of the television series *The Wonder Years* (1988–1993). The show was a coming-of-age drama set in the idyllic suburbs of America in the 1960s. His voice was the fictionalized voice of the Boomer generation; now he is the comedic fall guy for a young Gen Xer. As with the displacement of his parents, Kevin's besting of Harry and Marv for an extended period of time demonstrates the potential Generation X possessed in righting the world—if, and only if, the Boomers were off the stage.

Along Kate's journey to return as quickly as possible to her son, she encounters a group of polka players in Scranton, Pennsylvania, led by Gus (John Candy), who offer to drop her off in Chicago on their way to Milwaukee. She accepts, since there are no more flights, and ends up in the back of a rental van speeding through wintry landscapes back to her home. In one germane scene, she chats with Gus about her guilt as a bad mother for leaving her child at home and going to another country. He tries to console her by telling her that he did something similar. He had left his kid in a funeral home with a corpse for an extended period of time, adding that the boy started to talk again after six or seven weeks. "Kids are resilient," he concludes. It is this interaction between Boomer parents (the rest of the polka band, as Gus narrates, are likewise terrible parents) that the Boomer view of their Gen X kids is actually verbalized even while it is manifested in Kevin's character arc. Gen X kids are resilient but have been made so because, like the Silent Generation, they were forgotten and overlooked—without an identity, simply marked with a placeholder.

After much slapstick and not-so-comedic violence, Harry and Marv catch up to Kevin in a neighbor's house. By this point, they have gone through many of the outlandish traps Kevin has set up to defend his house. They have been burned, hit in the head with paint cans, lured onto ice and sharp objects, tarred, and more. They hang Kevin on a coat hook and start plotting their revenge when Marley comes in and knocks them both down with, ironically, a snow shovel. The police come and take them off to jail. Kevin returns home and sets out milk and cookies for Santa to the nondiegetic tune of "Have Yourself a Merry Little Christmas." At some point, he has apparently cleaned the entire house as well from the previous night's shenanigans, another mark of responsibility beyond the capacity of an eight-year-old kid. He wishes his family back and goes to sleep in his parents' bed.

The next morning, he awakes and sees it is snowing outside (another American Christmas trope: it must snow on Christmas morning for things to be "perfect"). Thinking his wish has come true, he runs downstairs but no one is there. Sullen, he turns away just as his mother comes in and finds him. Moments after they reconcile, the rest of the family rolls in with much noise and acknowledge Kevin in their own way. After the initial reunion has settled, Kevin walks to the window and sees Marley has taken his advice and is hugging his formerly estranged son and granddaughter. They wave to each other in friendship, a knowingness that they are both somehow not just responsible *to* their families but even responsible *for* them.

With a score by John Williams (*Jaws, Star Wars, E.T.: The Extra-Terrestrial, Indiana Jones*) score and a Christmas setting, *Home Alone* quickly cemented its place as one of the top American Christmas film traditions. Its self-conscious positioning as such is captured in one scene where some of the younger McCallisters in Paris are trying to watch *It's a Wonderful Life* on television, but it is in French and they cannot understand it. Here is a shining moment of the transition of one generational tradition to the next. Gen Xers are not positioned to fully understand the Boomer classic starring Jimmy Stewart; it is too distant and "foreign," but *Home Alone* is right up their alley—or perhaps their suburban cul-de-sac.

Benjamin Crace

See also: *Harry Potter and the Philosopher's Stone/Harry Potter and the Chamber of Secrets.*

Further Reading
Clarke, Gerald. 1990. "*Home Alone* Breaks Away." *Time* 136 (25): 94.
Ruiz-Casares, Mónica, and Cécile Rousseau. 2010. "Between Freedom and Fear: Children's Views on *Home Alone*." *British Journal of Social Work* 40 (8): 2560–2577.
Smith, Donna Marie. 2015. "*John Hughes: A Life in Film*." *Library Journal* 140 (6): 95.
Wilkinson, Amy. 2015. "*Home Alone* 25 Years Later." *Entertainment Weekly*, no. 1389 (November): 44–45.

Independence Day

Release Date:	1996
Director:	Roland Emmerich
Box Office:	$817.4 million
Main Cast:	Steve Hiller, played by Will Smith
	President Thomas Whitmore, played by Bill Pullman
	David Levinson, played by Jeff Goldblum
	Julius Levinson, played by Judd Hirsch
	First Lady Whitmore, played by Mary McDonnell
	Constance Spano, played by Margaret Colin

After Will Smith rebranded as a tongue-in-cheek action hero (*Bad Boys*, 1995), he solidified his position as an A-lister Gen Xer in *Independence Day*. As the youngest actor (b. 1968) on the set, Smith was still filming *The Fresh Prince of Bel-Air*, the quintessential coming-of-age/pauper-and-the-prince sitcom that moved Smith from rap to acting. Revolutionary in its own right for depicting Black Americans against type as cultured, complex, and capable, Smith's status as icon, nonetheless, went beyond ethnicity and imprinted a generation beginning to wake up from the racial intolerance that haunted the Boomers. His confidence in his performance as Captain Steve Hiller in the face of annihilation captured Gen X's sensibility that decisive action in the present, unhindered by the prejudices and anxieties of the past, is what truly matters. Thus *Independence Day* is, in a sense, a film of liberation for Gen X, setting them free from America's imperialistic past while reaching toward a new world order of cooperation and globalism. It also liberates them from traditional mores and Boomer expectations of family in pursuit of the American Dream.

Independence Day is a self-conscious alien invasion film. It ironically references *E.T.* and *Close Encounters of the Third Kind* and even goes as far as to show clips from *The Day the Earth Stood Still* (1951) playing on a television set. Moviegoers didn't go to the film to see a new twist on an old plot; they went for the pleasurable spectacle of destruction it promised. The '90s had brought in a new era in CGI, and the teasers for the film showed the White House, Capitol, and the Empire State Building all being destroyed. Here was finally a film that delivered, not just threatened, the apocalypse. In a nod to *Planet of the Apes* (1968), *Independence Day* shows the Statue of Liberty, facedown with a huge hovering spaceship overhead and a burning Manhattan in the backdrop. The sky is dusty and red. Aliens from another planet have destroyed not just America but the American Dream.

As the aliens approach Earth, their signal is picked up, but scientists and the military are not able to figure out what it is. At one point, someone comments, "It better not be another d—n Russian spy job," evoking the traditional enemy of Gen X and Boomer consciousness. A quick cut to the Iwo Jima memorial that then tracks to the Pentagon not only signals a new location but also the general anxiety both generations have of living in the shadow of the Greatest Generation. This alien threat will clearly prove to be more momentous and historical than all previous wars.

In turn, the audience is introduced to President Whitmore, who is sitting in bed with his daughter while his wife is on the phone in California. A single domestic, soft scene of parenthood is quickly balanced in dialogue that follows, giving the audience three important pieces of information: (1) this person is the president, (2) he was a fighter pilot in the Gulf War, and (3) there are questions about his age, that he is really young, even comparing him to Charles Dickens's young protagonist, Oliver Twist. Played by a young-looking Boomer (Bill Pullman, b. 1952), the film seems to go out of its way to make him seem younger, even surrounding him with a secretary of defense played by James Rebhorn who, despite being just three years older than Pullman, looks substantially older, as he is balding and has gray hair. Bringing in veteran actor Robert Loggia (1930–2015) as a consulting general who often shares scenes with Pullman further frames Whitmore as an older Gen Xer. But the inclusion of the subplot of Russell Case (Randy Quaid, b. 1950) as a Vietnam vet who ultimately sacrifices his life and finds the alien ship's weakness really pushes belief, since both are nearly the same age.

However, such artificial attempts to cover Whitmore's age also hints at the deeper meaning of the film; here is art managing the anxieties of a specific generation, a generation needing to find its identity as American but not in the same imperialistic sense that defined preceding generations. The Greatest Generation was defined by World War II, Boomers by Vietnam, and here Gen Xers, while acknowledging involvement in a small-scale conflict like the Gulf War, refuse to be defined by such a conflict. On the contrary, Gen Xers will be defined by a more encompassing and total war that supersedes and even obliterates other generations' identifying mythologies. And while Whitmore serves as the bridge between those white men who went to war and Hiller, ultimately, it is Hiller and conspicuously Jewish but ambiguously aged David Levinson (Jeff Goldblum, 1952–) who transgressively move Gen X beyond more of the same, imperialistic (read: Whit[e]more) Americanism.

The renegade qualities of both Hiller and Levinson are iterated multiple times in the film, even though Hiller is part of the military-industrial complex. Hiller is dating a stripper and promises to commit, is rejected by NASA, and takes on an alien fighter in one-on-one combat, finishing the battle with a punch to the alien's face and the line "Now that's what I call a close encounter." Later, he steals a military helicopter to save said girlfriend and volunteers on the probable suicide mission to upload a virus and launch a nuclear missile into the alien's mother ship. Levinson, too, though highly educated, works below his ability and literally goes against the flow, driving into an evacuating DC to tell his ex-wife that he has figured out the meaning of the signal (a countdown, as it just so happens). His concern and care for his father, played by Judd Hirsch (1935–), and for his father's Jewish faith (later in the film, he gives him a yarmulke and prayer book) place Levinson outside of the boundaries of the American hierarchy and Dream by locating him in the marginalized, distinctly older, and decidedly nonimperialistic Jewish tradition. In the unification of the minority and marginalized, Hiller and Levinson team up to literally save the world by first leaving it.

After Levinson proposes to upload a virus to the mother ship and deliver a nuclear payload to the same, he and Hiller volunteer for the mission. In *Star Wars* fashion, the idea is to shut down the shields of all the other ships in Earth's atmosphere by hitting the source. With the shields down, conventional weapons (through international cooperation and coordination) can take down the enemy. By this point in the film, the enemy has been dehumanized enough that proposed genocide is merely self-defense against its attempt at annihilation. (At one point, the aliens, in a possible biblical reference, are compared to locusts. At another, the alien uses a dead scientist's body to talk and make their mission clear: the destruction of all humanity.) Hiller and Levinson plan to accomplish this mission by flying a retrofitted alien fighter ship that just so happens to be the same one that was recovered at Roswell in 1947, thereby tying the film into a growing awareness of stigmatized knowledge and conspiracy theory that was beginning to proliferate on an earlier iteration of the internet.

After some trouble taking off, Hiller and Levinson's mythologizing for Gen X begins in earnest. The slate has already been cleared; all is in shambles—even the Statue of Liberty. Middle East peace has been achieved; Israelis prepare for battle alongside, not against, Arab armed forces (under the watchful eyes of the British, of course). Human wars are no longer of concern; the president gives a speech about how this is Independence Day for the whole world, and so forth. All is set. In many mythologies, there is the apotheosis of the hero, where the hero becomes a god. This is often accomplished by the hero ascending into heaven and taking a rightful place among deities or, as in the myth of the Prometheus, the hero ascends and descends again to bring mortals the invaluable gift of fire. Here Hiller and Levinson, purged of the cultural entanglements that thwarted the other generations, war, racism, and so forth, ascend to the heavens and enter the abode of the gods, symbolized by the mother ship of an advanced race. Once deceptively docked, they upload the virus and, when they try to leave, find that they are stuck and under investigation. Throughout their time in space, they become closer friends and prepare to face death together upon discovery. In mutual agreement, they launch the missile into and through some of the compartments of the alien craft, fully expecting to be obliterated by it as well. As they wait for it to detonate, they joke around that these aliens have no idea what's coming and then tell each other goodbye: "It's been a pleasure." At this point, they manage to break free from the docking area and begin to fly out. Now, because of their ascension, conflict, and willingness to sacrifice themselves in the heavens, their "immortality" is assured. They barely make it out alive as the Death Star—no, the alien mother ship—explodes. Their descent back to Earth and reception back into humanity is replete with a long shot of two swaggering heroes in flight gear smoking cigars as their respective women and leader welcome them home.

Meanwhile, the president leads his fighters against the aliens, and Russ sacrifices himself by flying into the primary weapon, thereby destroying the whole battleship and finding its Achilles's heel. There is a montage of various nations' armies attacking and defeating the other enemy crafts around the world. Again, this is all done because Hiller and Levinson, renegades, went beyond the various systems and limitations of the past to do the never-been-done.

There are other indications, too, that the appeal of *Independence Day* is not just along the superficial affirmations of America. In fact, it is precisely and paradoxically "American" in that it literally deconstructs, that is, destroys, America to reenvision it. As a generation without an identity, named with a placeholder, Generation X came to see its identity less as an heir to the Anglo-American dream and more in the emerging values of multiculturalism and the growing phenomenon of globalization. President George H. W. Bush had relaunched the idea of a "new world order," one in which cooperation and a balance of power would prevent further situations like the Cold War from occurring. In the post–Cold War America of the 1990s, this meant both nuclear disarmament and international cooperation. Interestingly, in the film, the nuclear option is used twice: once against a shielded alien battleship over Houston (ineffectively) and then against the alien mother ship in space (effectively), suggesting that the only place for such weapons is far away from Earth and not for humans against each other. Gen X's eclectic style and acceptance of outsiders and the culturally marginalized within American society suggests they took "X" as an amorphous identity in need of constant reshaping to match the ever-shifting, deeply interconnected landscape. X can be anything and needs to be anything to face the global threats that threaten all of humanity, such as global warming or even aliens.

Benjamin Crace

See also: *Close Encounters of the Third Kind*; *E.T.: The Extra-Terrestrial*; *Jurassic Park*; *Star Wars: A New Hope*; *Star Wars: Return of the Jedi*; *Top Gun*.

Further Reading

Davies, Jude. 2005. "'Diversity. America. Leadership. Good over Evil.' Hollywood Multiculturalism and American Imperialism in *Independence Day* and *Three Kings*." *Patterns of Prejudice* 39 (4): 397–415.

Dixon, John. 1996. "Aliens 'R' Us: A Critique of D4." *Film & History* 26 (1–4): 88–92.

Dvorak, Ken. 1996. "*Independence Day*: A Survival Guide for the Next Invasion." *Film & History* 26 (1–4): 90–91.

Hungerford, Kristen. 2010. "The Male 'White' House of Hollywood: A Feminist Critique of What It Means to Be Presidential." *Ohio Communication Journal* 48 (October): 55–75.

Molstad, Stephen. 2016. *The Complete* Independence Day *Omnibus*. London: Titan Books.

Jurassic Park

Release Date:	1993
Director:	Steven Spielberg
Box Office:	$912.7 million
Main Cast:	Dr. Alan Grant, played by Sam Neill
	Dr. Ellie Sattler, played by Laura Dern
	Dr. Ian Malcolm, played by Jeff Goldblum
	John Hammond, played by Richard Attenborough

Adapted from the novel by Michael Crichton, *Jurassic Park* is a potent mixture of adventure, science fiction, and horror, all held together by revolutionary visual effects. The film opens at night, with the delivery of a live velociraptor to a theme park. The shadowy jungle scenery is matched by equally shadowy glimpses of a large animal in a heavy-duty transport crate. When the raptor slams the back of the crate, an employee falls, his legs landing inside the open crate. The raptor eats him as security guards try in vain to Taser the animal. Thus the question is raised at the outset whether these animals, brought back to life by rapidly advancing technology, can be *controlled* by technology. The second scene takes us to an amber mine in South America, where we are told that the employee's (presumably poor) family is demanding payment for his death—an indication that economics, and the priorities of money over persons, will be a recurring theme. We are then shown a mosquito trapped in amber, the unexpected source of the monstrous animal trapped in the transport crate. What might happen when this mosquito and the animal whose DNA it carries are once again freed?

Compelled by the promise of endless research funding, Dr. Alan Grant and Dr. Ellie Sattler are recruited by John Hammond to visit his dinosaur park. Not knowing what to expect, they are flown to the park, where they and the audience encounter living dinosaurs for the first time. Dr. Grant drops to the ground, overwhelmed to see the creatures whose bones he had studied his whole life now walking before him. The audience, too, is treated to full-screen portraits of these creatures, whose lifelike enormity is driven by a combination of animatronic models and the new technology of computer-generated images (CGI). The advances in computer technology that enabled the creation of giant onscreen dinosaurs are immediately commented on in the film, which proceeds to explain, in a quirky computer-animated cartoon shown to the visitors, that the dinosaurs have been brought to life by computer-driven science. Computers analyze the DNA contained in ancient mosquitoes trapped in amber, those computers then replace any missing portions of those genes, and the dinosaurs are re-created. In the case of both the fictional science and filmmaking, what was trapped in the past is released into the present by the incredible power of modern computer technology.

But the park is not pursuing the science for its own sake. John Hammond is an entrepreneur and a showman, and the park is his great circus. Its purpose is entertainment and the money it will make. But capitalism is a dangerous and wild thing, and a rival company has arranged to steal dinosaur embryos by paying off an employee. To cover his tracks, the thief shuts down electricity to much of the park, forcing technicians to shut down power to the whole system in order to reboot it.

The visitors, including Hammond's grandchildren, are then stuck: the electric vehicles cannot run; the electric fence is useless, and they sit outside the tyrannosaurus enclosure waiting for the power to come back on. In the darkness, the tyrannosaurus emerges, eats a fearful lawyer, and injures Dr. Malcolm. Dr. Grant escapes into the jungle with Hammond's grandchildren. Their portion of the tale is, for a short time, an adventure story—they experience the wonder of (plant-eating) dinosaurs before avoiding a stampede and watching a tyrannosaurus hunt. Meanwhile, Hammond sends Dr. Sattler and the gamekeeper, Robert Muldoon, out to turn the power back on at a power substation located deep in the jungle. But the jungle is now patrolled by velociraptors. They kill Muldoon using clever pack-hunting techniques. The tone quickly shifts from adventure to horror, as Dr. Sattler finds herself in a dark, industrial hallway lined with cables and machinery. Just as she turns the lights back on a velociraptor attacks her. She escapes. Feeling a hand on her shoulder, she turns expecting to see Muldoon, only to find only a bloody, severed arm. This classic horror trope concludes with her running from the building.

Dr. Sattler finds Dr. Grant outside the main visitors' center, having left the kids inside. This sets up one of the most terrifying scenes in the film. The children discover that the velociraptors are hunting them inside the visitors' center, and they are chased into an industrial kitchen. They elude the raptors by hiding under tables, clanging spoons, and ultimately using a reflection to trick one raptor into colliding with a cabinet, while locking the other in a freezer. If the adventure scenes are marked by wide-open spaces and large colorful animals, such horror scenes are cramped, dark, and gray. The dimly lit stainless steel kitchen provides a washed-out pallet of colors, while the imagery evokes a feeling of entrapment. The dinosaurs have been freed from the past, and now the humans are trapped in a present filled with death and fear.

Ingenuity, however, saves the day, and the children make it out of the kitchen. They meet Dr. Sattler and Dr. Grant in the control room, where they cannot lock the doors because they are locked out of the computer system. Eventually, one of the children, Lex, is able to hack the computer system and get the doors to lock. But this computer-savvy solution only offers a brief reprieve: the dinosaur merely breaks through the glass windows, overcoming technical creativity with brute force. They escape through the crawl space in the ceiling and are finally cornered in the main lobby, ironically enough, beneath the massive, fossilized skeleton of a tyrannosaurus rex. When it appears that they, too, will soon be doomed to history, the living tyrannosaurus rex appears and does with brute strength what computer-savvy could not. As it kills the raptors, the humans escape to a waiting jeep outside, where they are taken to safety and flown home. In the end, the humans were not saved by ingenuity or technical acumen but by sheer good luck. "Life finds a way," as Dr. Malcolm memorably puts it, but that way is not through technological prowess and control: if *human* life finds a way, it is only through the chaos of a dino-eat-dino world.

If this seems like a gloomy conclusion, it is. *Jurassic Park*, like works of gothic horror going back at least to *Frankenstein*, seeks to expose the darkness that human progress is capable of. Human ingenuity combines with human greed to unleash unspeakable terror on the world. The wonders of computer-driven technological advancement enable humans to re-create the monsters of the past. And when those monsters are let loose, humans find themselves caught in the middle of the forces they created but that are too large for them to control. As the final scene shows, the humans are not capable of saving their own lives; rather, they are as subject to the chaos of nature as the raptors who are eaten by the T. rex. Indeed, the dinosaur conflicts are mirrored in the human conflicts between corporations battling for superiority. It is in animal nature to eat other animals, and it is the nature of modern American corporations to seek to destroy one another. The forces of nature here are not just animal but human, and human nature is no more noble than that of dinosaurs. The havoc this causes unleashes forces no one in the film can control, and survival has less to do with skill than on being on the right side of a happy accident. The dinosaurs are thus a kind of allegory for the corporate greed that created and unleashed them. And while humans survive, it is not without tragedy. The film thus chimes, with continued unease within Generation X, of unfettered capitalism. Belief in unrestrained free markets had nearly reached its peak, and the world it created was one of kill or be killed. The ideal of competition-induced efficiency was shown by the film to be little more than the brute instincts of a very hungry lizard: a leviathan, in classical terms. And while Generation X enjoyed many of the benefits of the society the leviathan produced, they also remained uneasy about its many tragic trajectories.

One of the most powerful and dangerous corporate forces at work in the film is that of entertainment. Jurassic Park is a circus whose technology has created an entertainment experience unlike any other. It is the relentless quest for a new experience that drives the re-creation of dinosaurs. And this is as true of the making of the film as of its content. The film received three Academy Awards for special effects and set the trajectory for all contemporary uses of CGI in film and media. It brought dinosaurs back to life in a way never seen before, opening new vistas for adventure and new opportunities for terror. Mirroring its own content, the film itself is the product of major corporations competing for resources and power: multiple studios competed for the production rights to the movie, with Universal Studios eventually paying Michael Crichton at least $1.5 million and substantial royalties as well as an additional $500,000 to write a screenplay based on the book. The film, moreover, is the product of an entertainment guru with a flair for technological genius: when he began directing the movie, Steven Spielberg had already established himself as one of the most technically and artistically compelling directors in Hollywood. There is perhaps a bit of self-critique involved in the film's themes. Can humanity survive its own entertainment, and is all society caught between corporate forces of financial manipulation and the human proclivity to crave new experiences? In short, will we all be eaten by our relentless need to be entertained?

Such questions are representative of numerous concerns that emerged in the mid-1990s. While the Cold War had effectively ended and the threat of nuclear war had greatly diminished, the technological age was only just beginning. The internet was beginning to emerge and change the texture of human interaction. It seemed that more and more of human life was being conducted in and through computer technology. This was the source of both optimism and anxiety. Would this technology erode human life, or would it sustain human life in new and exciting modes? This ambivalence is reflected in the film. Lex is a next-generation computer sleuth whose skills provide a crucial few seconds' reprieve from the attacking raptor. But that raptor was alive to attack them because of computer-driven scientific discoveries. So is the computer age something to be feared or embraced? The film does not answer this question. Computer technology, as with corporate culture and the entertainment industry, the film seems to suggest, merely provides another platform for the chaos of nature to play its life-and-death game; whether dinosaurs or corporations, life will find a way to survive. And whether *we* live to see it, *Jurassic Park* suggests, is not entirely up to us.

Josh Mobley

See also: *Close Encounters of the Third Kind*; *Independence Day*; *Jaws*.

Further Reading
Crewe, David. 2016. "Excavating Knowledge: *Jurassic Park* in the Classroom." *Screen Education* 83: 14–23.
Eaklor, Vicki. 2011. "*Jurassic Park*." In *Movies in American History: An Encyclopedia*, 1, edited by Philip C. DiMare, 284–286. Santa Barbara, CA: ABC-CLIO.
Michaud, Nicolas, and Jessica Watkins. 2014. Jurassic Park *and Philosophy: The Truth Is Terrifying*. Chicago: Open Court.

The Lion King

Release Date:	1994
Directors:	Roger Allers and Rob Minkoff
Box Office:	$1.084 billion
Main Cast (Voices):	Mufasa, played by James Earl Jones
	Timon, played by Nathan Lane
	Scar, played by Jeremy Irons
	Young/Grown Simba, played by Jonathan T. Thomas and Matthew Broderick
	Young/Grown Nala, played by Niketa Calame and Moira Kelly
	Pumbaa, played by Ernie Sabella

Like the animated/animalized version of *Robin Hood* (1973), Disney's *The Lion King* basically takes Shakespeare's *Hamlet*, reworks a few parts, and sets it in Southeast Africa. It adds a happy ending, of course, because the gloomy ending of the original play would never be marketable to families in the late 20th century. But like Shakespeare, Disney knows how to use generational conflict and tension to drive a narrative. Furthermore, the growing cultural concern for political correctness, multiculturalism, and diversity began to penetrate the overall Western whiteness of the Mouse's empire. And yet there is also, as with several other Disney films, a growing awareness of both spiritual longing and environmental concern.

For Gen Xers raised on environmentalism through cartoons such as *Captain Planet* (1990–1996), *The Lion King*'s aesthetic and depiction of the "circle of life" exhibits a world in which humans are excluded and Nature personified manages to maintain a type of species hierarchy, with lions on top. It is clear that as long as that hierarchy is properly maintained, Pride Rock and its surrounding kingdom will flourish with abundant food and water. When that hierarchy is broken, as it is when Scar (the bachelor uncle usurper) overthrows the legitimate ruler, Mufasa, with the help of the scavenger hyenas, the whole land suffers. Food disappears, water evaporates, bones are left scattered about, the ground and sky are dull grays and browns. In short, without proper management, the rich ecosystem becomes a wasteland until the proper manager comes back and restores everything by completing the circle of life, that is, taking responsibility as the next king and creating a nuclear family while providing care for his widowed mother.

Colonialism and Western Imperialism lay close at hand—side by side, as it were—to this environmental messaging. But Disney seems to be aware of this and tries to turn such criticism on its head by including African Americans as African proxies for key voices and by making an indigenous species the main characters. Robert Guillaume, famous for his roles as Frederick Douglas in the massive miniseries *North and South* (1985) and the main star for the long-running political sitcom, *Benson* (1979–1986), plays the mysterious baboon shaman Rafiki. Comic and television and film star, Whoopi Goldberg, hot off the success of her film *Sister Act* (1992), voices Shenzi, one of the hyenas. But for the majestic and powerful voice of Mufasa, Simba's dad and paragon of a lion king, Disney cast James Earl Jones. Besides voicing Darth Vader in *Star Wars*, Jones, interestingly enough, played Alex Haley in the sequel to the miniseries *Roots*. In it, he (as Haley) travels to Gambia to discover his ancestry beyond slavery. The gravitas of his performance lends the narrative both a sense of continuity between the generations (Mufasa, Simba, and other lion kings who look down from the stars) while also legitimizing and softening Disney's exploitation of African culture and customs for monetary gain. But Pride Rock's decline and the possibility of its return to its former glory rest squarely on the shoulders of Scar, voiced by white, English actor, Jeremy Irons, and Simba, voiced by Matthew Broderick, that fresh-faced icon of white, middle-class rebellion who made his mark in *Ferris Bueller's Day Off* (1986). One could say that Irons's Scar represents British colonialism and its plundering of Africa—especially of Kenya, where it seems most of the action takes place. This logic, however, sets up Broderick's Simba as the white, American savior who does colonialism even better than the British—so well, in fact, it looks a lot like a form of precolonial tribalism but with a white ruler: the circle of life thus takes on insipid imperialistic overtones instead of the foregrounded environmental mysticism. It is interesting to note that Disney's 2019 remake of the film replaced all of the main white speaking parts with British Africans and African Americans. Broderick is replaced by Gen Xer Donald Glover, whose alternate, musical persona Childish Gambino skewers American racism, classism, and socioeconomic disparity. Clearly, Disney was concerned to do things better the second time around. (It worked, too, earning $1.657 billion.)

Beyond issues of race and colonialism that freights any film made in Hollywood and set in Africa, *The Lion King* is also a coming-of-age tale that depicts Gen X anxieties about their place in the scheme of things, in the circle of life. In the beginning, a young prince, Simba, plays with his female friend, Nala, unaware of the larger and heavier responsibilities and expectations of adulthood that await them both. His father, Mufasa, continually tries to expound on what it is like to be a king, how one should act, and so on. But like the typical preteen/teen, Simba is more interested in exploring the world and being young than in monarchy and protocol. To Simba, as expressed in the song, "I Just Can't Wait to Be King," being king simply means complete freedom from restraint, freedom to "do it all my way." Enlightened Boomer parents, attending the film with their Gen X kids, would instantly recognize the folly of such thinking and later feel justified as Simba comes around to recognizing and enacting the wisdom of his elders.

Through Scar's machinations, Mufasa ends up dead and Simba in exile, believing his father's death was his fault. In exile, Simba attempts to rebrand himself, to find a new identity apart from his pride. In the film, this is depicted as a type of death and resurrection into a carefree paradise. After running away into the desert, Simba collapses, and just as the buzzards begin to descend to devour him, a warthog, Pumbaa, and a meerkat, Timon, rescue him. They indoctrinate him into their hedonistic, live-for-today lifestyle with the song "Hakuna Matata," an appropriated Swahili phrase that means "no worries." From the desert, they journey to an Edenic paradise where all they do all day is eat bugs, swim, sing, and lounge around. Through a short montage, Simba grows to early adulthood in just this fashion, singing "Hakuna Matata" throughout.

In terms of the audience, Simba, Timon, and Pumbaa's lackadaisical approach to life matches the reluctant embrace of adulthood, not only of teens but of Gen Xers as a generational cohort. Thrown into a globalized world only recently unshackled from Cold War anxieties (signaled by the fall of the Berlin Wall, 1989) only to be embroiled again in another foreign war (the Gulf War, 1990–1991) that would pave the way for the disastrous 9/11 attacks, responsible, routinized adulthood really did not seem like a palatable option. No, living off of whatever one could find and enjoying life with friends were clearly a better choice, a paradise of sorts. But as a Boomer/Gen X hybrid text, such an existence cannot extend indefinitely.

Nala, Simba's childhood friend and now potential mate, stumbles upon his little paradise while out hunting for food. Although the jungle area where Simba has been hiding is a long way from Pride Rock, the lions have had to go farther and farther afield for food, as their area continues to decay under the reign of Scar and the hyenas. Upon finding Simba, she is overjoyed and hopes he can come back and makes things right. During her stay in the oasis, a musical montage set to the Elton John song "Can You Feel the Love Tonight?" sets up their courtship and later marriage.

After Nala fails to convince Simba to return, Rafiki shows up and leads him on a journey of self-discovery through communion with his dead father. In a vision of sorts, Mufasa tells Simba, "You must take your place in the circle of life. Remember who you are. You are my son and the true king." Youthful hedonism must end, and Simba must take his place. In Gen Xer terms, that "circle of life" is really the numbing routine of the everyday nine-to-five job they saw their Boomer parents get sucked into. But here, such soul-killing prospects as becoming like one's father in terms of career and family are romanticized in terms of sexuality (Nala), power (become king), and even supernatural warrant (the dead/destiny). One's "true" identity, says the film, does not lie in self-expression or self-discovery but in doing what your parents tell you, and it just so happens to look a lot like what your parents did. Uncritically and unsurprisingly, Simba returns to Pride Rock.

Of course, there is opposition as Simba attempts to regain control. Scar tries to weasel his way out of being the bad guy by laying the blame for Mufasa's death at Simba's feet in front of the pride. Simba takes partial responsibility but then forces Scar to confess how he was actually the key agent behind it all. There is an epic battle between good and evil amid a huge fire that engulfs the Rock. Simba offers Scar exile, but he continues to fight until he ends up falling into the pack of hyenas who (presumably) eat him. It rains, the fire goes out, Simba walks to the ledge of the Rock, and roars, taking his rightful place.

The last scene is a near-perfect reproduction of the first, except this time it is Nala and Simba's cub that is held aloft by Rafiki for all the subservient animals to adore and pay obeisance. The song "The Circle of Life" crescendos, and a heavy drum beat transitions to the title card: "The Lion King." It is an emotional and satisfying ending; clearly in embracing his destiny, Simba has gained what most Americans—particularly males—want: a spouse, a child, property, and the deep respect of others, bordering on worship. Sure, it is the same "job" as Pop's was, but it is the only proper way to secure the goods that have been called into question by the upheavals of Gen X's cultural moment, or so the film says.

Josh Mobley

See also: *Black Panther; Star Wars: A New Hope.*

Further Reading

Edwards, Kim. 2018. "Coming Full Circle: A Study Guide to *The Lion King*." *Education*, no. 88 (January): 8–15.

Gavin, Rosemarie. 1996. "*The Lion King* and *Hamlet*: A Homecoming for the Exiled Child." *English Journal* 85, no. 3 (March 1996): 55.

Gooding-Williams, Robert. 1995. "Disney in Africa and the Inner City: On Race and Space in *The Lion King*." *Social Identities* 1 (2): 373.

Morton, John. 1996. "Simba's Revolution: Revisiting History and Class in *The Lion King*." *Social Identities* 2 (2): 311–317.

Ward, Annalee R. 1996. "*The Lion King*'s Mythic Narrative." *Journal of Popular Film & Television* 23 (4): 171.

Star Wars: Return of the Jedi

Release Date:	1983
Director:	Richard Marquand
Box Office:	$475.3 million
Main Cast:	Luke Skywalker, played by Mark Hamill
	Han Solo, played by Harrison Ford
	Princess Leia, played by Carrie Fisher
	Chewbacca, played by Peter Mayhew
	C-3PO, played by Anthony Daniels
	R2-D2, played by Kenny Baker

As the third installment of the original trilogy, *Star Wars: Episode VI—Return of the Jedi* closes the saga that burst onto the scene with *A New Hope* in 1977. Released three years after *The Empire Strikes Back*, Jedi picks up the same archetypal narrative of good versus evil: the Alliance (or the Rebels) fighting against the Empire. The actors, too, now six years older than in the first film, have progressed in their respective character arcs—all except, perhaps, Han Solo, who has been frozen in carbonite, as seen at the end of *Empire*.

As it turns out, Boba Fett, a bounty hunter, has transported Han to Tatooine, Luke Skywalker's home world, where he is hung up as a decoration in the palace of the Mafia-crime lord, Jabba the Hutt. The film begins with C-3PO, a humanoid protocol droid, and R2-D2, a smaller garbage-can-shaped droid that rolls along on its wheeled legs, arriving at Jabba's palace and requesting entry. They are there to deliver a message to Jabba from Luke, who is now considered to be a Jedi Knight—a significant development since *Empire*, where he suffered both an existential and physical defeat in battle at the hands of Darth Vader. In one of the most referenced and memed scenes in film history, *Empire* revealed that Vader was indeed Luke's father. Vader, who first appears at the beginning of *A New Hope,* is a large cyborg steeped in the ways of the Dark Side of the Force, the energy field that surrounds all living things. As a pawn of the Emperor, Vader is relentless in hunting down the Alliance members while seeking to turn Luke to the Dark Side. But as a frontier planet, Tatooine is ruled more by crime lords such as Jabba than by the tyrannical Empire.

Jabba is a large, sluglike entity that, before CGI, was staffed by several puppeteers working in unison. He is gluttonous, vengeful, and literally cold blooded. He derives his pleasure by enslaving various species, enjoying music, and watching a large monster in a chamber below his throne eat creatures he deems worthless. As a demonstration of his ruthlessness, early in the film, a slave dancer named Oola (Nigerian-born Brit, Femi Taylor) displeases Jabba by failing to succumb to his sexual advances, is made to fall through a trapdoor, and is devoured by the Rancor monster below. She is both scantily clad and chained by the neck; her Black skin has been painted over with green paint, and she has been fitted with a headpiece of two long pieces of flesh and horns to make her appear "alien." As the only female Black actor in the film, her quick disempowerment, dismemberment, and sexualization serves to solidify patriarchal othering narratives. That the franchise was targeted at children as a means of selling toys makes such depictions even further unsettling.

After C-3P0, R2-D2, Chewbacca (a large, Bigfoot-like creature who is Han's copilot), and Leia have all been captured, Luke finally shows up. Leia, just before her capture, has awakened Han from hibernation, so the whole core cast of the original films are now in Jabba's palace. Leia, however, has now taken Oola's place as the new provocatively dressed slave girl chained by the neck to Jabba. She remains in this overtly sexualized, dominated position for most of the time they are on the planet Tatooine. When Luke demands that Jabba release them all, Jabba attempts to kill him by the same trapdoor that killed Oola earlier. He avoids being eaten, killing the monster instead. However, Jabba then decides to execute them all by throwing them into the sarlacc pit in the desert.

Out in the desert, a large floating barge and two smaller ones arrive over the sarlacc pit. The droids and Leia, still chained to Jabba, are watching as the (male) others are being made to walk the plank over the living hole with teeth (insert Freudian overtones here). Along with some help from Lando Calrissian (Black actor Billy Dee Williams), Luke and the others manage to escape and even destroy Jabba's barge. Prior to their escape, in a rather strange moment of sadomasochistic erotic asphyxiation, Leia dominates Jabba, who has just called her a "slut," by choking the life out of him with her neck chain. Clad in alien lingerie, she stands strong and triumphant over his lifeless corpse.

Such scenes indicate the franchise's growing awareness that Gen Xer males were coming-of-age, and, given Leia's later commanding presence among her troops as a no-nonsense princess, Lucasfilm seems to want to have it both ways: eye candy and the independent, self-made woman of the '80s. Luke, too, no longer a teenager but a Jedi Knight, is a strong leader who makes his own decisions and is treated as an equal with now-general Han. They have all, like their audience, come of age.

As with many liminal films, that is, films that reflect generational transition, *Jedi* continues the *Star Wars* tradition of passing the torch. In *A New Hope*, Obi-Wan Kenobi, the old Jedi from Tatooine, passes the Jedi legacy to Luke and literally disappears to make room for him. *Jedi*, too, has Luke meet with Yoda, the small, old, elf-like Jedi master from *Empire*, for one last conversation. In overt signaling of the end of one generation, Yoda complains about being old (900 years) and needing to rest. He tells Luke that he needs to pass what he has learned on to someone else, and, just before fading away as Obi-Wan did, indicates that Luke has another family member that he does not know about. Luke leaves the small hut and walks outside, where the glowing ghost of Obi-Wan reveals more of the backstory about Vader and that Luke has a sister. Luke is briefly angry, because both he and the audience know that Obi-Wan had earlier said that Luke's dad was dead. When questioned, Obi-Wan cagily replies that he is dead, from a certain point of view. And then, in a line that could underwrite the whole hedonistic and turbulent decade of the '80s, he says, "Luke, you're going to find that many of the truths we cling to depend greatly on our own point of view." But Luke isn't swayed by the other generation's world-weary relativism and ultimately determines to face Vader but not to kill him as Obi-Wan suggests.

There is, then, a tight balance in the *Star Wars* universe between the exiting of the Greatest Generation (Obi-Wan is played by Sir Alec Guinness, a World War II vet; Vader, by David Prowse [1935–]) and the mantle being taken up by Boomers, who, as the audience already knows, are passing it on to Gen X through the film medium. It is, after all, a long, long time ago in a galaxy far, far away. This passing on the fight for freedom, personal destiny, good times with friends, and the restoration of the Jedi way (a mixture of Buddhism and medieval chivalry) is enacted over and over again in *Star Wars* through the father/son (Vader and Luke) and master/apprentice (Obi-Wan, Anakin/Vader, Luke) framing and the reunion technique. Numerous times in the film, the characters in the film are as excited to see each other as the audience is to see the actors/characters again after a three-year, cliff-hanging wait. Numerous scenes, too, are punctuated with celebrations of community and friendship, established by the iconic closing scene of *A New Hope*.

Significant, too, the Emperor appears far more in *Jedi* than in the other films. He is a very old, sarcastic, evil, white male who thrives on hate. Fittingly, the master villain is an old man, whose (spoiler alert) death causes the galaxy to celebrate. Obviously, a strong idealism and loyalty to one's friends trump the alluring power of the Dark Side. With strong echoes of fascism, Nazism, and communism, the Emperor and his Death Star exist solely to create coerced conformity in the galaxy, as shown by the homogenized Stormtroopers and near total lack of all color in Imperial uniforms. The exception here is the Imperial Guard, a blood-red–robed squad that protects the Emperor himself. The black-robed Emperor with unnaturally white skin, flanked by red guards is not dissimilar to the colors of the Third Reich of Nazi Germany. He does, after all, command legions of Stormtroopers, the exact same name as some Nazi military personnel, and the genocidal Death Star. His death, then, symbolizes the defeat of such totalitarian regimes, a cathartic release for an audience living in constant dread of World War III with Soviet Russia (*Red Dawn* would be released the next year, chronicling a "hypothetical" invasion of the United States by Russia). The Death Star's destruction, of course, is a spectacular display of nuclear disarmament out in space where no one is affected except the enemy. Recall, too, that President Reagan's initiative to weaponize space was announced and nicknamed "Star Wars" the same year *Jedi* was released. As usual, contemporaneous historical and cultural intersections bleed through into film, even science fiction.

Aside from counseling Luke (and the Gen X audience) toward relativism, Obi-Wan also counsels Luke to bury his feelings so Vader and the Emperor will not be able to manipulate him with them. Such counsel extends previous generational concerns with machismo, exemplified in the machinelike Vader and the Zen upthrust of Jedi training. Yet emotions and feelings are also problematized in the film as well, giving license to the type of emotional exploration that became entrenched in the self-help and therapy movement of the late '70s and '80s (and beyond). Han is openly jealous of Luke and wounded to think he could lose Leia to him. Han works this tension out with her as an equally empowered partner, where she explains Luke is her brother. The relieved Han accepts this and is clear on the status of their relationship as lovers. Even Vader, by the end of the film, is reconciled to Luke in a rare moment of tenderness and redemption. These scenes of intimacy and depth are a far cry from the emotional distance Luke has at his aunt and uncle's death in *A New Hope*. There, upon witnessing their charred bodies, he simply stares and looks away. Han, too, casually shot Greedo in *New Hope* and swaggered out of the cantina, but he seems remarkably vulnerable when his relationship with Leia is on the line in *Jedi*. Clearly, the characters have grown emotionally, but so has the franchise.

Once reunited (again), the Alliance determines to destroy the Death Star (again). But in order to do so, they must disable its protective shield (another self-referential nod toward Obi-Wan's disabling of the shield in *A New Hope*). The generator for the shield is on the forested planet Endor around which the Death Star is orbiting. While Lando and others prepare to fight a space battle and hit the

Death Star's Achilles's heel (again), Han leads the regular cast of characters and others on a strike team to Endor. Luke, of course, is planning to steal away and confront Vader at the opportune time.

On Endor, they encounter the Ewoks, small, furry aliens that resemble teddy bears. Yet these creatures are primitive and tribal; they use spears, wear skulls, and perhaps practice cannibalism. Some sources indicate that the Ewoks were so named in honor of the Native American tribe, Miwok, who lived in the redwood forest where Endor was filmed. Yet such a primitive and barbaric (even if "cute") depiction drains such an allusive reading of its force. Not only cannibalistic, the Ewoks are diminutive in height and mistake C-3PO as a god. Surely such representations cannot stand as honorific to local peoples.

Notwithstanding the troubling ethnic representations (a problem Lucas has again and again, especially in the prequels), the hiring of little people to act in the Ewok suits is equally problematic. Exploitation of little people has been a part of entertainment for generations; examples include "midget" wrestling and, into the film era, the Munchkins of *The Wizard of Oz* (1939). Lucas himself hired little people to portray the Jawas in *A New Hope*. In both *A New Hope* and *Jedi*, even their voices are muffled in chittering, animalistic languages. At one point, Leia picks Wicket up like a child, even though he is played by Warwick Davis, who was already a teenager at the time. Less problematic from a cinematic point of view is Kenny Baker's performance as R2, being completely invisible inside the robot.

But beyond exploitation of little people, the Ewoks remind us again that this is supposed to be a children's movie or at least a film for the whole family (erotic asphyxiation and strip teases aside). *Jedi* received a PG rating just prior to the updated rating system of PG-13 that came out the following year. And yet there are these Ewoks (capitalized on by Lucasfilm and Kenner in merchandise worth millions) who are in the action at relatively the same height as a large part of the Gen X audience. The Ewoks' successful defeat of the Imperial troops (with help), telegraphs that kids helped bring down the Empire. Such an overt audience identification maneuver successfully entrained a generation into the narrative of the franchise, boosted toy sales, and confirmed the perennial adolescent angst at constantly being misunderstood and underestimated. If etymology means anything, Endor or "eye of a generation" in Hebrew, truly captured the imagination, the inner eye, of a generation that would grow up and pass on the Jedi legacy and make the Star Wars franchise one of the most successful ever.

Good triumphs: Luke battles Vader while the Emperor goads him on, but Vader turns on the Emperor after he attempts to kill Luke for not joining the Dark Side. In the ultimate father-son moment, Vader throws the Emperor to his death and has a heart-to-heart with Luke just before he dies. Luke manages to get Vader's body onto the Emperor's ship and fly to Endor just in time, as Lando shoots the target that destroys the Death Star (again). Back on Endor, they all celebrate as Luke burns Vader's body.

Significantly, Lucasfilm added scenes and changed parts of the originals to match up with prequels. Thus when Luke sees all the past Jedis as apparitions, it is now Hayden Christensen (the actor who played Anakin Skywalker in *Star Wars: The Attack of the Clones* [2002] and *Revenge of the Sith* [2005]) who has been digitally inserted into the vision over Sebastian Shaw's portrayal from 1983 (when Christensen was two years old). But Shaw's face, not Christensen's, is the one behind the mask as well in the final conversation with Luke. Such editing raised and continues to raise questions of artistic vision versus audience expectations. And there is nothing as ire-inducing as tampering with a generation's memory—especially a generation that has sought and found its identity in such grand mythologies.

Benjamin Crace

See also: Indiana Jones and the Raiders of the Lost Ark; Star Wars: The Force Awakens; Star Wars: A New Hope; Star Wars: The Phantom Menace.

Further Reading

Berger, Arthur Asa. 1984. "*Return of the Jedi*: The Rewards of Myth." *Society* 21, no. 4 (May): 71–75.

Clark, Mark. 2015. Star Wars *FAQ : Everything Left to Know about the Trilogy That Changed the Movies*. Milwaukee, WI: Applause.

"Lucas, George W. Jr." 2018. *The Columbia Encyclopedia*. New York: Columbia University Press.

Meyer, David S. 1992. "*Star Wars*, Star Wars, and American Political Culture." *Journal of Popular Culture* 26 (2): 99–115.

Robb, Brian J. 2012. *A Brief Guide to* Star Wars*: The Unauthorised Inside Story*. London: Perseus Books.

Taylor, Chris. 2014. *How* Star Wars *Conquered the Universe: The Past, Present, and Future of a Multibillion Dollar Franchise*. London: Head of Zeus.

Terminator 2: Judgment Day

Release Date:	1991
Director:	James Cameron
Box Office:	$520 million
Main Cast:	Model 101 Terminator, played by Arnold Schwarzenegger
	Sarah Connor, played by Linda Hamilton
	John Connor, played by Edward Furlong
	T-1000 Terminator, played by Robert Patrick

James Cameron's *Terminator 2* set a new standard for sci-fi/action films. As one of the most expensive films ever made, it raised the bar for CGI and even won the Academy Award for Best Visual Effects. Cowritten by William Wisher and Cameron, it further entrenched Cameron's notoriety as a visual storyteller. Released at the tail end of the Cold War, the film pushes beyond contextual geopolitics to relocate humanity's enemy as the machine.

As a sequel, the film is highly self-referential to the Terminator universe established in the original film from 1984. In the original, humankind is in a fight-for-existence battle with an artificial intelligence known as Skynet. Skynet is a self-aware AI that evolved out of a computer built to manage the United States' nuclear arsenal. In 1997, it starts a nuclear war with the USSR and almost wipes out the human race. In the future setting of the film, 2029, it manufactures humanlike Terminators to destroy people. These Terminators have a metallic endoskeleton that can be covered with tissue. The Terminators of the future simply look like laser gun–toting, malevolent, metal skeletons who hunt and kill humans. As it turns out, Skynet figures out a way to time travel and sends a very human-looking Terminator (Schwarzenegger) back to 1984 to assassinate Sarah Connor (Hamilton), mother of John Connor (the leader of the human resistance in 2029). The human resistance of the future also manages to send one of its soldiers (Kyle Reese, played by Michael Biehn) back to protect her from the Terminator. What ensues is an extended cat-and-mouse game that ends with the destruction of the Terminator and the death of Reese, who has fallen in love with and impregnated Connor. All of this backstory is essential to understand the sequel.

In *T2*, the adult John Connor sends the now-outdated Terminator model (T1)—which looks exactly like the one that tried to kill his mother (Schwarzenegger)—to 1995 to protect his 10-year-old, younger self (Furlong) from Skynet's newest attempt to change the timeline. This time Skynet sends its latest Terminator, the T-1000, which is a form of liquid metal that can bend and mimic almost anything equal to its mass. The shape it ends up preferring is a California law officer (Patrick). The film rolls along with the same cat-and-mouse movement as the original—even going as far as to end in a factory, the same as the first film.

Also like the original, the film begins with Schwarzenegger appearing from the future completely nude. To fit in, he must find clothes, so he goes to a bar where, after beating up most of the people inside, he dons a black leather outfit, iconic sunglasses, and steals a Harley Davidson Fat Boy model parked out front. In the process, he also takes a shotgun from the bar's proprietor. The entire scene pays homage to the original while dutifully ticking off standard features of American masculinity: muscled, unfeeling, unflinching, emotion-hiding, and "cool." While reworking and affirming the motorcycle cultural ethos established early in American cinema (*The Wild One*, 1950; *Easy Rider*, 1969), the T1's use is less the young teenager's or hippie's act of social rebellion and more a middle-aged man's act of defying convention (Schwarzenegger was 43 at the time of filming). The T1 is older, wiser, has less time for inconveniences, and chooses the ultimate American symbol of individualism and freedom. However, as an aging Boomer in a now squarely Gen Xer franchise, the T1's constant upstaging by the T2 deconstructs the original film's portrayal of the T1 as nearly invulnerable.

Overlapping this competition is the continuation of Sarah Connor's story from the original. In the sequel, she has been committed to a mental health facility because she bombed the offices and labs of Cyberdyne, the company that created Skynet. She did so while claiming she was preventing Judgment Day, the day Skynet starts a nuclear holocaust. Up until her committal, Sarah had traveled extensively, preparing herself and John for future resistance. A frightened waitress in the first film, Sarah is now a tough and violent soldier; the first the audience sees of her, she is doing chin-ups in her hospital tank top and pajama bottoms. There is hardly any traditional femininity left; she has toughened up, the film suggests, by becoming like a man to survive. After the T1 saves John from the T2, John orders it to help him save his mom. Being the survivalist that she is, she decides to break out after the FBI brings pictures of the T1 taken at the mall early in the day—thinking that it has returned to kill her and John. The T2 anticipates that John will try to get his mother, so it meets him there as he and the T1 meet up with Sarah in the middle of her escape attempt. She is, at first, hesitant to go with the T1. Shades of the previous film and her terror converge briefly but are dispelled as John convinces her it is safe. The three barely escape as the T2 chases them down.

They end up traveling to Mexico, where Sarah has a friend and a cache of weapons. While there, she has a dream/vision of Judgment Day and decides that if she can kill the scientist in charge of developing Skynet, she can change the future. Paradoxically, Skynet's computer was reverse engineered from technology gleaned from the pieces of the Terminator from the '80s. Thus, Sarah has to destroy these parts as well.

Paralleling the contrasting deconstruction between the original film's Terminator and the aged T1, Sarah's transformation from waitress to soldier is constantly reinforced as the traditional gender tropes are upended. In the scene where she sees the nuclear holocaust, she sees her former self-immolated on a playground just before her present self is destroyed. Elsewhere, she is shown competently handling a variety of firearms and skillfully disarming and fighting various opponents. The film goes to great lengths to show that she is as much an agent as the machines are. The only vestige of traditional womanhood she receives is her odd way of being a mother.

After leaving John with the T1 safe in Mexico, Sarah travels to the home of the scientist (Miles Dyson, played by African American actor Joe Morton) and tries to kill him. Unable to finish him off as he is struggling on the floor with his wife and daughter, John and the T1 come in as Sarah falls to the floor, weeping at nearly becoming a cold-blooded killer. Once bandaged up, Sarah and the T1 tell Dyson about the future he is responsible for, and they all decide that the research needs to be destroyed.

The four of them travel to Cyberdyne, plant explosives all around the lab, and steal the original T1's microprocessor and robotic arm. In the process, they manage to fight off SWAT teams, the entire police department, and, of course, the rampaging T2. After an escalating chase scene, the T2 ends up in vat of molten steel at a processing facility. The T1, having now become much more human, in a Pinocchio-like fashion, has John and Sarah destroy the Terminator parts from the lab and then requests that they lower him into the vat as well—out of fear that his parts may result in the same future. The T1's descent into the molten metal is emotionally fraught: Sarah has found some kind of friendship with the machine, and John has found a surrogate father. As he melts, he gives one last thumbs-up to them and to the audience.

The film ends similar to the original, with a continuous, moving shot of a highway from the first-person point of view. Sarah's voice intones that she now has a sense of hope because "if a machine, a Terminator, can learn the value of human life. Maybe we can, too."

Perhaps the T1, and maybe the audience, has learned the value of human life, but the value of parental relationships in the film are mostly dysfunctional, reflecting the societal shifts of the '80s and '90s. These shifts come to the fore in John, an ATM-hacking, dirt bike–driving, Guns N' Roses–listening 10-year-old. Though difficult to imagine a 10-year-old behaving the way the film depicts John, he is a site of uneasiness for Boomers and resistance for Gen Xers. Defying his stepparents and living a largely independent existence with his friend, John adapts quickly to the ever-changing situation he finds himself in, like the Gen X audience transitioning out of the Cold War context into something unknown, themselves negotiating the rising divorce rates at home and tectonic shifts in geopolitics.

In *T2*, Los Angeles has replaced New York as America's center of gravity. It is from California that the apocalypse unfolds, not the East Coast, "old money," Europe-leaning side of the country. Schwarzenegger's Austrian accent here coming from the worn down but still protective sidekick perhaps signals this change or the obsolescence of NATO alliances. If nuclear war occurs, it will not be from Russia but from our own making.

Benjamin Crace

See also: *Avatar*; *Titanic*.

Further Reading

Collis, Clark. 2017. "*Terminator 2: Judgment Day* 3D." *Entertainment Weekly*, no. 1480 (September): 34–35.

"James Cameron Says *Terminator 2* as 'Timely as It Ever Was.'" 2017. *TechLife News*, no. 303 (August): 162–165.

Jolin, Dan. 2019. "*Terminator 2: Judgment Day*." *Empire* (September): 46–47.

Lash, Jolie. 2021. "James Cameron Reveals How a Sting Song and Ecstasy Inspired Teenage John Connor in *Terminator 2*." *Entertainment Weekly* (July). https://ew.com/movies/james-cameron-sting-song-ecstasy-john-connor-terminator-2.

Telotte, J. P. 1992. "*The Terminator*, *Terminator 2*, & the Exposed Body." *Journal of Popular Film & Television* 20 (2): 26.

Willis, Sharon. 1997. "Combative Femininity: *Thelma and Louise* and *Terminator 2*." In *High Contrast: Race & Gender in Contemporary Hollywood Films*, Sharon Willis, 98–128. Durham, NC: Duke University Press.

Titanic

Release Date:	1997
Director:	James Cameron
Box Office:	$2.195 billion
Main Cast:	Rose Bukater, played by Kate Winslet
	Jack Dawson, played by Leonardo DiCaprio
	Caledon Hockley, played by Billy Zane
	Brock Lovett, played by Bill Paxton
	Margaret Brown, played by Kathy Bates

As one of the highest-grossing films of all time and winner of eleven Academy Awards (a record), *Titanic* had a massive impact on the global consciousness and on Generation X specifically. DiCaprio's (1974–) performance in the MTV-esque *Romeo and Juliet* the previous year solidified his place among the edgy, self-confident, Gen X actors of the '90s in sharp contrast to the earlier, disaffected antiheroes of the '80s, such as the Brat Pack. Jack Dawson's carefree, seize-the-day yet sensitive approach to responsive people is at once very American and a projected antidote to Gen X insecurity in the face of crisis and coming into adult responsibility. Many Gen X audience members had just finished high school, started college, or were beginning families of their own. Another doomed story of star-crossed lovers, framed by Rose's denouncing of class and privilege, had a wide appeal for a generation dedicated to being different from the Boomers before them. Nominated for an Academy Award for Best Actress, Winslet (1975–), too, was launched to stardom by *Titanic*, her place among A-listers confirmed. But it was not simply the love story that entranced audience members to sit through a 3½-hour-long film.

Cameron's obsession with detail and historicity that richly layers the film with complexity and facticity undoubtedly contributed to its Oscar wins in Cinematography, Best Picture, Visual Effects, and Best Director. Cameron's own exploration and filming of the wreck are artfully interwoven into a frame-story narrative, a story within a story in the class Chaucerian tradition. The primary frame tells the story of treasure hunter Brock Lovett, who, like Cameron in real life, chartered a Russian research vessel and submersibles to explore the wreckage, which was originally found by Robert Ballard in 1985. Such cooperation between an American expedition and a Russian salvage company signals a remarkable shift from the heavy, anti-Soviet rhetoric Gen Xers had been bombarded with throughout the '80s. This post-Soviet, scientific cooperative spirit is further telegraphed by the name of one of the submersibles: *Mir 2*, an allusion to the space station that served as a symbol of cooperation between the United States and Russia. However, beyond the names of the vessels (Cameron used the actual name *Keldysh* of the main research vessel), there is little if anything recognizably "Russian" in the film.

Lovett's main goal is to find the Heart of the Ocean, a gigantic, 56-carat, blue diamond purportedly worth more than the Hope Diamond. After recovering a safe from one of Titanic's staterooms, he opens it to find that the diamond is not there. Disappointed, his team begins the arduous task of cleaning the documents that were found in the safe. As they clean one, it reveals a nude portrait of a lady wearing the Heart of the Ocean as a necklace. Later, in a TV interview, Lovett shows this portrait, which an elderly woman and her granddaughter see from their home. The grandmother calls Lovett and arranges to get onboard the *Keldysh*.

At first, Lovett and his crew are skeptical about the elderly woman. She knew that the necklace in the picture was the Heart of the Ocean, which had not been previously released information. She then claims to be the woman wearing it in the picture: Rose Bukater.

With a little more acceptance, one member of the crew, Lewis Bodine (played by Lewis Abernathy), shows Rose a computer-generated animation of how the

Titanic sank, a prolepsis to the audience's upcoming experience. She quips, "Thank you for that fine forensic analysis, Mr. Bodine. But the experience of it was a bit different." This old woman still has all her faculties and is consequently established as a reliable narrator for the audience. Lovett then invites her to share the experience. She walks over to some monitors on the wall, showing images from the wreck, sits down, and with Lovett recording, begins her story.

For the majority of the film, the frame story is only lightly referenced, usually with voice-overs and/or dissolve/fades from the wreck to its 1912 counterpart or vice versa. Much time is spent establishing the size of the ship and, of course, the size and scope of the production too. Obviously intended to be seen in a cinema, there are only a few places where one can detect the use of CGI and miniatures. Such realism reflects a growing consciousness of and generational concern with authenticity. Originally a term associated with the philosophical school of existentialism, authenticity became one of the core values of Gen Xers, who would rather appear as social failures than as sellouts. Cameron's attention to minute details fed into this felt need of being assured that what was seen in the film was not Hollywood fake but as close to "real" as a representation could be. Anecdotes and legends surround the movie precisely on this point—even down to the china and silverware. Part of the selling point for its '90s audience was that watching the film was as close to being on the ship as humanly possible. This further accounts for the plethora of pan shots of the ship and tracking shots of characters moving through every conceivable compartment of the vessel.

As part of Old Rose's retelling, we see Jack and his Italian friend, Fabrizio, use their winnings from a poker game (a pair of tickets from two Swedes) to board the Titanic as it leaves its English port. The air is full of excitement, and hundreds of people are milling about—some passengers, some just people saying goodbye. Jack is going home, back to America, and Fabrizio is immigrating to the New World of opportunity. Juxtaposed to Jack and Fabrizio, Rose arrives in a cavalcade of early automobiles. She pretends to be blasé about the ship and its size, while her fiancé, Caldeon Hockley (Billy Zane), tries to convince her of its size and significance, saying, "God himself couldn't sink it." As members of the upper class, the nouveau riche, they have porters and others to help them board. Jack and Fabrizio, meanwhile, barely make it past the steward at the lower-class entrance, who demands to know if they had had the scurvy and lice health screenings. Lying, Jack claims, "Of course. Besides, we don't have any lice. We're Americans, both of us." As standard, Hollywood fare, American exceptionalism and pride in diversity exceed the class anxiety of the Old World and the British-owned White Star Line specifically—a theme that is reiterated throughout the film, with Irish immigrants and workers serving both actually and metonymically as the authentic embodiments of American class disdain. This not-so-subtle, quasi-Marxist jab at both British and American aristocracy (Rose and Cal are both from rich American families) is overshadowed, however, by the "classless" love of Rose and Jack. Yet there is also the appeal of the working man and self-reliance that comes through the film that granulates easy dichotomies. That the audience knows something about the Titanic, that some people survive, means that their emotional investment in these characters may yield some kind of cosmic (even if artificial) justification for their own anxiety about living authentically in the face of Fate. Further, Rose's stubborn refusal to live life as a "kept" woman among the elite, signaled by her insistence on surviving and avoiding Hockley later, balances Fate with American self-determinism—even for women, who, at the time the Titanic sank, couldn't even vote.

As both a historical subplot and appeal to female empowerment, Cameron includes the character of the "unsinkable" Molly Brown, a wealthy American woman played by Kathy Bates. In real life, Brown is known not only for surviving but also for pleading (unsuccessfully) with the crew of her lifeboat to turn back and save others. As a character in the film, Brown serves as a bridge between Jack's and Rose's worlds, providing Jack with a tuxedo to attend a formal dinner that endears him more deeply to Rose while simultaneously rubbing Jack's carefree life of individualism in the face of the refined aristocracy trapped in their golden cages.

In a classic scene of comeuppance, Jack, the plebian who does not even know how to use all the silverware at the table, becomes the center of admiration after overcoming his self-doubt (through some coaching by Brown). In generational terms, the "old" vanguards of tradition, embodied in the other dinner party guests, such as Rose's mother and Hockley, are flustered in their attempts to pigeonhole Jack as a poor nobody. Jack primarily accomplishes this through wit and humor. When Rose's mother rudely asks how accommodations are in steerage, Jack quips, "The best I've seen, ma'am, hardly any rats"—to uneasy but general laughter. The young Gen X actor holding his own against stuffy formalisms and snobbery by his quick wit further entrenches the Gen X value of authenticity; being true to one's self doesn't have to be drudgery and can also effect a mild form of social justice by changing another generation's consciousness of possibilities and living alternatives. The scene ends with Jack's earthy philosophy: "Life is a gift. . . . Make each day count." Caught up in the moment, they all toast: "To make it count." With the exception of Hockley and Rose's mother, Jack has charmed them all.

Much could be said and has been said about the social and racial distinctions made on the actual vessel and in the film. The poor immigrants are literally under the feet of the rich and wealthy. The latter are also clearly prioritized when it becomes time to launch the lifeboats—which there are too few of anyway—and some leave only partly filled, to give the wealthy more space. There are several scenes of the lower classes literally caged in, prevented from getting to the top decks, at gunpoint. Jack, of course, with the help of Rose and Fabrizio, crashes through the barriers, physically and symbolically. At about the halfway mark, the film shifts from love story to disaster flick along the lines of *The Poseidon Adventure* (1972). This shift initially foregrounds class consciousness and conflict. As the ship sinks, in stages, class distinctions collapse into a general mess of humans simply trying to survive as long as they can. In a somewhat cathartic way, the flooding of the fancy dining rooms and staterooms of the rich is a manifestation of the general American suspicion of others' wealth, obviously acquired through "sin" and crime, needing purgation. Here, however, the ship's builder, unlike Noah, dies with his boat.

In a larger, metaphysical sense, the sinking of the *Titanic* on film (the runtime of which is longer than it took the ship to sink) telegraphs the message that money and fame are useless in the face of disaster; what matters is nobility of character and faithfulness to "true" love. Juxtaposed along images of Rose and Jack surviving are a mother and her kids in a bed, resigned to their fate but still loving each other. In perhaps one of the most poignant shots and one that somewhat counterbalances the unlikelihood of Jack and Rose's quick romance, Cameron shows an elderly married couple spooning on a bed as the water rushes in underneath and around them. This is a picture of "till death do us part."

Somewhat problematically, the romance story at the heart of the film is only made plausible by Rose's long life and her subsequent faithfulness to sharing Jack's vision of the world and of her.

Nevertheless, the ending of the film confirms the deeper values of love and character. In a scene after Rose tells her story, Brock, talking with Lizzy, Rose's granddaughter, says that he never "got it." He "never let it in." As a purported treasure seeker/pirate (with the requisite earring), it is obvious that he means the story of humanity that the tragedy of *Titanic* is really about. In his relinquishment of finding the Heart of the Ocean and through hearing Rose's story, he is poised to be more authentic. Later, Old Rose sneaks to the stern of the ship and tosses the Heart of the Ocean, which was in the pocket of the coat that Hockley had given to her those many years ago, into the ocean. Like her, the audience is now aware that the valuable things in life are not jewels but people.

In the closing scene, Rose either dies or dreams (there is some debate) of reuniting with Jack onboard the *Titanic*. In a scene that recalls theatrical productions that include all the cast bowing, the audience sees many of the people who died on the ship alive and well. What is significant in terms of the generational apparatus of interpretation is that she returns to her Gen X age in the afterlife, thereby confirming for the audience that the present young generation of 1997 and its mantra—"Make it count"—are the most significant and important.

Benjamin Crace

See also: *Avatar*; *Terminator 2: Judgment Day*.

Further Reading

Davis, Todd F., and Kenneth Womack. 2001. "Narrating the Ship of Dreams." *Journal of Popular Film & Television* 29 (1): 42.

Hurley, James S. 2001. "*Titanic* Allegories: The Blockbuster as Art Film." *Strategies: Journal of Theory, Culture & Politics* 14 (1): 91.

Kramer, Peter. 1998. "Women First: *Titanic* (1997), Action-Adventure Films and Hollywood's Female Audience." *Historical Journal of Film, Radio & Television* 18 (4): 599.

Masters, Kim. 2012. "*Titanic*'s Rough Seas: 'Glub, Glub, Glub.'" *Hollywood Reporter* 418 (13): 36–39.

Rushing, Janice Hocker, and Thomas S. Frentz. 2000. "Singing over the Bones: James Cameron's *Titanic*." *Critical Studies in Media Communication* 17 (1): 1.

Top Gun

Release Date:	1986
Director:	Tony Scott
Box Office:	$356.8 million
Main Cast:	Maverick, played by Tom Cruise
	Charlie/Charlotte, played by Kelly McGillis
	Ice, played by Val Kilmer
	Goose, played by Anthony Edwards
	Viper, played by Tom Skerritt

Released three years before the fall of the Berlin Wall, *Top Gun* is bathed in Cold War awareness. The Soviets are out there flying MiGs and replenishing the need for the U.S. Navy to recruit top pilots for an elite program to protect American interests all over the world. Roughly overlapping with and based on the actual navy program, the film uses real jets on loan from the navy as well as shots taken from the aircraft carrier, USS *Enterprise*. With its high production values and relatively positive, testosterone-driven representation of the U.S. military, *Top Gun* fits somewhere between propaganda and a recruitment film with a love story and bromance glaze.

The film begins on an aircraft carrier in the Indian Ocean. The alarm is raised, and the jets are scrambled. Maverick and his copilot, Goose, take off to support Cougar (John Stockwell) and Merlin (Tim Robbins). Together, they scare off the Soviet jets but not before Cougar has a panic attack and Maverick has to coach him back to the ship. Cougar's panic attack grounds him, and Maverick and Goose are slated to take his and Merlin's place in the Top Gun program. Even this early in the film, it is clear that the pilot/copilot relationship—especially that of Maverick and Goose—is a type of marriage. There is deep care and concern in and out of the cockpit. Early, too, the dynamic of the Boomer as authority and the Gen Xer as rebel is established. Stinger, the commander of the aircraft carrier, is played by James Tolkan, whose performance in *Back to the Future* just the previous year as the ageless, bald high school principal established him, if not typecast him, as someone to cast in the role of reprimanding the older cohort of Gen Xers. Later, the officer in charge of the Top Gun program, Viper (Boomer Tom Skerritt), takes on a similar role as father/mentor/commander to the young hotshot pilot couples.

While the pilots are introduced to the program, the audience learns that there is a competition during the training, and the winner will be part of the best of the best. Maverick makes it known that he is going to win, to the chagrin of Goose and the smiles of the other pilots. Later that same day, the pilots go to a navy bar to blow steam and meet women. It is here that Ice (Kilmer) and Slider (Rick Rossovich) try to intimidate Goose and Maverick. Here, too, Maverick puts the moves on Charlie (McGillis) on a bet from Goose that he cannot have sex with her in the immediate vicinity that night. Following her into the bathroom, he fails to make any headway with her, but as she leaves, she lies to a crestfallen Goose that

Maverick was fantastic. At this point in the film, neither Goose nor Maverick nor the audience knows that she is actually a consultant for the Top Gun program, and, although she does not actually have a rank higher than Maverick, he is expected to listen to her as an officer. Despite the agency given to her character (and the painful fact that McGillis was raped in 1982), the film makes clear she can only resist Maverick's egotistical, boyish charm for so long before having sex with him.

The next day, it is revealed to an astonished Maverick, during a Top Gun briefing, that Charlie is the consultant. Since Maverick has had an up close encounter with a Soviet MiG, he is immediately of interest to Charlie, who, as an academic and military consultant, wants to gather as much information as she can about the enemy. And, of course, she is attracted to Maverick sexually. After the lesson/briefing, the pilots practice air-to-air combat and Maverick, as the name indicates, breaks the program's rules to take out one of the instructors. He then does an illicit flyby of the air traffic control tower. Both actions send him and Goose straight to Viper's office, where they are chewed out (again, by a Boomer) and warned to follow protocol. Goose, too, is bewildered by Maverick and, like a spouse, endearingly shares his concerns about the negative consequences that await him and his family if he washes out of the program due to Maverick's recklessness. Goose also observes that Maverick seems to be flying against his dead father's ghost, trying to best his old man. Again, the Boomer/Xer generational conflict fuels the plot.

In a classroom scene, Charlie clandestinely gives Maverick her address and a rendezvous time on one of his papers. The scene then shifts to the classic, albeit cheesy, sand volleyball game between Goose/Maverick and Ice/Slider. Here the typical "male gaze" of films used to objectify women is turned around: three of the four characters are topless, sweaty and flexing for the camera. Maverick pulls on a white shirt and hops on his motorcycle to speed off to his date with Charlie.

The dinner scene at Charlie's rental mainly functions to increase sexual tension and give more of the backstory of Maverick's father. At one point, as they sit around drinking wine, the song "Sitting on the Dock of the Bay" plays, and Maverick comments on how much his mother liked the song, again, signaling his early Gen X credentials. He also talks about how his dad's disappearance and death in 1965 during Vietnam was hushed up and he never learned what really happened. After these few vulnerable moments of nostalgia, Maverick gets back onto his bike and speeds off. Aside from the visual chemistry between Charlie and Maverick, the classic song "Take My Breath Away" plays nondiegetically to underscore the growing attraction and love.

In another classroom scene, Charlie upbraids Maverick and rebukes him openly in front of the other pilots for flying recklessly—even though it all worked out. Petulantly angry, he rides off with her chasing him in her convertible. He pulls over and confronts her on the side of the road. She explains to him that she has to be mean to him in front of the others so the others cannot guess that she has fallen for him. They go back to her house and make love to "Take My Breath Away."

The next day, the pilots go out for another fighting simulation, during which Maverick gets beaten because he once again does things his own way. Ice asks him, "Whose side are you on anyway?" After the training, Maverick and Goose hang out in a bar with Goose's wife, Goose's son, and Charlie. Clearly Maverick is genuinely a part of the family and his and Goose's relationship includes simple things such as singing together at a piano. However, this is not to last.

With only two weeks left in the competition/training, they all go out again for more combat simulation. This time, however, Maverick pilots the plane into a situation that changes quickly, causing the plane to spin. He and Goose have to eject, but Goose ejects into the glass canopy, breaking his neck and killing him. As he floats in the ocean with Goose's body held tightly, the Coast Guard comes in with a helicopter and the rescuer tells Maverick, "You gotta to let him go, sir." This line, at the moment practical advice, is later repeated by Viper to pull Maverick out of his psychological spin over Goose's death. It also applies to Maverick's wrestling with his father's ghost. The messaging here extends beyond planes and pilots: Gen Xers have to forge their own path as individuals apart from family legacy and peer attachments.

Maverick's struggle to come to terms with Goose's death involves attending a military tribunal, where he is officially cleared of any wrongdoing, comforting Goose's widow and son, and, finally, quitting the Top Gun program. As he sits in a bar contemplating, Charlie finds him and says, "I'm too late. You already left and haven't learned a d— thing except to quit. You got that maneuver down real well. So long, Pete Mitchell." Here masculinity is reconceived as to not quit rather than dealing with one's emotions, to power through instead of taking time. If his and Goose's relationship fit the typical mold of the Boomer generation, such mourning would indeed seem out of place and quitting, a weak move. Yet in Gen X terms, in which friendship and family are coterminous, losing Goose and then dropping out of the program make sense in the face of the magnitude of the loss. But the film does not allow such "wallowing." He must man up and Boomer through, fulfilling the expectations of his Boomer commanders.

This journey into living out the values of the Boomers rather than his intrinsic project of self is underscored by Maverick finally learning about his father from Viper. He learns that his dad went down bravely, saving others and taking down enemies. This narrative pivoting away from Maverick the rebel to Maverick the scion of Navy pilots makes more sense when one imagines the film as approved by the military-industrial complex run largely by Boomers and their predecessors. *Top Gun*, in many ways, seeks to reconstruct a positive relationship between potential Gen X recruits and the U.S. military. Earlier war films, such as *Apocalypse Now* (1979), and later ones, such as *Platoon* (just a few months after *Top Gun* in 1986) and *Full Metal Jacket* (1987), wrestled with the moral ambiguity of U.S. involvement in Vietnam and as a global police force in general. If anything, these are anti-war war films. Here, however, Maverick's father is a war hero in the World War II–mode of fighter pilot and Maverick himself, a Gen Xer, is primed to take up his mantle.

After missing his Top Gun graduation ceremony, Maverick shows up to the after-party and gets orders to go back to the carrier where he was at the beginning of the film. In a recapitulation of the opening of the film, Maverick defeats his grief, his father's legacy, his own recklessness, and the Soviets to save Ice and the day. Back on the carrier after the mission, they are lauded as heroes, and Maverick gets the appointment of his choice. He, unsurprisingly, chooses to teach at Top Gun.

The final scene of the film has Maverick sitting in the same bar at the Top Gun base with his instructor's hat. He hears "You've Lost that Loving Feeling" (a song he had used earlier in the film to flirt with Charlie) playing on the jukebox and goes to inspect it. He turns around, Charlie is there, and they hold each other. The final shot is of two jets flying into the sunset to Kenny Loggins's "Danger Zone," the theme song of the movie. This final frame thereby seals the film as a revamped type of Western, with the good guys/cowboys ("maverick," is, after all, a cowboy term for a separated calf) as the U.S. military and the bad guys, the Soviets.

Despite being largely propaganda, *Top Gun* endures because it is a non–Vietnam War film for Gen Xers without an actual war. The "war" is between generational expectations and one's own sense of destiny and purpose. This war is fought relationally and communally. And, although at first glance it seems as though Boomer values of self-reliance and conservative conformity upend Gen X's value of autonomy from expectations, Maverick's advancement is really a result of peer-to-peer cooperation rather than of falling in line with Boomer orders. Two scenes in the final sequence are worth revisiting. When they return to the flight deck, Ice and Maverick banter as genuine equals, recognizing in each other friendship, rivalry, and professionalism. Surrounding them are all the other sailors, cheering them on. There is not a Boomer in sight; they are all in the control tower looking on. This recognition by peers resonates deeply within the Gen X psyche. Another short scene shows Stinger meeting Maverick in the locker room to talk to him about his fame and choice of job appointment. This is telling. The commander comes down from his office to meet the hero in his space; Maverick will be taking the reins of his own destiny and not just following orders from a fading (and balding) generation.

Benjamin Crace

See also: *Independence Day*; *Iron Man*.

Further Reading

Conlon, James. 1990. "Making Love, Not War." *Journal of Popular Film & Television* 18 (1): 18.

Modleski, Tania. 2007. "Misogynist Films: Teaching *Top Gun*." *Cinema Journal* 47 (1): 101–105.

Nashawaty, Chris. 2011. "How Does *Top Gun* Fly Today?" *Entertainment Weekly*, no. 1170 (September): 62.

Nelson, Elissa. 2013. "Beneath the Surface and the Excess: An Examination of Critical and Aesthetic Attacks on Films of the 1980s." *Journal of Popular Culture* 46 (5): 1029–1050.

Parker, Richard D. 2005. "The Armed Forces Need Another *Top Gun*." *U.S. Naval Institute Proceedings* 131 (12): 58.

Toy Story

Release Date:	1995
Director:	John Lasseter
Box Office:	$373 million
Main Cast (Voices):	Woody, played by Tom Hanks
	Buzz Lightyear, played by Tim Allen
	Rex, played by Wallace Shawn
	Hamm, played by John Ratzenberger
	Andy, played by John Morris

When released in the fall of 1995, *Toy Story* roughly coincided with the end of adolescence for the bulk of Gen Xers. And if not the end, for some, 1995 was the beginning of the transition from carefree childhood to the social pressures of peers (Randy Newman's "Strange Things Are Happening to Me" is acutely appropriate for puberty). The film's success, and its subsequent sequels, largely hinges on its tapping into of intergenerational commercial nostalgia, with a layer of animated spectacle for young Millennials.

For the Boomers, Pixar re-creates a sense of childhood colored by the Western genre, nursery rhymes, and exaggerated musical vocals. Woody, the cowboy doll, voiced by Tom Hanks, has a pull string that plays colorful phrases such as "There's a snake in my boot." He also has a detachable cowboy hat, handkerchief around the neck, and a vest. And he's a sheriff. Both Woody's facial features and outfit recall the Howdy Doody ventriloquist doll made famous on the *Howdy Doody Show* (1947–1960). The fact that Woody "talks," because of his pull string apparatus and as part of the film's secret life of toys plot, further accentuates the Howdy Doody overtones. Woody's love interest is a Little Bo-Peep (Annie Potts) toy who often speaks in innuendo to Woody and, later, to Buzz. One wonders why a rambunctious six-year-old boy in 1995 might have a ceramic or plastic doll of Little Bo-Peep; perhaps it was passed down from his parents. In any event, Bo-Peep and Woody serve as parents of a sort to the other toys in Andy's room, further underlining their Boomer-like status. On top of all this, Randy Newman's scratchy and distinctive singing style is reminiscent of the old gramophone recordings. His lyrics, too, are sappy and a little too on point, lacking the self-conscious irony of other '90s pop music but fully in line with the jaunty and sincere songs of the late '40s and '50s.

For the Gen Xers, *Toy Story* seeks to generate a patinaed nostalgia out of contemporary consumerism and popular culture. Pretending Nintendo's Game Boy (1989) or its Entertainment System (1983) had never been released, Andy's toy collection is littered with toys that predate those of any six-year-old of that era. There is an Etch A Sketch, first released in 1960, a Mr. Potato Head (1952), a slinky dog, based on the original Slinky (1942), and plastic toy soldiers, first sold in 1938. In the background on Andy's shelves, one sees both the *Candy Land* (1949) and *Battleship* (1967) board games. In short, many of Andy's toy "choices" are Boomer hand-me-downs. Many but not all. He also has a remote-control car.

There is a large, plastic tyrannosaurus rex dinosaur toy that is oddly coincidental with the 1993 blockbuster, *Jurassic Park*. And, of course, Buzz Lightyear of Space Command, whose backstory has him locked in an eternal struggle with an alien warlord named Zurg, is a thinly veiled reference to the Star Wars franchise. But an even more revealing reading of the film as an attempt to socialize Gen Xers more deeply into the Pixar animated universe is the casting.

All the main voices in the *Toy Story* universe are the voices of well-established '80s and early '90s television and film stars. Hanks's lovable and long-running older brother persona began with *Bosom Buddies* (1980–1982), moved through *Splash* (1984) and *Big* (1988), and climaxed with *Forrest Gump*, released just one year before *Toy Story*. Tim Allen, the voice of Buzz, had just hit widespread stardom with his family sitcom *Home Improvement* (1991–1999). John Ratzenberger, Cliff from the iconic series *Cheers* (1982–1993), voices Hamm, a toy pig. Others such as Jim Varney, Annie Potts, Laurie Metcalf, and Don Rickles round out the voices for the main set of toys. These are the voices of every Gen Xer's childhood and adolescence, regardless of their toy avatars.

The main theme and plot of the film are change. Andy's family is moving from one house to another. Andy's birthday adds another (disruptive) toy to the mix. Woody has to navigate sharing influence with Buzz and losing Andy's attention. In short, it is about growing and growing up, but it is mainly told through the plot device of living toy characters who also follow a toy code of sorts to become lifeless around humans. This in itself plays on every child's suspicion that toys have their own secret life, that they do things when no one is looking (This formula gets applied to pets in *The Secret Life of Pets*, 2016). This plot device sets the boundaries and parameters that enhance the dramatic irony of the film; the audience knows the toys have this life, but none of the humans in the film has any idea of what is going on. Part of the film's appeal is precisely in this sharing of a secret quality and the tension generated by the possibility of its being discovered. It also allows for the uncanny to break through. In one particular scene, Sid, the quintessential angsty Gen X teen next door, gets his comeuppance when the toys he has abused and destroyed for fun come to life in front of him, rattling him to his core. Thus this secret life is also a type of supernatural power.

Within this world of toys, Woody is the top dog until Buzz Lightyear (a space explorer toy) comes in. With Buzz comes a host of changes. Andy's room is no longer filled with cowboy-themed decorations and drawings of Woody's adventure but has transitioned to space-themed bedclothes and the like. Woody's interpersonal relationships are also reconfigured, as his jealousy marginalizes him in view of the other toys. What makes his loss of status even worse is that Buzz does not know that he is actually a toy, but, instead, believes that he is on an alien planet and must get back on mission. This makes Woody doubly frustrated since Buzz supplants him without even trying. The reality of this sets in when Buzz shows everyone that Andy has claimed him by writing his name on the bottom of his foot, just as he had done with Woody. Most of this action takes place in Andy's room or house.

After a trip to a spaceport-themed pizzeria/arcade, Buzz and Woody end up at Sid's house. Sid, as aforementioned, is notorious among Andy's toys as the teen who tortures and blows up other toys. They have seen him doing so in his backyard through their window. In many aspects, Buzz and Woody's sojourn at Sid's is akin to the mythical descent into the underworld where the hero must come to terms with life and mortality. For Buzz, he discovers that he is indeed just another toy. Woody learns empathy, both for Buzz and the other surviving, mismatched toys in Sid's room that ultimately help them escape. In generational terms, Sid's room aligns with the Gen Xer "shadow" side, that not-so-innocent, marginal awareness of the darkness adulthood brings. Black T-shirt–wearing, black light–using, metal-listening Sid recalls Sid Vicious of the Sex Pistols. At one point, one can see a Megadork band poster, a joke on Megadeath, the heavy metal band.

Sid's favorite pastime is torturing and destroying toys with explosives. At one point, he nearly quotes at length the dialogue from *Star Wars: A New Hope* to Buzz and Woody, where Darth Vader is questioning Princess Leia about the rebel base just before threatening her. This allusion thus frames Sid as Darth Vader himself, a master of the Dark Side. But it is not just Sid and his room that are the dark side in contrast to Andy's well-lit, innocent bedroom. The misfit toys that appear to help Woody and Buzz escape are equally terrifying in their grotesqueness and inability to talk. They are the products of Sid's experiments and are full of psychological potential—Freudian and otherwise.

After reversing the terror back on Sid, a chastened Woody and Buzz, now friends, race off to catch the moving van as it pulls out of Andy's drive. Woody manages to get the RC car out of the back and go back for Buzz, who has fallen behind. The other toys come out of the boxes and, still believing Woody to be at odds with Buzz, push him out. Woody and Buzz then climb onto the RC car, light the rocket Sid had attached to Buzz, and fly past the moving van, dropping deftly into the special box in the back seat of the car where Andy and his mother are leading the van. Andy is surprised that they are there, but his mother says, "See? Right where you left them," in typical mother fashion.

The closing scene takes place several months later, during Christmas. Like the birthday party that began the movie, the toys are all on edge about what new toys will be brought into their world. Through a soldier reporting via a baby monitor, the toys learn that Andy has received a Mrs. Potato Head, much to Mr. Potato Head's elation. This signals the sexual awakening of late adolescence, as does Bo-Peep kissing Woody under some mistletoe. The toys are growing up and starting romantic relationships. The film ends with the announcement that Andy has received a puppy—the toys' worst nightmare. It is significant that Buzz remains unattached romantically but grounded with the other toys as peers, since, for Gen Xers, potentiality, options, and friends are prioritized over and above the romance-to-nuclear family expectation of the Boomers.

The juxtaposing of the cowboy and the spaceman serves as a cipher for the Boomer to Gen X transition that was necessary for Pixar to solidify its place in the Disney empire. In a sense, then, Woody is old Disney, old fashioned and a bit out of date. He is an homage to the world Disney created for generations. Buzz, though, is the new, the technological. The high-quality computer-generated graphics Pixar innovated clearly surpassed earlier Disney animation. Poised as the then contemporary generation's "new" Disney, Pixar scored big with Gen Xers and earned Disney millions. Its high production values also appealed to upcoming Millennials and continues to attract them and the latest generational cohort, Generation Z.

Aside from all the generational work *Toy Story* accomplishes for its audiences, it is thoroughly American. Woody, the cowboy, reaches back to American Manifest Destiny, to explore in freedom. Buzz, the spaceman, reaches to America's future in outer space, the ultimate zone of freedom and possibility. American masculinity and individualism coalesce in both characters as friendship develops through competition for the respect and attention for others. The need to lead shared by Buzz and Woody is the very shape of the American alpha male. Beyond the frame of the film, the actual toys created, marketed, and sold concretizes the tight relationship between the toy industry and Hollywood within global capitalism. Merchandising, while not invented by Americans, certainly has paid off.

Benjamin Crace

See also: Forrest Gump; *Shrek*.

Further Reading

Crewe, Dave. 2019. "Cinema Science: Playing with Physics in the *Toy Story* Universe." *Education*, no. 96 (August): 38–44.

Hall, Lucia K. B. 2000. "Toy Stories for Humanists?" *Humanist* 60 (2): 38.

Meinel, Dietmar. 2016. *Pixar's America: The Re-Animation of American Myths and Symbols*. Cham, Switzerland: Palgrave Macmillan.

Scott, Ellen. 2014. "Agony and Avoidance: Pixar, Deniability, and the Adult Spectator." *Journal of Popular Film & Television* 42 (3): 150–162.

Wooden, Shannon R., and Ken Gillam. 2014. *Pixar's Boy Stories: Masculinity in a Postmodern Age*. Lanham, MD: Rowman & Littlefield.

4

Millennials and the American Myth Machine (1999–2009)

Avatar

Release Date:	2009
Director:	James Cameron
Box Office:	$2.79 billion
Main Cast:	Jake Sully, played by Sam Worthington
	Neytiri, played by Zoe Saldana
	Grace, played by Sigourney Weaver
	Colonel Miles Quaritch, played by Stephen Lang
	Norm Spellman, played by Joel David Moore
	Parker Selfridge, played by Giovanni Ribisi

Avatar is to Millennials what *Titanic* was to Gen Xers, an immersion into another world. But this time, it is not the world of the past but the world of the future. It does not take place on Earth, but out there, in outer space, on the appropriately named planet of Pandora. But like Cameron's *Titanic*, the film is as much about special effects and spectacle as it is story. The characters, like the audience, are absorbed by the epic scope of events and setting. For a generation raised in the digital world with their carefully curated social personas, the very idea of an avatar that interacts in one world while the other self is in another is almost second nature. But beyond this, through cutting-edge motion-capture techniques and 3D, the film itself provides an opportunity to become an avatar, a participant in another reality—a reality that films always invite the viewer into but not as blatantly as *Avatar* does. In a word: it is a world, not a film. In fact, after its release, there were reports that some viewers, once wrenched out of the fictitious world, were reeling with depression and even suicidal thoughts. The phenomenon came to be known as the "*Avatar* blues" and demonstrates the unprecedented power of this film.

The film centers on Jake Sully, a mobility-challenged, combat-wounded marine who is invited to take part in an ongoing experiment on Pandora. His twin, who had originally been slated to undertake the five-year, sleep-your-way-there journey through space, had been killed. The brother had been a part of the avatar program in which scientists linked one person's consciousness with an artificially created alien body that matched the Indigenous population of Pandora, the Na'vi. Since the avatar bodies were coded to a scientist's genetic code, the only other person who could be a part of the program was Jake. So he takes the place of his brother but is vastly underqualified to be a part of a team of scientists that study the Na'vi and the planet itself.

But the scientists themselves have a tenuous relationship with the mining company that sponsors their work. Ultimately, the company wants the Indigenous people out of the way so they can get to the unobtanium, the most expensive mineral in the galaxy ($20 million a kilo). For PR reasons (or as Selfridge, the company boss says, "Killing the indigenous looks bad. Find a carrot and get them to move"), the company wants to do this as humanely as possible, but if that does not work, they are ready to strong-arm their way to the natural resource using the ex-military mercenaries who provide security for the home base. At first, Jake, as a marine, is approached by the colonel in charge and tasked with humoring the scientists long enough to infiltrate the Na'vi and report back weaknesses and other vital intel. The colonel sweetens the op by promising to get Jake's legs repaired. Jake naïvely accepts the assignment.

The tension between the military-industrial complex and the scientists is scaled up in terms of humans versus the planet. Not only is the Indigenous race hostile but the air is also unbreathable, killing an unaided person in four minutes. Outside of the compound, the flora and fauna are also alien and deadly. It is a hostile world until Jake discovers its wonders through his avatar and through his relationship with the Na'vi princess, Neytiri.

At 2 hours and 42 minutes, much of the film is spectacle as the audience accompanies Jake on his journey from his wheelchair to the pod where the link to the avatar body is made, to the exploration of that body, and to the exhilarating exploration of Pandora and its people. After a while, the audience feels much the same way Jake does: the cold, sterile world of greedy humans on base is very dull and uninteresting compared to the rich environment and community of the Na'vi. As it is a completely alien world, it is hard to capture the essence of the film with mere descriptions of the intricately detailed trees, flowers, rivers, and animals.

But below the spectacle, there is a recognizable undercurrent here in terms of cinematic and American history. Akin to other films such as *Little Big Man* (1970) and *Dances with Wolves* (1990), *Avatar* takes its place as a critique of Western imperialism through the character journey of a white, establishment male "going native." The tale itself is ageless but recurs in the American mythos of white engagement with Native American populations. Here, too, the Na'vi are typified "savages": they wear little to no clothing, have bow-and-arrow-level technology, live in a tree, are close to the land, and are at one with their god/Nature, Eywa. And, of course, they are near defenseless against the marauding invaders.

Yet with the help of others in the avatar program, Grace (Weaver) and Norm (Joe David Moore), Jake is able to get close to the tribe. After being assigned to Jake as a teacher by her father, the chief, Neytiri trains Jake. In the process, he falls in love and loses his sense of connection to the other humans on the planet and his covert mission. Several crosscut scenes show this evolution taking place as he spends more and more time in his avatar body with the Na'vi than he does in his own in conversation with the colonel and others. Ultimately, he becomes part of the tribe and mates with Neytiri.

Things head south once Selfridge, a young and headstrong corporate ladder climber, decides to move in with bulldozers. Jake, in his avatar body, attacks one of the dozers, forcing the colonel to literally pull the plug on the avatar program. After disconnecting Jake and the others from their avatar bodies, there is a heated conversation and Jake says, "This is how it's done. When people are sitting on s—that you want, you make them your enemy. Then you're justified in taking it." Selfridge then gives Jake one hour to go back and convince the tribe to leave Home Tree because the largest deposit of unobtanium is directly below it.

In his avatar, Jake returns to the tribe and tries to convince them to leave. He reveals that that was his mission all along and tries to get to them to understand that he has changed in the process and is one of them. It is useless; the tribe decides to fight and stand their ground, much to Jake's dismay. The colonel and gunships show up, gas out the Na'vi, and then blow up the base of Home Tree, felling it as terrified Na'vi run away or are crushed. In the meantime, Jake and Grace have been tied up, but Neytiri's mother and tribal shaman, Mo'at, cuts them loose to help. Jake finds Neytiri standing over her dying father, and she tells Jake to leave and never come back. About the same time, the colonel again cuts the link between the team and their avatars and puts them all in the base's brig.

Later, a sympathetic pilot, Trudy (Michelle Rodriguez) breaks them free and helps them relocate an alternate lab with the equipment necessary to link to the avatars way off in the woods. In the process, Grace winds up shot in the gut by the colonel. Jake believes that the Na'vi can help, but he is on the outs with them ever since the Home Tree debacle. Then, remembering a legend Neytiri had told him of her ancestor riding the great Toruk (the largest flying, dragon-like predator on the planet) to unite the tribes by gaining their respect, he decides to follow suit and manages to ride the creature. Landing in the midst of the lamenting people, Jake is reconciled to the tribe and talks them into helping Grace. The Na'vi takes her to the Tree of Souls to do a soul transfer ritual between her dying human body and her avatar body; it fails and Grace passes away.

Jake and the new chief, Tse, agree to call all the tribes of the Na'vi and rally them with the Toruk against the humans (Sky People, as the Na'vi call them). In one telling moment, Jake, alone, prays to Eywa for help and transfers his memories of Earth through his neural organ, which resembles a ponytail, to the Tree of Souls. Not only has he become one of the tribe but he has fully adopted (albeit hesitantly and haltingly) their religion.

The rallying is successful, and there is an epic battle between the Sky People and the Na'vi. At one moment, it begins to look like the Na'vi are going to lose, but, in answer to Jake's prayer, Pandora's creatures join in the effort and beat back the attackers. After the colonel nearly kills Jake with his oversize robotic suit and exposes Jake's human body to the atmosphere, Neytiri spears the colonel to death. She then races to save Jake the human, getting an oxygen mask on him just in time.

The Na'vi and some of the sympathetic humans oversee the humiliating evacuation of the mining base. Jake posts one last video blog of his experience, signs off, and then goes to the Tree of Souls, where his soul is transferred to his avatar body. He has become fully "native." When the transfer is complete, he wakes up as a full Na'vi, and the film ends with his eyes opening, cut to black.

Post 9/11, Millennials have distanced themselves from a strong sense of patriotism and imperialism, attitudes that led to the disaster in the first place. This is explored in the film through the near-complete demonization of the military as nothing more than a tool of greedy corporations that fuel capitalism at the cost of environmental and cultural degradation. Unlike Gen Xer films such as *Top Gun*, there is no romanticizing of soldiering here. Both the military and the corporate world are thoroughly corrupt and even genocidal. The only options are to leave it (as Jake and Trudy do) or force them to leave. It is telling that the colonel is played by a Boomer (Lang was born in 1952) and Selfridge, a Gen Xer (Ribisi was born in 1973). Worthington's performance as a wide eyed, somewhat naïve and wonder-filled character (the actor was born in 1976) is, on camera without his avatar, much shorter in his wheelchair than the "adults." This effectively renders him much younger than his actual age suggests and more identifiable with Millennials in conflict with the preceding generations' obsessions with career success and military might/American status as a superpower.

But it is not just *Avatar*'s deconstruction of military service that resonates with Millennials; its nature mysticism is equally alluring. Having moved past the religious cynicism and nihilism of their Gen X parents and the perhaps naïve nominalism of their grandparents, Millennials seek authentic experience with the divine that also connects them with others. In short, deep interconnectedness *is* divine. This is nowhere more evident than in the religion of the Na'vi. They connect, literally, to trees, animals, and each other. Sure, Grace provides some scientific explication for this electrobiological network that frames it in a scientific register, but that merely makes the suprapersonal world of the Na'vi seem less foreign and more palatable to less postmodern Gen X and Boomer viewers. Through this web of interconnected spirituality, *Avatar* offers a less individualistic version of the American Dream that depended on the exploitation and rejection of others. On the contrary, the Millennial dream for justice, social engagement, and community as well as ecological stability can be had when we fully embrace a deep pluralism and reject the mechanistic materialism that drives those demonic engines.

Avatar thus serves as a type of high-water mark for the encoding of Millennial values into a cinematic text. And yet it, too, is part of the Hollywood machine that exists primarily for commercial reasons. The experience of Pandora for Millennials viscerally enacts their values, but in the cold light outside of the cinema, disillusionment sets in, possibly contributing to the *Avatar* blues or to the rise in popularity of independent films and streaming services among that generational cohort. Spectacle works, but for a generation seeking more than artifice, it does not suffice.

Benjamin Crace

See also: *Alien*; *Terminator 2: Judgment Day*; *Titanic*.

Further Reading

Benitez, Jorge, and Matt Wallin. 2011. "Rethinking the Silver Screen: Science, Film, and Art after *Avatar*." *International Journal of Science in Society* 2 (3): 45–54.

Dunn, George A. 2014. Avatar *and Philosophy: Learning to See*. Malden, MA: Wiley-Blackwell.

Erb, Cynthia. 2014. "A Spiritual Blockbuster: *Avatar*, Environmentalism, and the New Religions." *Journal of Film & Video* 66 (3): 3–17.

Holtmeier, Matthew. 2010. "Post-Pandoran Depression or Na'vi Sympathy: *Avatar*, Affect, and Audience Reception." *Journal for the Study of Religion, Nature & Culture* 4 (4): 414–424.

Klassen, Chris. 2012. "*Avatar*, Dark Green Religion, and the Technological Construction of Nature." *Cultural Studies Review* 18 (2): 74–88.

Nesbitt, Jennifer P. 2016. "Deactivating Feminism: Sigourney Weaver, James Cameron, and *Avatar*." *Film & History* 46 (1): 21–32.

Ødemark, John. 2015. "*Avatar* in the Amazon: Narratives of Cultural Conversion and Environmental Salvation between Cultural Theory and Popular Culture." *Culture Unbound: Journal of Current Cultural Research* 7 (May): 455–478.

The Dark Knight

Release Date:	2008
Director:	Christopher Nolan
Box Office:	$1.005 billion
Main Cast:	Batman/Bruce Wayne, played by Christian Bale
	Alfred, played by Michael Caine
	Joker, played by Heath Ledger
	Rachel, played by Maggie Gyllenhaal
	Harvey Dent/Two-Face, played by Aaron Eckhart

As the second in Nolan's rather confusingly labeled Batman trilogy (*Batman Begins*, 2005; *The Dark Knight*, 2008; and *The Dark Knight Rises*, 2012), *The Dark Knight* is, perhaps, the one of the three that can stand by itself. Like other Batman films, its in medias res beginning seems appropriate even if the viewer did not see Nolan's first film. Further, due to Heath Ledger's tragic death months after the release of the film, his performance as Joker gave it an added layer of attention that it might not otherwise have received. The significance of Ledger's death and now legendary performance underscores the blurring of art and life and meaning. For Millennials, a significant star was lost young, and his final legacy as a psychotic anarchist in a film that radically questioned the status quo, consensus narrative of modern America hit home and hit hard.

Ultimately, like much of its Millennial audience, *The Dark Knight* is concerned with identity. Batman is also Bruce Wayne. Harvey Dent, the district attorney and public crusader against organized crime becomes Two Face, a villain. Joker is without a past, and the few bits of his backstory he does give contradict and are unreliable. Rachel loves two men, both Wayne and Dent, and must put on another persona when she is around either. Alfred, Wayne's "butler," is at once staff but also a father figure and aged-out warrior. Lucius Fox (Morgan Freeman) is both Wayne's business manager at Wayne Enterprises but also his tech and equipment guru, helping Batman stay one step ahead of the criminals and the law. An additional layer of complexity in terms of identity is the fact that most of the cast are not just playing a character but are also hiding their national identities: Both Bale and Gary Oldman (who plays Commissioner Gordon) are English, and Ledger is from Australia. All three homogenize their accents to be "neutrally" American. Only Caine, perhaps due to his long career, is allowed to keep his British twang. Of course, Nolan himself grew up in London and yet still presumes to take an American myth and remake it. But the cast's feigned accents add to the overall, slightly off, tense atmosphere Nolan is known for. It is this freighted atmosphere and deconstruction of identity as a "thing" that aligns so well with Millennials. For a generation obsessed with authenticity and the curating of one's "true self," it is not so much a superhero film as it is a horror film. If we are all just layers and layers of roles, acting out parts given to us by the structures and systems and society, there is no self—it's just masks (or cowls) all the way down.

As one of the first feature films to use IMAX camera technology, *The Dark Knight* continues the spectacle tradition of cinema going. But it is not just the crispness and quality of the cinematography but also the camera's near-incessant movement that entrances the audience; scenes refuse to remain static. Many times, both character and camera are moving, but if the character is not moving, the camera is. This technique is especially clear in the opening scene as the shots move from a bird's-eye view of a cityscape to a rooftop to an over-the-shoulder point of view of criminals in clown masks breaking into a bank. Frequent back-and-forth cuts of the heist team doing their designated task and then killing each other afterward give the sequence a distinct and purposeful feeling. When there are only two criminals left, one shoots the other, offhandedly. The remaining criminal stands over the wounded bank manager, takes his mask off to reveal another mask, Joker's painted face. Joker drives a bus that has been backed into the bank through the wall back into a long line of other school buses going about their daily routes, effectively disappearing. The whole sequence takes less than a few minutes, as the heist goes according to meticulous timing and clockwork.

The heist sets in motion the rest of the film. The bank, as it turns out, was a mob bank, and Joker has stolen their money, which he will later offer back to them with his cut if they agree to kill Batman. Joker eventually kills one of the mob bosses, and the others agree to take down Batman so they can continue to run their illegitimate businesses. Ostensibly it seems as though Joker is motivated by the same inducements as other criminals: power and money. But as the film continues, it becomes much more twisted and less straightforward, as the Joker's simple love of anarchy manifests itself. Or as Alfred comments to Wayne, "Some men just wanna watch the world burn." For Joker, this way of living is in tune with the most fundamental, chaotic level of reality, and those who act differently are really the hypocrites and criminals. Thus the standard Joker versus Batman plot device changes key; it is not the good guy versus the bad guy who wants to hurt people but conflicting systems of morality. The police, mob, Joker, Batman, and Dent are all caught up in one long metaphysical moral battle for, as it is framed in the narrative, "the soul of Gotham." Thus both Batman and Joker are metonymized as parts of that soul, with Dent, after he is burned in a failed assassination attempt, becoming Gotham's visual emblem: half human, half monster, making decisions based on a coin toss.

Nolan thus inverts and subverts the typical superhero who fights for a city against an outside threat. In *The Dark Knight*, Batman fights as the city against the shadow of that city, manifested in Joker. This macrolevel psychological framing, which is really at the level of the sociological, scales both ways: up toward the "soul of Gotham" and down to the psyches of Batman and Joker. This deeply interconnected collectivism is important to note in terms of Millennials, who by 2008 had already begun to distance themselves from societal structures that supported unhindered egoism without a social consciousness. With the dot.com bubble bursting in the late '90s and the Great Recession of 2007–2008 making any semblance of the American Dream look completely unrealistic—not just in need of reform but in need of dismantling, as it was based in myopic self-interest and greed—Millennials became adept at side hustles, adapting, and continual rebranding. Also known for their frugality, there is a chastened quality to the Millennial outlook, here represented by Wayne's self-denial, expenditure, and self-sacrifice for others.

After Joker rallies/bullies the mob bosses behind him, he threatens the city with more murders if Batman does not reveal his identity. He then begins his rampage against important leaders in the city. Just as Wayne is about to reveal that he is Batman, Dent steps up and takes the credit and the blame. After Dent is taken into custody for being a moonlighting vigilante, the police decide to transport him to another holding place. En route, Joker tries to capture him but ends up captured himself. Although it looks like he has been defeated, Joker's men snatch Dent and Rachel, holding them hostage.

At this point, both Gordon and Batman interrogate Joker in a holding cell, and he reveals the locations of both Dent and Rachel. Both are tied up and surrounded with explosives. As Batman and Gordon race to free them, Rachel is killed, but Batman manages to save Dent's life despite the fact the explosion and subsequent fire permanently damage half his face. While out on their rescue missions, Joker escapes from police custody and plans more havoc for Gotham.

Joker's next move is to blow up a hospital unless someone kills a Wayne Enterprises whistleblower who has come forward with Batman's true identity. This, of course, sets the city on edge again, and the police begin evacuating hospitals. At

Gotham General, Joker visits Dent, who is recovering from his burns, and manipulates him further into his doctrine of chaos. "I'm an agent of chaos," he tells him. Leaving Dent with a gun and presumably time to escape, Joker walks out of the hospital and blows it sky high.

From here the narrative splits: Dent goes on his own vendetta, hunting down those responsible for Rachel's death. Joker sets up his next move: scare all of Gotham into evacuating. And Batman and Gordon race to hunt him down. Wayne, enlisting a reluctant Fox, deploys a new technology that turns every cell phone in Gotham into a listening device to catch Joker. Fox, concerned with overstepping and privacy invasion, at first refuses to use it until Wayne explains that he can destroy the whole thing when they are done.

Since Joker has made it clear that he is targeting roads and bridges out of the city, the scared populace evacuates via ferries. The police have decided that they need to move many of the criminals out of the city, so they will not join with Joker. Thus one ferry is mostly full of criminals and another ferry full of normal citizens. It is then revealed that Joker has rigged both ferries to blow unless one group detonates the explosives on the other. He gives them until midnight to decide before he destroys them all. In the meantime, Batman finally finds where Joker is operating from, bursts in, and catches Joker. Jumping back and forth between Batman's raid and the ferries, the film shows the moral dilemma being resolved on the ferries. On the citizen ferry, they take a vote, and it is to blow the felons up. On the criminal ferry, a large inmate takes the detonator and throws it out the window. The citizens, recognizing that the felons did not blow them up, cannot go through with destroying them. The clock moves past midnight.

Back on a skyscraper's edge, Joker and Batman fight it out, with Batman finally besting Joker by hanging him upside down by his feet. Without the detonator, Joker cannot execute that part of his plan. He tells Batman, "You truly are incorruptible, aren't you?" To which Batman responds, "This city just showed you that it's full of people ready to believe in good." Joker then laughs and reveals the other part of his scheme: to corrupt Dent. He says, "I took Gotham's white knight and brought him down to our level. Madness is like gravity; all it takes is a little push."

In the meantime, Dent has captured Gordon's wife and kid and is holding them hostage at the site where Rachel was killed. Gordon arrives and pleads for their lives. Batman shows up and, after getting shot in the stomach, saves the son and knocks Dent to his death. He and Gordon plan to pin all the murders Dent did in avenging Rachel's and Dent's deaths on Batman, in order for Gotham to keep its white knight. Batman explains, quoting a line from Dent earlier in the movie, "The Joker cannot win. Gotham needs its true hero. You either die a hero or you live long enough to see yourself become the villain." Batman self-sacrificially agrees to take on this burden and become even further misunderstood by the very people he longs to protect. As the police close in on the scene, he races off.

In the closing montage, as Fox destroys the technology, Gordon eulogizes Dent, and Batman goes on the lam, Batman offers an enigmatic voice-over: "Sometimes truth isn't good enough. Sometimes they need more. Sometimes they need to have their faith rewarded." For Millennials in the grip of the powerful postmodern deconstruction process, this rings true. Contextually, despite Dent's descent into criminality (the truth), Gordon and Batman manage to maintain his image as a white knight for the people (their faith), and they are thus rewarded with safety and security. In effect, if the image that covers the truth allows people to believe in good and feel secure, it is of the utmost importance that it be maintained. Problematically, the image is only partially true, and Batman taking responsibility for Dent's action is completely false. This gives weight to Gordon's closing voice over: "We'll hunt him . . . because he's not our hero. He's a silent guardian, a watchful protector, a dark knight."

This collapse of objective truth in exchange for pragmatic ends, as well as the willingness to embrace ambiguous complexity in terms of moral character both find purchase in the multilayered and often paradoxical Millennial worldview. Theirs is a worldview built on the collapse of American exceptionalism, deep digital and global connectivity, strong pluralism, and a justice-infused sense of relativism. In effect, then, there are no heroes left, just shades of darkness.

Benjamin Crace

See also: *Batman*; *The Dark Knight Rises*; *Joker*.

Further Reading

Brooker, Will. 2012. *Hunting the Dark Knight: Twenty-First Century Batman*. London: I. B. Tauris.

Ip, John. 2011. "*The Dark Knight*'s War on Terrorism." *Ohio State Journal of Criminal Law* 9 (1): 209–229.

Isaki, Bianca. 2009. "Anarchist Feelings: *The Dark Knight* (2008), a Love Story." In *Conference Papers—Western Political Science Association*, 1. Sacramento, CA: Western Political Science Association.

Russell, Patrick Kent. 2016. "Christopher Nolan's *The Dark Knight Trilogy* as a Noir View of American Social Tensions." *Interdisciplinary Humanities* 33 (1): 171–186.

Schimmelpfennig, Annette. 2017. "Capitalism and Schizophrenia in Gotham City: The Fragile Masculinities of Christopher Nolan's *The Dark Knight* Trilogy." *Gender Forum*, no. 62 (April): 3–20.

The Fast and the Furious

Release Date:	2001
Director:	Rob Cohen
Box Office:	$207.3 million
Main Cast:	Dominic Toretto, played by Vin Diesel
	Brian O'Conner, played by Paul Walker
	Letty, played by Michelle Rodriguez
	Mia Toretto, played by Jordana Brewster
	Johnny Tran, played by Rick Yune

As the first film in a franchise of eight, *The Fast and the Furious* was released just three months after the devasting events of 9/11. The narrative of the film is blissfully unaware of the changed global landscape, having wrapped up months before. It is, perhaps, one of the last Millennial films without that consciousness. As such, it offers one last look into a self-contained and self-centered Americana that recalls the Gen X classic, *Point Break* (1991). Although a bit archaic and tone-deaf by today's woke standards, it still hits all the American Millennial notes: freedom, importance of image, distrust of institutions, the all-pervasive drive toward authenticity, and reformulations of traditional notions of family.

The film begins with a series of shots showing a semi getting hijacked by some masked stunt drivers. It then cuts to Brian practicing street racing in a parking lot just before he goes to a café to flirt with Mia, Dominic's younger sister. As he flirts with her, Dom's crew comes in, and a jealous Vince (Matt Schulze) starts trouble. Brian pushes back, and Dom, who is stronger and older than everyone else, breaks them apart. He tells Brian to leave and that he is going to call Harry, the owner of a high-end car parts store known as the Racer's Edge, and tell him to fire Brian. This does not actually happen. As it turns out, Harry is under pressure to cooperate, since Brian is an undercover LAPD officer working with a joint LAPD-FBI task force to investigate the semi jackings, suspecting that Dom and his crew are involved. But, of course, in order to find out more, Brian must become an authentic street racer.

That night, Brian goes to a street race in order to impress Dom and get closer to his crew. The scene is a full-on assault of sexual objectification and racial stereotyping. Even though there are some women racers and Dom's girlfriend, Letty, is fairly liberated, most of the women are in microskirts and skintight tops. One even promises a threesome to one of the racers if he wins, placing his hand on her chest. Each LA subculture is represented almost like a museum exhibition: Black crews in their tight groups, Hispanics, and Asians too. Only Dom's crew is racially integrated and Brian, blond and blue eyed, stands out noticeably, drawing comments.

They race their modified cars, and Brian ends up losing his to Dom, but the cops come and all the racers scatter. Dom, separated from the others, drives off and parks in a parking garage and goes out on foot. He is then spotted by the police, but before getting picked up, Brian comes to the rescue, driving dangerously to avoid roadblocks. After evading the cops, a motorcycle crew surrounds them and forces them to stop near a Chinese market area. One of the cyclists turns out to be Johnny Tran, an Asian street racer/criminal, who hates Dom for sleeping with his sister. They shoot up Brian's car, Dom's prize, and the two are left to get back to town another way. After rendezvousing with the rest of the crew and others at Dom's house—where Dom openly accepts Brian and criticizes Vince—Brian and Mia develop their relationship a bit more, and she takes him home.

At this point in the film, the audience and Dom's crew still do not know that Brian is actually an officer. When he gets pulled over and handcuffed, one suspects it is for something legitimate, but it turns out that it is just a ruse to protect his cover. With his handler and some other agents, he goes for a meeting at a swanky LA house that had been repossessed and then repurposed as a base of operations. Here, Tanner (Ted Levine), Brian's boss, gives him the usual lecture, and Brian asks for more time to cultivate the relationships.

Over the course of the next few scenes, Brian and Dom take the beat-up racer for restoration to replace the car that was shot up, has a "family" dinner with the crew at Dom and Mia's house, asks her for a date, and investigates Johnny Tran as a possible suspect for the hijackings while trying desperately to maintain his cover. Pulled out of the field again, his superiors tell him that they are going to move on Tran and warn him again about Dom. Brian and Mia go on their date and, after sleeping together, he goes on the raid against Tran and his partner, Lance. Because Tran's family is well connected and rich, they all get out of jail, so the raid was pointless.

Brian is blamed for not being productive enough and is told he has 36 hours to crack the case. Interestingly, Tanner takes him aside and, after the typical cop-to-cop "you're too close" conversation, tells him, "There's all kinds of family, Brian. And that's a choice you're going to have to make." Tanner, a Boomer here, is more father than superior, and the statement is made with a kind of loving sternness, accented with uncertainty. And although Walker is a Gen Xer, Brian is situated as some kind of quasi-adolescent drawn toward the ersatz community of racers where "old" and revered Gen Xers such as Dom gather people like a force of nature.

Nonetheless, Brian redoubles his efforts to get Dom to let him in on the side business of hijacking. Dom ambiguously agrees but says Race Wars (a big convention of street racers out in the desert) will be the test. Like the shots for the races on the streets, the montage of Race Wars further objectifies women and pushes the reductionist imagery of racial stereotypes. One shot has a woman pulling off her pants and revealing a thong while wearing a white top that is being sprayed down for a wet, see-through look. She shakes her breasts while guys all around her take pictures, leer, and clap. It is a moment of irony and forced voyeurism since the film camera, too, is turning the audience into an extension of the crowd on the screen. Race Wars, and the whole film in general, takes the potent combinations of sex, violence, and speed and cycles them over and over, titillating the audience's basest instincts: connection, and fight or flight.

At Race Wars, one of Dom's crew, Jesse (Chad Lindberg) loses his car to Tran but refuses to hand it over. A fight ensues with Dom, and Tran accuses him of ratting him out to the police. Dom vehemently denies it and realizes that they need to move quickly to do one more hijacking before the net closes in. He and the rest of the crew (minus Jesse and Mia) leave the desert area where Race Wars are being held and get ready to rob the semi. Brian, seeing them leave and knowing that the truck drivers are now armed, wants to go and warn them. To do so, he has to reveal to Mia that he is actually a cop. Using his police resources, Brian tracks down Dom and the crew just in time to rescue Vince, who has been shot and is barely hanging onto the side of the speeding semi. Now that Brian has called in a life-support helicopter for Vince, everyone in the crew knows he is a cop, and they leave him alone in the desert.

Brian then races to Dom's house in time to stop him from hunting down Tran, who is pursuing Jesse for failure to relinquish his car. After Dom backs down, Jesse shows up, followed by Tran and Lance, who open fire on all of them, killing Jesse. Dom and Brian get into their cars and go after the two motorcycles. After taking them out, Brian knows he must decide about taking Dom in. They have one last race, in which they narrowly miss getting hit by a train, and Dom, in a moment of distraction, wrecks. Brian helps him out of the wreckage and, as the sirens close in on them, hands him his keys and lets him escape as he awaits the consequences. His choice of family has been made, and the franchise is set up.

Throughout the film, intergenerational awareness is sustained through the classic trope of father/son relationship. Jesse, one of the crew, wants to spend time with his dad when he gets out of prison. This desire leads him to race (and lose) his car. Dom, a racer like his father, almost killed the man responsible for his dad's death, even though it was a risk in stock-car racing. Brian, whose dad is completely absent from the narrative, relates to Tanner as a father-older brother. Since the film is largely pitched toward a male, Millennial audience, this absent-father legacy is reformulated in terms of peer-to-peer relationships, with Dom being at the center (his name meaning master/lord). And although both Dom and Brian are imaged as the typical Hollywood leading males, their "bromance" is charged with the type of mutually protective energies that permeate wider Millennial culture.

The contrast between Gen Xer and Millennial masculinities is more recognizable when the ending of the original *Point Break* is placed alongside this film. At the end of *Point Break*, Johnny Utah (Keanu Reeves), an FBI agent who has been undercover with a group of adrenaline-addicted surfer-bank robbers, catches up to the leader, Bodhi (Patrick Swayze), on a famous surfing beach in Australia. After struggling for a bit, Utah gets him in cuffs to take him in but lets him go to surf the once-in-a-lifetime wave, knowing it will probably kill him but he'd be better off dead than caged. The key difference here is that Utah allows Bodhi to escape by dying and justice is served; Bodhi and Utah live out their identities unto a higher purpose and larger philosophy (Bodhi being short for bodhisattva, the figure in Buddhism who postpones salvation to bring enlightenment to others). But Brian simply cuts Dom loose to continue to do whatever he wants without consequences or responsibility. In short, the Millennial man's bro-code is enablement unto personal fulfillment and individualist advancement whereas Gen X's is nihilistically tinged and metaphysical. Bodhi confronts the Void; Dom gets to keep doing juvenile street racing.

Also, like *Point Break*, *The Fast and the Furious* further advances the American narrative as ideally coastal, here California. Many films, for various and sundry production and narrative reasons, are set either in New York or Los Angeles. But there is more to that decision than just these things. The West has always served as a symbol for American expansion, and the sense of new possibility hangs palpably in the air in California, drawing thousands of immigrants from all over each year. It is a space to re-create and explore one's identity apart from the "old" strictures of America's tainted past in the East. This is why the film underscores the mostly friendly rivalry between racial groups, although there is some Asian exploitation here with Johnny Tran and Lance's ruthless portrayals without any further softening or comment. But California also allows the film to be escapist; it all happens somewhere else—over there, where life is always fast and furious.

Benjamin Crace

See also: *Avatar*; *Fast and Furious 7*.

Further Reading

Beltran, Mary C. 2005. "The New Hollywood Racelessness: Only the Fast, Furious, (and Multiracial) Will Survive." *Cinema Journal* 44 (2): 50–67.

Beltran, Mary C. 2013. "Fast and Bilingual: *Fast & Furious* and the Latinization of Racelessness." *Cinema Journal* 53 (1): 75–96.

Crewe, David. 2017. "Cinema Science: *The Fast and the Furious* and the Mechanics of Dangerous Driving." *Screen Education*, no. 87 (October): 32–39.

Davé, Shilpa. 2017. "Racial Accents, Hollywood Casting, and Asian American Studies." *Cinema Journal* 56 (3): 142–147.

Finding Nemo

Release Date:	2003
Directors:	Andrew Stanton and Lee Unkrich
Box Office:	$871 million
Main Cast (Voices):	Marlin, played by Albert Brooks
	Dory, played by Ellen DeGeneres
	Nemo, played by Alexander Gould
	Gill, played by Willem Dafoe

In 2003, Pixar produced a breakthrough animated film whose lush graphics and entertaining storytelling made it an instant classic. *Finding Nemo* tells the story of a young clownfish and his overprotective father. When Nemo is taken from the Great Barrier Reef for a fish tank in a dentist's office, his father Marlin sets off to find him, eventually joining forces with a regal blue tang named Dory. Along the way they must overcome Dory's short-term memory loss, avoid predators, ride the East Australian current with surfer sea turtles, be blown from a whale's spout, and be carried in a pelican's mouth, all while Nemo and his aquarium-mates scheme ways to escape their dental prison. With stunning visual effects, a compelling story, and well-paced action, the film has been lauded as one of the finest animated films of all time.

The film opens with two clownfish, Marlin and his wife Coral, surveying their new home, an anemone perched on the edge of the Great Barrier Reef. Beneath them, in a hole in the coral, their brood of eggs slowly develops. But their home, with its "ocean views," turns out to be a dangerous place: a barracuda knocks Marlin unconscious and—we infer from the scene that follows—eats Coral and her brood of eggs. Marlin awakes to find them gone, with one lone egg remaining. That egg eventually becomes a young fish, named Nemo, with one malformed fin, over whom Marlin broods with extreme protectiveness. This establishes the cultural and generational axes on which it will turn: a happy suburban family discovers that life is not risk-free, even in the suburbs, and overprotective parenting collides with ambitious adolescence. The film thus encodes the concerns of the Millennial generation and their parents. Marlin is the quintessential "helicopter parent," Nemo the classic sheltered but enthusiastic Millennial. The upsetting of this equilibrium sets the story in motion.

On a field trip, Nemo is goaded into swimming out into the open ocean as his friends challenge him to prove his bravery. They spot a boat, which the fish think is called a "butt," floating just out past the edge of the reef. As they observe the boat, Marlin arrives and yells at Nemo for risking his life out in the open ocean, pulling him back to the safety of the reef. Embarrassed and frustrated at Marlin's lack of confidence in him, Nemo swims all the way to the boat and touches it ("He touched the butt!"). Everyone gasps, shocked by this display of courage and anger. But as Nemo swims back, he is caught by a scuba diver. Marlin swims after the boat as it speeds away but cannot catch it.

Marlin trails the boat into the open ocean, the technicolor splendor of the reef giving way to a grayscale ocean floor. He meets Dory, a regal blue tang fish who suffers from memory loss, an issue that makes their partnership hilarious and complicated. Together they find the diver's goggles, with an address written on them, while attending a shark-support group and accidentally setting off a cluster of underwater mines. Meanwhile, Nemo is taken to a fish tank in a dentist's office. The burly dentist brags to a patient about "rescuing" the poor clownfish from the ocean as he proceeds to inflict serious pain on the poor man in the chair. The quirky gang of creatures in the tank welcome Nemo. It is eventually revealed that in one week, Nemo will be given to the dentist's terrifying niece, Darla, who kills the fish given to her by shaking them too much. A key plot goal becomes rescuing Nemo before Darla can kill him too. When Nemo survives being sucked into the return-pipe of the tank's circulation system, a mysterious fish named Gill formulates a plan to have Nemo jam the circulation system with a rock. This will cause the aquarium to mold, forcing the dentist to put the fish in individual bags while he cleans the tank. They will then push themselves through the open window and into the harbor. If Marlin is a classic suburban father of the Boomer generation, Gill is a tough-love war veteran, whose willingness to let Nemo risk himself is both inspiring and terrifying to the young fish. But the plan fails, and Nemo nearly dies. Gill is ashamed and despondent.

After chasing the goggles into a deep-sea trench, surviving an attack by an anglerfish, and receiving instructions from a school of moonfish, Marlin and Dory go in search of the East Australian current to find Nemo in some place called Sydney. However, the moonfish had instructed Dory to swim *through* a trench on their way to the current, not over it. Dory forgets, but when they find the trench, she tries to convince Marlin to go through it because she has a feeling that they should. Marlin's unwillingness to trust anyone again intervenes, and he overrides his friend, tricking her into swimming above the trench. Marlin's inability to trust others leads them straight into a dangerous cloud of jellyfish. The animation of the jellyfish's translucent pink bodies and tentacles is wonderous, but they pose a serious danger to Dory. Being a clownfish, Marlin is somewhat immune to their stings, but a sting would mean certain death for Dory. Marlin is able to save Dory from being eaten by the jellyfish, carrying her unconscious body out the other side of the swarm. But the stings are too much even for him, and he passes out as a dark shadow approaches their listing bodies. His inability to trust others has seriously endangered Dory, but his surprising courage has saved her.

Marlin awakens on the back of a green sea turtle named Crush, who acts like a surfer who smokes too much marijuana but whose carefree confidence, especially toward his son, inspires Marlin to relax. The story of Marlin's heroic quest for his son through sharks, explosions, and jellyfish passes through the group of travelers and then the broader ocean, eventually making its way to Nigel, a pelican in Sydney Harbor. Nigel knows the fish in the tank at the dentist's office and flies to tell them that Nemo's father is on his way. Inspired by news of his father, Nemo jumps back into the filter, jams it with a rock and swims back out. The plan works this time, and the tank turns green with algae. Marlin, the scared suburban dad has apparently turned into a heroic adventurer, and his bravery inspires Nemo as well.

Marlin and Dory "bale out" of the East Australian Current somewhere near Sydney. But being close to a large city, the water is murky and barren. They are eventually swallowed by a blue whale. Dory apparently speaks whale, but Marlin again does not trust her to do so. When the whale tells Dory to swim to the back of his mouth, Marlin thinks it is simply trying to swallow them. Eventually Dory convinces him, saying, "Just let go." And here Marlin's personal story arc reaches its climax. He is forced to trust the instincts and abilities of his friend, forced to loosen his controlling grip and (literally and figuratively) let go. He does so, and the whale launches them out of its blowhole and into Sydney Harbor.

Once in the harbor, they are rescued by Nigel the pelican, who flies them to the dentist's office. Just before they arrive, the animals in the tank awaken to a clean tank: the dentist had purchased an expensive cleaning system, thwarting their escape plan. The dentist scoops Nemo into a net, but the fish all work together, swimming away from the dentist to pull the net from his hand. They celebrate, only to have Nemo scooped into a plastic bag, pulled from the tank, and handed to the petulant niece, Darla. Nemo thinks quickly and plays dead in the hopes of being flushed down the toilet. At that very moment, Marlin and Dory arrive with Nigel at the window. Seeing Nemo, they assume he is dead. Instead of the toilet, the dentist moves to throw Nemo in the trash. Gill loads himself into the bubbling volcano, launching himself out of the aquarium and causing panic in the room. The dentist drops Nemo onto a dental tray, and Gill lands next to him. Gill flips Nemo into a drain.

Marlin, Nemo, and Dory meet in Sydney Harbor, but Dory is caught in a fishing net. Nemo convinces Marlin to once again "let go" and let him swim through the fish telling them to swim together downward. They all work together, snap the line holding the net and are all set free. The film ends with Marlin, Nemo, and Dory (and three support-group sharks) happily together back in the reef.

The film is an adventure film, telling a timeless tale of coming-of-age, of leaving a comfortable home, of facing and overcoming dangers and temptations along the way. But the setting reflects very particular concerns of the wealthy Western world at the turn of the millennium. The incredible economic growth of the 1990s led to lives of isolated comfort for those who could afford the suburbs. Great schools, great views, and the sense that risk could be minimized if not dissolved dominated wealthy Western consciousnesses. But a life without risk is hardly worth living, and Millennials chafed at the overprotectiveness of their parents. At any rate, all was not well. In particular, the suburban lifestyle is one of extreme waste, requiring enormous energy and financial resources to sustain. The environmental impacts of such a life were only just beginning to be felt. The film makes those impacts palpable. Immersive animation enables viewers to experience the colorful glory of coral reefs, the vast expanse of the ocean, the darkness of the deep sea, and the murky, polluted haze of industrial waters. One cannot but feel sorrow for the polluted mess of Sydney Harbor as the human desire for total comfort wreaks havoc on the natural world. This can also be seen in the film's critique of the pet trade, interpreted as the human desire to capture and control. Marlin's desire for a comfortable suburban life is mirrored in the brutish dentist who "rescued" Nemo from the wild. Both thought that sterile isolation would protect Nemo, but in the end, it only stifled him. Our desire for control ends up killing the very things we hope to preserve, and only by allowing others to risk the wilds of life can we actually help them grow.

One clear purpose of the film was to inspire an empathetic devotion to the wild spaces of the ocean world and an awareness of the negative human impacts on such environments. But this purpose was not without irony. Some have argued that there was actually a spike in tropical fish sales after the film's success, further depleting wild fish populations. While it is not clear that the "Finding Nemo effect" was a statistically significant phenomenon, it underscores the complex relation between entertainment and environmental concerns. By making the ocean entertaining, the film increases a curiosity that may lead to greater conservation and greater exploitation. Entertainment, like the ocean, is a beautiful and dangerous thing.

But behind the fish, the coral, and the pelicans is a very human story, one about fear, control, and trusting others. The world is a beautiful and dangerous place, and it takes courage to work together and trust others. Only in doing so can we hope to find our way to maturity. To see this human story told in an unfamiliar landscape, made palpable by extraordinary animation, constitutes this film's enduring appeal.

Josh Mobley

See also: Toy Story; Zootopia.

Further Reading

Bruckner, Lynee Dickson. 2010. "*Bambi* and *Finding Nemo*: A Sense of Wonder in the Wonderful World of Disney?" In *Framing the World: Explorations in Ecocriticism and Film*, edited by Paula Willoquet-Maricondi, 187–208. Charlottesville, VA: University of Virginia Press.

Brydon, Suzan B. 2009. "Men at the Heart of Mothering: Finding Mother in *Finding Nemo*." *Journal of Gender Studies* 18 (2): 131–146.

Higgs, Sam. 2017. "*Finding Nemo* in the Three-Act Structure." *Screen Education* 85: 90–97.

Militz, Thane A., and Simon Foale. 2017. "The 'Nemo Effect': Perception and Reality of *Finding Nemo*'s Impact on Marine Aquarium Fisheries." *Fish and Fisheries* 18 (3): 596–606.

Harry Potter and the Philosopher's Stone/ Harry Potter and the Chamber of Secrets

Harry Potter and the Philosopher's Stone		Harry Potter and the Chamber of Secrets	
Release Date:	2001	Release Date:	2002
Director:	Chris Columbus	Director:	Chris Columbus
Box Office:	$317 million	Box Office:	$262 million
Main Cast:	Harry Potter, played by Daniel Radcliffe Hermione Granger, played by Emma Watson Ron Weasley, played by Rupert Grint Albus Dumbledore, played by Richard Harris	Main Cast:	Harry Potter, played by Daniel Radcliffe Hermione Granger, played by Emma Watson Ron Weasley, played by Rupert Grint Albus Dumbledore, played by Richard Harris

It would be hard to overestimate the global cultural impact of the Harry Potter series. While the books are credited with getting an entire generation of children interested in reading, the release of each film in the series was almost as eagerly awaited as the novels. To this day, there are animated discussions among fans as to which is better, the books or the movies.

Harry Potter and the Philosopher's Stone (2001; henceforth *Philosopher's Stone*; Sorcerer's Stone in its U.S. release), was released a mere four years after the novel of the same name. It is the first of eight films based on the seven books of the series (the final book was made into two films), and the popularity of the original series has resulted in the filming of a five-film prequel series tracing the beginnings of the Wizarding world. The second film, *Harry Potter and the Chamber of Secrets* (2002; henceforth *Chamber of Secrets*) came out the next year, again only four years after the publication of the novel. In fact, the seven-book series (1997–2007) and the eight-film series (2001–2011) were published or released like clockwork over a period of little more than a decade. For the films, this was crucial in order to avoid having to replace any of the young stars who might have aged out of the roles should there have been a significant delay in release.

The first two films (*Philosopher's Stone* and *Chamber of Secrets*) were both directed by Chris Columbus, known for his lighthearted touch in the *Home Alone* films (1990 and 1992) and *Mrs. Doubtfire* (1993). The remainder of the series would see a total of four different directors, which some critics said led to a somewhat uneven feel to the series while others said worked well due to the increasingly dark atmosphere of the later stories.

Both of the Columbus-directed films were well received by fans and critics alike, with *Philosopher's Stone* earning seven BAFTA Award nominations, including Best British Film and Best Supporting Actor, and winning a Saturn Award for costume design. *Chamber of Secrets* was nominated for four BAFTA awards, was nominated for seven Saturn Awards (including Best Director and Best Fantasy Film), and won a Grammy for John Williams's score. Despite its status as the second highest-grossing franchise in film history (over $8.5 billion) and receiving twelve nominations across the eight films, no Harry Potter film was ever awarded a single Oscar. There are several theories for this: among the more compelling are the franchise being pigeonholed as a children's series and its blockbuster status.

The first two books and films follow the unlikely hero Harry Potter during one year of his life both in the Muggle (non-Wizard) world of London and the Wizarding world of Hogwarts School of Witchcraft and Wizardry. Harry was orphaned as a baby when the evil lord Voldemort (he who must not be named) kills his parents in a murderous rampage to destroy any wizards who have not followed Voldemort to the dark side. Miraculously, Harry survives the attack but is left with a lightning-shaped scar on his forehead, which serves as a warning of impending danger at times and also marks him as different and special to his fellow wizards and witches. Dumbledore, the headmaster of Hogwarts, realizes he must protect Harry from Voldemort and decides that the best place to hide him is with his Muggle family: his mother's sister, Aunt Petunia, her husband, Uncle Vernon Dursley, and his porcine cousin, Dudley. They keep Harry's origins secret from him, and for the first 11 years of his life, he leads a safe yet miserable existence, sleeping under the stairwell and being treated as an annoyance.

The first film is a triumph in world building, as Harry and the audience are shown through a series of amusing incidents that there is a parallel and much more exciting world than the mundane Muggle existence. This world is also one full of danger and one in which the quintessential struggle between good and evil play out externally and internally in our hero's life. He is "the boy who lived," the only one known to have survived a direct attack by the Dark Lord, and is determined and destined to fight him and avenge his parents' death. But Harry is also connected to Voldemort through his scar (which in a later film we learn is a Horcrux, containing a fragment of the Dark Lord's soul) but also through their ability to speak the snake language, Parseltongue, and by sharing feathers from the same phoenix as the core of their wands.

The guide to much of the early journey as Harry prepares to begin his wizarding studies at Hogwarts is Hagrid, the half-human, half-giant groundskeeper who plays a key role in the lives of Harry and his friends, Ron Weasley and Hermione Granger. The Weasley family is introduced, and they become a surrogate family for Harry and also for Hermione, whose own parents are Muggles. While the transition into the Wizarding world begins on the train, the key moment for Harry happens during the "sorting" into houses, which is based on a student's proclivities and potentials, when the Sorting Hat debates whether to put him into Slytherin or Gryffindor (where he is eventually placed along with Ron and Hermione).

We are then introduced, along with the first-year students, to daily life at Hogwarts, which is an amusing combination of the mundane and the magical. The potential danger lurking beneath the amusing surface is revealed to the three friends when they become lost and accidentally encounter the three-headed Cerberus, a doglike beast named Fluffy (which, it turns out, is extremely faithful to Hagrid). It is also revealed, in a moment of Gryffindor impulsiveness, that Harry possesses the qualities to make an excellent Seeker in the game of Quidditch, the wizard equivalent of football, played in the sky on brooms. Harry's father, James, had also been a Seeker, and so we see one of the tropes of the film, the importance of heredity and bloodlines, play out in a positive manner.

Dangers reemerge when it is discovered that there is a troll loose in the school. Hermione, who had annoyed the boys with her air of superiority, overheard them mocking her and had been hiding and crying in the girl's bathroom all afternoon. Harry and Ron realize they must warn her of the presence of the troll, who had made his way to Hermione's hiding place. The children fight off the troll and cement their friendship, which will be needed for them to survive in upcoming adventures in this film and throughout the series.

Much of the remaining action of the film revolves around the trio's desire to protect the philosopher's stone and their mistaken notion that Snape is fighting on the side of Voldemort. Their mistake is not revealed to them or the audience until they enter an underground chamber and discover the real villain. It turns out that a weakened Lord Voldemort was living parasitically off the body of Quirinus Quirrell, professor of defense against the dark arts. Voldemort reveals himself to Harry, who has, through the magic of the Mirror of Erised ("desire" spelled backward), found that the philosopher's stone is now in his pocket. Voldemort tries to entice Harry to join him on the dark side, telling him that there is no good and evil, only power and those too weak to seek it, and that if Harry will join him, together they will bring Harry's parents back to life—perhaps the one thing that the boy has yearned for his entire life. Harry resists, and when Quirrell tries to kill Harry at Voldemort's command, it seems that the stone has given Harry powers to turn anyone he touches into stone. Quirrell crumbles, leaving Voldemort without a host body. As his black essence flees, it flies through Harry, intensifying the connection between the two, which will be employed as part of the boy's struggles in future encounters with the Dark Lord.

Chamber of Secrets repeats the basic structure of the first film, opening with Harry's suffering at the hands of his unbearable family, but he is quickly rescued by the Weasley boys, who have stolen their father's flying car and whisked him away to their magical home. While we are constantly introduced to new magical delights (such as floo powder), there is not the same world-building necessity as in the first film. We are also introduced to discrimination within the Wizarding world, in the slavery of Dobby the house elf and in concerns over miscegenation and purity of blood found in Tom Riddle's diary (Tom Marvolo Riddle invents his evil pseudonym as an anagram, "I am Lord Voldemort"). While the matter of "Mudbloods" is strongly condemned, slavery is a more complicated matter, and many readers remain unconvinced by Rowling's treatment of the matter (which is left out of the films entirely). Some critics have noted the introduction of darker issues, such as self-harm, mistreatment of animals, and bullying, which they feel are not adequately addressed in book or film.

The main plot of the second film is the unsealing of the Chamber, which had been closed since Slytherin had had a falling-out with the other cofounders of Hogwarts. Residents of the school are being petrified (turned to stone) as part of an evil plan to rid the school of Mudbloods and other undesirables, and Harry

Potter is under suspicion, in part because his Parseltongue abilities are accidentally revealed to others. But Harry himself has self-doubts and keeps secret from the headmaster the murderous whisperings he has been hearing as well as his communications with Riddle's diary. Although the audience does not yet know that Riddle and Voldemort are one, Harry's connection to Riddle is revealed when a much earlier moment between Riddle and Dumbledore is reenacted between the headmaster and Harry. This is part of the series's appeal: Harry's connection with and attraction to the Dark Lord. For as Dumbledore tells Harry at the end of the film, it is not our abilities but our choices that matter.

It turns out that Ginny, Ron's younger sister, had earlier been seduced by Riddle's diary and is being held captive in the Chamber. When it is revealed that the defense against the dark arts professor Lockhart is a fraud, the trio, minus Hermione (who has mistakenly turned herself into a cat hybrid), can only rely on themselves to rescue Ginny. They open the Chamber with the help of Moaning Myrtle (whom they had met while killing an ogre in the girls' bathroom in *Philosopher's Stone*) and who had been one of Riddle's earliest victims. The diary turns out to be another Horcrux, and it was Ginny (not Hagrid, who was unfairly blamed) who had opened the Chamber while under the diary's spell. Harry is wounded while fighting the Basilisk but is still able to plunge the snake's tooth into the diary and kill that part of Voldemort's soul with the help of the Gryffindor sword and Dumbledore's phoenix, Fawkes, whose tears also heal Harry's near-mortal wound. It is also revealed that Voldemort left a bit of himself in Harry's scar (although it is not clear until later films that this is also a Horcrux containing part of Voldemort).

Harry Potter remains an anomaly in many ways. It was and remains a global craze that is firmly based on a conservative and even paternalistic view of the world and of Britain. There was even a requirement that the main cast had to be British. While arguably a form of British soft power, it mostly escapes criticism of cultural imperialism that is often launched at Hollywood. There is, however, something nostalgic about the British boarding school that brings to mind (and then dismisses) other classics such as Lindsay Anderson's film *If* (1968) or even George Orwell's essay "Such, Such Were the Joys" (1952). However, a closer look reveals many colonial and imperial symbols and storylines (including its treatment of the Muggles, its somewhat fascistic fixation on purity of bloodlines, and its treatment of the house elves and the topic of slavery) that deserve more consideration.

The Millennials grew up identifying with the Harry Potter franchise, in part because it reflects their core values of diversity and acceptance, resistance to authoritarianism, distrust of government, and the belief in skepticism rather than cynicism. One critic's book-length study even argues that the series may have influenced their generally "liberal" values, which was then expressed in their overwhelming vote for Barack Obama in 2008. A study of Generation Zers also found them to be more empathetic and less prejudiced than their peers if they were immersed in the *Harry Potter* universe. While the Gen Z generation has moved on to TikTok, Millennials are reluctant to let go of the comfort of *Harry Potter*, despite enthusiastic disagreements over whether Snape is a misogynist or just misunderstood and whether characters such as Malfoy or Dumbledore are wholly bad or good, respectively. Millennials are also more reluctant than other generations to let go of the security of their childhood (evidenced by "I did laundry—adulting is hard" posts) and are often enabled by their Baby Boomer or Gen X parents. Gen Zers, however, seem to outgrow *Harry Potter* as they reach their adolescence, and many have moved on to the superhero as a better model for the work they need to do to save the planet from conflict and climate change.

The popularity of the good versus evil theme of these films (and others, such as the first film of the *Lord of the Rings* trilogy, released in 2001) must on some level be seen through a lens of a post-9/11 War on Terror worldview. The community Harry found at Hogwarts and his special friendship with Ron and Hermione, which empowered them and enabled them to fight off evil, resonated with a Millennial generation scarred by the 9/11 attacks.

Despite its undeniably conservative ideology, the films did draw the ire of some religious communities, primarily the Christian Right in the United States, whose members argued that their children were being taught to worship Satan and practice witchcraft. There is, of course, a history in the United States of "satanic panic" dating back to the Salem Witch Trials of the 1690s, exemplified in the satanic ritual abuse that some believed was happening in daycare centers in the 1980s, and demonstrated in QAnon today. There is also a subgenre of Christian-themed fantasy, such as that by C. S. Lewis or even J. R. R. Tolkien. The pro- or anti-Christian (or Muslim) elements perceived by adults in the narratives were not of great importance to most fans of the Millennial or Generation Z generations.

The film franchise, starting with the two films directed by Columbus, have also been credited as being in the vanguard of a new approach to blockbusters: for some because they were based on primarily unknown authors, directors, and actors, and for others because they mark a shift toward established media franchises. They also mark the shift in focus on using children's or young adult literature (a newly coined category) as a basic for films, and a linking of the book and film series in order to capitalize on this growing fan base. Since then, fantasy or dystopian sci-fi book series have been the place to look for the next blockbuster film.

Angelica Maria DeAngelis

See also: *The Lord of the Rings: The Fellowship of the Ring.*

Further Reading

Gierzynski, Anthony, 2013. *Harry Potter and the Millennials: Research Methods and the Politics of the Muggle Generation.* Baltimore, MD: Johns Hopkins University Press.

Lauer, Emily, and Balaka Basu. 2019. *The Harry Potter Generation: Essays on Growing Up with the Series.* Jefferson, NC: McFarland.

Patterson, Diana, ed. 2009. *Harry Potter's World-Wide Influence.* Newcastle upon Tyne, UK: Cambridge Scholars.

Whited, Lana A., ed. 2002. *Ivory Tower and Harry Potter: Perspectives on a Literary Phenomenon.* Columbia: University of Missouri Press.

Iron Man

Release Date:	2008
Director:	Jon Favreau
Box Office:	$585.3 million
Main Cast:	Tony Stark/Iron Man, played by Robert Downey Jr.
	Pepper Pots, played by Gwyneth Paltrow
	Rhodey, played by Terrence Howard
	Obadiah Stane Quaritch, played by Jeff Bridges
	Happy Hogan, played by Jon Favreau
	Raza, played by Faran Tahir

Other than relaunching Robert Downey Jr.'s acting career, *Iron Man* also kicked off the Marvel Cinematic Universe (MCU), which has continued to expand since 2009, when Disney acquired Marvel Studios. Part of a complex and intricate mythological landscape, the MCU's premier film contains the seeds of its subsequent productions. Tony Stark/Iron Man will be reprised by Downey over and over again until his last "appearance" 11 years later in *Spider-Man: Far from Home* (2019). Such longevity of a single character portrayed by the same actor is a feat in itself but also gestures toward a deeper need embedded in the Millennial psyche: the need for familiar heroes that are part of a larger, almost transcendent story.

It is difficult not to contextualize *Iron Man* within the Marvel mythos. At one level, there is the comic book legacy, which supplies the "lore" or "canon" of character consistency and backstory Favreau reshapes to fit into the film media while pleasing a spectrum of fans from the obsessed to the mildly interested. And there is quite a bit of this canon: Iron Man first appeared as a character in 1963 and had his own comic by 1968. But Iron Man's narrative gets splintered in the comic book world into many diverse narratives and plot twists involving other planets, the future, and other universes. The challenge for a film, and one that recognizes its fan base, is to choose from the embarrassment of riches surrounding the character while setting up the commercial dominos for future MCU productions. By all accounts, *Iron Man* succeeded, launching a franchise that has netted more than $22.56 billion to date. To put that into perspective, that is almost double the GDP of Nicaragua.

The narrative begins with Stark riding in a military convoy of Humvees in Afghanistan. As the audience learns later, he has just left a successful demonstration of Stark Industries' Jericho Missile to the U.S. government. The convoy is attacked by a local warlord, Raza, using Stark's own weaponry. Stark is wounded in the firefight and secreted back to a network of caves where the fighters are living. Another prisoner, Yinsen (Shaun Toub), an Afghan scientist, helps save Stark's life but has to connect him to an electromagnet powered by a car battery in order to prevent pieces of shrapnel from getting to his heart and killing him. Both Yinsen and Stark are tasked with re-creating the Jericho Missile from the parts

Raza has salvaged and bought elsewhere. Instead of building a missile, they build a crude robotic, armored suit that enables them to escape but not before Yinsen is killed in the process, interestingly dying on top of a pile of bags with American flag images and the words: "Not to Be Sold or Exchanged." Stark thanks Yinsen for saving his life, and Yinsen, just before passing, admonishes Stark to not waste his. Stark leaves the cave, destroys a large cache of stolen Stark Industries weapons, and flies off, crashing in the desert. He is later picked up by the U.S. military and his friend, Rhodey.

Between the attack on the convoy and Stark's captivity, the film jumps back a day and a half to show Stark blowing off a banquet held in his honor to shoot dice in Las Vegas. Outside the casino, a reporter, Christine (Leslie Bibb) confronts him about his involvement in war and violence. He tells her, "Peace means having a bigger stick than the other guy," just before going down a list of the good things that the military has done. This Stark is clearly nonplussed by his contributions to the military machine. To further underscore his lack of ethics and his playboy lifestyle, he sleeps with the reporter. The next day, his assistant, Pepper Pots, dismissively shows Christine out and walks Stark through his schedule and various rich-man entanglements. Stark then leaves and joins Rhodey on a private jet. They drink and watch the air hostesses pole dance all the way to Afghanistan, where the film brings the narrative back to the attack on the convoy.

At this point in the film, it has already hit some standard Millennial concerns. Having a protagonist who begins as both a militaristic, chauvinist pig and a narcissistic capitalist begs for some kind of transformation. The military-industrial complex is not to be trusted (as shown by Obadiah [Bridges], the dirty, double-dealing, second-in-command at Stark Industries who will betray Tony). Tony Stark and his flippant, detached attitude of "cool" is repulsive, yet his underlying confidence is paradoxically magnetic. The viewer wants him to change but not too much and in just the right ways, those ways being attuned to Millennial sympathies of a global consciousness, gender equality, authentic relationships based on vulnerability, and secret but pragmatic genius.

This transformation, of course, takes place through suffering. As Stark narrowly escapes death with the help of an Afghan whose country he has helped ruined, there is somewhat of a Jean Valjean of *Les Misérables* redemption taking place. In exchange for his life, Stark begins to come to terms with the cost of his weapons manufacturing. When he returns home after the three months of captivity, and to the dismay of Obadiah, his military contacts, and his shareholders, he announces that Stark Industries will no longer make weapons. Later, after the press conference, Obadiah confronts Tony and the need to keep order in the world. Tony listens and hints that more can be done with the arc reactor (an energy supplying machine that powers Stark Industries). It seems, in Tony's mind, that development of arc reactor technology can replace the money lost from closing the weapons division of the company. He knows that the tech can be further refined because, as he shows Obadiah, he has miniaturized the arc reactor and used it to replace the electromagnet cum car battery that had been keeping the shrapnel out of his heart. It is the glowing ring in his chest that will later become the power source for the Iron Man suit.

The clash between Obadiah and Tony is itself rooted in generational conflict. Obadiah is a member of the old guard, the generation that helped Howard Stark build the company, full of moral and ethical compromises. War is good for business. Tony's recent experience of trauma (he suffers PTS throughout the franchise), however, has wrenched him out of this world of profiteering and placed him on the path of reformer if not moral crusader. But it is a naïve crusade, as he realizes that simply not participating in weapons manufacturing is not enough to bring order and peace to the world. So as an already tainted and guilty individual who has much to atone for, he begins work on the Iron Man suit.

After several scenes showing Tony building and testing the suit, he leaves for another benefit, where Obadiah tells him that he has locked him out of the company and that they have resumed selling weapons. At the same benefit, his and Pepper's relationship develop a bit beyond boss and assistant, and Christine, the reporter from earlier in the film, asks him about the disaster in Gulmira, a town in Afghanistan. As it turns out, Raza has attacked the city using weapons Obadiah sold him. Tony has had enough, not just because it is against his newfound sense of purpose but also because Gulmira was the hometown of his friend, Yinsen. He sets off in the new Iron Man suit to save it, which he does—single-handedly—to the chagrin and confusion of the U.S. military and his friend, Rhodey, who had been monitoring the situation.

A side scene shows Obadiah meeting with Raza, and the audience learns that he had paid off the warlord to capture Tony so he could take control of the company. Raza and his men had also picked up the proto–Iron Man suit's pieces and were trying to reconstruct it. Obadiah, seeing this, takes the pieces and takes over the project. He leaves Raza's camp after killing everyone, showing his truly dark nature.

Eventually, Obadiah finishes his version of the suit and takes the arc reactor out of Tony's chest to power it. Tony barely survives and uses an older version of the arc reactor (the one he had made in the cave) to power the Iron Man suit so he can combat Obadiah. With Pepper's help, they defeat Obadiah, whose suit looks a lot like the robotic suit used in *Avatar* a year later. In terms of Easter eggs (or subtle clues that are meaningful for attentive audiences), Favreau re-creates two iconic scenes from other films. First, after Pepper initiates an overload of the big arc reactor as Stark and Obadiah fight above, the resultant blue beam sends a gigantic shaft of light that strikes Obadiah's own arc reactor, killing him. A long shot shows the bright blue light shooting up to heaven, recalling the end of *Indiana Jones and the Raiders of the Lost Ark* (1981); here, though, it is not the ark but an *arc* reactor. Second, after dying, Obadiah in his suit falls forward down into the reactor, causing it to explode—again, much like the death of the Emperor in *Stars Wars: Return of the Jedi* (1983). Surely such decisions by Favreau, a Gen Xer himself, are more than coincidental.

The final scene has Tony revealing that he is Iron Man with the words: "Truth is. I am Iron Man"—a phrase that will round out his character's arc over a decade later. But this is not the end of the film, for like every MCU production, there is an end of credits scene that shows Nick Fury (Samuel L. Jackson), the leader of

SHIELD (a secret agency that helps defend the world from alien attacks and other superpowers) offering Tony a place in the Avengers' Initiative, thus forecasting the rest of the MCU. Inclusion of these "end of credits" teasers/scenes not only adds something unique to the viewing of an MCU film but also registers deeply with the Millennial value that everyone's contributions matter, no matter the size. Inviting moviegoers to sit through the generally skipped credits of a major motion picture offers them the chance to see the names of people who would otherwise go unnoticed. This is clear virtue signaling and a smart marketing move for their target audience.

But is Tony remade in the Millennial image? Not by the end of *Iron Man*, no. Despite the boy-like characterization, Stark remains a stained hero (recall that his nemesis's last name is actually Stane, Obadiah Stane). He has innocent blood on his hands and cannot fully and authentically be a Millennial god. However, as a Gen X, cynical realist with a romantic soft spot and ironic sense of humor, he serves an important mythological function within the MCU. He is the arbiter between one generation's heroes and the next. Nowhere is this more clearly displayed than in his mentor relationship with Peter Parker or Spider-Man, but that does not come until later. Thus the unfinished nature of *Iron Man*'s ending is not just a setup for the franchise but also the lingering effect of the distance between the audience's desire for a more thorough transformation of Tony and his actual development.

Iron Man is also another contribution in the intergenerational project of coming to terms with the American military and the decline of the modern mechanistic worldview. Every generation has its films that celebrate, normalize, or demonize our armed forces. Here it is somewhere between a necessary evil and an inept, overly bureaucratic organization. Nevertheless, the sense that the United States and even the earth itself need something more than just a military is pervasive. That need for "something more" from somewhere unexpected taps into the occult roots of the superhero/comic book genre and the postmodern (including many Millennials) project of re-enchantment. The modernist materialist military, with its guns and tanks and planes, is incapable of fighting evil. Evil must be fought with magic sorcerers, Nordic gods, scarlet witches, and a man with a glowing heart, like that of Jesus.

Benjamin Crace

See also: *The Avengers*; *Black Panther*.

Further Reading

Beck, Bernard. 2009. "Something for the Boys: *Iron Man, Transformers*, and *Grand Theft Auto IV*." *Multicultural Perspectives* 11 (1): 27–30.

Kripal, Jeffrey. 2015. *Mutants and Mystics: Science Fiction, Superhero Comics, and the Paranormal.* Chicago: University of Chicago Press.

McSweeney, Terence. 2018. *Avengers Assemble! Critical Perspectives on the Marvel Cinematic Universe.* London: WallFlower Press.

Robinson, Ashley Sufflé. 2018. "We Are Iron Man: Tony Stark, *Iron Man*, and American Identity in the Marvel Cinematic Universe's Phase One Films." *Journal of Popular Culture* 51 (4): 824–844.

Travers, Peter. 2008. "Superhero Smackdown." *Rolling Stone*, no. 1052 (May): 73–76.

The Lord of the Rings: The Fellowship of the Ring

Release Date:	2001
Director:	Peter Jackson
Box Office:	$888.3 million
Main Cast:	Frodo Baggins, played by Elijah Wood
	Gandalf, played by Ian McKellen
	Legolas, played by Orlando Bloom
	Strider/Aragorn, played by Viggo Mortensen
	Samwise Gamgee, played by Sean Astin

Released in the United States just three months after 9/11, *The Lord of the Rings: The Fellowship of the Ring* took on a changed significance for its American audience. Eerily, its nearly prescient voice-over prologue could just as easily have been uttered by any shattered American: "The world is changed. I feel it in the water. I feel it in the earth. I smell it in the air. Much that once was is lost." *LOTR*'s dualistic worldview, itself a result of J. R. R. Tolkien's Catholicism, World War II, and Cold War experiences, elides well with the post-9/11 Millennial malaise of a lost paradise; there is no Shire (tranquil home of the hobbits) to return to. And yet, *LOTR* also offers Millennials a curious antidote to overcoming evil, be it socioeconomic, militaristic, or in the form of existential threats to one's authenticity. Contrary to the isolationist trends of Boomers and many Gen Xers, greater multiculturalism and deeper interconnectedness ("fellowship") are offered as means to fighting evil in the present age. This also means accepting intergenerational wisdom, although it needs to be done critically.

The plot of the fantasy film is fairly simple once one has a sense of the backstory, which is given in the first five minutes of the film. It takes place in Middle Earth, perhaps our earth (it is, after all, called earth) but a long time ago. This Middle Earth is divided into different realms belonging to different races: elves, orcs, goblins, wizards, humans, hobbits, and dwarves. They mostly keep to themselves in their own territories. Thousands of years prior to the beginning of the film's narrative, Sauron, a Satan-like figure, tricked the leaders of the elves, humans, and dwarves into receiving magic rings to help them rule their respective people. Unbeknown to them, Sauron had created a separate ring, the ring of power, one that more or less controlled all the other rings ("one ring to rule them all"). He had kept this ring to himself and intended to dominate all of Middle Earth, enslaving the other races. In a spectacular battle, Sauron loses this ring, and it is then taken by one of the human kings, who also loses it. It sits in the bottom of a river for 2,500 years when Gollum (Andy Serkis) finds it and hides with it in a cave for 500 more years. The ring's immediate powers give long life and even invisibility to whoever puts it on and possesses it. However, those powers come at a cost; since it contains Sauron's evil, it poisons the mind of its user. Gollum, a pathetic and now ghoulish creature, loses the ring to Bilbo Baggins (Ian

Holm), a hobbit, who wanders into his cave on one of his own adventures and finds it. Hobbits, in terms of physical characteristics, are only about three to four feet tall, walk barefoot everywhere, and live in homes under the earth. They are miniaturized English village folk, basically. Bilbo takes the ring back to the Hobbiton, the region of the hobbits, specifically to his village, the Shire, and keeps it there for decades. It gives him extraordinary long life, but since he does not wear it, it does not poison him to the same degree as it did Gollum. And given the country heartiness of hobbits, he manages to have a relatively stable and good life. And as the voice-over tells us, "And some things that should not have been forgotten were lost." So this is where the film's main action begins, and through various narrative techniques, the audience learns that although Sauron's body died long ago, his spirit has survived and is now awake, looking for the ring from his hellish home of Mordor.

With this backstory, Gandalf, an aging wizard, visits the Shire to see his old friend, Bilbo for his 111th birthday and to catch up with Bilbo's nephew, Frodo. Gandalf loves being around hobbits and their simple and direct mannerisms. At Bilbo's big birthday celebration, Bilbo disappears, using the ring. Gandalf is alarmed and suspects that there is more to it. He confronts Bilbo before he tries to sneak off to Rivendell (the home of the elves) with the ring, convincing him to leave it. When Frodo comes back to Bilbo's house from the party, he finds the ring on the ground, and Gandalf tells him to hide it while he figures out what it may be. Frodo obediently does so, and when Gandalf does come back to the Shire sometime later, he confirms that this is the ring of power and everyone is in danger. He sends Frodo and his friend, Samwise, out on a journey out of the Shire and promises to meet them in a human village at a pub/hostel called The Prancing Pony. Meanwhile, Mordor has caught and tortured Gollum until he gave up who took the ring, thereby surmising its location in Hobbiton. Nine Ringwraiths (or semighost riders on horseback) are dispatched immediately to get it. This adds another level of danger and urgency for the hobbits.

Along their journey to The Prancing Pony, Sam and Frodo meet up with two other ne'er-do-well hobbits, Merry (Dominic Monaghan) and Pippin (Billy Boyd). Together, they manage to escape the Ringwraiths twice and make it to the pub, hoping to meet Gandalf there. However, Gandalf, as the audience knows but the hobbits do not, has been taken prisoner by another wizard he had assumed was on the side of good but, had, in fact, taken the "realist" option and joined up with Mordor. Nevertheless, a ranger (a human who roams around the country) named Strider (who later turns out to be the lost king of Gondor, named Aragorn) decides to help the hobbits after he sees Frodo disappear when the ring finds its way onto his finger. Knowing the danger that is coming, Strider has the four hobbits change rooms so when the Ringwraiths appear, they stab decoys in the beds. Strider then leads the four to Rivendell, the home of Elrond (Hugo Weaving), the elvish king and an ally.

After some time in Rivendell, it is decided that the ring of power must be taken to Mount Doom in Mordor (where it was originally forged). Together with the four hobbits, two men (Aragorn and Boromir, played by Sean Bean), one dwarf, Gimli (John Rhys-Davies), and one elf, Legolas. They form the fellowship of the ring.

Given Frodo's history and apparent lack of destructive ambition, he is the primary ring bearer. Gandalf volunteers to accompany them on their journey as well.

It is interesting to note here the use of the term "fellowship" to describe the group tasked with saving Middle Earth. It is not a very likely term; it is not militaristic, nor does it have security force overtones—even though the members are all armed and prepared for battle. Perhaps Tolkien had in mind his group of academic and artistic friends, the Inklings, who thought that England needed a new way of thinking about the Christian tradition in a postwar culture. The religious undertones of "fellowship" as a key term to describe Christian community in the New Testament are indeed present here, especially when one considers the sacrificial nature of the quest and the obvious Satanic imagery associated with Sauron and Mordor, death and doom. But beyond fidelity to the original subtitle, Jackson's decision to keep the language in the film adaptation further signals a Millennial shift away from the strong, individualist hero, one who stands up against evil, to the value of friendships as a source of inherent good in the midst of darkness. And it is this theme of friendship, of the hard-to-define brotherly affection between them, that remains an attractive feature for a socially conscious generation. They are out to save not just Middle Earth but each other.

Setting out from Rivendell, they are chased by Ringwraiths and armies from the turncoat wizard, Saruman. At one point, they are forced to go underground, through the dwarfish kingdom of Moria. Disappointingly, goblins and orcs have preceded them, and all the dwarves have been killed. But there is one quiet moment during their Dantean, underground journey where Gandalf and Frodo talk about Gollum, who has been following them, and their quest. Frodo has just blurted out that someone should destroy Gollum. Gandalf says, "Do not be eager to deal out death and judgment . . . the pity of Bilbo may rule the fate of many. . . . All we have to decide is what to do with the time that is given to us. There are other forces at work in this world . . . besides the will of evil. . . . Bilbo was meant to find the ring which means that you were meant to find it. And that is an encouraging thought."

Here is perhaps the only direct reference in the film to some kind of transcendent, good Providence that is far more subtle in its machinations than those of evil and has a much longer endgame in mind than immediate subjugation through force. While skirting close to the bromide "Everything happens for a reason," the dialogue here realistically asserts both individual responsibility ("All we have to decide is what to do with the time that is given to us") and the presence of evil working in the world. But there is also the encouraging sense of purpose and meaning behind the events, even if they are not always obvious. This is exactly the kind of tempered, complex worldview that offers a counter to Millennial disillusionment and nihilism. Gandalf might as well be speaking directly to a 9/11-traumatized audience, offering hope. However, as the fellowship leaves the Mines of Moria, Gandalf falls off a ledge after battling a giant demon. Demoralized, the remnant visits some wood elves, whose witch queen is tempted by the ring.

Refreshed and sent on their way, they journey into the realm of men, where Boromir also makes a play for the ring, but Frodo evades him. A hunting party of Uruk-Hai (monster supersoldiers) sent from Saruman catches up to them, and Boromir redeems himself by holding them off long enough for Frodo and Sam to escape. The Uruk-Hai, thinking that Merry and Pippin were the main targets, kidnap them and race back to Isengard. Frodo and Sam head on to Mordor; Legolas, Gimli, and Aragorn decide to chase down the Uruk-Hai and save the two captive hobbits but not before Gimli asks if everything they had gone through had been in vain. Aragorn replies, "Not if we hold true to each other." Again, friendship and loyalty remain as good in the world despite the short-term efforts and successes of evil.

Twenty years on, the film clearly has some deficiencies in terms of the more developed social consciousness of Millennials and Gen Zers. There is not a single BIPOC represented in any substantial way. Heteronormativity prevails, with the exception of some homoerotic overtones of the fellowship and the relationship between Frodo and Sam. But by and large, it is a white, middle-class epic that offers a wider mythology to imagine than the mind-numbing possibilities of the work commute from the suburbs. On an ecological level, the contrast made between the harmonious relationship hobbits and elves have with the earth versus the strip mining of the dwarves and clear-cutting of the orcs drives home the message that saving Middle Earth means saving more than just its sentient inhabitants.

Shot mainly in New Zealand with a British director and based on a British novel series, *The Lord of the Rings* is not brimming with the type of American exceptionalism and triumphalism one associates with other Hollywood films about good and evil (see *Independence Day*). Perhaps the thin and attractive cast members, over-the-top special effects, and epic journey all link into the image-conscious, imperialistic military-industrial-entertainment complex's agenda for generating massive income (which this film and the others in the series undoubtedly have). But beyond the box office, *LOTR*, for Americans, reclaims something of what those early Americans felt about each other and the open future when they named a city, Philadelphia, the city of brotherly love.

Benjamin Crace

See also: *Indiana Jones and the Raiders of the Lost Ark*; *The Matrix*; *Pirates of the Caribbean: The Curse of the Black Pearl*; *X-Men*.

Further Reading

Bassham, Gregory, and Eric Bronson. 2003. *The Lord of the Rings and Philosophy: One Book to Rule Them All*. Chicago: Open Court.

Degim, Iclal Alev. 2013. "The Ents Will Rise Again: The Representation of Nature in the Film *The Lord of the Rings: The Fellowship of the Ring*." *Journal of Social Studies Research* (January): 91–97.

Knaus, Christopher. 2005. "More White Supremacy? The Lord of the Rings as Pro-American Imperialism." *Multicultural Perspectives* 7 (4): 54–58.

Laird, Raymond J. 2014. "J. R. R. Tolkien: Theologian in Disguise? Small Is Powerful: A Guiding Principle of *The Lord of the Rings*." *Evangelical Review of Theology* 38 (1): 81–90.

Morgan, Alun. 2010. "*The Lord of the Rings*: A Mythos Applicable in Unsustainable Times?" *Environmental Education Research* 16 (3–4): 383–399.

Thompson, Kristin. 2007. *The Frodo Franchise: The Lord of the Rings and Modern Hollywood*. Berkeley: University of California Press.

The Matrix

Release Date:	1999
Directors:	Lana and Lily Wachowski
Box Office:	$465.3 million
Main Cast:	Thomas Anderson/Neo, played by Keanu Reeves
	Trinity, played by Carrie-Anne Moss
	Morpheus, played by Laurence Fishburne
	Agent Smith, played by Hugo Weaving
	Cypher, played by Joe Pantoliano
	Tank, played by Marcus Chong

Released less than a month before the tragedy of Columbine, where 2 students gunned down 13 people before killing themselves, *The Matrix* has, rightly or wrongly, been associated with it. In some people's minds, the black trench coat style of Neo and others in the film is directly correlated to the events in Colorado, though footage clearly shows neither shooter wearing them. Less directly relatable is the excessive amount of gun violence in the film that may or may not have inspired the shooters—and not just the Columbine ones, for others have claimed subsequent shootings have been inspired by the films. More to the point, the potent suggestion that the real world is really an illusion we are all enslaved within does provide the philosophical framework for an already disassociated teen to further derealize others in addition to self. But aside from the controversies, the film is a watershed text in terms of the unfolding of American generational consciousness.

It begins with Neo getting recruited through various means by a team of people who all know that the real world is actually a computer simulation. Neo, a computer hacker, represents the hinge on which the Industrial Age swung into the Information Age. The hero is a computer nerd who must do battle with his mind instead of his body; the world itself is a computer game that must be hacked. As part of his recruitment, the audience, too, learns that there are agents (who look and sound a lot like FBI agents) who are out to stop the team from waking people up to the reality of the real world outside of the simulation; that is, the comatose human race is being used as an energy source by sentient robots in a dystopic future radically different from the "present-day" world of experience. At first, Neo is reluctant, but his curiosity (and budding attraction to Trinity) drives him on. He finally meets up with Morpheus, who offers him a choice in the form of two colored gel capsules that have now entered popular culture: the red pill or the blue pill. The blue one, apparently, will allow Neo to go back to the simulation. The red pill, however, will begin the process of disentangling his consciousness from the Matrix. He, of course, takes the red pill.

He awakes in the real world, inside a body-sized capsule among billions, where the BTUs of human biology are converted to energy for the robot overlords. In this nightmarish reality, the system rejects him since he is awake, and he is flushed down the sewer, where he is saved by the dingy, real-world counterparts of his new friends, Morpheus, Trinity, and others. Over time, he is rehabilitated and acculturated to the real world, which consists of riding around in their ship, the *Nebuchadnezzar*, hiding from squid-like, robot sentinels, and eating awful gruel. Life in the real world is so bad, in fact, that one crew member, Cypher, hates it so much he makes a deal with the ruling artificial intelligence to be put back into the Matrix in exchange for Morpheus, who knows where the last human city, Zion, is located. There is also talk of a prophecy about someone who will come and save humanity from its slavery. Morpheus and Trinity believe Neo to be this messiah, although he is very doubtful himself.

On board the *Nebuchadnezzar*, Neo receives martial arts and weapons training via a spike that goes into his brain through the access point that had him plugged into the original Matrix. All the training is intended for him to learn how to survive in the Matrix and to train his mind to see past the illusion of it. Not only does the crew have their own sandbox version of the Matrix but they also have access to the real one as well. It is then revealed to the audience and Neo that what happens to the mind in the Matrix affects the body outside of it. The mind-body link is so strong, then, that if someone dies in the Matrix, the person's body dies in the real world. These raised stakes help keep the whole plot from devolving into just a scaled-up video game.

The team decides to take Neo to the Oracle, a lady who lives in the Matrix but is aware of what it is and what will happen. She is the one who speaks prophecies and tells people their fate. When she meets with Neo, she lies to him that he is not the One (O-n-e/N-e-o anagram) but that he will have to make a decision about saving Morpheus, who believes that Neo is the one to the degree that Morpheus will sacrifice himself for the sake of this belief. Neo is relieved but worried about what may happen. As they try to leave the Matrix and return to the ship in the real world, Cypher, first back onboard the *Nebuchadnezzar*, betrays them, allowing the AI to capture Morpheus just before Tank (Marcus Chong), another crew member, kills him.

Neo and Trinity return to the ship and make plans to rescue Morpheus, whose body is showing signs of abuse from his captured avatar. They get as many guns as possible, go back into the Matrix, and make a raid on the building where the lead AI, known as Agent Smith (Hugo Weaving) is interrogating Morpheus. It is successful; they rescue Morpheus, and he and Trinity return to the ship in the real world. Unfortunately, Neo did not get out in time and is left to face Smith alone. They fight, but ultimately Neo cannot win, because an agent can become anyone within the simulation. So as soon as he kills one incarnation, the system just takes over the consciousness of another person and attacks. Thus, when Smith comes right back, Neo decides to run instead of fight again.

Three agents, including Smith, chase Neo through the city as he looks for a landline phone, the means through which they enter/exit the Matrix. He does not make it in time, and the agents catch him, shooting him while his body apparently dies in both worlds. Onboard, Trinity kisses him, and he resurrects in the Matrix. After stopping some bullets fired by the agents, he jumps inside Smith and explodes him. The other agents run. A point of view seen through Neo's eyes shows the audience that he now sees the code for the Matrix, the vertical, trickling green writing that indicates his godlike abilities.

The film ends with Neo in a phone booth, making a call to the governing AI. His closing speech is poignant:

> I know you're out there. I can feel you now. I know that you're afraid . . . you're afraid of us. You're afraid of change. I don't know the future. I didn't come here to tell you how this is going to end. I came here to tell you how it's going to begin. I'm going to hang up this phone, and then I'm going to show these people what you don't want them to see. I'm going to show them a world without you. A world without rules and controls, without borders or boundaries. A world where anything is possible. Where we go from here is a choice I leave to you.

He then steps out of the phone booth (here reminiscent of Superman) and (again, like Superman) flies off to the sounds of a heavy metal track by the band (appropriately named) Rage Against the Machine.

Unpacking the above speech, one hears the echoes of a vision of a kind of grassroots globalization away from bureaucratic and corporate hierarchies—an anarchist vision perhaps. But at the same time, there is a deeply American "don't tread on me," laissez-faire sense of possibility. The Superman parallel (who fights for truth, justice, and the American way) is more than coincidental. The last line, "a choice I leave to you," is foregrounded by the film's taut theme of free will versus fate/control clearly and finally falls on the side of autonomous choice, that central concept so cherished by all Americans. He may have been acting according to the prophecy, but he chose it all the way along. Neo made his own fate; it was not handed to him. It was, to recall a phrase from American history, his Manifest Destiny.

In terms of generational shifts, *The Matrix* is another of the pre-9/11 transitional texts of postmodernity. Boomers, perhaps telegraphed by the world-weary Cypher, would rather keep the illusion going, eat steak every day, and be rich (part of Cypher's deal with the AI)—basically, have the best version of the American dream. Gen Xers and Millennials can both identify with Neo, cubicle slave by day in an office (oddly paralleling the "real" world dystopia) and hacker by night with a secret identity as the messiah of the human race. Here the generations split: Xers want the embodied self to matter, to do physical things in the analog world. Neo needs to know how to use his fists. Millennials need to know that ultimately the Age of Information belongs to the digital savvy and not just the rebellious analogs. Neo "wins" by learning the code.

The worldview of *The Matrix* offers an alternative sci-fi metanarrative to the religious metanarratives of the past. Gods of the past litter the filmscape, mainly through allusive names: Morpheus, Greek god of sleep; Trinity, the inscrutable doctrine of Christianity; Nebuchadnezzar, the pagan, idol-making king of the Hebrew Bible; the Oracle, the Delphic fountain of paradoxical revelation. It is significant, too, that the only other candidate for messiah-ship whom Neo interacts with in the waiting room of the Oracle is a Buddhist monk (a shaved, Caucasian child with an English accent wearing a robe that is white instead of the typical saffron color). Cultural appropriation aside, it is clear that the Wachowskis want to centralize Buddhist philosophy as closest to the "reality" of things. This stands in marked contrast to Western Christian doctrines of sin and redemption. Neo, then, is less Jesus and more a bodhisattva, the Enlightened One who forgoes nirvana to help others achieve enlightenment. (Oddly enough, Reeves's character in his earlier film *Point Break* [1991], is friends with Patrick Swayze's Bodhi, short for bodhisattva.) *The Matrix* thus signals an ongoing, transgenerational fascination with the East, what writer Jeffrey Kripal calls "orientation," with an emphasis on Orient. But at the same time, the film offers a reconfigured spirituality without clear formal religious trappings. Sure, the world of the Matrix is an illusion, and the cold hard reality of the dystopic world seems to be thoroughly secularized—except that prophecies are believed and are fulfilled in *both* worlds. With more and more Millennials professing spirituality but not religion as part of their postmodern identity, the film navigates the fine line between complete modernistic materialism and the possibility of a post-postmodern magical realm of meaning and potential. It is a vision, ironically enough, that seems to run on the same tracks as any other religious vision: belief now reframed as belief in yourself and as others' beliefs about you.

Coming full circle, then, despite its unique version of a sci-fi dystopia, groundbreaking special effects, slick aesthetic, and hard-hitting philosophical underpinnings, *The Matrix* is as American as it gets. The black trench coat costumes are less some kind of weird tie-in to Columbine as they are an updated version of the Western gunslinger. The cult of the gun, of course, is alive and well in this film as well as the other two in the trilogy. It is romantic love that brings Neo back from the grave, and the salvation of the human race depends on a strong sense of self and the embracing of undiluted individualism. Only sleeping slaves are part of a wider community; individuals are the ones who really change society. The final shot speaks volumes: Neo, alone, the One, soaring above all others.

Benjamin Crace

See also: Lord of the Rings: The Fellowship of the Ring; Superman.

Further Reading

Díaz-Diocaretz, Myriam, and Stefan Herbrechter. 2006. The Matrix *in Theory*. Amsterdam, Netherlands: Rodopi.

Kimball, A. Samuel. 2001. "Not Begetting the Future: Technological Autochthony, Sexual Reproduction, and the Mythic Structure of *The Matrix*." *Journal of Popular Culture* 35 (3): 175.

King, C. Richard, and David J. Leonard. 2006. "Racing *The Matrix*: Variations on White Supremacy in Responses to the Film Trilogy." *Cultural Studies/Critical Methodologies* 6 (3): 354–369.

Lavery, David. 2001. "From Cinespace to Cyberspace." *Journal of Popular Film & Television* 28 (4): 150.

McFarlane, Brian. 2006. "*The Matrix*: Cult Classic or Computerized Con?" *Screen Education*, no. 41 (January): 105–109.

Purse, Lisa. 2005. "The New Spatial Dynamics of the Bullet-Time Effect." In *Spectacle of the Real: From Hollywood to "Reality" TV and Beyond*, edited by Geoff King, 151–160. Bristol, UK: Intellect Books.

Pirates of the Caribbean: The Curse of the Black Pearl

Release Date:	2003
Director:	Gore Verbinski
Box Office:	$654.3 million
Main Cast:	Captain Jack Sparrow, played by Johnny Depp
	Barbossa, played by Geoffrey Rush
	Will Turner, played by Orlando Bloom
	Elizabeth Swann, played by Keira Knightley
	Governor Weatherby Swann, played by Jonathan Pryce
	Anamaria, played by Zoe Saldana

Pirate stories of one stripe or another have been a staple in the Anglo-American world since Daniel Defoe penned *Robinson Crusoe* in 1719. Countless books and films have been made in the genre, which could also be recast, now in American terms, as a Western on water, featuring gunplay, treasure, a near limitless frontier, constant movement, and ongoing conflict between order and chaos. But few films have been adapted from an attraction at a theme park. Long before the film series, visitors to Disneyland (starting in 1967) and, later, Disney World (1973), could participate in the Pirates of the Caribbean experience. Set in the West Indies in the late 18th century, both the rides and the films reproduce a kind of capitalistic profiteering that accompanies militaristic imperialism and colonialization. In terms of the former, Disney's decision to introduce the attraction at both of its sites in the thick of the Vietnam War suggests that such a narrative offered a justification for America's involvement: the freedom- and adventure-loving, for-profit pirates are not pillaging and raping "bad" guys but are the marginalized and misunderstood heroes who navigate their way between empire and the "real" threat of the type of pirates who are incapable of having fun. Generations of Americans returned again and again to the pirate-as-hero attraction, and in 2003, when the first film was released, America was, yet again, involved in another war in another place. This time, it was Afghanistan. Distancing themselves from American militarism, Millennials were thus attracted to the film for many of the same reasons their Boomer grandparents stood in line for hours to ride the ride: Americans have an undying need to see themselves as the scrappy underdog, resisting empire and conformity at every turn.

The film begins with a rescue of an unconscious boy floating on wreckage, saved by a passing British vessel. Onboard is the governor of Port Royal, his daughter, Elizabeth, and Norrington (Jack Davenport), the captain. Roughly the same age as the castaway, Elizabeth takes and secretes away a gold medallion from the boy, who later turns out to be Will Turner. She is afraid that if the adults see the medallion, they will think the boy is a pirate.

The film then cuts to a few years later, and Elizabeth is grown but still in the house of her father. She has kept Turner's medallion near her bed, and she looks at it before the hustle and bustle of the day begins. There are many preparations being made as she and her family get ready for Norrington's promotion. Turner, now a blacksmith, comes in and presents the governor with a sword he has made as a commissioned present for Norrington. Meanwhile, Captain Jack Sparrow barely makes it into the harbor, as his boat sinks up to a few feet left of the mast. For the next few scenes, the movie cuts back and forth between the promotion ceremony at the citadel and Sparrow confusing some bumbling dock guards about stealing one of the British ships. He almost succeeds until he has to abandon his plan and rescue Elizabeth, who, due to the constriction of her corset, has passed out and fallen off the citadel into the sea. Her contact with the water, while wearing the mysterious medallion, initiates some kind of supernatural signal through the water that will eventually bring the *Black Pearl*, a pirate ship, to the town. Before the *Pearl* arrives, however, Jack is captured but escapes, only to get into a sword fight with Turner, whose boss ultimately knocks Jack out, leading to Jack's imprisonment.

At night, the *Black Pearl* sails in. The pirates are looking for the medallion, and the audience learns that there is something not quite right with these pirates: in moonlight, they appear as skeletons. Apparently, they are under a curse for stealing Aztec gold that was originally taken by Cortés. The curse means they live in a state of immortality but are unable to taste or smell or enjoy anything of life. The only way to break the curse is to get all the pieces of gold back to the treasure chest and offer the blood of the thief (or a near relative will do) to the offended gods. The colonial overtones here are obvious; both Cortés and Barbossa (the captain of the *Pearl*) are "cursed" for stealing from the Indigenous population of Central America. Perhaps unsurprisingly, little is made of enslaving and pillaging the Indigenous populations of the Caribbean and its natural resources. Only the Aztecs can curse gold, apparently. Other than underwriting the *Pearl*'s quest, the cursed-gold narrative allows the plot to supernaturally distance itself from directly critiquing empire; the British Navy just happens to be around and are the ones in charge of the town and the surrounding waters. They are there to add dramatic tension and a touch of historical realism but not much else. By way of contrast, Jack and his motley crew of women and POC offer a subtle American critique of the uniform lack of diversity in their British rivals. Jack's crew is democratically empowered; Barbossa's crew is cursed; and Norrington's all fall in line with the aristocratic British hierarchy.

For the rest of the film, these three spheres each receive various amounts of attention in a rather confusing pastiche of action and crosscutting. Barbossa mistakenly takes Elizabeth as a potential sacrifice and speeds toward the Isla de Muerta, where the treasure awaits both its final piece and blood. Will breaks Jack out of jail, and together they raise a crew to save Elizabeth, Will's true love. Jack is more concerned with getting the *Pearl* back, claiming that he is the true captain. Norrington and the governor also set out to chase down the fugitive Jack and the kidnapped Elizabeth. After a series of captures and escapes, and one marooning, the curse is lifted and the now-mortal Barbossa dies after being shot by Jack.

Always with an eye to law and order, Jack is taken back to Port Royal and ordered to be hanged. As the noose is lowered around his neck, Will, now a full-fledged pirate, helps him escape but is ultimately caught (again) by Norrington and his men. Elizabeth stands between them, declaring her love for Turner. Jack manages to dive into the sea, where he is rescued by his crew on the *Pearl*. They sail away as Norrington, now a bit more sympathetic to the "good" pirates, decides to give them a day's head start before chasing them down. The film ends with a medium shot of Jack, behind the wheel of the ship, looking off into the distance and saying, "Now, bring me that horizon."

Another way of thinking about this last closing scene is in terms of the American automobile mythology explored elsewhere in this text. The freedom to literally steer one's own destiny to new places of never-ending possibilities is an intoxicating part of the American car cult. Our very rites of passage center around receiving our driving licenses or, perhaps, making love in the back seat. Here, Jack Sparrow might as well be behind the wheel of a car instead of a large pirate ship. Like the cowboy riding off into the sunset, the driver and captain can leave the past behind and head West, that mythical realm of fully realized freedom and independence. This lust for independence symbolized by the car seems to, at least superficially, transcend generational distinctions. However, there is a growing trend of Millennials delaying this aspect of purported maturation, preferring digital freedom and socialization instead of the physical. Instead of chasing a literal horizon, they are staying home longer and opting for faster internet speeds. The car, then, is slowly being deconstructed as a status symbol and freedom archetype as the curated self, generated through expensive digital technologies, replaces it. Cell phones and social media accounts have replaced somewhat and will continue to slowly replace the driver license.

Additionally, like other blockbusters, *Pirates* also taps into the need for disillusioned generations to experience the uncanny. Yes, it is about piracy in the West Indies. Yes, the ships, soldiers, and costumes are all historically accurate and of the period. But the old gods' power in the precolonized Americas is still operative in the curse laid on Cortés' gold. It is a curse that seems not to fade with time but only with restitution and sacrifice. Could it also be the fear that increasingly haunts many Americans' minds as usurpers of the very land itself? Are restitution and sacrifice still possible to break our curse? Perhaps, too, the franchise's further amplification of the supernatural in later films offers even postmortem possibilities for setting things right in the spiritual world. As the spiritual but not religious moniker increases among Millennials and Gen Zers, their deep interconnectedness of transpersonal spirituality presently experienced in the digital world will refract backward toward our collective historical responsibility for the way things are. *Pirates*, then, offers a way forward, noted earlier: diverse democracy with leaders but not kings.

With a series box office of $4.542 billion, the mythos of the Pirates franchise and Disney's meteoric rise as a superconglomerate with its Marvel Comic Universe domination is not likely to collapse in the near future. These films continue to replenish the American, cross-generational need to see ourselves as underdogs against empire and as independently making our own destinies. The unease of actually being the new British Empire continues to be negotiated and renegotiated through these texts of popular culture.

Benjamin Crace

See also: *Avatar*; *The Lord of the Rings: The Fellowship of the Ring*.

Further Reading

Grabarek, Daryl. 2018. "The Real Story: *Pirates of the Caribbean*." *School Library Journal* 64 (5): 56.

Patton, Craig D. 2012. "From Depp to Breadth: Teaching World History with *Pirates of the Caribbean*." *World History Connected* 9 (1): 13.

Telotte, J. P. 2008. *The Mouse Machine: Disney and Technology*. Urbana: University of Illinois Press.

Williams, Jennifer R. 2006. "Pirates and Power: What Captain Jack Sparrow, His Friends, and His Foes Can Teach Us about Power Bases." *Journal of Leadership Education* 5 (2): 60–68.

Zhanial, Susanne. 2020. *Postmodern Pirates: Tracing the Development of the Pirate Motif with Disney's* Pirates of the Caribbean. Leiden, Netherlands: Brill/Rodopi.

Shrek

Release Date:	2001
Directors:	Andrew Adamson, Vicky Jenson
Box Office:	$484.4 million
Main Cast (Voices):	Shrek, played by Mike Myers
	Donkey, played by Eddie Murphy
	Princess Fiona, played by Cameron Diaz
	Lord Farquaad, played by John Lithgow

As a pre-9/11 film, *Shrek* is a watershed animated film that not only won the first Academy Award for Best Animated Feature but also became the foundation of a multibillion-dollar franchise. Based on the children's book *Shrek!* by William Steig, the film collates many of the disparate Gen X memes, solidifies them, and repackages them in a foundational mythological structure for Millennials. This process of refinement and retrenchment of values is achieved primarily through subverting the fairy tale and its accompanying expectations. The subversion is kept from being threatening by continually applied layers of humor: scatological, gross-out, slapstick, innuendo, and wordplay. Built on the back of years of irreverent animated television programs such as *The Simpsons*, *South Park*, and *Beavis and Butthead*, *Shrek*'s box office success is partly attributable to its Gen Xer wry detachment and pessimism as social critique and its borderline child-friendly packaging. The exaggerated accents and tonal registers of the two main characters, Shrek and Donkey, further accentuate the bombastic nature of the project. Myers's *Saturday Night Live* run and success through the Wayne's World films and Austin Powers parodies shaped Gen Xer consciousness; the Scottish accent he uses for Shrek almost exactly matches that of his Fat Bastard, from *Austin Powers: The Spy Who Shagged Me* (1999). Murphy's well-known penchant for speed-talking and insult (usually generously laced with expletives) is toned down to sidekick banter. In sum, *Shrek* did what Disney could not, locked as it was into propping up and producing the traditional fairy tale.

The film begins with someone reading an old, leather-bound, illustrated book that gives a brief exposition of a princess locked in a tower, foreshadowing the Fiona character, who is introduced later in the film. The film then shifts to indicate that Shrek, a green ogre with a round head and little fluted, hornlike ears in peasant dress, has been reading the fairy tale book while in an outhouse, using its pages for toilet paper. As he exits the outhouse, he picks at his buttocks and shakes off a page of the book from his foot. Smash Mouth, a popular alternative-rock band of the time, sings its hit "All Star." The nondiegetic, unexpected rock music accompaniment instead of the earlier orchestral tune underscores the fact that this is not the typical fairy tale. From this opening and through the credits, Shrek engages in his daily routine, which is full of disgusting activities such as a mud bath with farts and so on. As the main character, Shrek the ogre turns the fairy tale on its head; the "bad guy" is the lovable good guy, the antihero who just wants to be left alone.

Also in the opening sequence, the common trope of townspeople getting into a mob to go get the monster becomes a laughable escapade as Shrek sneaks up behind them while they plan to attack his borough in a tree stump. He clarifies that ogres are scarier than giants, that ogres will "make a suit from your freshly peeled skin." The mob backs away and Shrek roars, extinguishing their torches. Frozen, they don't run away until Shrek whispers to them, "This is the part where you run away." Despite being a humorous twist on the trope, the additional gore-horror suggestion of skinning someone alive retrieves the grotesque elements of the traditional fairy tale (see *Grimm's Fairy Tales*, which suggest cannibalism and other taboo acts) that usually get sanitized (or Disney-fied) in modern retellings. But at the same time, Shrek is making a disturbing intertextual allusion in his speech. Immediately after telling the mob that ogres "will make a suit from your freshly peeled skin," he continues to delineate the other horrible things ogres like to do, including "shave your liver and squeeze the jelly from your eyes. Actually, it's quite good on toast." Shrek's speech here alludes to a scene and line from *The Silence of the Lambs* (1991), where the infamous, cannibal serial killer, Hannibal, quips, "I ate his liver with some fava beans and a nice Chianti." Later in that film, Jame Gumb is shown to have skinned overweight women to make suits of their flesh. Given, too, that *Hannibal* (2001), the sequel to *The Silence of the Lambs*, was released three months prior to *Shrek*, such a reference would have hardly been lost on its audience. Again, this is not your parents' fairy tale, and from here and on throughout the rest of the film, idyllic childhood innocence is subverted.

Elsewhere in the world of the film, Lord Farquaad has issued rewards for fairy tale creatures because he believes them to be "fairy tale trash, poisoning my perfect world." His Final Solution soldiers sit in the woods at tables to receive incoming bounties. Characters from all sorts of fairy tales (e.g., the bears from *Goldilocks*, the three little pigs, witches, elves, fairies, dwarves from *Snow White*, etc.) are brought forward and then locked into horse-drawn wagons that look a lot like train boxcars. Despite the decontextualized appearances of stock fairy tale figures that make it somewhat humorous, it recalls the systematic collection and execution of Jews in the Holocaust. Neighbors are turning their fairy tale character neighbors in for money. One lady in particular, attempts to get Donkey taken, claiming he can talk. Donkey refuses to talk but then, when he thinks he is going to be able to escape, he starts chattering away, proving his identity to the soldier/henchman, who now sees him as the type of character that needs to be imprisoned. The concept of an identity that others suspect but that can remain hidden unless self-disclosed through circumstantial entrapment echoes many anecdotes of Jews on the run from the Nazis but who are betrayed by friends or break under interrogation. The Jewish/betrayal overtones of the scene are further hinted at by the reward for a witch: 20 pieces of silver—the exact amount and coinage Judas was paid to betray Jesus.

Donkey does indeed escape and manages to hide with Shrek. During the night, all sorts of fairy land creatures show up on Shrek's doorstep, looking for sanctuary. Perturbed that his life of peace and solitude has been upended by Lord Farquaad, whom he doesn't even know, Shrek determines to find him and clear things up so he can have his swamp back. He and Donkey begin their quest to Duloc, the human city of Lord Farquaad.

Meanwhile, in Duloc, Lord Farquaad is torturing the Gingerbread Man to give up more of his fairy tale friends for extermination. He is soaking him in milk and has already taken his legs. A magic mirror is brought in so Farquaad can see different, stereotypical princesses as candidates for marriage. He apparently needs to marry someone of royal lineage in order to become king. Reminiscent of *The Dating Game*, the mirror offers candidates in a game show format. Farquaad choses Fiona, who is stuck in a castle guarded by a dragon. Farquaad plots to send someone else to rescue her and bring her to the city. To decide whom to send, he plans a tournament.

Donkey and Shrek show up the day of the tournament and, after scaring everyone, end up in the arena. Farquaad initially has them attacked, but after they successfully defeat all the other contestants, he seizes the opportunity to make a bargain with Shrek. He promises him to give his swamp back if he goes and saves Fiona for him. Shrek agrees, and he and Donkey go on to the second part of their quest.

When they arrive at the castle where Fiona is prisoner, there is a large mountain with lava and fire surrounding it. They manage to get inside, narrowly miss getting burned and eaten by the dragon that guards it, and free Fiona. Fiona, perhaps like much of the audience, is hoping for a fairy tale hero and saving but instead gets Shrek, who says things like, "I have to save my ass." He is not a knight in shining armor, but she doesn't know he's an ogre since he wears a helmet with a face covering during her rescue. Donkey manages to subdue the dragon a bit by flirting with it, and they all escape. Afterward, Shrek reveals he is an ogre, which confuses Fiona because her true love is supposed to be the one who rescues her and Shrek is merely on a mission on behalf of Farquaad. She refuses to go along with it, so Shrek unceremoniously picks her up and carries her on his shoulder as they start their journey back to Duloc.

Along the way, there are some indications that Fiona is hiding something and that she is not the typical princess. At one point, she hides in a cave just as the sun goes down. At another, she defeats Robin Hood and his Merry Men who want to "save her" from Shrek, whom she is beginning to like. She uses martial arts, and the scene is a near-perfect parody of Trinity's combat in the opening scene of *The Matrix* (1999), another R-rated movie reference for the parents. In terms of character development, there is much dialogue devoted to judging people about their appearance. Fiona tells Shrek, "Maybe you shouldn't judge people before you know them." Here the ogre is not the misunderstood one, as the film has indicated, but even the beautiful stock princess may be more than meets the eye. It is also here that the subtle moralism of the film begins to emerge. Self-acceptance and a nonjudgmental approach to others' bodies are telegraphed in terms of their blossoming relationship (this despite the fact that numerous jokes are made about Farquaad being short). Such messaging elides well with the self-esteem movement of the late '70s that so shaped Gen X consciousness and the then-growing awareness of how body shaming could lead to a host of other dysfunctions such as eating disorders and so on. Essentially the feel-good message is that being you and being different are OK, but don't be quick to judge others with the criteria they may be tempted to use to judge you. This comes out much more clearly as it is revealed that Fiona is also an ogre as part of the spell a witch placed on her. But she is only an ogre from sundown to sunup. Not knowing this, Shrek initially thinks she wants to be away from him as quickly as possible, having overheard only part of her conversation with Donkey in which she expresses her self-loathing and Shrek mistakes it for her loathing him.

In sight of Duloc, Farquaad shows up to their camp with his men. He gives Shrek the deed for his swamp, as promised, and takes Fiona away on his horse. Fiona, unable to understand Shrek's cold shoulder, wants to get married as quickly as possible before she is exposed as a part-time ogre. She rushes Farquaad. Her departure depresses Shrek, and he distances himself from Donkey as well. A montage and several cut scenes show how hurt and lonely each character is: Shrek returns to his swamp, Donkey meets up with the lonely Dragon, and they comfort each other. Donkey goes back to the swamp and tries to build a fence on his half of the land. After arguing with Shrek, Donkey reveals the truth about Fiona and together, with the dragon, they fly off to stop the wedding.

In Duloc, Shrek succeeds in stopping the wedding. Moments later, after Farquaad mocks Shrek for falling for someone out of his league, she turns into an ogre in the fading light. Aghast, Farquaad proclaims that he is a king and demands Fiona and Shrek be taken prisoner. Donkey and the dragon break through the window and save the day by consuming Farquaad. Shrek tells Fiona he loves her, and he kisses her. When he does so, she is lifted up (much like Beast in *Beauty and the Beast*, 1991) in a golden magical light, and one expects her to transform back into her princess state. Instead, as she is gently lowered, she sees that she's still an ogre. She is confused; she says, "I'm supposed to be beautiful." To which Shrek replies, "But you are beautiful." From here, the fairy tale trope is reinstituted and they are married, "and they lived ugly ever after." The film ends with various characters dancing around to Smash Mouth's cover of the Boomer-era Monkees' "I'm a Believer," cementing *Shrek* as less than a perennial retelling and subversion of the fairy tale and more of a product of its cultural moment, replete with the now-dead Macarena dance.

As with most Hollywood blockbusters, the common American tropes are all here. There is the rough individualism of the alpha male who is followed around by a near-sycophantic buddy. There is concern about land and property: possessions. Following its early '00s cultural changes, women are not merely sidekicks or romantic objects but equal partners with similar amounts of agency as their male counterparts. Even the subversion of Disney (among other things, Duloc looks a lot like the Magic Kingdom, with stanchions for lining up and costumed characters at the entrance) is "American" in the sense that reinvention through mockery and parody have played an important role in the development of the modern American identity. Even *Shrek*'s crass humor draws on America's long tradition of vaudeville, Chaplin, and the Three Stooges—in seemingly an intentional departure from its British cultural roots that demand more of a subtle witticism. Loud, with an obviously pretend Scottish accent meant to grate on one's nerves, green as the American dollar, without manners, and larger than life, Shrek is an American ogre, the composite stereotype of the average American for the rest of the world.

Benjamin Crace

See also: *Beauty and the Beast*; *Beverly Hills Cop*; *The Matrix*.

Further Reading

Brabham, Daren C. (2006). "Animated Blackness in *Shrek*." *Rocky Mountain Communication Review* 3 (1): 64–71.

Caputi, Jane. (2007). "Green Consciousness: Earth-Based Myth and Meaning in *Shrek*." *Ethics & the Environment* 12 (1): 23–44.

Evely, Christine. (2004). "*Shrek*: A Study Guide." *Screen Education*, no. 36 (September): 70–81.

Roberts, Lewis. (2014). "'Happier Than Ever to Be Exactly What He Was': Reflections on Shrek, Fiona and the Magic Mirrors of Commodity Culture." *Children's Literature in Education* 45 (1): 1–16.

Zeenat, Afrin. (2017). "'You Are All Wrapped up in Layers': Pastiche, Paradox, and *Shrek*." *Studies in American Culture* 40 (1): 109–123.

Spider-Man

Release Date:	2002
Director:	Sam Raimi
Box Office:	$825 million
Main Cast:	Peter Parker/Spider-Man, played by Tobey Maguire
	Mary Jane Watson, played by Kirsten Dunst
	Norman Osborn/Green Goblin, played by Willem Dafoe
	Harry Osborn, played by James Franco
	Aunt May, played by Rosemary Harris
	J. Jonah Jameson, played by J. K. Simmons

Spider-Man, released the year after 9/11, is crawling with the larval archetypes that would later metamorphose to define Millennial consciousness and social sensibility. Already a naïve and slightly ironic antihero from his first appearance in another period of cultural upheaval, 1962, Raimi's Spider-Man is filled with both a deep sense of social responsibility ("friendly neighborhood Spider-Man"/"With great power comes great responsibility") and Millennial hustle in a downturned economy. Peter Parker's side job is photographing himself (the Selfie) as Spider-Man and selling the photos to an ignorant Boomer (the editor of *The Daily Bugle*, Jameson). He lives in the city, takes public transportation or walks everywhere, and ostensibly does not even have a license, which further distances him from American car culture as a symbol of independence in both the Boomer and Gen X generations. The few times he is in a car is when he is with Uncle Ben, his Boomer uncle. As Spider-Man, of course, his authentically unique way of transportation is to sling his webs from one building to another and swing along, high above the plebeians confined to their workaday, nine-to-five existence. And although a Gen Xer himself, Maguire's youthful looks allow him to play an 18-year-old when, in fact, he was already 26 when they started filming. His unique style of acting and form, not ruggedly good looking or suave or built, makes him less of a traditional "leading man" and more of the Millennial Everyman: greatness is within, changing the world is possible, but . . . it's complicated.

As the first in a trilogy, *Spider-Man* begins with the hero's origin and takes him up against a sinister bad guy, the Green Goblin. The first scenes show Peter as a bit of an outcast but whose marginal status allows him to be friends with dashing and rich Harry Osborn—himself on the margins because of his status as the son of Norman Osborn, a billionaire with a weapons contract with the Pentagon. The film loses no time in getting Peter bit by a genetically modified spider that begins his transformation process. Here is a clear updating from the original canon, where the spider was radioactive. Further, Harry is shown to be a bit of a romantic rival as well as Peter's friend; he flirts with Peter's lifelong crush, Mary Jane Watson (her name an obvious throwback to Spider-Man's creation in the 1960s, as Mary Jane is a euphemism for marijuana).

A cut scene shows Norman Osborn demonstrating a glider weapon to some Pentagon brass. It is basically a short, horizontal wing surfboard that can fire missiles and allow a lot of maneuverability for the single pilot. The military officers are unimpressed and want updates on Osborn's other project: supersoldier performance enhancers. One general tells him that they need to see human trials or he will lose his funding. This foreshadows Osborn desperately injecting himself and thereby creating his evil alter ego, the Green Goblin.

But here in 2002, we see the inklings of the Marvel Cinematic Universe beginning. Even though the Spider-Man character wouldn't appear in the MCU until 2016 in *Captain America: Civil War*, already we have some typical Marvel comic book-to-film tropes. For some reason, the U.S. military is always involved in one way or the other, as in *Iron Man* (2008). There is a plan to make some kind of supersoldier, as in *Captain America: The First Avenger* (2011) and *Captain America: Winter Soldier* (2014). There is also the heavy urbanization of setting; New York looms large, not only home to Spidey but to Stark Tower and the Sanctum Sanctorum of *Dr. Strange* (2016). More traditional to the genre, of course, is the love interest, the problem of identity (hence masks), and so on.

Parker, a modest, middle-class kid from the suburbs who uneasily transfers to life in the city, is the only one who can defeat the Green Goblin. This is intergenerational class conflict at its finest. Harry, who later takes up his father's mantle as Goblin, is depicted as a betrayer to his generation, giving undue weight to his father's legacy instead of his friendship (the bond that replaces the dissolved nuclear family among Millennials) with Peter.

But before his showdown with the Goblin, Peter discovers his powers and, embarrassed, tries to hide them at first. This awkwardness with regard to powers clearly parallels the unease and discomfort of adolescents coming to terms with their sexual development. As if to telegraph this point, he spends a lot of his time in his room alone, shooting white stuff out of his body everywhere. His aunt, worried about him, knocks on his door, and he tells her he is undressed. This same teenage awkwardness comes across in his communication with Mary Jane (MJ). When he does finally get to have a conversation with her (she is actually his neighbor), he is overly sincere and flattering: "You're gonna light up Broadway."

Trying to impress her, he decides he wants to buy a car, which seemingly represents the temptation to the path of inauthenticity rooted in the illusion of a slowly crumbling American Dream: first the car, then the girl, then the marriage, and so forth. To do so, he needs money and so decides to enter a wrestling contest for prize money. After beating the professional wrestler with his newfound powers, Peter is tricked out of the money by a managerial technicality. On his way out of the office to the elevator where he was supposed to have been paid, a criminal on the run asks to go first. Seeing that this guy has stolen from the manager who conned him, Peter steps aside and lets him pass. The manager exasperatedly demands to know why he did it. Peter throws his words back at him: "I missed the part where that is my problem." Later, it is revealed that this same thief is also a carjacker who ends up shooting Peter's beloved Uncle Ben—at the end of a series of events that was set off by his failure to stop the guy at the elevator. Peter, understandably, feels responsible.

Yet at a deeper level, it was the decision to follow the classic American path to adulthood that began the chain of events that led to his uncle's death in, of all places, a car. Here then is the deconstruction of the car as mythic American archetype; rather than a place of freedom unto success, it becomes the site of death and a symbol for what happens when one places one's own pursuit of the Dream ahead of social responsibility. We live in a networked and interconnected world where one's own actions reverberate into the lives of others. With a post-9/11 New York as backdrop, the messaging here is clear: the world itself is deeply interconnected, and actions somewhere else to someone else bring the problems back to our own doorsteps. The solution: the younger generation must step up, deny the false ideology of happiness in life in the suburbs, and defeat the Green Goblins (read: terrorists) that the Boomer military inadvertently but somewhat intentionally created. Recall, too, that the Goblin's preferred way of bringing terror is by flying and creating explosions. One scene where he destroys a balcony full of his enemies is a little too on the nose of blown-up buildings in Manhattan.

After Ben passes, Peter goes after the perpetrator as Spider-Man, now losing his innocence and becoming the rogue, near-vigilante crime fighter. He catches the guy who, in classic Hollywood fashion, ends up falling to his death instead of dying at Peter's hand. Later, he goes home and tells his Aunt May what happened, signaling the end of his childhood. This is further underscored by a high school graduation and then a move to the city, where he rooms with Harry, who is secretly dating MJ. But he has his own secret too. As Spider-Man, he begins to gain a reputation for catching criminals.

Over a series of scenes, Harry and Peter drift apart over MJ, who believes she is in love with Spider-Man after a post-rescue kiss. Norman fully embraces the Goblin, tries to recruit Spider-Man to his side to no avail, and deduces that Peter is Spider-Man. He then scares Aunt May to the point of hospitalizing her. At the hospital, Peter realizes his love for MJ and that Osborn knows who he is. Harry, too, figures out that MJ is in love with Peter and tells his father, who vows to make things right.

The climax of the film occurs when the Goblin forces Peter to choose between saving MJ or a tram full of kids dangling off a bridge. Peter manages to do both and wins a brief respite from the Goblin's attack, because New Yorkers as a crowd attack him in a powerful display of post-9/11 solidarity against terrorists. But the moment is short lived; Peter and Norman resume fighting elsewhere, and the latter ends up dead when Peter moves out of the way of the Goblin's glider aimed at him. Peter/Spider-Man carries Norman's body back to his penthouse where Harry sees him, believing he is responsible.

The film ends with Norman's funeral. Harry, not knowing Peter is Spider-Man, vows revenge. MJ wants more of a relationship with Peter, but since he knows that he must remain unattached for her safety, he rejects her. She is heartbroken at being sent to the friend zone, but she realizes from their last kiss that he is Spider-Man. He offers this monologue: "With great power comes great responsibility. Who am I? I'm Spider-Man." Thus the first *Spider-Man* film in nearly a quarter of a century ends with what later becomes a signature MCU line.

But this isn't quite the end. The closing shots show Spider-Man web slinging and swinging around New York and coming to a perch on top of a building with a giant American flag streaming behind him. Here is the final shot that recapitulates the rest of the film: America and New York are back on top, our collective and national anxieties expunged through the defeat of the Goblin. This defeat is at the hands of a committed Millennial hero who not only eschews romantic love but even riches, those generational temptations that must be refused to save the world. A hero is now one who is defined ("I'm Spider-Man") by service to others rather than in service to a dismantled American Dream.

Benjamin Crace

See also: *The Avengers*; *Iron Man*.

FURTHER READING

Burke, Liam. 2015. *The Comic Book Film Adaptation: Exploring Modern Hollywood's Leading Genre.* Jackson: University Press of Mississippi.

Koh, Wilson. 2009. "Everything Old Is Good Again: Myth and Nostalgia in *Spider-Man*." *Continuum: Journal of Media & Cultural Studies* 23 (5): 735–747.

Meyer, Michaela D. E. 2003. "Utilizing Mythic Criticism in Contemporary Narrative Culture: Examining the 'Present-Absence' of Shadow Archetypes in *Spider-Man*." *Communication Quarterly* 51 (4): 518–529.

Richardson, Niall. 2004. "The Gospel According to *Spider-Man*." *Journal of Popular Culture* 37 (4): 694–703.

Sanford, Jonathan J. 2012. Spider-Man *and Philosophy: The Web of Inquiry.* Hoboken, NJ: John Wiley & Sons.

Star Wars: Episode I—The Phantom Menace

Release Date:	1999
Director:	George Lucas
Box Office:	$1.027 billion
Main Cast:	Padmé Amidala, played by Natalie Portman
	Qui-Gon Jinn, played by Liam Neeson
	Obi-Wan Kenobi, played by Ewan McGregor
	Mace Wendu, played by Samuel L. Jackson
	Anakin Skywalker, played by Jake Lloyd

As an attempt to reboot the Star Wars franchise for the Millennial generation, *The Phantom Menace* was the first *Star Wars* film since the release of *Return of the Jedi* in 1983. Just two years prior to its release, however, Lucas made additional changes to the original trilogy that appeared in a special edition. Unlike the previous films, *Menace* relies less on puppet and in-camera special effects and more on CGI characters and settings. Further, rather than carrying the events of the original trilogy forward, it, and the sequels that follow, are all prequels to the originals. However, the events are not so far back in time as to not be able to feature some of the original cast: Kenny Baker reprised his role as R2-D2, Anthony Daniels as C-3PO, Frank Oz as Yoda, and Ian McDiarmid as Senator Palpatine (later, the Emperor). There is, then, some measure of continuity and nostalgia with these cast members, Lucas as director, and John Williams providing the music. A large part of the film takes place on Tatooine (Luke Skywalker's home planet in *A New Hope*), and even the Hutts (giant, sluglike gangsters from *Return of the Jedi*) make an appearance.

But despite all the appearances of continuity and rebooting, *Menace* is a product of its American cultural moment. Gone are the echoes of the twin specters of Nazism and communism that resounded through the originals. Instead, the America of the last decade of the last millennium had to face its own status as the surviving superpower sliding further toward its own dark imperialism and erosion of democratic standards: a bombing campaign in Iraq and President Clinton's impeachment. In the background, too, of the film's attempted genocidal slaughter of the Gungans on Naboo (perhaps a veiled allusion to the ancient African culture of Nubia), and the much-criticized, purported racist portrayal of the Gungans' language, is the Rwandan Genocide of 1994. However, the opening scroll frames the narrative primarily in bureaucratic and economic terms: "Turmoil has engulfed the Galactic Republic. The taxation of trade routes to outlying star systems is in dispute. Hoping to resolve the matter with a blockade of deadly battleships, the greedy Trade Federation has stopped all shipping to the small planet of Naboo. While the Congress of the Republic endlessly debates this alarming chain of events, the Supreme Chancellor has secretly dispatched two Jedi Knights, the guardians of peace and justice in the galaxy, to settle the conflict." One could just as easily read "United States" for "Galactic Republic" as the dominant superpower that heavily influenced globalization and the real-life "Trade Federation" known as the World Trade Organization. Here, too, are allusions to presidents using the military at their own discretion—overriding or avoiding Congressional approval—recalling both Nixon's bombing of Cambodia (1969–1970) and the Battle of Mogadishu or the Black Hawk Down incident in 1994. Here, Jedi knights are no longer the stalwart defenders of the Rebel Alliance in the face of a fascist threat but, rather, pawns of an unwieldy bureaucracy on the brink of collapse (which takes place in the other two films after *Menace*).

As the scroll indicates, the film begins with the Trade Federation blockading the planet of Naboo—which is inhabited by humans called the Naboo and an amphibious frog-crossed-with-a-dog humanoid species known as Gungans. Traditional enemies, the Gungans and Naboo, must learn to work together to defeat the Trade Federation, which, as it turns out, is merely a tool for political leverage for Senator Palpatine of Naboo to gain power. He has orchestrated the whole thing so as to get himself placed as the supreme chancellor and from there, like Julius

Caesar, become emperor. Palpatine's political schemes are fueled by his devotion to the dark side of the Force (this creates his alter ego: Lord/Darth Sidious), that cosmic energy field that embraces all things. He is the antithesis of a Jedi; he is a Sith lord who has trained another Sith in the ways of the Dark Side. His enemies are the Jedi and Queen Amidala of Naboo, to whom he must pretend deference. Throughout the film, however, neither the Jedi nor Amidala figure out who he is or what his plan is, setting up the rest of the prequels.

The main Jedi characters, Qui-Gon Jinn and Obi-Wan Kenobi, escape the Trade Federation's plan and ship to land on the surface below. After teaming up with obnoxious Gungan Jar Jar Binks, they secure passage to the main city of Naboo. There they warn the queen and tell her that she needs to go plead Naboo's side of the blockade to the Senate on the planet Coruscant, the seat of government for the Galactic Republic. She reluctantly agrees and, together with her retinue, departs with the two Jedis. In the process, however, the Trade Federation's ships damage their craft, and they are forced to land on Tatooine for repairs.

On Tatooine, the two Jedis, accompanied by Padmé (supposed handmaid to Queen Amidala, who is actually the Queen herself playing her decoy) and Jar Jar, go into a parts dealer to negotiate for the things they need. The owner, a large-nosed, flying creature called a Toydarian but named Watto is not very helpful and tells them that their money won't work on the planet. Even after Jinn attempts to change his mind with a Jedi mind trick, he laughs and says, "Mind tricks don't work on me. Only money." Here, again, is another possible racial stereotype cropping up in the least likely of places. The name of his species looks surprisingly Armenian or Eastern European, while the caricatured facial protuberance and attachment to money (being too smart for Jedi mind tricks to work) suggest a subtle anti-Semitism at play. Watto, as it is quickly discovered, owns Anakin (the future Darth Vader, i.e., Luke Skywalker's father) and his mother as his slaves. Anakin, a nine-year-old boy, fixes and cleans parts in the shop. He is taken with Padmé, and the outsiders leave. Once outside, a storm rolls in, and Anakin invites them to his house, where he lives with his mom.

At his house, Jinn begins to suspect that Anakin may have the capability of being a Jedi after he talks about pod racing, a form of entertainment akin to Grand Prix. Jinn explains their mission, and Anakin offers to help them through gambling on his piloting of a pod in the upcoming race. They make a deal with Watto, and there is a brief but controversial scene where Jinn speaks to Anakin's mother, Shmi, about him. Apparently, Anakin has no father, and, as revealed later, was conceived directly by the midi-chlorians, microscopic organisms that mediate the Force to their hosts. This origin story for Anakin was widely contested and hotly debated by Star Wars fans for years. Additionally, Lucas's appropriation of Jesus's virgin birth for a character that turns into less a messiah and more of a devil became religiously problematic. It does, however, signal the areligious but spiritual turn of the late 1990s. As more and more Gen Xers left organized religion, perennial systems of philosophy and spirituality gained wider acceptance and traction. And even though it is science fiction, the Force has a deep similarity to spiritual thinking involving the chi or qui—further suggested by Qui-Gon Jinn (the latter name a reference to Islamic spirits). Thus, a virgin birth by the Force, to many in the audience, seemed as plausible as one by the Holy Spirit, both operating at the mythic and cosmic levels.

After Anakin wins the pod race, he is set free to join the Jedis, and after a brief battle with another Sith, Darth Maul, the entourage travels to Coruscant. There the queen, with the prompting of Senator Palpatine, helps lead the vote against the supreme chancellor while the two Jedis discuss training Anakin as a Jedi with the Jedi Council. The senator ends up as a nominee, and Queen Amidala decides to go back to be with her people, who are suffering under the blockade and a subsequent invasion.

What is interesting here is the amount of backstory Lucas provides with regard to the Force and the strange prophecy of one "who will bring balance to the Force." There are also some heavy Buddhist overtones that further *Star Wars'* amalgam of science fiction with a plausible "New Age" spirituality. At one point, Yoda, riffing on the Four Noble Truths of Buddhism, delineates not only the path to the Dark Side but also the plots of the next two films. He tells Anakin, "Fear leads to anger, anger leads to hate, and hate leads to suffering." Later, as a mix of the Law of Attraction and scientific mysticism, Jinn tells Anakin, "Your focus determines your reality." And he then explains the midi-chlorians: "[They are a] microscopic life-form that resides within all living cells . . . and we are symbionts with them. Without the midi-chlorians, life would not exist and we would have no knowledge of the Force. They continually speak to us, telling us the will of the Force. When you learn to quiet your mind, you'll learn to hear them." This is as close as the *Star Wars* canon gets to an explanation of the Force and how Jedis/Siths interact with it.

From here, it plays out much as one expects of a sci-fi opera. The Jedis, Queen Amidala, and the others all return to Naboo. They recruit the Gungans to help them fight off the droid army of the Trade Federation and end up retaking the Naboo capital city. In the process, Darth Maul, the assassin for Darth Sidious, kills Jinn but is later cut in two by Kenobi and falls, presumably, to his death. Before his last breath, Jinn reiterates Anakin's future, asking Kenobi to train him: "He's the chosen one. He will bring the balance."

The film ends in much the same way as *Return of the Jedi* and *A New Hope* do. There is a funeral pyre for Jinn, and the queen officiates an award ceremony for the hero survivors. There is reconciliation between the Gungans and the Naboo, and the Jedi are suspicious of who the other Sith may be. Yet for all their powers and clairvoyance, they can't figure out that it's Senator Palpatine. Thus the stage is set for *Attack of the Clones* and *The Revenge of the Sith*, the final films in the prequel trilogy.

Like *The Matrix*, released the same year, *Phantom Menace* has the same type of prophecy of a powerful individual who will do great things. This individual must realize his destiny through his own free choices and the inscrutable power of Fate, thinly disguised as the Force (with no unsubtle telegraphing of coercion and determinism). This paradox of choice and destiny lies at the very heart of the American psyche and even governs the two-party political system: Democrats often want to address societal issues that transcend individual choice while Republicans tend toward viewing individuals as responsible for their own way in the world, systems be damned. Further, the pioneering and freedom-loving dimensions of American culture push against such ideas as Fate except when confronted with a destiny that upholds its individualistic emphasis. Important people are born for greatness, for such a time as this, and so on. We like our heroes a little flawed and not completely responsible but responsible enough to get credit. Anakin's narrative as a young, innocent boy who becomes Darth Vader but ultimately destroys the Emperor plays carefully on this edge of destiny and choice. And in the spirit of American entrepreneurship, the saga made Lucas billions.

Benjamin Crace

See also: *Star Wars: The Force Awakens*; *Star Wars: A New Hope*; *Star Wars: Return of the Jedi*.

Further Reading

Brooker, Will. 2001. "Readings of Racism: Interpretation, Stereotyping and the Phantom Menace." *Continuum: Journal of Media & Cultural Studies* 15 (1): 1.

Meyer, David S. 1992. "*Star Wars*, Star Wars, and American Political Culture." *Journal of Popular Culture* 26 (2): 99–115.

Morris, Kathleen. 1999, July 19. "This Phantom Is a Menace to Toymakers." *BusinessWeek*, no. 3638: 42.

Robb, Brian J. 2012. *A Brief Guide to* Star Wars*: The Unauthorised Inside Story*. London: Perseus Books.

Taylor, Chris. 2014. *How* Star Wars *Conquered the Universe: The Past, Present, and Future of a Multibillion Dollar Franchise*. London: Head of Zeus.

Taylor, Ella. 2000. "Cyberreality Bites. Boys, Toys and Girl Trouble in 1999's Top Ten." *Nation* 270 (13): 30–34.

Transformers

Release Date:	2007
Director:	Michael Bay
Box Office:	$1.027 billion
Main Cast:	Sam Witwicky, played by Shia LaBeouf
	Robert Epps, played by Tyrese Gibson
	William Lennox, played by Josh Duhamel
	Seymour Simmons, played by John Turturro
	Mikaela Banes, played by Megan Fox

Many Gen Xers grew up watching Saturday morning cartoons in a near ritualistic fashion. And between the years 1984 and 1987—in the middle of the decadent generation of the Reagan era—*Transformers* was a weekly staple. However, perhaps given the special effects and computer graphic capabilities of the time, a live-action version of the series seemed a remote possibility. But what was not remote was the possibility of owning the toys based on the animated series that were produced by Hasbro. In the world of play, then, young Gen Xers could create their own storylines with their favorite Autobots (the Transformers who want to protect humanity) and Decepticons (the Transformers who want to destroy humanity). As was the case with the Star Wars franchise, *G.I. Joe*, and others, *Transformers* was as much about the toy industry as it was television. Bay's film in 2007 superficially seems to be an attempt to reactivate all these nostalgic elements for an older Gen X audience while offering an entry point for them to initiate their children into the lore. Yet there is much more to the film than a reboot for Gen Xers and their kids. In fact, there is a set of complex underlying meanings that makes the film a quintessential Millennial production that outstrips its Gen X glossing.

The film begins its exposition with a religiously laden alternative narrative to the Judeo-Christian Genesis story. In a voice-over by Optimus Prime (the leader of the Autobots, voiced by the same voice actor from the '80s series, Peter Cullen), we are told, "Before time began, there was the Cube. We do not know where it comes from, only that it holds power to create worlds and fill them with life. That is how our race was born. For a time, we lived in harmony, but like all great power, some wanted it for good, others for evil. And so began the war, a war that ravaged our planet until it was consumed by death, and the Cube was lost to the far reaches of space." Here is a new cosmology, edging out the dead or dying gods of human mythology. The Cube is a mysterious object that has the power to "create worlds and fill them with life"—like the God of Genesis 1. And, again, similar to the Genesis account, power becomes the source of conflict between these superhuman beings, and a war results, an allusion to the angelic revolt described in Revelation 12: "And there was a war in heaven [read: outer space on the Transformers home world of Cybertron]: Michael and his angels [read: Optimus Prime and the Autobots] fought against the dragon [read: Megatron, the leader of the Decepticons, voiced by Hugo Weaving]; and the dragon fought and his angels [the other Decepticons] . . . and the great dragon was cast out . . . he was cast out into the earth, and his angels were cast out with him [the battle moves to earth from outer space]." Yet at this point in American history, fewer and fewer Americans were identifying as religious, so these clear rescriptions of Christian apocalypticism probably went mostly unnoticed. But all the pieces are there, even in the naming: Optimus Prime, the best and the first, like Michael, the most powerful archangel; and Megatron's name and lore connects him with a mysterious Metatron, the name of another archangel in mystical Judaism. And although Autobots "deceive" by hiding in plain sight as things other than what they are, only the "bad guys" are called Decepticons, thus linking them to one of the names of Satan, the Deceiver.

The blurring and wholesale appropriation of these traditions in the series and film follows a rather long arc within American popular culture that extends back to beginnings of comic books and is carried forward into film through the strenuous efforts of filmmakers, in particular, Steven Spielberg. This arc could be described as the E.T. as cosmic brother. Spielberg's early films, *Close Encounters of the Third Kind* and *E.T.: The Extra-Terrestrial*, explore this idea. That he was also the executive producer for Bay's movie is no small coincidence. In comic books, as worked out through the films that constitute both the Marvel Cinematic Universe and the DC Universe, the religious overtones are as overt as described above; these entities are not just alien superheroes but were thought to have been gods by older human cultures (e.g., Thor). Ridley Scott, too, through his *Alien* films but especially in his *Prometheus* films (2012 and 2017), props up the idea that humans themselves are the product of alien science or a reformulation of the theory of panspermia, that is, life came to earth from outer space (perhaps the Cube?). Each generation, then, has had its own contact with this meme; *Transformers* is but another iteration for the Millennials.

After the audience witnesses the Cube crashing to Earth, the film's cosmic scope narrows down to the small, Middle Eastern country of Qatar. Here is the U.S. military's forwarding base of operations for the region in a post-9/11 world of militaristic retaliation. A dark helicopter lands without permission at the base, transforms into a giant robot, and starts attacking everything, eventually destroying the whole base. A few soldiers escape to tell the tale.

Meanwhile, the story shifts to Sam presenting a genealogy project in front of his high school history class. It is not as much a presentation as it is an advertisement: he is trying to sell his great-great-grandfather's Arctic exploration artifacts for money to buy a car (a very American thing to want to do, apparently). His dad picks him up after class, and they go to a used car dealer. Very quickly, sex, freedom, and driving are connected. Sam argues with his dad about various models, telling him one is a "forty-year-old virgin" and another a "fifty-year-old virgin." Clearly, a "hot" car leads to sexual possibilities in the present without waiting until middle age. This linkage of sex and machine is a consistent trope in the film. Mikaela (Megan Fox), his love interest, is repeatedly objectified and shows her cleavage, midriff, and bare legs throughout the movie. In one scene, the camera leeringly follows her body as she looks under the hood of Sam's car. And although she has some empowerment, the film fails the Bechdel test left, right, and center. In media studies, the Bechdel test is a quick way to determine female representation. It asks: Does the film have more than two women who talk to each other about something other than a man? Here and elsewhere in the film, women rarely if ever appear together on screen without a man present, and when they do, they are talking about one of the male characters. Mikaela's solo objectification in scene above ranks as sheer voyeurism. In any event, the used car Sam ends up with is, in fact, Bumblebee, one of the Autobots.

It takes some time for Sam to work this out, of course. In the meantime, the U.S. government prepares for an attack on what it thinks is a foreign power by sending out its ships into the Arabian Gulf and the Yellow Sea. Young hackers, recruited by the Pentagon, figure out that it is not a foreign power that has attacked the base but an extraterrestrial enemy. This is later confirmed by some soldiers who survived the attack (Lennox and Epps). Sam figures out his car is an Autobot and he and Mikaela are contacted by Optimus Prime and others to help them find Sam's great-great-grandfather's glasses, which have, through a rather confusing process, been imprinted with the location of the Cube, or AllSpark. Apparently, Megatron, when he was looking for the AllSpark millennia before, had crashed in the Arctic (like *The Thing from Another World*, 1951). When Sam's ancestor found him, he transferred the location to him—a process that left him insane—as well as the treasure map on the lenses of his glasses.

Sam, Mikaela, and the Autobots eventually team up with a secret government agency known as Sector 7 and travel to Hoover Dam, where the government has been hiding both the Cube/AllSpark and the inactive body of Megatron since 1913. The Dam was apparently built around the AllSpark to hide it from detection. At the Dam, they also meet up with Lennox and company while trying to decide what to do. The Decepticons, through spying, have also figured out where the AllSpark is and prepare to attack. Megatron, of course, is brought back online, and the good guys evacuate with the AllSpark, which has now been reduced down to a portable size. They flee to Mission City nearby, and there is a lengthy battle scene between the military, Decepticons, and Autobots. The main battle is between Optimus and Megatron. Eventually, Sam pushes the AllSpark into Megatron and destroys him and it. A single leftover shard remains that Optimus takes to set up the sequel.

The film ends with the bodies of the Decepticons being dropped into the Laurentia Trench, one of the deepest places in the ocean. The Autobots determine to stay on earth and protect humanity. Sam and Mikaela kiss and make out on the hood of Bumblebee on an overlook at sunset, suggesting that the car indeed enhances sexuality and masculinity. At this point, Bumblebee is no longer a broken down, used Chevrolet Camaro but a brand new one, so the scene is more akin to a car commercial than simply the end of the film.

Aside from the spectacle of a typical Michael Bay film (*The Rock*, 1996; *Armageddon*, 1998; *Pearl Harbor*, 2001), what anchors this film into Millennial generational consciousness is Shia LeBeouf's performance and the direct carryover of Optimus Prime's character and voice from the animated series. Unlike their Gen X predecessors, who value ironic detachment and cynicism, neither Sam nor Optimus speaks or does anything other than with sincerity. This cultural shift, noted by critics, is even named the New Sincerity and emerges most forcefully in the texts of the popular culture (and even the "high-brow" art) of Millennials. Sam says exactly what he thinks and feels without dissimilitude toward anyone. He is, in other terms, authentic. Optimus, too, with his deep voice and matter-of-fact tone, does not have a hidden agenda but clearly means what he says; we are prone to trust him without qualification (think, too, of Captain America/Steve Rogers). Thus the Witwicky family motto that recurs through the film, "No sacrifice, no victory," comes off as a genuine summation of Sam and Optimus's values rather than a cheap platitude or mantra used to steel oneself for bravery. LeBeouf's quirky performance, half-comedic and half-dramatic, generates a new type of heroic confidence based more on the primacy of personality and character than on looks and actions, as for other heroes. There is a sense in which his adoption of the clichéd beliefs of the typical American teenager, that is, nice car = sex, seems humorous precisely because of his authentic nature. The audience knows he does not really believe the equation, and if he does, we know it is naïvely.

Despite the New Sincerity qualities inherent in the film, its American bravado is on full display, leaning heavily on tropes and clichés previously mentioned: teenagers, cars, sex, freedom, and so on. The square-jawed, blond soldier, Lennox, is the typical American hero, a foil to the sincere but "weaker" Sam. Subtler nods to Americentrism are also here: the AllSpark crashed in, of all places,

Nevada—despite the fact that the earth is 71 percent water. Even Bumblebee, a German-made Volkswagen Beetle originally, becomes the quintessential, American-made muscle car. And, given, too, Bay's partnership with Hasbro, there is no doubt that the film continues the tradition of maximizing the franchise's profits through the toy and video game industry. The almighty dollar is perhaps the true cosmology behind *Transformers*.

Benjamin Crace

See also: *The Avengers*; *Close Encounters of the Third Kind*; *E.T.: The Extra-Terrestrial*; *The Lord of the Rings: The Fellowship of the Ring*; *The Matrix*.

Further Reading

Bacon, Simon. 2012. "(S)Mothering Reproduction: Procreation, Gender and Control in the *Transformers* Films in Michael Bay." *Femspec* 12 (2): 47–65.

Beck, Bernard. 2009. "Something for the Boys: *Iron Man*, *Transformers*, and *Grand Theft Auto IV*." *Multicultural Perspectives* 11 (1): 27–30.

Dudenhoeffer, Larrie. 2017. *Anatomy of the Superhero Film*. Cham, Switzerland: Palgrave Macmillan.

Mirrlees, Tanner. 2017. "Transforming *Transformers* into Militainment: Interrogating the DoD-Hollywood Complex." *American Journal of Economics & Sociology* 76 (2): 405–434.

Sperb, Jason. 2016. *Flickers of Film: Nostalgia in the Time of Digital Cinema*. New Brunswick, NJ: Rutgers University Press.

Twilight

Release Date:	2008
Director:	Catherine Hardwicke
Box Office:	$407.1 million
Main Cast:	Bella Swan, played by Kristen Stewart
	Edward Cullen, played by Robert Pattinson
	Jacob Black, played by Taylor Lauter
	Rosalie Hale, played by Nikki Reed
	Alice Cullen, played by Ashley Greene
	Jessica Stanley, played by Anna Kendrick

Every generation has its cinematic vampires, going all the way back to *Nosferatu* (1922) and the classic *Dracula* (1931) with Bela Lugosi. But Gen Xers and Millennials seem to have a particular fascination with them. The '80s saw *Fright Night* (1985) and *The Lost Boys* (1987), and in the '90s, *Bram Stroker's Dracula* (1992) and *Interview with a Vampire* (1994). The most famous TV vampire series, *Buffy the Vampire Slayer* (1997–2003), seeded the minds of millions of Millennials and paved the way for the success of the Twilight series—a five-film saga that netted more than $3.3 billion. As with many films, there is an author behind them. For Gen Xers the vampire author extraordinaire was Anne Rice, who penned eight Vampire Chronicles over three decades. Only two of the series, *Interview* and

Queen of the Damned (2002), were made into films. The former featured mega superstars Tom Cruise, Brad Pitt, and a young Kirsten Dunst. The latter starred the late R and B superstar, Aaliyah, in its titular role. Following Rice's legacy, Stephenie Meyer released the first novel in her Twilight series, *Twilight*, in 2005. The anthologized version's cover depicts white, feminine hands cradling a bright red apple over a stark black background, offered to the reader/viewer as a gift but obviously recalling the Garden of Eden narrative where Eve gives Adam the forbidden fruit, thus accomplishing the fall of humankind. The novel's cover is significant in that it presages a central theme of the book series as well as the film. In this first film, the vampire genre is reframed as a coming-of-age story where the forbidden fruit is teen/premarital sex. Thus, *Twilight* does what previous vampire stories did not: it centralizes what was always latent in the genre (sex) while humanizing vampires and thereby downplaying the typical horror overtones. Against the grain of its contemporaneous culture but in keeping with Meyer's conservative Mormon values, *Twilight* offered young, Millennial women a third option between promiscuity and a cold purity: erotic abstinence.

The film begins with Bella providing a voice-over about her death: "I've never given very much thought to how I'd die." There is then a cut scene where someone is chasing down a deer in the woods, foreshadowing her own plight of being hunted later in the film. The narrative then moves to Phoenix, Arizona, where Bella's familial situation is laid out: her mom (Renée Dwyer, played by Sarah Clarke) and dad (Charlie Swan, played by Billy Burke) are divorced (a common experience for Millennials) and mom is moving to Jacksonville, Florida, with her new husband, Phil Dwyer (played by Matt Bushell). Bella chooses to live with her dad, Charlie, in Forks, Washington, a small town of 3,000 people where he is the chief of police. This Pacific Northwest setting, vastly different from the sunny climes of Arizona and Florida, provides much of the atmospheric sense of brooding, teen angst that characterizes the film.

Since Bella has not spent a lot of time with her father, her relationship is somewhat awkward, and neither really know-how to relate well to one another. When she first arrives, he gives her a newly renovated, classic truck that a childhood friend, Jacob, helped rebuild with his dad, Billy Black (played by Gil Birmingham). The Black family, part of a local Native American tribe, are only tangential to the plot of this particular film, but their roles grow substantially over the course of the series. At this point, though, Jacob simply seems to be a possible friend for Bella. Unfortunately, he goes to school on the reservation, so she will not be seeing him regularly.

The next day, Bella goes for her first day at her new school in Forks. Some of the other teens try to get her to talk, but she is reluctant. During gym class, she quasi-joins up with some other teens and ends up sitting with them at lunch. At lunch, the teens narrate the drama of the Cullen family as each member comes in mysteriously and sits down at a nearby table. Both Bella and the audience learn that they are all foster kids of the same family and that the males have coupled off with the females, leaving one, Edward, unattached.

Already, here, the bizarre hint of pseudo-incest is used to increase their aloofness, as is the fact they all look way older than high schoolers. Significantly, this scene underscores an ongoing trope in the film, that is, the lack of a romantic partner means someone is fundamentally incomplete. And, despite her tough, independent act, Bella's character is depicted in such a way that she only finds fulfillment in Edward and being a part of his family, although it is not exactly clear why she feels such a draw toward them. Simply being a new kid in town or vampire magic does not seem to be adequate explanations. No, this goes rather problematically beyond the external to something more essential to her very femininity, sending a rather stark message to the female audience that one's meaning is inextricably tied to having someone long for you.

Bella then is assigned a seat next to Edward in biology class, where he looks unwell and refuses to talk to her. It turns out later he was overwhelming desirous of her blood. After school, she eats lunch with her dad, goes home, and talks to her mom on the phone before going to bed.

Parallel to the development of Bella and Edward's relationship, there is a side narrative of random murders in the town. These murders, at first, appear to have been done by animals, but as the movie progresses, it turns out there is a group of three vampires who still feed off humans, unlike the Cullen family, who drink animal blood.

After having a promising conversation with Edward at school, Bella walks out into the parking lot. A van pulls in too quickly, hits a patch of ice, and skids toward Bella. Edward, using his vampire strength and speed, covertly saves her. She knows he did it but neither she nor others can really see how he did it. After she is checked out by Edward's "dad," a doctor at the hospital, she confronts him about it, and he refuses to concede that he has any kind of powers.

Later, Bella joins up with her human peers for a trip to a beach the Cullens never go to. Jacob, her Native friend, is also there, surfing, and he explains to her the legend of the conflict between the Cullens and his people. Part of the legend is that the beach belongs to his tribe, a group of people descended from wolves (hint, hint: werewolves). The story piques her interest, and she begins doing research on the myth.

As she delves deeper into the mythology, Bella travels to a larger city nearby, Port Angeles, where she buys a book on Native myths from an Indigenous bookstore. As she is leaving the bookstore, she gets harassed by some guys until Edward drives up recklessly in his car, growls, and scares them off. Her friends go back to Forks, leaving her to dine with Edward, where he suspiciously refuses to eat. He also tells her that he can usually read people's minds but he cannot read hers. Edward reveals that he does not have the strength to stay away from her anymore. She says, "Then don't."

Back at home, she does more research and pieces together the fact that the Cullens are vampires. The next day at school, she follows Edward into the woods and tells him that she knows what he is. He asks if she is afraid. She turns around to him and says no. He asks her to ask him what they eat. She says, "You won't hurt me." He takes her up the mountain at superspeed for her to see what he looks like in the sunlight. He walks to a shaft of light, and his skin dazzles in the light. She says it's like diamonds. Then he says he wanted to kill her, that he never wanted human blood so much in his life. He tells her that she is his heroin and that he cannot stay away from her, from her scent. Bella, too, has fallen in love.

Eventually, Bella goes to the Cullens' house, where she is tentatively accepted on Edward's behalf. Despite the fact that Edward is at least 100 years old (he became a vampire in 1918), they talk and stand around awkwardly in his room for her visit—that is, until he puts her on his back and jumps around from tree to tree through the forest.

Later on, he visits her in her room, where they kiss. As things heat up, he throws himself back against the wall and says, "I'm stronger than I thought. I could never lose control with you." And from that point on, they simply sit and talk until she falls asleep on him. Again, abstinence is instrumentalized as a means to develop eroticism between individuals, suggesting that waiting to have sex creates a bond that goes even beyond sex. Further, Bella appears to be more responsive and passive rather than owning any agency of her own; Edward must control himself and even boast about how strong he can be. She must simply live with disappointment.

As their asexual but erotic relationship develops, Bella joins Edward and his family for a game of vampire baseball during a thunderstorm. The thunder, apparently, masks the sound of how hard vampires can hit baseballs. During the game, the three human blood–drinking vampires show up, and one sets his sights on Bella. The Cullens know that he will hunt her down no matter what, so they help her escape.

Nevertheless, despite the Cullens' best efforts, James, the hunter vampire, tracks her down to her hometown, Phoenix, where she confronts him at an old dance studio where she used to take lessons. For most of the scene, there are strong hints of rape: he wants to record himself killing her, she sprays pepper spray in his face, he holds her down, and so on. He does end up biting her wrist, thereby beginning her transformation into a vampire. Edward catches up to them and fights James. The other Cullens arrive; they defeat and kill James, and Edward sucks the venom out of Bella before she can change. Again, the overtones here are that "becoming a vampire" means losing one's virginity, an irreversible event.

The film ends with Bella and Edward attending prom. They dance with the others for a while and then they go out to a gazebo and dance alone. She says she has decided to be like him: "I dream about being with you forever." He asks if she is ready right now, tilts her back, goes in for the throat, but kisses her instead. He then asks, "Is it enough to have a long and happy life with me?" She replies, "Yes, for now." The closing scene shows one of the evil female vampires watching them.

As intimated, abstinence and patriarchy are key aspects of this film. In generational terms, the consequences of the Boomer's sexual revolution of the '60s and '70s fell into the laps of Gen Xers, who could neither keep the earlier trajectories nor fully depart from them. Further, beginning in the 1990s, Conservative Americans launched what has since been called purity culture. Spreading mainly through evangelical churches and communities, this culture was, in some ways, a return to purported 1950s American gender roles and sexual mores. Conflated politically with the Moral Majority, authoritarian patriarchy preached the virtues of intact families, abstinence, male leadership, and monogamy after marriage. *Twilight* aligns with this culture in a variety of ways: Bella does not have much of an identity because she does not have a male partner, initially. Her parents' divorce, too, has made her a loner of sorts. Once she is "adopted" into the Cullen family, she experiences acceptance and protection under Carlisle's (the father of the Cullens) leadership. Bella's mom is known mainly through phone calls only. At a more theological level, it is only within the family structure of the Cullens and in her relationship with Edward that she can potentially achieve "immortality."

But *Twilight* is also a classic coming-of-age film in the American key. Teen culture, born and nurtured in America, is on full display. Teens prefer each other's company over adults, there are cliques at the school, the open road signifies freedom, and all the other simulacra of preadulthood hold the film together, ending, of course, with the great American teen rite of passage: prom.

Benjamin Crace

See also: The Hunger Games.

Further Reading

Bode, Lisa. 2010. "Transitional Tastes: Teen Girls and Genre in the Critical Reception of *Twilight*." *Continuum: Journal of Media & Cultural Studies* 24 (5): 707–719.

Caperton, Jessica. 2014. "A Gender Role Analysis of Twilight." *Kentucky English Bulletin* 64 (1): 66–67.

Chaplin, Susan. 2017. *The Postmillennial Vampire: Power, Sacrifice and Simulation in* True Blood, Twilight *and Other Contemporary Narratives*. Cham, Switzerland: Springer International Publishing.

Clarke, Amy M., and Marijane Osborn. 2010. *The Twilight Mystique: Critical Essays on the Novels and Films*. Jefferson, NC: McFarland.

Edwards, Kim. 2009. "Good Looks and Sex Symbols: The Power of the Gaze and the Displacement of the Erotic in *Twilight*." *Screen Education*, no. 53 (March): 26–32.

Simmons, David. 2017. *American Horror Fiction and Class: From Poe to Twilight*. London: Palgrave Macmillan UK.

X-Men

Release Date:	2000
Director:	Bryan Singer
Box Office:	$296.3 million
Main Cast:	Wolverine, played by Hugh Jackman
	Charles Xavier/Professor X, played by Patrick Stewart
	Eric/Magneto, played by Ian McKellen
	Storm, played by Halle Berry
	Jean Grey, played by Famke Janssen
	Mystique, played by Rebecca Romijn

Released months before 9/11, *X-Men* is perhaps one of the few superhero films to prominently feature preattack New York as a key location. Originally a comic book (1963), *X-Men* also ran as an animated series from 1992 to 1997. The film, which was released in 2000, was the first of 13 in the series and netted $6.083 billion total. And although X-Men run in the same universe as other Marvel characters, so far there has not really been any overlap, with the possible exception of Marvel's character, Wanda, who appears to be a mutant crossover from the world of the X-Men to the world of the Avengers. In generational terms, the film is transitional, solidifying Gen X concerns and identity while foreshadowing Millennial preoccupations prior to their more crystalized expressions later in the decade.

The movie is fairly straightforward and self-conscious as the launchpad of a franchise. It introduces the three central characters who will anchor the franchise: Professor Xavier or X (Stewart), Magneto (McKellen), and Wolverine (Jackman). Magneto, as the beginning of the film makes clear, was alive during the Holocaust, and the trauma of being separated from his parents at one of the concentration camps activated his latent mutant powers of being able to control metal. Professor X, though in a wheelchair, has the ability to control people's minds, read their thoughts, and, when using Cerebro (a giant computer), locate mutants anywhere in the world. He is responsible for bringing mutants together and training them to live peaceably with nonmutants at his Xavier's School for Gifted Youngsters. He also trains and funds older mutants to fight against those who would try to cause a war between humans/mutants, namely Magneto, an old friend and nemesis with a different view of things. These defenders are called the X-Men. Wolverine, however, leads a solitary life and is recruited by Professor X to help join the fight. He is a marginalized loner-rebel at first and must learn how to live with and care for others before really becoming a part of the X-Men team. His powers include rapid healing, superstrength, and sharp claws that exude from between his knuckles. As the film foreshadows, he was also the victim of a secret military project that coated all his bones with an indestructible element known as adamantium. The other X-Men in the film are Storm (Berry), a female who can control weather; Cyclops (James Marsden), a man who shoots a destructive laser beam from his eyes but wears a protective visor; and Jean Grey (Janssen), who has similar psychic abilities as Professor X. Magneto's "team," in contrast, includes Mystique (Romijn), a blue woman with barely there prosthetics who has the ability to imitate anyone; Sabretooth (Tyler Mane), a strong, near-animal-like superhuman, and Toad (Ray Park), who can use his tongue to move things, spits green goo, and can climb anywhere. The plot revolves around another young mutant who has just become aware of her abilities. Her name is Rogue (Anna Pacquin), and she can absorb another mutant's powers for herself temporarily or suck the life out of humans and mutants. After nearly killing her boyfriend, she goes on the run, winding up at Professor X's home. Xavier wants to train and nurture her; Magneto wants to use her powers to mutate New York.

The characters thus represent several generations. Magneto and Xavier belong to the subset of the Greatest Generation that is often referred to as the Silent Generation. Skipping over the Boomers, Wolverine, Storm, Cyclops, Jean Grey, Sabretooth, Toad, and Mystique are all Gen Xers. Rogue and her classmates at X's school all appear to be Millennials. Clearly, they are being trained to take over after the other generations disappear. The one prominent Boomer in the film is

Senator Robert Kelly (Bruce Davison). Kelly is the stereotypical conservative and suspicious Boomer; he uses his political platform to endorse the Mutant Registration Act, a law that is supposed to count and describe all mutants and their abilities in the United States. At one point, just before he is kidnapped, he says, "We're America. Let the rest of world deal with mutants in their own way. If it were up to me, I'd lock them all away." His comeuppance in the film is to be transformed into a mutant himself, a process that ultimately kills him. In contrast, both Magneto and Xavier are portrayed rather sympathetically as having phased out of mere conservatism and moved toward a strong social activism, albeit in opposite directions. The real heir apparent to their respective visions is not the Gen Xers in their employ but the contested Millennials who are part of X's school and, of course, Rogue herself. Thus in the film, we have the outlines of a Millennial social consciousness developing that is underwritten and legitimated by the august and deeper roots of World War II survivors. Both Xavier and Magneto want to change the world for people who no longer feel as though they fit in it; the Gen X characters are fine to live by their own unique vision (Wolverine) or toe the line with someone else's. But the real key to changing the future, as Magneto and Xavier know, lies in the power of the Millennials.

Once Rogue and Wolverine end up at Xavier's home, Wolverine is given a tour and Rogue participates in some of the courses taught by the X-Men. Wolverine is anxious to leave, but Xavier offers him a chance to learn what has happened to him. He cannot remember the process or the people responsible for coating his skeleton with metal. Wolverine agrees to stay on for a couple of days and help him figure out why it seems Magneto is looking for him. However, as it turns out, Magneto does not want Wolverine but Rogue, who is deceived by Mystique posing as a handsome classmate and runs away. Xavier plugs into Cerebro and finds her at a train station. The team goes after her, but Magneto and his henchmen get her first. Meanwhile, Mystique, still disguised as a student, tampers with Cerebro and then escapes.

Later, Xavier and others figure out Magneto's plan to mutate New York using Rogue. When he tries to locate her again using the sabotaged machine, he ends up in a coma, while the team races to Bedloe's Island, where the Statue of Liberty has been used to hide Magneto's mutant-making machine. After a showdown with Magneto's people, they manage to destroy the machine just before its wave of radiation mutates the city. Rogue, however, is killed in the process. Or so one is led to believe. Wolverine sacrificially touches her, transferring his healing abilities to her to bring her back from the dead (again, this is how important Millennials are to the future). Briefly, it looks as though the sacrifice was fatal for him, but he wakes up in recovery along with Xavier, who has also recovered.

The film ends with Wolverine going out to look for and reckon with his past while Xavier and Magneto play chess together in a plastic cell. Magneto says the cell won't hold him and the war is still coming. Xavier tells his "old friend" that he will always be there too. The camera then shows that Xavier has checkmated him with only a pawn.

As with many of the superhero films, "mutant powers" are simply various permutations of sexuality. Perhaps more so than in other superhero films, there is a clear and subversive subtext against heteronormativity. Simply put, mutants are queer. They are rejected and despised by the wider society and seek to find recognition and acceptance with others. They band together to bring this acceptance about. McKellen, himself a member of the LGBTQ community, further signals the film's messaging. Later films in the series will add to this ethos; telling one's family and friends about one's mutant abilities is paralleled with coming out. Heterosexuality is also explored through Wolverine's flirting with Jean Grey, who is engaged to Cyclops. Rogue's powers, of course, come to the fore as she begins experimenting with her sexuality.

Race and gender are fairly standard for Hollywood blockbusters. Storm (Berry) is the only person of color with a significant role. Perhaps somewhat problematically, she is not allowed to have her own hair but, rather, wears a straight, white wig, thereby whitening the character. Her eyes, too, glow white when she exercises her abilities, another subtle nod to the linkage between whiteness and power. She and Rogue are unattached romantically. Jean Grey is engaged to Cyclops but desired by Wolverine. It is not clear why Storm is not a potential romantic partner in the film, although she does become one much later in the comic lore, both with the Black Panther and with Wolverine. Rogue, apparently, is incapable of romantic attachments because of her powers. Yet despite the fact that Jean Grey, Storm, and Rogue make up a significant part of the plot, the fate of the world is ultimately decided, as perhaps it too often is, by two old white men.

Patriotism and "militartainment" are rather conspicuously absent from the film. The U.S. government is portrayed as rather ineffectual and full of xenophobes. The cops who try to stop Magneto end up with their guns aimed back at them. There is thus no glorification of law enforcement or the U.S. military as is commonplace in other films. Magneto is a Jewish immigrant played by a Brit; Professor X, supposedly a native New Yorker in the comic lore, speaks with a distinct British accent (rightly so, Stewart is English); and Wolverine is initially found in Canada but is played by Aussie Jackman. Such distancing from "things American" aligns well with the emerging global identity of Millennials. Even more so, when the Statue of Liberty's torch is destroyed to reveal Magneto's machine, it seems less sacrilegious than simply necessary. And there is also Rogue's Millennial attitude to Magneto's question about the icon: "I've seen it." Its true meaning lies elsewhere, beyond the American Dream of bygone generations, in the future evolution of humanity.

Benjamin Crace

See also: *The Avengers*; *Black Panther*; *The Lord of the Rings: The Fellowship of the Ring*; *Spider-Man*.

Further Reading

Baron, Lawrence. 2003. "X-Men as J Men: The Jewish Subtext of a Comic Book Movie." *Shofar: An Interdisciplinary Journal of Jewish Studies* 22 (1): 44.

Bucciferro, Claudia. 2016. *The X-Men Films: A Cultural Analysis*. Lanham: Rowman & Littlefield Publishers.

Burke, Liam. 2015. *The Comic Book Film Adaptation: Exploring Modern Hollywood's Leading Genre*. Jackson: University Press of Mississippi.

Claverie, Ezra. 2019. "Storm and the Angels of History: Blackness and Star Image in the X-Men Films." *Journal of American Culture* 42 (1): 55–69.

Davis, Blair. 2018. *Comic Book Movies. Quick Takes: Movies and Popular Culture.* New Brunswick, NJ: Rutgers University Press.

Duncan, Pansy. 2020. "'Journeys of Adventure among Its Far-Flung Debris': Three Theories of the Blockbuster Explosion Spectacle." *JCMS: Journal of Cinema & Media Studies* 59 (2): 1–22.

McSweeney, Terence. 2020. *The Contemporary Superhero Film: Projections of Power and Identity.* New York: WallFlower Press.

5

Gen Z Finds Its Heroes (2010–)

The Avengers

Release Date:	2012
Directors:	Joss Whedon, Joe Russo, Anthony Russo
Box Office:	$1.081 billion
Main Cast:	Iron Man/Tony Stark, played by Robert Downey Jr.
	Captain America, played by Chris Evans
	The Hulk/Bruce Banner, played by Mark Ruffalo
	Thor, played by Chris Hemsworth
	Black Widow/Natasha Romanoff, played by Scarlett Johansson
	Hawkeye/Clint Barton, played by Jeremy Renner
	Loki, played by Tom Hiddleston
	Agent Phil Coulson, played by Clark Gregg
	Nick Fury, played by Samuel L. Jackson

The Avengers is one of the top-grossing films of all time, and two of its three sequels, *Avengers Infinity War* (2018) and *Avengers Endgame* (2019), grossed even more. Only the highest-grossing film in history, *Avatar* (2009)—another close-encounter-with-an-alien-civilization movie–topped *Endgame*. The 2012 *Avengers* is the culmination of other films in the Marvel Cinematic Universe (MCU): *The Incredible Hulk* (2007), *Iron Man* (2007), *Iron Man 2* (2010), *The First Avenger: Captain America* (2011), and *Thor* (2011), all of which constitute phase 1 of an ever-emerging MCU. *The Avengers*'s three directors—the Russo brothers and Joss Whedon—impressively managed to maintain a continuity in characters while helping establish the firm cinematic foundation needed for future MCU phases.

As of 2021, there have been over 20 blockbuster MCU films, with many more planned, as well as TV series, video games, toys, and comics. This Disney-owned franchise is an intergenerational phenomenon in itself. Boomers grew up on Marvel comics, and very few Millennials or Gen Zers are unfamiliar with the mythos of the Avengers, the most successful film franchise in history. Disney, who has been capturing the hearts and minds of Americans with its magic since Mickey Mouse and the Greatest Generation, continues to cast its spell on all ages in a globalized world.

In contrast to prior low-budget film and TV adaptations of Marvel comics, the quality MCU produced by Kevin Feige appeals to a multigenerational audience. And unlike many of the near-perfect DC comic characters, such as Superman and Wonder Woman, Marvel comic characters are flawed and endearingly relatable yet just as capable of saving the world from existential threats. A reimagining of the comic *The Avengers*, which debuted in 1963, the 2012 film stays true to the comic of the American Cold War era but adapts to and reflects a post-9/11, 21st-century society.

In the 2012 MCU *The Avengers*, the superheroes Hawkeye, Black Widow, Hulk, Captain America, Iron Man, and Thor are assembled by SHIELD—Marvel's secret CIA/NASA-like agency led by Nick Fury—in order to save our planet from an alien invasion led by the Norse god Loki, Thor's brother. Loki has come to get the Tesseract, a glowing blue cube of almost unlimited energy, to deliver to another cosmic supervillain, who MCU fans will learn in *Guardians of the Galaxy* (2016) is Thanos. In exchange, Loki will receive the extraterrestrial Chitauri army for his conquest of Earth. Loki goes to Earth and with the help of Hawkeye, whose mind Loki has controlled, steals the Tesseract from SHIELD. He is later captured by three of the Avengers and held captive by SHIELD, on its flying aircraft carrier. Loki's allies attack, and he then escapes and sets up a Tesseract-powered device on top of Stark Tower that opens a portal to space, allowing the alien Chitauri army to invade New York City. There, in the Battle of New York, the Avengers fight Loki and his intergalactic army. The World Security Council tries to nuke Manhattan, but Iron Man diverts the missile to destroy the Chitauri mother ship and save the world. In the end, Loki is in custody of Thor to face Asgardian justice, and the Tesseract is returned to Asgard.

In the opening scene on some foreign world, the then-unknown Thanos and Loki discuss their deal over the Tesseract and Earth. This eerie scene is set to the ominous music of Alan Silvestri, whose tone-setting magic used by Hollywood since the early '70s would be familiar to a multigenerational audience. The Tesseract, which first appeared in the comic *Tales of Suspense* in 1966, made its first appearance in the MCU in *Captain America: The First Avenger* (2011). It drives the plot of multiple MCU films, as it is one of the six infinity stones with which one can rule the universe. Used in World War II by the Nazis to power weapons against the Allies, it eventually falls into the hands of SHIELD, who keeps it at a secret government installation in New Mexico, the birthplace of atomic weaponry. The Tesseract easily allegorizes nuclear energy. In the wrong hands (i.e., not in the United States' possession), it can destroy the world, whether in the hands of Nazis, Russians, North Koreans, or Iranians. When the Avengers discover that SHIELD plans to develop weapons of mass destruction with it, they confront Fury, using rhetoric similar to what had been used against Iraq for its alleged development of

WMDs. After the thawing of the Cold War, Millennials and Gen Z have had little sense of the nuclear doom of previous generations, but apocalypse was in the minds of media-saturated audiences in 2012. With lingering imagery of 9/11 and talk of WMDs, the ongoing War on Terror and conflicts in Iraq and Afghanistan, and the continual reminders of environmental catastrophe, our world appeared under siege. As in Cold War comics, in 2012, cinematic superheroes battled world-destroying supervillains to save a frightened world.

The film introduces each Avenger in successive scenes. The first Avenger introduced is the most downplayed Avenger, SHIELD black ops assassin, Clint Barton, a.k.a. Hawkeye, who has been mind-controlled by Loki to help in stealing the Tesseract. Hawkeye, MCU fans will later learn, was sent to assassinate the Marvel comic Cold War creation, Natasha Romanoff, a.k.a. Black Widow, the Russian KGB superspy. Instead of killing her, he recruited her by exploiting her guilt for past atrocities. Now a SHIELD agent, she is the first to be summoned to address the existential crisis brought on by Loki. She gets the call while she is being interrogated by Slavic arms smugglers. Actually, it is they who are being interrogated by her, as she deceives them into divulging intel. She grudgingly relents to the SHIELD order—as if she has been enjoying the torture—and easily overpowers her male interrogators. Her order is to fetch the nuclear scientist Bruce Banner, the calm alter ego of Hulk, the monstrous freak of a radiation mishap. Banner, too, is a Cold War creation seeking redemption through action, now engaging in medical work in India to atone for having become a monster. In addition to Romanoff's and Banner's distinctly American redemptive archetypes, this Dr. Jekyll and Mr. Hyde character reflects Americans' conflicting relationship with technology; science is both loved and feared, much as the Hulk is, in the Beauty and the Beast relationship he and Romanoff would develop in sequels. Banner reluctantly relents as Romanoff explains the destructive nature of the Tesseract and how his expertise in radiation is needed to find it.

The director of SHIELD, Nick Fury, played by Samuel L. Jackson, convinces the World Security Council that these independent-minded Avengers are humanity's only hope of saving the world from an alien invasion. This Avengers initiative is an American initiative. Though these superheroes represent America the superpower, whose technological might can save the world, they hardly represent American society. The diverse but not-so-diverse Avengers are assembled by Fury, who resembles Shaft in *Shaft* (2000, 2019), also played by Jackson. This is no accident. In one scene in *Captain America: The Winter Soldier* (2014), Fury even wears the exact same purple hoodie and black leather jacket as Shaft. Both Fury and Shaft are aptronyms suggestive of the stereotypical aggressive, defiant Black masculinity that helped the original *Shaft* (1971) define '70s blaxploitation films. Yet because Fury applies his streetwise aggression toward security, he is the model minority. Likewise, the tough, hyperfeminine Romanoff is a faux representation. As an appendage of the security state, she is a model emigrant. Though adapted to the 21st century, she is not quite suited for the feminist sensibilities that have grown with each successive generation. Black Widow may represent female empowerment to those viewers who appreciate the allusion to the myth of female spiders eating their half-size mates, but in the so-far sexist MCU, her sexualized hyperfemininity is a product of a hypermasculine agenda in which physical strength, lying, and killing are what empower. In the post–Cold War cinematic version, she is, like Fury, furthering America's role as the world's policeman, fighting against weapons of mass destruction, terrorism, and underworld arms smugglers who are in competition with legitimate arms dealers, such as Tony Stark. The United States, through the Avengers, now not only polices the world but protects it from other worlds. Instead of representing Americans, they represent American exceptionalism but fail to represent the self-consciously feminist and most racially diverse generation in American history.

Fury summons the next Avenger, Steve Rogers, or Captain America, the Nazi-fighting literal throwback to the Greatest Generation of World War II. Captain America, an icon of Americana, combines romantic nostalgia for past values as well as American qualities that have endured. The almost continual warlike stance of America, like Rogers, has been frozen in time. World War II continues in spirit. Since thawing from his 66-year frozen state, Captain America obeys Fury like the good, patriotic supersoldier of the good old days, when the line between good and bad was clear. But he does so reluctantly, as he finds himself lost in a new world where such distinctions are often blurred. Since the protest era of the '60s, the American value of questioning authority has only grown.

SHIELD agent Phil Coulson is sent to Stark Tower, which Tony Stark, a.k.a. Iron Man, has just made energy self-sufficient, a nod to the green-energy-conscious Millennials and Gen Z. Stark is preoccupied with his date, his entrepreneurial genius/personal assistant, Pepper Potts. She, like Romanoff, defies traditional female stereotypes but plays into them as well as she helps define Stark as a playboy. Stark the defense contractor is a military-industrial complex poster boy, embodying much of what America idolizes, polarizing a society that also worships the moralistic countervalues of Captain America. Stark is a melding of rich playboy Hugh Hefner, creative tech entrepreneur Steve Jobs, and genius atom bomb creator J. Robert Oppenheimer. The cyborg Iron Man is a melding of high-tech AI weaponry and humanness, and like Hulk and Captain America, a transhuman and thus superhero, reflecting Americans' faith in technology to solve its problems. Like the rest of the Avengers, Iron Man is at first very reluctant to join but gives in quite willingly when he quickly grasps the potential of the Tesseract.

Like the lumpy melting pot that is America, the assembled team is a divisive though effective power when called to war. Black Widow, Captain America, and Iron Man team up to capture Loki in Germany just as he tells a crowd that they "were born to be ruled" and demands that they kneel before him. One man old enough to remember Hitler remains standing and says, "Not to men like you." Loki responds with a blue beam from his scepter, which is intercepted by Captain America's shield. Once again America intervenes and deposes a tyrant in Germany. Though an effective team fighting against a common enemy, the Avengers often clash with one another. When Thor, the god of thunder, has come to get Loki, the god of mischief, he battles Captain America and Iron Man. Thor is the only Avenger without a dual identity. The rest of the Avengers are akin to the digital native Gen Zer, who lives in the duality of virtual online and real offline personas. Thor is an anomaly, a god representing little more than an Aryan bodybuilder who doesn't fit in with the team of humans. Neutralized by each other's power, they agree to cooperate, but once all of the Avengers assemble, they begin to bicker, pointing out each other's foibles. The reluctant superheroes are sometimes more like a dysfunctional family than a team. It is easy to empathize with this realistically imperfect bunch and perhaps especially appealing to Generation Z's preference for nuanced complexity. This is not the Greatest Generation's black-and-white world of Captain America.

The Avengers effectively take on the alien terrorists that pour down from the sky and, in cooperation with NYC policemen and firemen, attempt to save civilian lives. The parallels of the Battle of New York with 9/11 terror attacks 10 years earlier are unmistakable. As the iconic Manhattan skyscrapers explode and debris falls from the sky, the camera focuses on frightened faces looking upward. NYC policemen scurry about as NYC firemen tend to traumatized bystanders with dust on their faces. The parallels go beyond similarities with the terrorist attacks themselves; the whole narrative speaks of and to the post-9/11 War on Terror era, creating and feeding into a particularly American postmodern mythology yet recycling generations of similar war mythologies.

The World Council overrides Fury and the Avengers' efforts by launching a nuke for use for the first time since Hiroshima and Nagasaki, against Manhattan. Fury's defiance of the World Council and Iron Man's interception of the nuclear missile may be a reflection of America's ambiguous, growing relationship with supranational entities. Ultimately the alien terrorists are destroyed, and Iron Man falls like an avenging angel safely to Earth below, having saved the world from destruction. New York, like Pearl Harbor, is avenged. Humanity is saved by a nuclear weapon literally in the hands of an American transhuman billionaire military contractor. Violent vengeance wins, and capitalism, mercenary militarism, technology, and the American way save the day.

As the credits roll, the Millennial grunge band Soundgarden sings a Gen Z messianic refrain of timeless Hindu life-and-death cycles: "Like the sun we will live to rise, like the sun we will live and die, and ignite again." The postcredits scene returns to the film's opening outer-space scene, where standing beneath a distant sun, Thanos turns toward the camera and reveals his grinning face and identity, as if to say, "I am death, destroyer of worlds." This suggests that in a sequel, the Avengers will once again need to avenge.

The Avengers is a superhero of film franchise history and a mythology of a superpower and its transgenerational values. It is an epic alien invasion tale that speaks of and informs the United States' self-perception as flawed and divisive as a society yet exceptional as a provider for global security in a scary world. America and Disney have dominated the entertainment industry for decades, and now especially so through the MCU, which has captured the hearts and minds of its international fan base. *The Avengers* is not only a signifier for and of Gen Z but is a defining film for all who face the uncertainties and unprecedented complexities of the 21st century.

Derek Parks

See also: Black Panther; Iron Man.

Further Reading

Darowski, Joseph J., ed. 2014. *The Ages of the Avengers: Essays on the Earth's Mightiest Heroes in Changing Times.* Jefferson, NC: McFarland.

Hagley, Annika, and Michael Harrison. 2014. "Fighting the Battles We Never Could: 'The Avengers' and Post–September 11 American Political Identities." *PS: Political Science and Politics* 47 (1): 120–124.

Irwin, William. 2012. *The Avengers and Philosophy: Earth's Mightiest Thinkers.* Hoboken, NJ: Wiley.

Jenkins, Tricia, and Tom Secker. 2021. *Superheroes, Movies, and the State: How the US Government Shapes Cinematic Universes.* Lawrence: University Press of Kansas.

McSweeney, Terence. 2018. *Avengers Assemble! Critical Perspectives on the Marvel Cinematic Universe.* New York: Columbia University Press.

Sterba, Wendy. 2015. "Avenging American Arrogance: Joss Whedon's Filmic Post-9/11 Superheroes in *The Avengers* (2012)." *Revue Francaise D'Etudes Americaines* 4 (145): 21–30.

Black Panther

Release Date:	2018
Box Office:	$631 million
Director:	Ryan Coogler
Main Cast:	T'Challa/Black Panther, played by Chadwick Boseman
	N'Jadaka/Erik "Killmonger" Stevens, played by Michael B. Jordan
	Nakia, played by Lupita Nyong'o
	Okoye, played by Danai Gurira
	Everett K. Ross, played by Martin Freeman

Steeped in an Afrocentric sensibility, *Black Panther* (2018) was a cultural sensation like no other superhero film. Part of the Marvel Cinematic Universe (MCU) franchise, the film was direct by Ryan Coogler, a young but already well-respected director following the critical accolades for his first film, *Fruitvale Station* (2013), which had won the top audience and grand jury awards at the 2013 Sundance Film Festival. This 2018 film was very much inspired by the recent volume of the comic written by prominent African American author and journalist, Ta-Nehisi Coates. The character T'Challa/Black Panther had first appeared in comics in 1966, a creation of the unsurpassed Stan Lee and Jack Kirby writing team. Not only was T'Challa the only mainstream superhero of African descent, he predated African American superheroes such as Marvel's Falcon (1969) or Luke Cage (1972) or DC's Green Lantern (1971). The film broke numerous box office records, including the highest-grossing film in history by an African American director. It was nominated for seven Academy Awards and won three. Although it did not win Best Picture, it was the first superhero film to be nominated for this highest award.

The film opens with the mythological backstory of the Black Panther, introducing this relatively unknown superhero to a mainstream audience and setting the story within an Afrocentric tradition of storytelling and orality. It introduces two key elements of the Black Panther's powers: the heart-shaped plant that, when ingested, allows the human to transform into the Black Panther, and the meteorite Vibranium, the indestructible metal that is used to make his costume and weapons. African-inflected English voice-overs of a father and son speaking continue as the screen shows the superimposition "1992 Oakland California." There we learn of King T'Chaka's betrayal by his own brother N'Jobu, whom he correctly accuses of stealing Vibranium and selling it on the black market to arms dealer Ulysses Klaue. While all the twists and turns are not immediately revealed to the audience, it turns out that N'Jobu's intentions may have been more righteous than originally believed, as his "partner" (another Wakandan working for the monarchy) later tells the new king and T'Chaka's son, T'Challa (the Black Panther) that N'Jobu had wanted to share the technology of Vibranium with other African nations so they could fight off their oppressors. This is only one of the ambiguous thematic threads of the film that will be considered below. Another twist that is revealed later is that N'Jobu's death leaves behind a son in America, Erik Stevens, a black ops U.S. Navy SEAL who takes on the name "Killmonger" and later becomes Black Panther's doppelganger and arch enemy.

Killmonger hooks up with arms dealer Klaue, they steal a Vibranium weapon mislabeled in a London museum, and then they travel to South Korea to sell it to a CIA agent, Everett K. Ross. Ross is seriously wounded in a battle involving the arms dealers and Wakandan warriors and, against custom and the law, is brought back to Wakanda, where their superior technology and medical science can save his life. Wakanda purposefully presents a picture of itself to the outside world that fulfills Orientalist stereotypes of the impoverished and backward African nation. Yet inside its protective shield is a country that has advanced on its own path, separate from "advances" imposed on other African nations by European colonialism and development projects. It has maintained authentic cultural and aesthetic values, as seen in its dress, architecture, and symbology. It is also a cinematic expression of Afrofuturism, a literary and film movement that combines futuristic or science fiction themes with Black history or culture. Wakanda is a majestic composite of many African nations, with a cutting-edge scientific bent (personified by T'Challa's younger sister, Shuri) and a rich tradition of tribal customs, as seen when a member of the Jabari tribe challenges T'Challa's succession to the throne, an early foreshadowing of what will be the later and more devastating challenge by Killmonger.

T'Challa wins the early challenge and then partakes in the ceremony where he consumes the magical plant that enables him to regain the powers of the Black Panther and to meet his father on the ancestral plane. T'Challa is also able to defeat Killmonger with the help of the Jabari warrior whose life he had earlier spared, despite Killmonger also having partaken of the heart-shaped plant and now possessing Black Panther powers and a nanotechnology suit of armor. The film ends with a return to Oakland to establish an outreach center to help

Wakanda's oppressed African American brothers and with a visit to the UN, where T'Challa reveals Wakanda's truth. There is an aftercredit scene of Shuri and Bucky Barnes/Winter Soldier (from the Captain America franchise) that strengthens the tie-in to the MCU, preparing the viewer for a deeper association in future films of the Black Panther narrative within the larger Marvel universe.

Black Panther is a film that speaks to its cultural moment. Released into a tense moment in American racial history, the #BlackLivesMatters activists and allies were ready to welcome with open arms this Hollywood superhero film that seemed to decenter Eurocentrism and patriarchy. Millennials have praised the movie's diversity and representation, as has the even more diversity-minded Generation Z. Based on its representational aesthetics, which should not be underestimated given the 2015 social media movement #OscarsSoWhite, an outgrowth of the fact that all nominees for the 20 major acting awards were white, *Black Panther* represented what seemed to be a paradigm shift of racial representation. This was, after all, a mainstream Hollywood superhero movie, not only with a Black director, a Black lead and other Black characters but with an Afrocentric grounding as seen not only in its casting but also in its costuming, linguistics, architecture, and other cultural or symbolic choices. Here was a film that showed a wide range of possibilities to Black (and white) viewers alike, where both the hero and villain were Black, and where the scientist and the general were not only Black but were women too.

Some of the most important public members of the African American community, such as Michelle Obama and Oprah Winfrey (both Boomers), tweeted their approval of the film and its positive and powerful impact. Obama wrote, "Young people will finally see superheroes that look like them on the big screen. I loved this movie and I know it will inspire people to dig deep and find the courage to be heroes of their own stories" (Babb 2020, 95), while Oprah noted the film resonated in "layers and layers." For African Americans, the film engaged both with the past and with the future, just as Africa itself has functioned within the African American imagination since the days of slavery. Wakanda is the imagined homeland that has been spared the violence of European colonialism and has proven itself to be a traditionally proud and technologically innovative nation that can offer psychological healing to African Americans, a homeland to the African diaspora that is not only a place of a nostalgia past but also of a speculative future. Boomers who grew up during anti-war and civil rights struggles in the United States and in anti-colonial struggles globally would have relished the idea of a technologically advanced African nation that was fiercely independent of Western imperialism.

While most superheroes, even those from other planets (and franchises) seem to wind up in America fighting for some version of the "American way," for African Americans, this Africa-to-America connection seems more purposeful and meaningful than in other superhero movies, not just to audience members but within the film itself. The rising action of the film takes place in Oakland, California, in 1992, the very year when the city of primarily African Americans received the dubious recognition of being the "bloodiest" year in its history, with a murder rate three times that of neighboring San Francisco. Oakland is also the birthplace of the Black Panther civil rights movement, which, although founded three years after the character was created, still resonates in the minds of many audience members. Aside from the CIA agent (more on him below), the inner-city boys playing basketball are the only Americans we meet in the film, and it is to their impoverished neighborhood that the Wakandans return at the end of the film to establish an outreach center. It seems, then, that the oppressed Africans Wakanda needed to assist were not in the motherland but in this African American diasporic community of Oakland.

Millennials have long appreciated the mythic MCU world and the way in which their allegorical certainties provide stability and meaning in a postmodern chaotic world and allow them to dream of a better world, the way the lyrics of '60s rock did for a Boomer generation. It was also the first superhero movie that seems to reach across generational, racial, and national divides, resulting in musing by Boomers, admiration for its post-ironic sincerity by Gen X, and gifs and memes by Millennials and Gen Zers on why the film is so culturally important. Of course, there was some room for criticism: a poorly edited and dimly lit early fight scene that made the action hard to follow, for one. And the CIA character, who was part of the original comic book series and whose life is saved by the Wakandans and their superior medical technology, still seems to function as a kind of "white savior"—not simply because he is white but also because he is a member of an organization whose goal is ostensibly to maintain American hegemony throughout the globe. And there does seem to be a coordinated mainstream media effort, on television and now in Hollywood cinema, to recuperate the agency's reputation. While Shuri at first questions Ross's presence in Wakanda, after this initial questioning his white benevolence seems to be assumed by all. This easy recuperation of the CIA was an uncomfortable element of the film for many Boomers, whose suspicion of the government has grown over decades of endless wars, first in Asia and more recently in the Middle East. Another limitation noted in the film is the impossibility of lasting Black liberation. Two possibilities of Black nationalism are represented in the film: one by the radical (and what Frantz Fanon would call Third-World nationalist) Killmonger and the other by the more reasonable isolationist T'Challa. Yet neither path proves tenable, and in the end, they must be brought back into the global and U.S.-centered, neocolonial fold.

The tragedy of Chadwick Boseman's death in 2020 has provided an opportunity to rethink how the Black Panther character and his Afrocentric narrative should move forward. While fans (and investors) are assured that a second installment, *Black Panther 2: Wakanda Forever* is on schedule for a 2022 release, it will focus on other character narratives rather than continuing T'Challa's Black Panther using another actor. So while this is a welcome addition to the MCU cinematic franchise, it remains for viewers to decide if its representational aesthetics go more than skin deep.

Angelica Maria DeAngelis

See also: The Avengers; Iron Man.

Further Reading

Babb, Valerie. 2020. "The Past Is Never Past: The Call and Response between Marvel's *Black Panther* and Early Black Speculative Fiction." *African American Review* 53, no. 2 (Summer): 95–109.

Holland, Jesse J., ed. 2021. *Black Panther: Tales of Wakanda*. London: Titan Books.

Johnson, Jordan L., and Kristen Hoerl. 2020. "Suppressing Black Power through Black Panther's Neocolonial Allegory." *Review of Communication* 20 (3): 269–277.

The Dark Knight Rises

Release Date:	2012
Director:	Christopher Nolan
Box Office:	$1.081 billion
Main Cast:	Batman/Bruce Wayne, played by Christian Bale
	Alfred, played by Michael Caine
	Commissioner Gordon, played by Gary Oldman
	Bane, played by Tom Hardy
	Selina Kyle/Catwoman, played by Anne Hathaway
	John Blake, played by Joseph Gordon-Levitt
	Miranda Tate/Talia al Ghul, played by Marion Cotillard
	Lucius Fox, played by Morgan Freeman

Released just four years after Nolan's second *Batman* film, *The Dark Knight*, and seven years after the first in the trilogy, *Batman Begins*, *The Dark Knight Rises* completes Christian Bale's tenure as the Caped Crusader. And although it is mostly drenched in Gen X and Millennial ethos, its dismantling of wealth and social classes, inclusion of female main characters, reconfiguration of the role of romance, and emergent social consciousness make *The Dark Knight Rises* a potent and symbolic text for American Gen Zers.

After a brief voice-over and montage of Commissioner Gordon reflecting on Harvey Dent (who died in the previous film as a villain but was projected to be a martyr), the film moves to Bane hijacking a plane midflight in order to kidnap a nuclear scientist, Dr. Pavel. At one point, one of Bane's followers is preparing to leave with him, but Bane tells him, "They expect one of us in the wreckage, brother." The acolyte then remains behind to his death. Given the setting, such fanatic loyalty and devotion to a leader and cause undoubtedly conjures up 9/11, thereby firmly establishing Bane's movement as a terrorist organization.

The scene then turns back to Gotham, at Wayne Manor, where the mayor continues to eulogize Dent. Gordon deliberates about whether to tell the truth about Dent and Batman, who, in the wake of Dent's descent into villainy, volunteered to be a scapegoat. However, Gordon decides against it and focuses on the achievements of the Dent Act, which has helped put away members of organized crime. Meanwhile, Selina (a.k.a. Catwoman), in disguise as a maid, manages to make her way to where Wayne has been hiding out. After some brief banter with Wayne, she steals his mother's pearls and escapes out the window, ultimately with a congressman (Brett Cullen).

With the congressman officially missing, policeman Blake talks with Gordon on the roof of the police department about starting a search and about what really happened the night Dent died eight years prior. Gordon evades the questioning.

Intrigued by Selina's stealth, Wayne goes to the Batcave to do research on her. Alfred finds him there and upbraids him for hiding away. As a father figure of sorts, Alfred explains how he wanted more for him. Here the Boomer admonishing the Gen Xer to get off his screen and out of his cave and to "get out there" serves as a prototype of the Gen Xers to the Gen Zers, alone in the dark with their digital devices. Part of Alfred's rebuke is that Wayne has not really lived. It is also revealed that when Wayne was off training with the League of Shadows, Alfred would visit Florence, Italy, sit in a café, and hope that he would see Wayne with a wife and kids: "But we'd both know that you'd made it. That you were happy. I never wanted you to come back to Gotham." The wishes of the previous generation for the younger are thus often unfulfilled and full of disappointment.

Blake investigates a body in the sewer system, which leads him to a boys' home where he finds out that something is going on underground. Shortly after, Selina and the congressman meet up with another criminal who has paid her to get Wayne's prints. The criminal double-crosses her, and there is a short shootout as the police also get involved after having been tipped off that the missing congressman was there. During the shootout, Commissioner Gordon chases one of the bad guys into the sewer and eventually comes face to face with Bane. However, just before Bane can do anything more than take his "truth about Dent speech" out of his pocket, the now wounded Gordon rolls into the sewer water and escapes.

Blake visits Wayne at the mansion and tells him of Bane and Gordon's escape. Blake relates how he and Wayne had met before, when he was younger, at the boys' home. He then reveals that he knows Wayne is also Batman and that he still believes in him. Before leaving, he tells Wayne that the boys' home has lost its funding due to his business negligence; Wayne was unaware, and Alfred fills him in later with additional details on how his negligence has been detrimental to his company. It also turns out that Bane and a wealthy businessman, John Daggett, are connected.

After visiting Gordon in the hospital, who tells him of Gotham's need for Batman, Wayne goes to a charity event and follows Selina around. At the charity, he runs into Miranda Tate, the philanthropist who is hosting the event. She cryptically tells Wayne, "You have to invest if you want to restore balance to the world." He then dances with Selina, who rebukes him for being so rich: "How could you live so large and leave so little for the rest of us?" In an ironic and humorous twist, Selina leaves by stealing Wayne's supercar by claiming she is his wife.

Together with the subplot of the boys' home, one gets a glimpse of the emergence of the wider social conscience required by Gen Zers, injected into the Batman/

Bruce Wayne mythology. It is not sufficient to fight crime in the dark or delegate someone else to contribute to charities. Selina thus succinctly draws the line between insider and outsider, upper class and working class. This reconfiguring of Batman's efforts as patronizing dismantles the tension of Wayne's wealth and "heroic" efforts to save "the city." Instead, Nolan reconstructs a more palatable narrative for Gen Z through the subplot of the rise of Detective Blake—an honest, working-class orphan unafraid to speak truth to power. In addition, Selina and Blake's character arcs align with American distrust of inherited wealth and sympathy for the disadvantaged underdog. In order, however, to sustain the myth of Batman, Wayne must be brought all the way down before being eventually replaced—his wealth and even physical condition reduced.

Wayne Enterprises' business manager, Lucius Fox, and Wayne discuss the lack of profits. It turns out that they had sunk a lot of money into developing a nuclear fusion generator that Wayne had shut down for fear that someone could weaponize it. Together with a loss of profits, Bane's manipulation of the stock exchange, and Daggett's attempts to take over Wayne Enterprises, Wayne essentially goes bankrupt and his properties go up for sale. Fox encourages him to talk to Tate about the generator, believing her to be someone who could do something with it and help the city.

Selina, as it turns out, was hired by Daggett to get Wayne's prints. She goes to confront him, while Batman has his hands full with Bane's hijacking of the stock exchange. Apparently, Daggett had promised Selina a program that could wipe out one's identity from all records: a program aptly named "Clean Slate." Daggett insists it doesn't exist, and just before his men can kill her, Batman comes to her rescue. At this point, it seems as though Bane is still working for Daggett to oust Wayne from Wayne Enterprises.

Back at Wayne Manor, Wayne and Alfred have yet another heart to heart. Alfred now reveals to Wayne that Rachel, his friend and lover from the previous film, had actually chosen Dent over him. This is in reference to a letter Rachel had given Alfred in *The Dark Knight* but which he had destroyed. This moment signals the end of Wayne and Alfred's relationship, and it is full of the kind of pathos one would expect in such a charged relationship. But Alfred's exit is just another level of loss Wayne must suffer to become a more sympathetic character for a new generation.

Wayne eventually steps down from Wayne Enterprises, allowing Miranda Tate, who is also a board member, to take control in order to stop Daggett from taking over. He shows her the reactor with absolute trust, thinking he has kept it from the enemy. Later, she shows up at his now shuttered and unbutlered mansion, where they sleep together.

However, Bane kills Daggett and arranges a meeting with Batman through Selina/Catwoman. But it turns out to be a trap, and as Bane beats Wayne to a pulp, he reveals that he is fulfilling the destiny of Ra's al Ghul (Liam Neeson), linking his mission to the leader of the League of Shadows from the first film in the series. He then sends Wayne to an overseas prison known as the Pit, where, as it is revealed later, Bane was born and raised. There, an injured and defeated Bruce at the bottom of a hole will be forced to watch the demise and destruction of Gotham without being able to do anything about it.

Bane then tricks all the police into going underground, where he traps them all. He then forces Tate and Fox to show him the reactor and to turn it on. The scientist from the beginning of the film, Dr. Pavel, is brought in to weaponize it. After blowing up a football field in the middle of a game, Bane announces to Gotham and the world that there is a nuclear bomb ready to detonate in the city. Bane then tells the crowd that someone in the audience has the trigger. If someone tries to run or people try to interfere, they will trigger the bomb. He tells them to go home and wait. This leads to the military locking down the city, cutting off all avenues of escape. The president announces on TV, in a broadcast again eerily similar to both 9/11 and *The Dark Knight*'s plot, "The people of our greatest city are resilient. They have proven this before and they will prove it again. . . . We do not negotiate with terrorists."

Here the film takes a decidedly Marxist turn, the tempting, anti-capitalist ideology of Gen Z. Bane reveals Gordon's complicity in covering up Dent's failures. He goes on to monologue about how the rich have "kept you down with the myth of opportunity." The city is thrown into chaos in a way that parallels the French Revolution. The rich are kicked out of their homes, a kangaroo court is set up to "try" the wealthy and privileged, and so on. All the while, the bomb is ticking down; it will explode in less than two months. Bane's men keep it moving around the city, so it can't be found. Nonetheless, Gordon, Blake, and a few others who have managed to hide from the takeover, try to figure out its movements.

As the days roll on in Gotham, Wayne is nursed back to health by a blind prisoner. He does some training and manages to do the impossible—climb out of the Pit. Upon escaping, he returns to Gotham, meets up with Tate, Fox, Selina, Gordon, and Blake to overthrow Bane. The police, once liberated, lead an attack, brawl-style, on Bane and his men. Batman comes in to help and takes on Bane, man to man. After briefly winning the upper hand, Tate stabs Batman and also reveals that she is Ra's al Ghul's daughter. She mocks him, saying that the bomb cannot be stopped and then leaves him to fight Bane while wounded. However, Catwoman comes to the rescue, killing Bane and demonstrating that women can be both villains and saviors in a reversal of the typical superhero trope that necessitates the presence of a man as really the only one smart enough to be a boss or hero. Here the aspirations of the previous generation's feminists have come to fruition as both Tate/Talia and Selina/Catwoman are empowered characters that play key roles in a matter-of-fact way without having to be directly empowered and authorized by men. Bane works for Talia, and Selina is clearly shown as choosing to help instead of running off from the challenge. Their respective capacities and capabilities as female characters are never questioned onscreen due to their sex.

While Batman manages to get the bomb, fly it out of the city, and detonate it over the water, presumably killing him, Blake has been trying to get a bus of orphan boys across one of the bridges, but the military will not allow it. The military blows the bridge up so they can't cross. While stuck, Blake and the boys see the bomb explode on the horizon as Batman saves the city. Later, Blake throws his badge off the bridge in apparent disgust with working inside a corrupt system—a system that would blindly follow orders, even stranding a bus full of orphans.

In gratitude, the city erects a statue of Batman. There is a funeral for Wayne, and Alfred is left with a sizable amount of money. The mansion, again in line with the emerging social conscience ethos, is given to the boys' home. Blake, whose other name is revealed to be Robin, follows Wayne's clues to discover the Batcave; he becomes the next Dark Knight. The final scene has Alfred's wish, expressed earlier in the film, come true. He is sitting in a café in Italy and sees Wayne and Selina at a table just down from him. They make eye contact, nod, and Alfred walks off happy. Clearly Wayne has survived—he apparently had turned on the autopilot on the plane as he flew the bomb out. So his resurrection appearance here is somewhat a surprise, but his Italian holiday with Selina and loss of wealth have somewhat normalized him into another guy. His direct look into the camera and nod is as much a goodbye to the audience as it is to Alfred. Wayne—and the rest of Generation X left behind—will be OK.

Pausing briefly, however, on Blake's character, one notices that he embodies the American sympathy for the hard working, came from nothing, rose up through the ranks, and then eventually rebelled against the system mentality so common with other Hollywood cop dramas and heroes. On top of that fact, he is basically fearless, unimpressed with authority, and as much a patriot as he is the new Batman. But unlike Wayne and Selina, his sexual energy and charisma are directed toward doing the right thing instead of building romantic attachments. His real asceticism, in contrast to Wayne's fake, Howard Hughes type, imbues him with a type of authenticity, independence, and pragmatic detachment that so deeply characterizes Generation Z. He is not reliant on the old order of things but will change and shape them unto his own vision. That the Batcave he inherits is underneath the new Wayne Home for Boys speaks volumes: societal change for the marginalized is built on self-sacrifice, not sublimated sadism seeking revenge for a shattered childhood.

Benjamin Crace

See also: *Batman*; *The Dark Knight*; *Joker*; *Superman*; *Wonder Woman*.

Further Reading

Brooker, Will. 2012. *Hunting the Dark Knight: Twenty-First Century Batman*. London: I. B. Tauris.

Fradley, Martin. 2013. "What Do You Believe In? Film Scholarship and the Cultural Politics of the Dark Knight Franchise." *Film Quarterly* 66 (3): 15–27.

Ghumkhor, Sahar. 2019. "'To Veil the Threat of Terror': Law and the Other's Question in *The Dark Knight Rises*." *Law, Culture & the Humanities* 15 (3): 862–878.

Hancock, Will. 2013. "*The Dark Knight Rises* to Face America's New Fears." *Kentucky English Bulletin* 63 (1): 47–48.

Russell, Patrick Kent. 2016. "Christopher Nolan's *The Dark Knight Trilogy* as a Noir View of American Social Tensions." *Interdisciplinary Humanities* 33 (1): 171–186.

Schimmelpfennig, Annette. 2017. "Capitalism and Schizophrenia in Gotham City—The Fragile Masculinities of Christopher Nolan's *The Dark Knight Trilogy*." *Gender Forum*, no. 62 (April): 3–20.

Despicable Me

Release Date:	2010
Directors:	Pierre Coffin and Chris Renaud
Box Office:	$543.1 million
Main Cast (Voices):	Gru, played by Steve Carell
	Vector, played by Jason Segel
	Dr. Nefario, played by Russell Brand
	Gru's mom, played by Julie Andrews
	Margo, played by Miranda Cosgrove
	Edith, played by Dana Gaier
	Agnes, played by Elsie Fisher
	The Minions, played by Pierre Coffin, Chris Renaud, and Jemaine Clement

In 2010, Chris Renaud and Paul Coffin's *Despicable Me* disrupted the animated film scene by refusing to tell a morality tale or a narrative of triumphant heroes and instead tell a story that celebrates a villain: Felonious Gru. *Despicable Me* became a defining movie of the 2010s and influenced subsequent animated films. The movie was distinct in exploring people's capacity for change, the meaning of family, and its embrace of joy. The film is bookended by heists—first a pyramid and then an attempt to steal the moon—but under the guise of thievery, Gru transforms from a failing villain desperate for recognition into a loving single father.

Despicable Me centers around Gru—whose name is also the acronym of the Russian intelligence agency. He has distinctly sharp facial features, a pseudo–Eastern European accent, and an all-black aesthetic. He lives in a large, gothic house with a dying yellow lawn and drives a monstrous metallic vehicle, both standing in stark contrast to the white-picket-fence houses and family minivans that populate his neighborhood. Gru's image evokes the Cold War villain stereotypes only to subvert them through his redemption.

In the opening scene, we see Gru attempting to soothe a crying boy by making a balloon animal—a shocking act, considering he is supposed to be the villain. However, as soon as the boy calms down, Gru pops the balloon and walks away with a grin. He then walks into a café and steals a pastry, but he leaves a tip for the terrified barista. The contrast between cruel and kind acts characterizes Gru as a new type of villain: evil with a hint of compassion.

At home, Gru's solitary, stolen breakfast is interrupted when three little girls (Margo, Edith, and Agnes) ring his doorbell and try to sell him cookies; he pretends to be a recording machine and sends them away. Returning to his living room, Gru receives a call from his assistant, Dr. Nefario (Russell Brand), telling him that a criminal stole the pyramid—we later learn that Vector (Jason Segel) was the culprit. Vector looks like an ordinary suburban American boy, not a criminal mastermind, in his bowl cut and orange tracksuit, but Gen Z grew up in a world of school shootings and domestic terrorism; for them, the real threat is not foreign but from within. This is compounded by their diverse demographics and rejection of isolationism, making their generation less likely to view foreignness as a red flag compared to earlier generations.

After speaking with Nefario, Gru rushes to his lab, where we meet his henchmen, the Minions—10,000 or so inept, denim-overall-clad, goggle-wearing, pill-shaped yellow creatures who embody the essence of Gen Z humor: absurd, bizarre, and nihilistic. Gru tells the Minions his idea for the crime of the century—stealing the moon—and shares his plan, which involves stealing a shrink ray and building a rocket ship.

While the Minions and the whimsical plot are targeted toward Gen Z, the older generations are drawn in by the movie's cast. Take Julie Andrews, who voices Gru's mother; Gen Z might not recognize her, but she is an iconic figure for earlier generations for her roles in *The Sound of Music*, *Mary Poppins*, and *The Princess Diaries*. We first hear Andrews when Gru's mother calls him, saying, "I wanted to congratulate you for stealing the pyramid. That was you, right? Or was it a villain who is actually successful?" Gru sighs, promising to make her proud, but she laughs at him and hangs up. Her call prompts a series of flashbacks: we see a child Gru in a cardboard astronaut suit watching the moon landing on TV. He tells his mom that one day he will go to the moon, but she replies, "It's too late; NASA is not sending monkeys anymore." The glimpse into Gru's past and his inner psyche humanizes him. Unlike his villain predecessors, he is not motivated by hate or greed but by a desperate need for recognition from his cruel mother, which creates space for the character to move beyond the binary of good and evil.

By showing Gru to be a product of his environment and not an inherently bad person, *Despicable Me* became one of the first animated movies to address trauma and emotional abuse, marking the shift in the conversation around mental health that is spearheaded by Generation Z. Gru's trajectory reflects Gen Z's nonjudgmental and nuanced understanding of mental health as an explanation rather than a justification of actions—his mother's abuse motivates his evil plans but does not excuse them. To show that, the movie offers two villainous foils with no trauma: Mr. Perkins (Will Arnett), who is the director of the "Bank of Evil," and his son Vector.

For Gen Z, the evil archetype is not a Russian spy but a rich (and mediocre) white man. Generation Z is critical of capitalism and has repeatedly challenged the notion of American meritocracy by calling attention to systemic injustices and generational wealth. We see that in the discrepancy between the effort Gru puts into his work versus Vector. When Gru meets Perkins to request a loan for his lunar heist, Perkins denies him, claiming he already invested too much with little returns. Gru is expected to prove that he deserves the money; meanwhile, Vector's failing piranha and squid launchers are funded by his wealthy father even though he spends his days playing Wii and eating popcorn.

After meeting with Perkins, we see Gru and three Minions breaking into a "secret testing lab in East Asia" the location of the shrink ray. However, as soon as they steal it, Vector swoops in and poaches the stolen ray. It eventually becomes a pattern, Gru does the hard work, and Vector reaps the reward and claims the credit. Undeterred, Gru goes to Vector's lair to steal back the shrink ray; he tries to sneak into the lair multiple times, but Vector's elaborate security system defeats him repeatedly. Finally, while crushed under a rocket, Gru sees Margo, Edith, and Agnes walking into Vector's lair to deliver cookies, which gives him the idea of using the girls as a trojan horse to get the shrink ray back.

Shortly afterward, Gru goes to Miss Hattie's Home for Girls to adopt them. His application is approved, and the girls go home with him. Gru shows them the house and then leads them into the kitchen, where he has put out a bowl of water, another filled with candy, and a newspaper instead of a toilet. He points at the setup saying, "As you can see, I have provided everything a child might need." It is a comedic moment that illustrates Gru's incompetence when it comes to childcare—the incompetence of adults eventually becomes a viral meme among Generation Z.

In true Gen Z manner, Margo meets Gru's Boomer attitude and idiosyncrasies with sarcasm and wit. She mocks his accent and pushes back against his house rules. When he tells the girls not to touch anything, Margo antagonizes him, saying, "Uh-huh, what about the floor? What about the air?" She questions his authority to reveal the subjectivity of his rules and demands, the same way Gen Z's rejection of the status quo sheds light on the archaic and arbitrary nature of social norms imposed by older generations.

Overwhelmed by the girls, Gru retreats to his lab. Moments later, the girls find their way into the lab, where they (unintentionally) wreak havoc. Despite his frustration, we see Gru being gentle and not reproducing his mother's patterns. Later that night, Gru puts the girls to bed without bedtime stories or goodnight kisses, his detachment and stoicism reminding us that he is still the villain. The next day, Gru takes the girls to Vector's lair with the boxes of cookies, including robot cookies that allow Gru and the Minions to sneak in and successfully get the shrink ray. On the drive back, the girls ask to go to an amusement park, and Gru agrees, seeing it as an opportunity to get rid of them now that he has the shrink ray.

Once there, the attendant tells Gru that kids cannot be left alone at the park, so he is forced to accompany them. They walk past a shooting game kiosk, where Agnes sees a fluffy unicorn and begs Gru for it. He tries to buy it for her, but the kiosk operator tells them they have to win the game by hitting the spaceship if they want the unicorn. The girls win after the second round, but the operator abruptly changes the rules and says they need to knock down the spaceship, not just hit it. This angers Gru, so he takes out his large laser gun and blows up the entire kiosk—the whole encounter is an analogy of the illusion of meritocracy, where hard work and effort are always rewarded.

Back at home, Gru informs Perkins that he acquired the shrink ray and walks him through the steps of his plan, but tucked between his blueprints is a drawing the girls made of Gru on the toilet, which he does not realize until he hears himself saying, "Then I sit on the toilet" out loud. The contrast between seriousness and playfulness in a minimalist format characterizes early Gen Z humor.

Gru finishes explaining his plan but is denied again; this time, Perkins says, "I love everything about the plan except for you, Gru." Perkins's words trigger another series of painful flashbacks to Gru's childhood, where his mother dismissed him with indifference every time he excitedly showed her his inventions. These memories serve to add depth to his character and explain the impetus behind his criminal lifestyle.

Without the loan, Gru can't steal the moon to instate himself as the greatest villain and make his mother proud. He tells the Minions the sad news, and hopelessness overwhelms the scene until Margo and her sisters approach Gru, offering him their piggy bank. This is a pivotal moment in their relationship. In supporting Gru, the girls give him the love and recognition his mother never did, illustrating how Gen Z values emotional support and interdependence over individualism and a bootstrap mentality.

We then witness the integration of the girls into Gru's life—they are no longer instruments for his plan but now are his family. One night, while tucking them in bed, Gru agrees to read them a bedtime story. He reads Agnes's puppet book, *Sleepy Kittens,* complaining the whole time about the quality of the writing until he gets to the last page and reads: "Goodnight kittens . . . though while you sleep, we are apart, your mommy loves you with all her heart." These lines move Gru to tears. He leaves the room quickly, startled by his own reaction. Gru's discomfort with emotions represents Boomer sensibilities about vulnerability and masculinity, but his redemption hinges on dismantling these sensibilities and accepting vulnerability.

Gru's fatherly commitment is put to the test when his daughters' recital conflicts with the moon heist. He asks Nefario if they can change the date of the heist; angrily, Nefario replies, "[This is] your chance to make history, become the man who stole the moon! But these girls are becoming a major distraction." The tension between the two men is symbolic of changing American values and the shift from prioritizing personal gain to collaborative care. Without Gru knowing, Nefario calls the orphanage and asks Miss Hattie (Kristen Wiig) to collect the girls. She arrives the next day, surprising Gru and his daughters, who were enjoying a tea party—another subtle subversion of gender norms representing Gen Z's conception of masculinity. The loss of the girls puts Gru and the Minions in a state of mourning.

Heist Day: Gru puts on his pink spacesuit, and one of the Minions plants the recital ticket in Gru's pocket. The rocket leaves the atmosphere, and Gru successfully shrinks the moon. But as he celebrates his success, the recital ticket floats out of his pocket, and Gru's expression changes—the joy of his triumph is replaced by the fear of missing his daughters' recital. He rushes back to Earth, crashing his rocket a few feet away from the recital hall, but it is too late. Not only did he miss the recital, but Vector has taken his daughters hostage. Once again, we see how Vector reaps the benefits of Gru's efforts—characterizing the stereotypical American boy as the (lazy) villain and the foreign character as the ethical hero illustrates Gen Z's changing attitudes toward American exceptionalism.

Vector demands that Gru hand over the moon in exchange for the girls, and Gru does. Vector doubles back once he has the moon and flies off with both the moon and the girls. Gru wastes no time and follows Vector in his plane. In midair, the Minions launch a grappling hook to connect the two planes while Gru climbs onto the wing to save his daughters. The girls step out onto the door of Vector's plane; Gru instructs them to jump into his arms. Edith yells, "Are you insane?" and Margo protests, "But you gave us back!" and he replies, "I know, and it is the worst mistake I ever made." Edith and Agnes jump successfully, and Margo is more hesitant. Gru assures her, saying, "Margo, I will catch you, and I will never let you go again." Moments before jumping, Margo slips, and Gru jumps after her with fatherly instinct. This final act of heroism completed Gru's redemption, but it was his admission of fault and expression of affection that transformed him.

On the news, the man who returned the moon is declared a hero, but Gru doesn't revel in his heroism because he is too busy reading his daughters the bedtime story he wrote for them, *One Big Unicorn*. The girls listen as Gru narrates the story of a unicorn whose life has been turned upside down by the arrival of three kittens that "made him laugh and made him cry—he never should have said goodbye. And now he knows he can never part from those three little kittens that changed his heart." This thinly veiled memoir brings up the earlier tension between vulnerability and stoicism. The movie ends with the whole family dancing in the lab, and in the final scene, we see Gru and his daughters on the rooftop watching the moon.

While this film's predecessors often featured the death of a parent (e.g., Mufasa, in *The Lion King*) as a character's defining moment that marks the fall from innocence to despair, *Despicable Me* takes on a new framework. It is one of the first movies to deal with characters whose trauma took place offscreen and who are now trying to live their lives and form a found family. *Despicable Me* shows a generation that a family can consist of an ex-villain single dad, his three daughters, a mad scientist, and a hoard of hyperactive, incomprehensible Minions who are id incarnate. The movie offers a message of healing, change, and growth without compromising joy or humor.

Dina Alqassar

See also: *Finding Nemo*; *Frozen*; *Shrek*; *Toy Story*.

Further Reading

Brown, Noel. 2021. "Crossing Boundaries." In *Contemporary Hollywood Animation: Style, Storytelling, Culture and Ideology Since the 1990s*, by Noel Brown, 41–77. Edinburgh, UK: Edinburgh University Press.

Deamer, David. 2016. "*Despicable Me, Despicable Me 2* and Minions." In *Deleuze's Cinema Books: Three Introductions to the Taxonomy of Images*, by David Deamer, 193–195. Edinburgh, UK: Edinburgh University Press.

Fattal, Isabel. 2018, January 4. "Why Do Cartoon Villains Speak in Foreign Accents?" *The Atlantic*. https://www.theatlantic.com/education/archive/2018/01/why-do-cartoon-villains-speak-in-foreign-accents/549527.

Feldman, Brian. 2015, June 23. "How Minions Destroyed the Internet." The Awl. https://www.theawl.com/2015/06/how-minions-destroyed-the-internet.

Keen, Richard, Monica L. McCoy, and Elizabeth Powell. 2012. "Rooting for the Bad Guy: Psychological Perspectives." *Studies in Popular Culture* 34 (2): 129–148.

Fast and Furious 7

Release Date:	2015
Director:	James Wan
Box Office:	$1.516 billion
Main Cast:	Brian O'Conner, played by Paul Walker
	Dominic Toretto, played by Vin Diesel
	Letty, played by Michelle Rodriguez
	Luke Hobbs, played by Dwayne Johnson
	Deckard Shaw, played by Jason Statham
	Mia Toretto, played by Jordana Brewster

Perhaps one of the defining characteristics of the world for Generation Z is rapid change on a global scale. This change has been both fast and furious. It has included members from diverse backgrounds and dissolved static conceptions of identity, replacing them with dynamic and complex relational ones. In many ways, the seventh installment of the Fast and Furious franchise reflects these fundamental changes in a hyperrealist vision that ultimately coalesces around the collapse of the fourth wall as it memorializes the diegetic departure of Brian O'Conner and the real-life death of Paul Walker.

Like the other films, 7's narrative begins in static dissolution, tightens up, dissolves, and reunites. In line with its now globalist context, it begins with Shaw, in London to see his kid brother in the hospital, going on a killing spree. He blames Toretto and his crew for his brother's condition, and he clearly has revenge on his mind. There are then other update scenes for the rest of the main characters: Dom and Letty are racing again at Race Wars, featured in the first film. She is suffering from amnesia, and all of it is only vaguely familiar to her. Brian is living a life of domesticity with Mia, a kid, and a minivan. Shaw, who has killed Han, one of Dom's friends, visits Hobbs to find out where the Dom and the rest of the crew are. After a rather over-the-top fight, Shaw escapes, and Hobbs is hospitalized.

Later, Shaw sends a package bomb to the Toretto house. It explodes and demolishes the house that served as the center of the Toretto gang since the first film, nearly killing Dom, Mia, and Brian. Dom then visits Hobbs in the hospital, who briefs him about Shaw and warns him about how dangerous he is. The plan to stop Shaw is set into motion. But first, Dom gets Brian and his family to leave LA and stay with a friend in the Dominican Republic. With his family safe, Brian then returns to LA to help Dom and the others stop Shaw.

In the meantime, Dom has gone to Tokyo to get Han's body and return it to LA. At the funeral, the entire gang is reunited, but during the service, Dom sees Shaw watching them from a distance and goes after him. After an intense car chase that ends with the two of them playing a game of chicken with both of their cars smashed, they fight. Shaw gets the upper hand, but then some government agents, led by Mr. Nobody (Kurt Russell), come in, save Dom, and scare Shaw off. Nobody wants to recruit Dom and his crew for a mission.

At a covert base, Nobody offers an exchange: if Dom and his people will help him get a terrorist named Jakande, a hacker named Ramsey, and a computer program called God's Eye, which allows the user to find and track anyone on the planet, he will help Dom take Shaw down. Dom agrees, and the whole crew arrives at the base to help plan their assault on Ramsey's caravan.

In typical *Fast and Furious* action, the mission features unbelievable maneuvers with cars, planes, buses, and trucks. Stunts—jumping from one car to another, driving off cliffs, and the like—also fuel the scene. After rescuing Ramsey from Jakande, the crew escapes, but not without interference from Shaw. Seeing an opportunity, Shaw decides to team up with Jakande to help him take out his revenge. Afterward, Ramsey tells Dom and the others that a friend of hers in Abu Dhabi has the God's Eye program. They make plans to go immediately.

Once in Abu Dhabi, Safar, Ramsey's friend, tells them that he thought she wanted him to sell the program, which he did. He then tells them that he gave it to a Jordanian prince, who has hidden the program in a chip inside his supercar that he keeps in his penthouse in one of the local skyscrapers. Upon learning the prince plans to have a party, the crew decides to carry out a sophisticated heist. But things go wrong during their attempt when Shaw shows up and starts shooting. Ultimately, Brian and Dom drive the Lykan HyperSport out the window and into another building. Then, barely escaping, they send it out another window to crash on the ground below.

Having escaped Shaw (temporarily), the crew meets up with Nobody and give him God's Eye, which Nobody uses it to find Shaw for Dom. Nobody and his team, Dom, and Brian then go to get Shaw, who knows they are coming and, after another extended fight scene, manages to steal the program and hand it over to Jakande. Brian, Nobody, and Dom barely escape. They end up leaving Nobody in the desert to get picked up by his agency's helicopter. The film then cuts back to LA.

In LA, the team make plans for how they will evade and take down Shaw and Jakande. Their plan involves moving Ramsey around from car to car as they drive around the city, in order to give her time to hack God's Eye while drawing out Shaw. The plan works with a few flaws, and Hobbs joins in to help. In the end, Jakande dies, and Shaw is taken into custody. After a moment of believing Dom to be dead, he wakes up, and Letty regains her memory. But of course, this isn't the end.

On an empty beach somewhere, the crew are all there watching Mia, Paul, and Jack, their son, play in the ocean. Here is where the film starts to memorialize Paul Walker's contributions to the franchise. There is a real blurring between the characters' fondness for Brian and the actors' love for Paul. Interspersed with some flashbacks from the other films, Brian and Dom end up in two different cars at a four-way stop. They take off and race for a short distance, but then Brian takes a different road than Dom does. Meanwhile, Dom, through a voice-over, says, "You'll always be with me, and you'll always be my brother." The film ends with a white screen and "For Paul" in black letters.

Since Paul Walker passed away in a car crash midproduction, the ending of the film carries with it a deep sense of loss and a surprising amount of sincerity. Such an earnest expression of grief for both the character and the actor signals a significant cultural and generational shift. Generation X, known for using irony as a type of shield, became, perhaps, one of the more jaded and cynical generations. Millennials, on the other hand, in their quest for authenticity, launched the quest for more honest representations of a panoply of human emotions. And with Generation Z, a lengthy goodbye for a character/actor simply makes sense—despite the fantastic and over-the-top nature of the film and franchise. Real toughness is not simply loyalty but sincere loyalty.

This new, un-ironic sincerity arises out of the evolution of the friends as family meme that is shot through the franchise. Playing on the Italian-as-family-gangster stereotype, 7 reconfigures it, transforms it from East Coast godfather to West Coast crew leader. With Dom and Mia at the center, the rest of the crew are invited into their orbit, with Brian eventually marrying into the family. With Letty's healing, the film officially offers a matriarch and patriarch for future installments, roles they have been playing from the beginning anyway. In the wake of the decades-long decline of the American "nuclear" family, the Torettos' charisma and ability to integrate outsiders offers viewers an alternative vision of what belonging looks like. The ethnic and socioeconomic diversity of the crew, too, increases the size of the table, so to speak. Given their backgrounds, activities, and run-ins with the law, the way the ersatz family is represented further provides images of protection from criminal retribution and police harassment. With its constant action, speed, and location shifting, the message is clear: family remains when all else is in flux.

Or at least that is true on one level. At another level, Brian is clearly dissatisfied with domestic life and misses the action of the FBI and street racing. There is an underlying tone throughout the film—perhaps due to Walker's death and CGI replacement—that his and Mia's relationship is deteriorating. The collapse of the realization of their rather idealized romance sits uncomfortably alongside the bombastic action and Dom and Letty's relationship. It is, perhaps, one of the few "real" parts of the film. Thus in terms of Generation Z Americans, the film offers yet another alternative to interrelatedness; one can look for and maybe even find self-fulfillment outside of both traditional marriage and friends.

Nonetheless, while the film forecasts and reflects some of Generation Z's concerns, it promotes and, in some ways, actively subverts its values. Perhaps more than any of the preceding generations, Gen Z is especially socially conscious and sensitive to a variety of forms of disempowerment. And while 7 is careful to include ethnic and socioeconomic diversity, it still promotes toxic forms of masculinity and body image. In a throwback to earlier cinematic representations of "tough guys," 7's males are muscular, thin, and strong, with angular jaw lines. None of them even wears glasses. The women, too, are thin with curves in the "right" places. The scene in the billionaire's penthouse seems more like a chance to showcase beautiful people than anything that has to do with the plot.

Contrary to the pragmatic and frugal ethos of Gen Z (possibly inherited from Millennials), the film also glamorizes materialism, symbolized by that quintessential American status symbol, the automobile. This is not done so much through featuring expensive cars as through destroying them over and over. Such a representation of the disposable nature of one of America's most costly commodities underscores both the consumeristic need to have the symbol and to also be unsatisfied with it. This admiration of the automobile and then quick destruction cycle literally drives the franchise.

Like many films, and given the for-profit nature of the cinema industry, 7 is not just aimed at Generation Z any more than any of the films in this volume are targeted exclusively to a single generation's profile. While Boomers are probably the most underrepresented in the film, Kurt Russell's role definitely allows for a sense of continuity between the generations. And like other films, the relationship between the generations is dynamic: the old is fading and the new is coming, but it requires the ones in the middle to step off the stage. And while Russell is in the film, his character does not do much more than make deals and plans. In his one action scene, he takes down a few bad guys, but then he's wounded. After that, he is left in the desert. But even more significant is the fact that the single Boomer featured in the film is named Nobody.

Benjamin Crace

See also: The Fast and the Furious.

Further Reading

Beltran, Mary C. 2005. "The New Hollywood Racelessness: Only the Fast, Furious, (and Multiracial) Will Survive." *Cinema Journal* 44 (2): 50–67.

Beltran, Mary C. 2013. "Fast and Bilingual: *Fast & Furious* and the Latinization of Racelessness." *Cinema Journal* 53 (1): 75–96.

Crewe, David. 2017. "Cinema Science: *The Fast and the Furious* and the Mechanics of Dangerous Driving." *Screen Education*, no. 87 (October): 32–39.

Davé, Shilpa. 2017. "Racial Accents, Hollywood Casting, and Asian American Studies." *Cinema Journal* 56 (3): 142–147.

Gutiérrez, Peter. 2015. "Safety in Numbers." *Screen Education*, no. 79 (Spring): 38–45.

International Business Times. 2014, February 27. "*Fast and Furious 7* Tyrese Gibson: 'Paul Walker's Absence in the Film Is Extremely Difficult to Cope Up With.'" *International Business Times*.

Stock, Kyle. 2015. "Six Reasons *The Fast and the Furious* Franchise Became an Unlikely Global Hit." Bloomberg.Com (March). https://www.bloomberg.com/news/articles/2015-03-31/six-reasons-the-fast-and-the-furious-franchise-became-an-unlikely-global-hit.

Frozen

Release Date:	2013
Directors:	Jennifer Lee, Chris Buck
Box Office:	$1.28 billion
Main Cast:	Queen Elsa, played by Idina Menzel
	Princess Anna, played by Kristen Bell
	Kristoff, played by Jonathan Goff
	Olaf, played by Josh Gad

Loosely based on the fairy tale *The Snow Queen* by Hans Christian Andersen, *Frozen* tells the story of a magical queen terrified of her own power to create ice and snow. It is this fear that drives the plot of the story, leading her into self-imposed exile, creating an accidental blizzard in the middle of summer, and the unintentional freezing of her sister's heart, a freezing that only an act of true love can thaw. *Frozen* is widely considered one of Disney's greatest animated films, and its soundtrack formed the background music of an entire generation of young filmgoers.

While previous Disney-princess films juxtapose good and evil (Snow White, Cinderella), or love and evil (Beauty and the Beast), *Frozen* makes love the enemy of fear, and the overcoming of fear the central aim of the plot. The opening scene of workmen cutting ice on a remote mountain lake declares the theme:

Strike for love and strike for fear.
There's beauty and there's danger here.
Split the ice apart; beware the frozen heart.

The audience is then immediately introduced to the beauty and danger of young Elsa's magical ability to produce snow and ice from her hands. This begins with an innocent game in which the children Elsa and Anna build a snowman in a palace ballroom, but it ends when Elsa slips and, in a desperate attempt to save Anna, hits her in the head with a blast of ice. The girls' parents take Elsa and an unconscious Anna to the king of the trolls deep in the forest. The troll king tells Elsa that fear will be her greatest enemy, and they all agree to keep her powers secret. Anna's head is healed, her memories of Elsa's powers replaced with anodyne memories of playing in the (nonmagical) snow.

But the plan to keep Elsa's power hidden results in uncontrollable fear and anxiety for Elsa. She shuts Anna out of her life, afraid of hurting her again. Years go by, narrated by Anna's repeatedly rebuffed question, "Do you wanna build a snowman?" When their parents die at sea, Elsa is forced to enter public life at her coronation as queen. The now teenage Anna, overjoyed that the palace will be open again, is dreaming of the coming party, longing to meet prince charming, and afraid that this may be her only chance. "For the first time in forever," Anna will have the opportunity to live the classic Disney-princess life she's dreamed of. But her extravagant dreams of romance contrast to Elsa's terror that her power will be discovered. Elsa steels herself to make it through this one event, narrowly completing the coronation ceremony without revealing her powers.

But her secret would not last the night. Anna meets a handsome prince named Hans, and the two share a hilariously sappy and awkward love song before deciding to get married. When they ask for Elsa's permission to marry, she says no, apparently doubtful that Anna could possibly love someone she's only just met, but more importantly, terrified of what expanding the circle of family members might mean for the keeping of her secret. Elsa and Anna argue and, in the heat of the argument, in an attempt to keep Anna away from her, Elsa creates a jagged wall of ice around herself. The intimacy of sisterhood—even the intimacy of arguing—is simply too terrifying for the young queen. Her secret now publicly revealed, she flees the palace toward the North Mountain, leaving a trail of steadily increasing ice and cold behind her.

Once on the mountain, Elsa sings possibly the most recognizable anthem in film history. "Let It Go" charts the exhilaration Elsa experiences as her long-held secret is unmasked, freeing her from the anxiety and fear of being found out. It is an evocative display of Elsa's power, a public announcement of her hidden identity. The terrified teenager transforms into the Snow Queen: confident, assertive, beautiful, and brash. It is tempting to see this song as *the* central lesson of the film—be who you are; discover yourself; forget the world and its expectations; the cold never bothered you anyway. *Frozen* gives voice to all those trapped in society's expectations, who now have a role model for throwing all those expectations to the wind. But that is only a partial reading. For as Elsa declares to Anna, she is certainly free . . . but she is alone. And as necessary and exhilarating as Elsa's liberative moment is, she cannot be free as long as she is alone. This connects with a tension in Generation Z culture more broadly, namely, that for all the talk about self-liberation, there is also a discernible desire for community and connection. It is not possible to completely disregard the opinions of others, as Gen Z reliance on social media attests, and so Gen Z must find a way to be both self-expressive and bound together with others in community, a tension that *Frozen* seeks to resolve.

While Elsa rejoices in the freedom her isolation brings, she is unaware of the consequences her actions are unleashing on others. In running to the North Mountain, she has, in Anna's words, "kind of set off a never-ending winter." Apparently, Elsa can run away from others, but she cannot absolve herself of responsibility toward others. Anna therefore teams up with Kristoff, an ice dealer, and his reindeer pal, Sven, to find Elsa. They set off up the mountain, where they meet Olaf, the snowman Anna and Elsa made when they were children. Olaf serves as a reminder that Elsa's powers are capable of creating great joy, and what a joy Olaf turns out to be. Olaf is a swinging lounge singer; he is festive and silly and dreams of seeing summer. He is also apparently very naïve.

The four set off up the mountain, where Anna and Elsa finally meet in the ice palace Elsa has created. Elsa is under the impression that Anna is better off without her—she can enjoy the palace with open gates and rule as the beautiful and gregarious queen Arendale needs. Anna informs her that her action has buried Arendale in "deep, deep, deep, deep snow." And all the fears that Elsa thought she left behind come rushing back. Overcome by panic, she again attempts to shut Anna out, this time hitting her heart with an icy blast. Once clear of the palace, Kristoff sees that Anna's hair is turning white, and she begins to grow faint. Kristoff must take her back to the troll king.

If there is a "gospel" to *Frozen*, it is the song "Fixer Upper" sung by the trolls. The song itself is stylistically a kind of Broadway-meets-Black gospel chorus. Unfortunately, the trolls are the closest approximation the film has to nonwhite people. While we should not expect much diversity in 18th-century Scandinavia, the film nonetheless may darkly portray white culture as standard, with African culture sitting outside the approved mainstream and providing an occasional injection of spunk, rhythm, and spiritual vitality. These Black-gospel trolls represent a wild, untamed, pagan side of Scandinavian culture and are thus *abnormal* in their otherwise white context. Nonetheless, they prophetically announce what is surely the central theme: we are all a bit of a mess. We are powerful, capable of great good or great harm, and only the love of a family can direct that power in constructive ways: "Father, sister, mother, brother, we need each other to build us up and round us out." Thus, inasmuch as "Let it Go" involves an affirmation of self as the rejection of others, "Fixer Upper" wants to affirm the self but only in the context of others. The deep bonds of family are the issue, and it is a firm commitment to each other that sustains and perfects all our powerful and dangerous capabilities. The only thing that can thaw the inadvertent effects of Elsa's powerful and dangerous ice is the power and strangeness of sisterly love. Here the film resolves the tension between Gen Z liberation and need for community. Both may be achieved if we broaden our understanding of love beyond the princess-meets-boy Disney model to include other forms of affection and care.

But Anna is a classic *Disney* princess, and so she naturally assumes that an act of true love is a kiss from Prince Charming—her would-be fiancé, Hans. But Kristoff, the blue-collar ice salesman, is clearly in love with Anna. Nonetheless, he sacrifices his love for her, racing her back to Arendale for Hans to kiss her. But when Hans has Anna alone, he reveals that he has been manipulating her and leaves her to die of a frozen heart while he takes over the kingdom. He had previously captured Elsa on a mission to "save" Anna, and when he now sends guards to execute Elsa, she escapes out onto the frozen fjord.

Meanwhile, the blizzard whips into a frenzy, and Olaf rescues Anna, who now turns her search for an act of love to Kristoff, who loved her enough to leave her with Hans. She ventures onto the fjord to meet Kristoff, who is racing back to Arendale on Sven. Everyone converges out on the dangerous, icy waste. Anna is slowly succumbing to her frozen heart, staggering toward Kristoff, when she sees Hans preparing to kill Elsa with a sword. With her last breath, Anna places herself between Hans and Elsa, turning completely to ice just as Hans' sword strikes her. Elsa is saved. And this act of sacrificial, sisterly love is what saves Anna. The act of love has been her own act. Elsa recognizes that love is the solution that overcomes her fear, and she uses the power of love to lift the eternal winter. She becomes a magical queen, Anna and Kristoff kiss, and Prince Hans is shipped home in chains.

This film represents a bundle of cultural anxieties around Disney's typically patriarchal portrayal of women, gender roles, and sex. Pressure had been building for some time for Disney to change the overtly patriarchal and girl-needs-boy romance of past princess stories. In response, the film contrasts a typical Disney princess with a new kind of heroine, decentering romantic love in favor of sisterly sacrifice, and implicitly chiding the princess-saved-by-the-prince story arc of old. Anna is, in nearly every way, a typical Disney princess. She is a vivacious dreamer with a singing voice as clear as a glass slipper. But her dreams of an old-fashioned princess plot turn out to be deeply misguided, causing her to nearly give away the kingdom to a manipulative man. Elsa, by contrast, has no such dreams. She shuns the limelight, wants nothing to do with adventure, and does not seem interested in romance at all. Even her voice is untypical—powerful, with a slightly raspy edge that makes her more assertive and provocative. Above all, she does not need to be saved by a man.

This new take on the Disney princess has been received as a mixed bag of progressive ideals and regressive residue. Elsa's independence and self-generating power call into question traditional gender roles. Given Elsa's atypical character arc and her apparent disinterest in romance, the film has also been seen as creating an imaginative space for sexual minorities. "Let It Go" was received by LGBTQ+ communities as a powerful depiction of both the fear and the liberating thrill of coming out to one's friends and family. And yet the story retains much of the old order. Elsa's moment of liberation is also her moment of sexualization as she transforms from shy princess into a boisterous diva, implying that female power is still dependent on sexual appeal. Moreover, Elsa's power might come at the *expense* of romantic interest, implying that female authority is incompatible with romantic appeal, reinstantiating patriarchal presuppositions about the limits of feminine power and attraction.

Disney has enormous financial interest in moderation—on a spectrum of social values, Disney aims for something neither too conservative nor too progressive. *Frozen* settles for an uneasy mixture. The film is unlikely to please puritans on either side of the political spectrum. Nonetheless, the film's primary point seeks—whether successfully or not—to transcend the spectrum. Whether you are a typical Disney princess caught in a plot you did not expect, an atypical Disney princess navigating expectations you cannot fulfill, an ice salesman selling ice in a snowstorm, or a snowman who longs for life in the summer, there is no substitute for community. Whether that is sufficiently progressive or conservative depends on the viewing context.

Josh Mobley

See also: *Beauty and the Beast*; *The Lion King*; *Toy Story*.

Further Reading

Heit, Jamey. 2020. "True Love in *Frozen*." In *Disney and Philosophy: Truth, Trust and a Little Bit of Pixie Dust*, edited by Richard B. Davis, 185–192. Hoboken, NJ: John Wiley and Sons.

Law, Michelle. 2014. "Sisters Doin' It for Themselves: *Frozen* and the Evolution of the Disney Heroine." *Screen Education* 74: 16–25.

Rudloff, Maja. 2016. "(Post)feminist Paradoxes: The Sensibilities of Gender Representation in Disney's *Frozen*." *Outskirts* 35: 1–20.

Streiff, Madeline, and Lauren Dundes. 2017. "Frozen in Time: How Disney Gender-Stereotypes Its Most Powerful Princess." *Social Sciences* 6 (2): 38.

The Hunger Games

Release Date:	2012
Director:	Gary Ross
Box Office:	$152 million
Main Cast:	Katniss Everdeen, played by Jennifer Lawrence
	Peeta Mellark, played by Josh Hutcherson
	Haymitch Abernathy, played by Woody Harrelson
	President Coriolanus Snow, played by Donald Sutherland

The Hunger Games (2012) is a postapocalyptic, dystopian film based on Suzanne Collins's novel of the same name. It tells the story of Katniss Everdeen and Peeta Mellark, who are sent as Tributes to the Hunger Games to represent District 12 as they fight other Tributes to the death as punishment for a previous rebellion against the capital. It is the first story in a trilogy of novels (*Hunger Games* [2008], *Catching Fire,* [2009], and *Mockingjay* [2010]) and will result in a total of six feature films. A prequel, *The Ballad of Songbirds and Snakes*, was published in 2020, and at the time of this writing, a movie is in the works. The entire series has been a favorite with audiences and critics and, whether book or film, consistently appears on lists of the best apocalyptic or dystopian young adult (YA) fiction. *The Hunger Games* film set records for opening-day sales and is presently the third highest-grossing film in the United States.

YA literature is aimed at the teenage market between children's and adult literature and in the late 20th century began to be recognized as its own category. Today it has gained both critical and financial legitimacy, with a loyal reading and viewing public of teenagers, young adults, and not-so-young adults. Some mark the start of the YA category with the publication of the first *Harry Potter* book in 1997, although the book is considered children's literature. Others consider Lois Lowry's *The Giver* (book, 1993; film, 2014) as the first contemporary YA novel. Because the vast majority (if not all) contemporary YA films are adapted from novels and audiences seem to overlap, it is difficult in discussion to separate them entirely. Marketing them as a separate category has been financially lucrative, although critics continue to debate whether YA is a category or a genre. Either way, YA narratives such as *The Hunger Games* can be classified as sci-fi, which in the YA category first concentrated on stories of dystopias posing as utopias (*The Giver*; *Uglies* [book, 2005; film upcoming]) and later on as postapocalyptic societies (*The Hunger Games; Maze Runner* [book, 2009; film, 2014]; *Divergent* [book 2011; film 2014]). Some common themes include a teenage protagonist, adults who are either politically impotent or collaborators, an authoritarian government (which can be manifested through religious, political, or technological control), and some kind of geographic destruction that can be caused by war or environmental devastation, whether in the present or in the past. It is precisely attention to these themes that resonates with Gen Zers, who seem to have more of an apocalyptic worldview than other generations and who have driven the incredible financial success of these YA dystopias.

The film's opening crawl tells the backstory of the dark and dangerous world we are about to enter, its former uprising and "the Reaping" of Tributes for the Hunger Games as penance. The film opens with an interview of the Gamemaker and the Master of Ceremony (MC) discussing the meaning of the Hunger Games today. We are immediately struck by the unusual haircuts and outfits, which only become more and more outlandish as we enter deeper into the world of the capital in the film. There is a sharp break, and we find ourselves hearing and then seeing a screaming child in District 12, which is a gray and grim world, as are many of the Districts. Through establishing shots, we follow a teenager traversing a village reminiscent of an Appalachian mining town during the Depression era: faces of destitute children gazing through holes in a wooden fence, women fetching water in buckets, men heading into the mines with their metal lunch pails. There are also signs of the uprising and resultant militarization mentioned in the opening crawl, in the form of electrified fences and guard towers. We see a teenager who is different from others in her village: she is dressed in masculine clothing, is running actively through the village, and slips through a hole in the fence in an act of defiance to the posted warnings. The characteristics of rebelliousness, independent thought, and bravery make her a strong female lead, other characteristics shared in many YA narratives.

We meet the Everdeen family, comprised of Katniss, her younger sister Primrose, and their mother. As Prim has reached the age of 12, her name will now be included in the Reaping as a potential Tribute from the District. When Prim is chosen, Katniss altruistically offers to take her younger sister's place. Peeta is chosen as the male Tribute from the District, and soon they are on their way by train to the capital. The security men from the capital present as similar to the fascist Stormtroopers from *Star Wars*, while the MC sent from the capital is nothing short of carnivalesque, cheerfully spouting off the formulaic lines "Happy Hunger Games" and "May the odds ever be in your favor" to a group of teenagers waiting in silence and dread to hear of their fate. On large screens is projected a film with the voice-over narration of Big Brother President Snow, who tells the story of the nation and the treachery of the Districts, which has led to their current predicament.

From then, the two Tributes will be kept under guard until they enter the Games. Through flashbacks, it becomes clear to the audience that Peeta and Katniss have a backstory that involves his saving her from starvation by a gift of bread, for which he is punished by his mother. As we move toward the capital by train, we are reminded of the obscene opulence of the capital compared to the severe privation of the Districts. We are also reminded of the insensitivity of the residents of the capital who celebrate the Hunger Games and are immune to the deadly fate of all but one of the Tributes, who are often seen looking on in shock and silence.

The pre-Game celebrations are orchestrated by the Gamemaker from a command center, and the opening ceremonies seem to channel an imperial Roman ambience of chariot races (and, later, gladiator training) with a blend of Nazi architecture and aesthetic, made even more grotesque by the carnivalesque spectators. Even the name of the capital, Panem, references the decadence of the latter period of imperial Rome, using the Roman poet Juvenal's phrase *panem et circenses*, or "bread and circuses" for inspiration, a phrase referring to a superficial appeasement of the masses as a way to maintain control.

Peeta proves the importance of being liked (according to Mentor Haymitch Abernathy, played by the veteran actor of film and television, Woody Harrelson, who helps draw in the Gen X audience who grew up with him from 1982 to 1993 on *Cheers*), which will be crucial to garner sponsors and receive gifts during the Games—gifts that could actually influence whether a Tribute survives or not. Katniss does not possess this skill of likability, so she must demonstrate another way to gain points (and sponsors) before entering the arena, which she does in a dramatic pre-Game moment. Although known for her archery skills, she fails to hit the target her first try, losing the attention of the sponsors. In a potentially dangerous act, she aims the arrow instead at the feast being enjoyed by the sponsors in their box seats and shoots an apple out of a roast pig's mouth. She earns a score of 11 out of 12, but she also earns the attention of the President, who reminds the Gamemaker that while a little bit of hope might be good, too, much hope is dangerous, setting up animosity between Katniss and Snow that will last throughout the film franchise. It also confirms that she is different from the other contestants, that she is not afraid to take a chance, and that she has the dangerous potential to rally others against the capital by giving them hope. Her skepticism toward authority figures speaks not only to generational attitudes toward authority but perhaps also to American values in general, which include a healthy skepticism toward political authority, part of our national narrative. While Boomers were more likely in their youth to resist authority openly, Gen Xers are less impressed and more likely to test its limits, as will Millennials (unless they happen to agree with or like the individual authority figure). Thus we see Katniss is not afraid to fire the arrow at the judges before the Games, yet she and, especially, Peeta seek Haymitch's guidance.

The Games finally begin, and the violence of children as young as twelve years old killing and being killed for survival is shocking, even to an audience exposed to a high level of violence in film and despite it being another commonality of YA films. Rated PG-13 for violence, the camera's use of the cutaway to avoid showing the goriest moment does little to diminish the fact that the characters look a lot like the audience's friends at school. Recent studies have shown American audiences have become more accepting (or perhaps desensitized) toward violence in films, and many films today that receive a PG-13 rating would have gotten an R rating in the past. As the Games progress, it becomes clear that the Gamemaker does more than orchestrate the ceremonies, that he and the team in the command center manipulate what is going on in the arena, creating dangerous situations such as fireballs when the action slows, or forcing Tributes into close proximity—all in order to keep the viewing public of the capital entertained. Katniss and Peeta must enact a televised romance, the veracity of which becomes one of the tensions throughout the franchise. Katniss displays not only courage and ingenuity but also humanity as she teams up with Rue, a young Tribute her sister's age, and later honors Rue's death by surrounding her body with flowers. This does not go unnoticed by the people in her District nor by the other Tribute from her District who spares Katniss's life because of her deed. Nor does her sign of the Mocking Jay, which Katniss makes to the camera (the same sign the people in her District had made to honor her volunteering in her sister's place), and which is returned by Rue's people, inspiring them to begin revolting against the capital's control—yet another plotline that is followed in subsequent films.

In one of the many instances of interference, the capital changes the rules of the Games, allowing a team of Tributes to be spared and declared winners rather than just a single Tribute as in the past. More than one critic and several memes have noted the negative parallels of these games to the Olympics, citing things such as dehumanization and corporate domination. The Olympics trace their origins to the foundations of Western culture and democracy, which then and in the film is a very selective universal citizenship indeed. Institutionalized racism and classism are on display in the districts farthest from the capital, and Millennials are noted to be less tolerant of this than their older peers are. When the team from District 12 (Katniss and Peeta) are declared winners, the capital tries to rescind the rule change, but this backfires, as the star-crossed lovers follow the Romeo and Juliet story to almost the very end, threatening to eat poisoned berries and die in a suicide pact. Afraid to risk the wrath of the audience, the capital relents and allows them both to be declared victors, which cements the wrath of President Snow, a major motivation in the upcoming films, which are clearly set up in this film's ending.

So why is *The Hunger Games* such a popular and important film? It has attractive and relatable leads and an exciting storyline with elements of adventure and romance. It is immediately accessible to an audience, which is a feature praised by teenagers, but it also has deeper concepts that go beyond the surface didacticism common in children's literature and in some other YA literature and film. A book-length study has been done of the film's connection to philosophy and the ethical issues it raises, such as morality and luck, social Darwinism, the ethics of militarism and the "just war" tradition, and mimetic and monstrous art (to name only a few). The issue of mimesis (imitation of the real world by art) has been brought up in many discussions of the film, suggesting that it operates as a commentary on our fixation on reality TV and the dangers inherent in this manipulative form of entertainment.

The film provides girls and young women a powerful postfeminist role model, one that at times engages with a strong masculinity but also embodies an ethics of care traditionally associated with the feminine. She can be pretty when necessary, but never in a way that distorts her true self. In fact, the entire world of Panem and the Districts often appears gender-neutral or gender-fluid, reflecting less rigid thinking about this issue by young people today. The film also addresses many issues that resonate with Generation Z: climate change and the destruction of the planet, endless wars and increased militarization of the police, the global increase in authoritarianism, and technology's role in restricting individual freedoms. Adults, as every teenager knows, are incapable of understanding things or fixing things, in part because they are responsible for causing the problems in the first place. It will be up to the youth to fix the problems of the world. Perhaps the clearest message in *The Hunger Games* and YA narratives in general can be heard in the declaration of Filipino nationalist Jose Rizal over 100 years ago: "The youth is the hope of our future."

Angelica Maria DeAngelis

See also: *Harry Potter and the Philosopher's Stone/Harry Potter and the Chamber of Secrets.*

Further Reading

Carpenter, Caroline. 2015. *Guide to The Hunger Games: The World of The Hunger Games.* Medford, NJ: Plexus Publishing.

Michaud, Nicolas, and George A. Dunn, eds. 2012. *The Hunger Games and Philosophy: A Critique of Pure Treason.* Hoboken, NJ: John Wiley & Sons.

Miller, Laura. 2010, June 7. "Fresh Hell: What's behind the Boom in Dystopian Fiction for Young Readers?" *New Yorker*. https://www.newyorker.com/magazine/2010/06/14/fresh-hell-laura-miller.

Inception

Release Date:	2010
Director:	Christopher Nolan
Box Office:	$838.8 million
Main Cast:	Dom Cobb, played by Leonardo DiCaprio
	Arthur, played by Joseph Gordon-Levitt
	Ariadne, played by Elliot Page
	Mal, played by Marion Cotillard
	Saito, played by Ken Watanabe
	Fischer, played by Cillian Murphy

As another one of Christopher Nolan's mind-bending, psychological thrillers, *Inception* mirrors the growing complexities of a globalized world and increased sensitivity toward questioning the nature of material reality. In terms of the generational framework, it is a transitional film that mirrors the aging anxieties of Gen Xers, gives space for Millennial expectations and contributions, and sets new standards of cinematic spectacle for the new generation of moviegoers: Generation Z.

Despite its convoluted nature, the basic plot of the film is fairly straightforward. Cobb (DiCaprio) wants to return to the United States to be reunited with his children. He has been on the run ever since his wife, Mal (Cotillard), died and he was suspected of being the killer. While on the lam, he has continued his job as an information extractor within the world of transnational, corporate espionage. In order to do this, he enters the subconscious of an individual through a shared, induced dream state. In that state, he engages with the subconscious of the "mark" and extracts secret data for his "client"—usually another competitor on the global market. In the film, the subconscious dreamworld is similar to the real world; however, if one starts making changes to it, the mark's subconscious begins to attack via "projections." These projections are simply the people that inhabit the dreamworld and are there to protect the subconscious of the individual.

Cobb, of course, is not alone. He is accompanied by a team of people who help him do various things such as design the dreamworld for the mark to occupy, drug the victim, and wake the other team members when the time is up, the mission complete, or some dire circumstance occurs. But only very little time is spent in the real world; most of the action sequences and dialogue occur in a dreamworld of some kind.

Although the audience does not know it from the outset, the film begins in a dreamworld where Cobb is trying to get an elderly man to make a deal with him. After a quick cut, in the same setting—a Japanese-style beach mansion—Cobb and Arthur (Gordon-Levitt) are talking to the same Asian man, Saito (Watanabe), but now he is young. They are trying to get Saito to reveal some hidden information. After an unsuccessful attempt, that dreamworld spectacularly collapses and Cobb, Arthur, Saito, and more associates wake up to find themselves in an apartment building with a riot descending on them. This, too, turns out to be another constructed dreamworld, built to get Saito to reveal his hidden information. The dream-within-a-dream, however, does not work, and they all return to the waking world.

Saito then hires Cobb and his team not to extract an idea but to implant an idea into the mind of the heir of a competing company, Maurice Fischer (Murphy). Saito wants to convince Fischer that he should dissolve the company after his father passes and he is made CEO. Implanting, or inception, is near impossible, but Cobb is convinced they can do it, incentivized by Saito's offer to clear his criminal record and allow him to return home.

What follows is a rather confusing sequence of frame stories, dreams within dreams within dreams. Each time the main characters go deeper into Fischer's psyche, they leave someone behind, and the physics of each dreamworld are increasingly complicated by the other layers. Thus, at the "lowest" level, dream time is significantly different from real time, the former moving much faster than its prior levels up to reality, where they are all asleep on a plane.

All the while Cobb is attempting to implant the idea, he is also dealing with his own struggle in his own subconscious, which threatens to derail the whole project. As it turns out, Mal killed herself because her and Cobb's numerous trips and stays in the shared dreamworld blurred the line between dream and reality. She committed suicide thinking she would wake up somewhere else while Cobb watched. Predictably, he manages to reconcile with her memory, implant the idea, and return to the real world to join up with his family—a somewhat ambiguous ending notwithstanding.

Like the multilevel plot it presents, *Inception* has multigenerational appeal. For Gen Xers, Cobb's motivations hit home. He wants to grow old with Mal, something he accomplishes in the dreamworld before she commits suicide. He wants to be with his young kids and watch them grow up. He wants to be the best at what he does and to take on challenges that others think impossible, namely, inception. Cobb is also comfortable with being more than just an American; his wife is French, and he travels internationally. He is the epitome of what the yuppies attempted but so few succeeded. And like all Gen Xers, he is anxious and conflicted about what to do with his inner world, unsure of who to let in.

Arthur, Cobb's sidekick, is the Millennial's psyche writ large. He cares about style, buffers Cobb's rashness, and can operate as a team member or independently. These qualities and more are infused in one of the most famous scenes of the film: the rotating hallway fight. At this point in the film, Cobb and the rest of the team have gone to a different level of dreaming, leaving Arthur with their sleeping bodies in a different dreamworld. However, this level of the dreamworld is within another level, that of the van. When the van at the top level of the dreamworld goes off a bridge, the hotel setting of Arthur's dreamworld tumbles around. Arthur is faced with the dilemma of fighting off projections, keeping his team secure, and waking them up in time while the whole world is literally spinning upside down and falling. He does all of this in a collected, deliberate fashion, intrinsically driven despite circumstances. Thus for the Millennial viewer, a helter-skelter world is to be engaged with through patience and determination and by taking responsibility for others. This is in deep contrast to Cobb's Gen Xer egocentrism, concerned mainly with his own goals and his own family.

Its multigenerational appeal is evident not only in the plot and structure but in its casting as well. Gen Xer DiCaprio, no longer the youthful face of *Titanic* fame, carries the dramatic weight of the narrative as a father and mourning widower as well as the leader of the team of extractors. His dead wife, who appears mainly as a projection of his subconscious, is likewise played by Marion Cotillard, herself born in 1975, a year after DiCaprio. Together they form the existential ballast that gives weight to the film's gravitas. Brief scenes with veteran actor Michael Caine (1933–) do little more than accentuate the Gen X base on which the film's cast is built. This also includes Tom Hardy (1977–), Cillian Murphy (1976–), and Dileep Rao (1973–).

Millennials, too, are well represented in terms of casting. Youthful-looking Joseph Gordon-Levitt and Elliot Page both provide a mature beyond their years but still energetic atmosphere. Whereas the older actors have a world-weariness, these two portray characters that are not just drones in a generational hierarchy but creatively offer and enact solutions to near intractable problems. Cobb's (DiCaprio) taking of Ariadne (Page) as his protégé in the extraction business is as close a passing of the torch as it gets in terms of generational transitions. The consciousness, too, that a young woman could hold a significant place within an all-male team further links up to the egalitarian sobriety that characterizes Millennials.

As young moviegoers in 2010, when the film was released, Gen Zers may not have been in need of all the existential, social, and psychodynamic work that art performs for the other generations. And yet *Inception* launches a type of storytelling and cinematography that set the standard for the next decade or more. For children of the internet, the multitiered and virtual realities the film presents align with their lived experiences of instant communication, digital worlds, and social media. While globe-hopping may be central to an older kind of film, the quick-paced continual change of not just geography but whole realities echoes the compression of time and space brought about in the Information Age. The central plot, that of trying to insert an idea into others' minds and make them think it is theirs, is essentially the movement of data—an upload of sorts—from one mind to another.

Further, for a generation entranced by constant visual stimulation and movement, *Inception*'s near constant dynamism seems like familiar territory. The scenes where the camera or actors are not moving simply allow for a break from the constant motion. At its climax, the narrative frames of the plot all include this perpetual motion: one frame story is during a flight; the next level, in a van; the next, a race toward a fortress on foot and snowmobile, and at the deepest level, the entire setting is crumbling in the background. Nolan's continuous crosscutting does not allow the audience to forget all of this simultaneous motion; it stays lodged in the viewer's mind in a visceral sort of way. Perhaps one theme that could be derived from the film that fits well with the Gen Z experience is that change is constant. Even so-called material reality is ephemeral and secondary to information that is always moving. That Cobb's totem, his means of determining whether or not he is in a dream, is a spinning top is deeply emblematic.

Finally, in terms of the film itself, the visual and special effects set and, in some ways, met the expectations of Gen Z viewers. Whereas Gen Xers and Millennials allow more space for the so-called magic of Hollywood to work its wonders, Gen Zers are already adept at manipulating digital images and have seen behind the curtain. In this sense, filmmakers in the '00s and '10s (and even now) had to produce films that were better than what could be found on other, noncinematic platforms and small screens. For a more attentive audience with the technology to rewatch a film and pause, rewind, zoom in, and so forth, filmmakers such as Nolan had to up their game, so to speak. Given, too, the higher production values that television began utilizing in the early 2000s to compete with both Hollywood and streaming services, a movie at the theater had to create a different kind of experience beyond merely having a bigger screen. Within this ecosystem, Nolan has thrived, preferring to do most of his visual effects in camera and almost seamlessly incorporating CGI. The final product looks more like a playful realism than a computer creation. Thus Gen Z expectations have significantly shaped the movie industry's attention to detail and use of special effects.

Another way in which the film reaches deep into the psyche of Gen Zers while pulling Gen Xers and Millennials along is its fascination with causality and connectivity. In the film, what happens at one level reverberates throughout all levels. For example, when, at the first level of the dreamworld, the van the team is in falls off a bridge, the next dreamworld level down is inverted, and at the deepest level, an avalanche occurs. In the Information Age, Gen Zers are acutely aware, perhaps more than their parents are, of the damage a single keyboard stroke can make across virtual and real worlds. This causality can really only have these aftershocks because of the level of connectivity of the people involved. Not only are the characters physically connected to the same device that induces and maintains a dream state but they are also literally sharing a consciousness. In much the same way, Gen Zers share the same consciousness, not just as a generation but as a collective identity attached to each other through rapidly progressing and engrossing forms of social media that are not limited to national boundaries or time zones.

Benjamin Crace

See also: *The Dark Knight*; *The Dark Knight Rises*; *Titanic*.

Further Reading

Antrim, Taylor. 2010. "Making of *Inception.*" *Hollywood Reporter* 416 (55): 50–53.

Bernard, Catherine. 2017. "Christopher Nolan's *Inception*: Spectacular Speculations." *Screen* 58 (2): 229–236.

Corliss, Richard. 2010. "Whose Mind Is It, Anyway?" *Time* 176 (4): 59–61.

Hiatt, Brian. 2010. "Leo Faces His Demons. (Cover Story)." *Rolling Stone*, no. 1110 (August): 46–86.

Johnson, David. 2012. Inception *and Philosophy: Because It's Never Just a Dream*. Hoboken, NJ: Wiley.

Joker

Release Date:	2019
Director:	Todd Phillips
Box Office:	$1.074 billion
Main Cast:	Arthur Fleck, played by Joaquin Phoenix
	Sophie Dumond, played by Zazie Beetz
	Murray Franklin, played by Robert De Niro
	Penny Fleck, played by Frances Conroy
	Thomas Wayne, played by Brett Cullen
	Gene Ufland, played by Marc Maron
	Detective Burke, played by Shea Whigham

As a complete revision of the Joker mythology, Phillips's incarnation carries the deconstructionist tendencies of Generation X to their logical conclusions. However, it isn't as thoroughly Gen X as it may appear, nihilism and cynicism aside. Despite the fact that the film is a character study that focuses on Phoenix's performance as an individual actor, the communal and social dimensions of the film offer an X-ray of Gen Z consciousness. This consciousness carries with it a sensibility that the complexities of mental health victimization that result in violent action are similar energies that emerge in the protests of the proletariat. The synecdochic nature of Fleck as every[working-class]man is contextually telegraphed over and over throughout the film. And while there is not a particular antagonist, Fleck's revolt is precisely against the concretized Boomer values perpetuated by Gen Xers. In a sense, then, *Joker* is the punch line to the American Dream.

The film starts with Fleck working as an advertising clown in a run-down part of Gotham City. There is garbage everywhere; from a radio announcement in the background, one learns that the waste collectors are on strike. As Fleck is spinning his sign, some mean teens steal it and make him chase them. They end up beating him with it in an alley. This opening sequence ends with the title card for the film in large, narrow letters that cover the entire screen: "JOKER."

This early sequence of undeserved hostility telegraphs the exact opposite of what one typically associates with clowns and jokers: humor. There is nothing "funny" about the way Fleck has been treated nor about his subsequent response to the humiliation. Phillips is doubly aware here of working within a genre and a canon of sorts but only enough to subvert it; Fleck/Joker exists not as a villain balanced out by Bruce Wayne/Batman but as a synecdoche of the complex dark side of the American psyche. Further, as the first few minutes of the film reveals, Fleck has serious mental health issues, which he tries to treat through therapy and an assortment of pharmaceuticals. These seem to be the only tether he has to the harsh reality of working-class life. Upon losing his social worker therapist, he descends even deeper into his psychosis. This combination of social commentary, mental illness, and estranged comedy converge in Fleck's ambition to become a standup comic. America has a long history of male standup comedians who tell the truth a little too straight: Lenny Bruce, Andy Kaufman, George Carlin, and, the latest incarnation, Dave Chappelle. We, as Americans, love to laugh at our faults while simultaneously being kicked in the teeth. Our nationalistic, sadistic tendencies possibly come from a number of different sources. Perhaps it is our prized value for free speech or our uncomplicated and necessary discomfort with being as global and domineering an empire as the one we revolted against in the 18th century. Perhaps it is, too, as the film suggests, our cognitive dissonance generated from holding the everyman as ideal and then treating him like dirt through exclusive social hierarchies and greed (here Thomas Wayne looms large). Thus as the film ironizes what one typically thinks of "comedy," it becomes a "bit" on its own within this "offend the mind to win the heart," urban, underground comedy tradition.

This reading of the film as a sketch or bit is supported by Phillips' inclusion of "safe" and mainstream comedy in the figure of Murray Franklin, a late-night TV show host. Serving as a foil to the unwholesome and tormented Fleck, Franklin, in some ways, is the reassuring presence, a father figure for Fleck, Gotham, and the targeted American audience. At first, Fleck idolizes Franklin and enjoys watching the Johnny Carson/Jay Leno/Jimmy Fallon-esque program he fronts. *The Murray Franklin Show*, like the Carson show, has an aging host and a conservative, late-1950s aesthetic, closer to Carson and Ed Sullivan than to Conan. The casting of De Niro as Franklin adds just enough austere gravitas to create an ordered space of genteel entertainment, a space, like its aesthetic, that never really existed. Fleck initially sees an appearance on the show as the goal of any comic's career. At one point, Fleck poorly performs his comedy at a small club, but the footage of his act makes it to Franklin, who ends up skewering and mocking it to his audience. Fleck is outraged but, nevertheless, when offered a chance to appear on the show, he takes it. However, between the time Fleck accepts the invitation and his appearance on the program, he takes on more and more of the psychotic murderer persona.

In addition to Fleck's dreams of becoming funny (as a clown and standup comic) and Murray Franklin's sanitized but cruel humor, Phillips inserts another disquieting element to Fleck's character: a rare disorder that makes him laugh uncontrollably. In fact, Fleck carries a card with him that he shows to strangers when in a laughing fit to help them understand that he cannot help it. On the front, the card reads, "Forgive my Laughter: I have a Condition. MORE ON BACK." And the back reads, "It's a medical condition causing sudden frequent and uncontrollable laughter that doesn't match how you feel. It can happen in people with a brain injury or certain neurological conditions. Thank You! KINDLY RETURN THIS CARD." Perhaps a form of hebephrenia, where the sufferer is prone to the types of behavior one sees in Fleck, this condition, like many of the elements in the film, is laden with significance. In terms of the plot, we're asked as the audience to give him a pass; he can't help it. But where, exactly, does his responsibility begin? Does it begin when he kills three men who were tormenting him on the subway? Does it begin when he smothers his mother? Does it begin when he murders a former colleague? Are these all the result of a "condition"? Yet here, too, the parallel tension with the *Murray Franklin Show* foil is evident. Shows like

Franklin's tell people when to laugh and applaud and when to stop (the darkened "APPLAUD" sign appears in several shots of Franklin's stage). Franklin's monologue, too, is scripted, on a card next to the camera. The contrast couldn't be clearer: Fleck's unscripted, spontaneous, incongruous laughter requires a written explanation for societal acceptance. Franklin's comedy, and the societal vision he represents, requires others to conform, dictating when and what is acceptable, appropriate, and funny.

Joker's concern with the meaning of humor/humorlessness as a phenomenon is not only a central theme of the film but keyed into the burgeoning social conscience and ethos of Generation Z. Peter McGraw and Joel Warner, in their book, *The Humor Code*, elegantly define humor as "benign violation." They argue that "humor only occurs when something seems wrong, unsettling or threatening (i.e., a violation), but simultaneously seems okay, acceptable, or safe (i.e., benign)" (2014, 10). In *Joker*, Franklin is benign and Fleck, the violation. However, the balance is out of whack: the violation overpowers, colonizes, and kills, sparking riots. And this is part of the point: there isn't anything funny about the world *Joker* mirrors, because there isn't an authentic, benign balance for true humor to emerge. Murray Franklin is a joke; he is supposed to be funny but is cruel, mocking a mentally ill individual for ratings. His real-world counterparts are the hollow, canned, and curated MCs of America's late nights from the Boomers' Jack Paar and Johnny Carson to Gen X's Leno and Letterman to the Millennials' and Fallon. Add a global pandemic, climate change, and the urgent calls for justice and equality, and there appears to be no reason for laughing for Gen Z; there are far too many uncertainties and pressing issues. Here, then, Fleck is a dark Gen Z fantasy: his violence is not his fault and is even necessary, he sparks reformation and anarchy, and he disrupts the oppressive order of rich, white Boomers in suits. Phillips thus transmutes the Joker mythology into a cautionary tale of what happens when Gen Z's social concerns are not heeded, summed up nicely in Fleck's last "joke" just prior to shooting Franklin in the head on live television: "What do you get when you cross a mentally ill loner with a society that abandons him and treats him like trash? I'll tell you what you get, you get what you f—ing deserve!" Significantly, with the studio in chaos immediately afterward, Fleck genuinely laughs.

Although the majority of the film is a character study and social commentary, there a quite a few nods to the Batman/Joker mythology. It is a type of origin story, after all—or at least that's what the audience expects, given the name of the film, the location (Gotham), Fleck's costume and facial paint, and so on. In one chilling scene, Fleck visits a young Bruce Wayne through the bars of the entrance gate of Wayne Manor. At first, Fleck roams along the outside wall, signaling his outsider position. He sees Bruce in a cupola, puts on a red nose and gets his attention, calling him over to the gate. After doing some lame magic tricks with trick flowers, they introduce themselves and, through the gate, Arthur pushes the corners of Bruce's lips up into a smile, saying, "That's better." Alfred runs over and tells him to go away. Arthur then argues with Alfred about how his mother, Penny, was Thomas Wayne's lover and thus Wayne is his father. Alfred insists Penny is delusional, and Fleck briefly chokes him through the bars before running off. Bruce, here, is just a side character that helps to establish a deeper connection between the Waynes of Gotham, its subversive working class (Fleck), and subservient guardians (Alfred). The generation-yet-to-be, Bruce, as the audience knows, will become the Dark Knight who is as emotionally and psychological disturbed as the Joker and the city he defends. Toward the end of the film, Bruce's narrative is picked up again as one of the clown-masked rioters, set off and inspired by Fleck's murder on the subway, follows the Waynes into a dark alley and murders his parents. The well-known element of Martha Wayne's pearl necklace being ripped and spilling everywhere is perhaps Phillips's most classically Batman shot. But aside from these moments and nods, *Joker* is all Fleck.

In addition to the fact that much of the film is Fleck doing things alone, another key layer of the film that makes it difficult to simply summarize is the blurring of the world of the story and the fantasy world of Fleck. This also confuses the audience: a significant part of the movie is simply Fleck's fantasy of a relationship with a single mother named Sophie in his apartment building. In the delusion (before the audience knows it is not real), Sophie and Fleck's relationship seems to be a means of healing and redemption for him. He begins to act fairly "normal": they sleep together and go on dates; she goes to his standup performance and comforts him in the hospital after his mother is admitted. Yet all of these activities with Sophie are only in his mind, which only becomes evident later in the film, suggesting that many of the things the viewer has seen were also delusions. Fleck, then, as an unreliable narrator of sorts calls into question the earlier sympathy elicited by his condition and abuse. But at the same time, deceiving the audience through inclusion into his mind gives one a sense of what it feels like to experience the world through his perspective. Together with the many, tight, long close-ups, we are psychically stitched into the character, making it nearly impossible to simply dismiss him and his actions, for they have, in some way, become our own.

At the end of the film, he is in Arkham Asylum. The scene recapitulates one of the opening scenes between Fleck and his therapist. However, he is fully Joker now, and Arthur Fleck is gone. As he sits with the psychologist in a white room with handcuffs, he starts laughing. When she asks what he is laughing about, he says he was thinking of a joke. The counselor asks him to tell her, and he responds with, "You wouldn't get it" just before killing her. Gone is the nervous Fleck looking for help, stumbling over himself to get his card to explain his laughter. No. Joker needs no understanding, no shared empathy, no help.

Unlike many of the other films in this text, *Joker* is not as much a blockbuster as a mirror. Its blockbuster status was probably achieved because of the controversy it generated, its usage of the Batman mythology, and Phoenix's acting. It isn't, however, as entertaining as it is disturbing, reflecting our present cultural moment in ways that disrupt any escapist cinephile. Like *V for Vendetta* (2005) and its main character's Guy Fawkes mask, Joker and his makeup became a symbol of protest against oppression around the world soon after its release. Such real-world appropriation and mass identification makes the film less of a fun American blockbuster and more of a reservoir of vast symbolic potential.

Benjamin Crace

See also: *Batman*; *The Dark Knight*; *The Dark Knight Rises*.

Further Reading

Çöteli, Sami. 2020. "The Concept of Social (In)Justice and Its Portrayals in Todd Phillips's *Joker.*" *Communication Today* 11 (2): 36–44.

Jürgens, Anna-Sophie. 2020. "The Pathology of Joker's Dance: The Origins of Arthur Fleck's Body Aesthetics in Todd Phillips's 2019 *Joker* Film." *Dance Chronicle* 43 (3): 321–337.

Kaur, Harmeet. 2019, November 3. "In Protests around the World, One Image Stands Out: The Joker." CNN. https://www.cnn.com/2019/11/03/world/joker-global-protests-trnd/index.html.

Lane, Anthony, and Richard Brody. 2019. "No Laughing Matter." *New Yorker* 95 (30): 65–67.

McGraw, Peter, and Joel Warner. 2014. *The Humor Code: A Global Search for What Makes Things Funny*. New York: Simon & Schuster.

Peaslee, Robert Moses, and Robert G. Weiner. 2015. *The Joker: A Serious Study of the Clown Prince of Crime*. University Press of Mississippi.

Tietze, Tad. 2020. "Populist Panic at the Movies." *Modern Age* 62 (2): 31–36.

Skyfall

Release Date:	2012
Director:	Sam Mendes
Box Office:	$1.109 billion
Main Cast:	James Bond, played by Daniel Craig
	M, played by Judi Dench
	Raoul Silva, played by Javier Bardem
	Eve Moneypenny, played by Naomie Harris
	Gareth Mallory, played by Ralph Fiennes
	Bill Tanner, played by Rory Kinnear
	Q, played by Ben Whishaw

In *Skyfall*, Daniel Craig reprises his role as the iconic British spy for the 50th anniversary of the James Bond franchise. *Skyfall* quickly became the most successful in the franchise, amassing over $1 billion in revenues and winning two Oscars. While infused with Gen X cynicism and Boomer nostalgia, "*Skyfall* triumphantly reinvents 007" to become the defining Bond movie for Gen Z (Ebert 2012). Mendes's soft reboot of the franchise situates a traumatized Bond in the globalized, post-9/11 digital world and marks an ideological departure from the previous movies.

The film opens with Bond's silhouette walking down a dark hallway, suit pressed and gun in hand, toward a room where he finds MI6 agent Ronson (Bill Buckhurst) critically injured and a laptop gutted of its hard drive. Speaking into Bond's headpiece, M insists that he run after Patrice (Ola Rapace), the mercenary who took the hard drive. The disposability of agents is critiqued in a way that we have not seen before in the Bond movies. We are introduced to a central issue: the value of an agent's life measured against the mission. Craig's Bond ignores M's insistence as he attempts to stabilize Ronson and cover his wounds. His hesitation, which comes in conflict with his instinct to complete the mission, shows his capacity for expressing basic human compassion.

Bond walks out into the busy streets of Istanbul and into a car with Eve Moneypenny to chase Patrice. The chase leads to a fistfight between Bond and Patrice on top of a moving train, while Moneypenny assumes sniper position. Because of their proximity, taking a shot at Patrice has a high risk of hitting Bond, but M gives Moneypenny the order. As feared, the bullet hits Bond, and we see him fall off the train and into the river below, presumed dead.

Bond survives the fall and washes up on a beach. We see him first in bed with a woman and then at a local bar drinking whiskey, with a scorpion on the back of his hand while the bar patrons cheer him on. The debauchery and hedonism, cornerstones of the Bond mythology, rather than being symbolic of leisure, highlight the extent of Bond's hurt and unmoored state—adding a depth to his character unseen in previous iterations of 007.

Meanwhile, MI6 comes under attack from a hacker, later revealed to be Raoul Silva, a scorned former MI6 agent. Silva infiltrates MI6's central network to decrypt the stolen hard drive and sends a taunting message to M, saying, "Think on your sins." Moments later, MI6's base is blown up, firmly rooting *Skyfall* in the 21st century, where the War on Terror has subsumed the Cold War. The nature of the attack reflects contemporary fear: the looming threat of terrorism that has now migrated from an external threat to an invisible and omnipotent one enabled by cyber technology and made communal by the media.

After the attack, M meets the new Intelligence and Security Committee chairman, Gareth Mallory. In that meeting, they reveal that the hard drive contained a classified list of undercover NATO agents (a PR disaster and political scandal as much as a security threat). As a result, Mallory implies, M should retire with dignity. Prompted by the news of the attack on MI6, Bond returns to England. He breaks into M's apartment and waits for her in the shadows with bloodshot eyes and an unshaven face. Craig's Bond is broken and battered, returning reluctantly out of a sense of duty. We later learn that M recruited Bond when he was young and vulnerable; she even says, "Orphans always make the best recruits." This casts a dark shadow over their relationship, which had the subtle air of familial intimacy but now appears to have an exploitative dynamic.

Following the strained reunion with M, Bond goes to the new MI6 headquarters for evaluations to clear him for fieldwork. In the Bondian narrative structure, the first act is where Bond gets debriefed and prepared for his first mission; but here, rather than an external mission, Bond's first mission is himself. Forcing Bond to undergo these tests in place of the first mission highlights the movie's self-reflexive and introspective impulses.

During the evaluation, Bond visibly struggles to complete the physical tasks and ends his psychological evaluation abruptly after being triggered at the mention of his childhood home, Skyfall Manor. To show Bond emotionally triggered by something so intimate adds another dimension to his character, showing the audience that there is more to him than being a "blunt instrument" with a "license to kill."

Age is a central motif in *Skyfall*. The Bond movies rarely acknowledge the agent's age because that would affect the timelessness and mythology of Bond. Highlighting his age here is a metatheatrical moment that acknowledges the change of audience and their paradigms of heroism. That becomes evident when Bond meets the new Q (Ben Whishaw) at the National Gallery in London. Q has appeared in a majority of the Bond films (except for *Live and Let Die*, *Casino Royale*, and *Quantum of Solace*). Often portrayed by an older British actor, Q serves as the head of research and development of the British Secret Service, who faithfully briefs Bond on the gadgets for his mission. This time, Q comes in the form of a Gen Z representative, a young, scrawny, bespectacled, digital native.

We see Bond and Q in front of J. M. W. Turner's painting *The Fighting Temeraire* (1838) at the museum. The painting is of an old warship being towed away unceremoniously to be scrapped and its parts used to fuel new industries. Q, who had not introduced himself yet, initiates small talk with Bond, who meets his friendliness with antagonism. This hostility on Bond's end continues when Q introduces himself and Bond doubts Q's qualifications because of the latter's age and the remote nature of his work. Q responds, "I'll hazard I can do more damage on my laptop sitting in my pajamas before my first cup of Earl Grey than you can do in a year in the field . . . [but] now and then a trigger has to be pulled." Q challenges Bond unprecedentedly and places a higher value on remote cyber work over fieldwork. In the digital world of network and surveillance, "not the gun but the computer as weapon renders Bond's physical action anachronistic" (Jeong 2020, 214). This exchange brings us back to the main question *Skyfall* raises: Is James Bond relevant in the age of technology?

After the biting exchange, Q gives Bond the classic Walther PPK and a radio transmitter. Disappointed by the functional yet not flashy equipment, Bond says, "Not exactly Christmas." Q replies, "Were you expecting an exploding pen? We don't go in for that anymore." Here we see another metatheatrical moment, where Q refers to his predecessors and their taste for extravagant gadgets contributing to Bond's ostentatious presentation. This is further developed in how Q designed the gun: it has dermal recognition to make it "less of a random killing machine, more of a personal statement."

Trying to absorb this "brave new world," Bond exits the museum and flies to his next destination, searching for Silva. To get to Silva, Bond goes to several exotic locations: Shanghai, Macau, and eventually to Hashima Island, where Silva is. It's a journey characteristic of the Bondian narrative, but like most tropes in this movie, it is subverted, and "his world tour is no longer hedonistic but breathless with unpredictable widespread threats," which is another way Mendes reconfigures 007 for its contemporary moment (Jeong 2020, 216).

Meanwhile, Silva hacks M's laptop again and sends her to a YouTube video, where he releases the names and images of the first five agents from the list while promising to reveal five more each week. Soon, one of the compromised agents is found and executed on live TV. This scene shows how Silva can destabilize an entire espionage agency and compromise the national security of multiple nations with a single video, thus highlighting how the contemporary villain can wreak havoc from a remote distance and without an arsenal. There are no nuclear warheads, no plans of infecting livestock or irradiating gold, and no space laser beams. It is a simple video that sends the entire nation and its allies into a frenzy and instigates tensions between them. Silva emphasizes that later, when he boasts about his ability to manipulate stocks, disrupt spy satellites, and rig elections with one button. Furthermore, this scene highlights how spectacle characterizes the violence Gen Z has been exposed to, which is a sharp break from the secrecy and shadows of the Cold War.

Despite sharing the classic characteristics with other Bond villains (visible marks of difference, a secret lair, and a taste for the dramatic), his motivation is unique. We find out later that he was captured and tortured for five months but remained loyal to M throughout the whole time, only to learn that M had forsaken him and agreed to a prisoner exchange. After a failed suicide attempt with a cyanide capsule left him permanently disfigured, he says, "It burned all my insides, but I didn't die. Life clung to me like a disease." In addition to the physical damages, Silva emerged from that imprisonment with symptoms of PTSD, which is a revealing moment indicative of the awareness and importance placed on the psychological effects of war. In addition to adding nuance to Silva's character, his relationship with M sheds light on the corruption of MI6 and specifically M's role in it. The distinct nature of her relationship with both Bond and Silva shows the dark underbelly of the agency that preys on and exploits vulnerable young people and molds them into "blunt instruments" in service of the state. In addition to destabilizing the binary of good and evil, M's role and the nuances allowed to Silva show how Gen Z has moved away from a Manichean morality and embraces a more complex worldview.

The video's release and the consequential executions renewed the questions about the relevance and efficiency of MI6 as an espionage agency in the 21st century. In a meeting between Mallory and M, the chairman describes the agency as "many antiquated bloody idiots fighting a war we don't understand and can't possibly win." When the prime minister requests M's presence, M describes it as having to "stand in the stocks at midday." While Mallory can appear as a symbol of an older and more conservative stance, his position here is comparatively progressive: "We're a democracy; we're accountable to the people we're trying to defend. We can't keep working in the shadows. There are no more shadows!" While M, the defendant of the agency and the old ways, says, "You don't get this, do you? Whoever's behind this, whoever's doing this, he knows us! He's one of us! He comes from the same place as Bond, a place you say doesn't exist—the shadows!" The same discussion is heightened at the inquiry, where the board interrogates the relevance of an espionage agency post–Cold War. Their question to M highlights the main problem that the movie is grappling with: MI6 is built on a premise and upheld by values that directly conflict with the values upheld by contemporary society with the emphasis on privacy, transparency, and democracy.

In response, M gives an impassioned speech, imbued with a carefully constructed patriotism: "Well, I suppose I see a different world than you do, and the truth is that what I see frightens me. I'm frightened because our enemies are no longer known to us. They do not exist on a map. . . . Our world is not more transparent now, and it is more opaque! It is in the shadows. That is where we must do battle. So, before you declare us irrelevant, ask yourselves, how safe do you feel?" The logic M presents "renews the Cold War rhetoric of fearmongering politics in the post-historical (and post-9/11) age in which global networks generate the schizophrenic multitudes of stateless hackers and ghost-like terrorists. In this world that lacks transparency, secret agencies would become more vulnerable and ineffective under open scrutiny and public interference.... The terms of criticism are then inverted.... The agency is not oppositional to, but rather protective of the open democratic system from behind" (Jeong 2020, 217).

The irony lies in watching M, who accused Bond (Pierce Brosnan) in *GoldenEye* (1995) of being a "relic of the Cold War," become that relic herself by re-creating Cold War rhetoric for the 21st century. However, unlike *GoldenEye*, *Skyfall* "offers an emphatic defense of the secret state against such interferences, not only deflecting calls for accountability and oversight but positioning the secret intelligence officer, not the politician or citizen, as the true defender of democracy in this time of ubiquitous threat" (Smith 2016, 156).

Once M ends her speech, Silva barges into the courthouse and starts shooting, aiming for M, but Bond's timely arrival thwarts the prodigal son. In the iconic Aston Martin, Bond saves M and takes her to Skyfall Manor. The return to his childhood home forces Bond to come to terms with his past, which is crucial to his journey of identity re-formation. Silva follows them and viewers witness the final battle between M's two golden boys.

In the final act, inside a dark and dilapidated chapel, Silva holds a gun to a terminally injured M's head but is unable to pull the trigger and ends up collapsing into her arms, allowing him to be vulnerable in his final moments despite being the antagonist. At that moment, Bond walks up and stabs Silva in the back before stepping over his body unceremoniously. The camera angle changes, and we see Bond transformed from being the ruthless agent to a man hurting, holding the dying body of his maternal figure. M looks at him and says, "I did get one thing right," giving him the validation Silva died for. She takes her last breath and the rugged, steely-eyed Bond is further reduced to a bereaved man. The camera angle changes again, this time showing us his back only and slowly panning out of the chapel almost as if to give Bond a moment of privacy. This is not the suave and stoic James Bond of Sean Connery or Timothy Dalton, nor is it the campy Roger Moore or superhero-like womanizer Pierce Brosnan that gave birth to the Austin Powers spoofs; "this is a brand-new Bond with love and respect for the old Bond" (Ebert 2012).

In his previous incarnations, Bond was characterized by a "fantastical flamboyance," but that is replaced by highlighting the extent to which Craig's Bond is characterized by his emotional and physical vulnerability (Gaine 2016b, 130). In many ways, this iteration of Bond, emphasizing vulnerability and human flaws, responds to the growing trend during the mid- to late 2000s of realistic, dark, and gritty films reflective of the disillusionment with the American Dream by Gen Xers and older Millennials alike. This shift is often attributed to Christopher Nolan's *Batman* reboot (2005–2012), which shaped the contours of a new superhero and even espionage genres. The impact Nolan had was in presenting a character "that employs self-seriousness, a tone of morbidity, real-world context, and a kind of existing material so that the new version of the character is an amalgamation of older qualities and other iterations" (Robertson 2020). More importantly, this trend is marked by the move toward reckoning with murky ethical grounds, which feed into the protagonists' distress. The refashioning of Bond as a tragic hero haunted by his demons and the dark and gritty atmosphere in general highlight the rising (and sustained) interest in trauma and interiority in the post-9/11 era.

Skyfall branches out in mode and tone without sacrificing the iconography and narrative structure present in its predecessors. Craig, whose "blue eyes were less suggestive of matinee-idol seductiveness than a subzero temperature, chilling everything right beneath the surface," gives us a more human Bond with physical limitations and inner demons, indicating the cultural shift and interest in trauma and interiority replacing the spectacle of large-scale heroics with the body (Fear 2021).

Dina Alqassar

See also: *The Dark Knight*; *The Dark Knight Rises*.

Further Reading

Dodds, Klaus. 2014. "Shaking and Stirring James Bond: Age, Gender, and Resilience in *Skyfall* (2012)." *Journal of Popular Film and Television* 42 (3): 116–130.

Ebert, Roger. 2012, November 7. "The Best Bond in Years." Roger Ebert.com. https://www.rogerebert.com/reviews/skyfall-2012.

Fear, David. 2021, October 8. "Daniel Craig Is the Best James Bond—It's Not Even Close." *Rolling Stone*. https://www.rollingstone.com/movies/movie-features/daniel-craig-best-james-bond-1234978.

Gaine, Vincent M. 2016a. "It's Only a Film, Isn't It? Policy Paranoia Thrillers of the War on Terror." In *Cycles, Sequels, Spin-offs, Remakes, and Reboots*, edited by A. A. Klein and R. B. Palmer, 148–165. Austin: University of Texas Press.

Gaine, Vincent M. 2016b. "'Not Now That Strength': Embodiment and Globalisation in Post-9/11 James Bond." In *American Cinema in the Shadow of 9/11*, edited by Terence McSweeney, 127–146. Edinburgh, UK: Edinburgh University Press.

Hasian, Marouf, Jr. 2014. "*Skyfall*, James Bond's Resurrection, and 21st-Century Anglo-American Imperial Nostalgia." *Communication Quarterly* 62 (5): 569–588.

Jeong, Seung-hoon. 2020. "Global Agency between Bond and Bourne: *Skyfall* and James Bond in Comparison to the Jason Bourne Film Series." In *The Cultural Life of James Bond: Specters of 007*, edited by Jaap Verheul, 207–226. Amsterdam, Netherlands: Amsterdam University Press.

Murray, Jonathan. 2016. "'I've Been Inspecting You, Mister Bond': Crisis, Catharsis, and Calculation in Daniel Craig's Twenty-First-Century 007." *Cinéaste* 41 (2): 4–11.

Robertson, Dane. 2020, August 18. "How Christopher Nolan Changed Superhero Movies (for the Better)." The Latch. https://thelatch.com.au/christopher-nolan.

Smith, James. 2016. "How Safe Do You Feel? James Bond, *Skyfall*, and the Politics of the Secret Agent in an Age of Ubiquitous Threat." *College Literature* 43 (1): 145–172.

Verheul, Jaap, ed. 2020. *The Cultural Life of James Bond: Specters of 007*. Amsterdam, Netherlands: Amsterdam University Press.

Star Wars: The Force Awakens

Release Date:	2015
Director:	J. J. Abrams
Box Office:	$2.066 billion
Main Cast:	Rey, played by Daisy Ridley
	Finn, played by John Boyega
	Poe Dameron, played by Oscar Isaac
	Kylo Ren, played by Adam Driver
	Maz Kanata, played by Lupita Nyong'o
	Supreme Leader Snoke, played by Andy Serkis
	General Hux, played by Domhnall Gleeson
	Captain Phasma, played by Gwendoline Christie

In *A New Hope* (1977), Obi-Wan Kenobi explains the Force to Luke Skywalker as "an energy field created by all living things. It surrounds us and penetrates us; it binds the galaxy together." Much like the Force, the mythos of *Star Wars* surrounds the collective American consciousness and binds the foundation of modern folklore. The release of a new *Star Wars* movie is a generational milestone and a shared foundational memory that shaped—and reflected—identities and cultural discourses. The seventh installment of the Skywalker saga, *The Force Awakens*, initiates Generation Z into the *Star Wars* universe. Directed by J. J. Abrams, *Awakens* tells the story of an orphan from Jakku, Rey (Daisy Ridley), and a rogue Stormtrooper, Finn (John Boyega), who, with the help of Han Solo (Harrison Ford), help the Resistance find Luke Skywalker (Mark Hamill) and join the fight against the evil First Order. Essentially, the film is a pastiche of the original *Star Wars* movies that is structured to address "questions of identity, inclusion, and representation," creating a cultural bridge between Gen Z and their predecessors while introducing a new chapter to the beloved saga (Golding 2019, 91).

Cultural critic bell hooks argued that "movies not only provide a narrative for specific discourses of race, sex, and class, they provide a shared experience, a common starting point from which diverse audiences can dialogue about these charged issues" (2008, 3). We see how movies provide a shared narrative in the way *Awakens* addresses sociopolitical and cultural discourses. Consider Han Solo's attitude toward the Force; in *Hope*, set against the background of the Vietnam War, Han proclaims, "Hokey religions and ancient weapons are no match for a good blaster at your side." His self-confidence and distrust of spirituality reflect traditional American values of individualism and material work, with undertones of Orientalism and American exceptionalism. But a pivotal shift happens in *Awakens* when Rey asks about the Jedi, and Han says, "I used to wonder that myself. I thought it was a bunch of mumbo-jumbo: a magical power holding together good and evil, the dark side and the light. The crazy thing is, it's true. The Force. The Jedi. All of it." Han's acknowledgment of the Force reflects the changing religious landscape of America, where a growing number of people, especially Gen Z, are identifying as spiritual, not religious. Moreover, it shows how the Force "serve[s] as a kind of secularized American religion," as an alternative to organized and institutionalized religion (Saiman 2017).

The Star Wars franchise's success stems, in part, from its ability to transport its audience to a galaxy far, far away, and its enchantment extends beyond the story to the experience of watching it, as stories of watching the movie for the first time are part of the legend and appeal. But growing up during a time when films are available on demand, Gen Z fans could easily access the catalog of Star Wars films and experience them as a single collection, not as monumental events that punctuate their lives with anticipation and enchantment. Rey is not unlike a Gen Z fan of *Star Wars*—she has heard the stories but never experienced the magic herself. Early on, we see her wearing a Rebel pilot's helmet and pretending to fly an aircraft, with the implication that she often daydreams about Rebels and the Galactic Wars. Rey's daydreaming mirrors the way Gen Z's experience with *Star Wars* was primarily through action figures, toy lightsabers, or video games without knowing much about the narrative of the movies itself.

Abrams also captures Gen Z's experience through Rey and Finn's interactions with Han Solo. For instance, when Rey tells Han she stole the Falcon, he says, "You tell [Unkar Plutt] that Han Solo just stole the Millennium Falcon back for good." Rey beams with excitement and asks, "This is the Millennium Falcon? You are Han Solo?" Her reaction gestures to the legendary status of Han and the Falcon in pop culture. The subsequent conversation between her and Finn gives us insight into the characters' backgrounds. Also, it mirrors the different frames of reference Gen Z has regarding *Star Wars* that shaped their introduction to the franchise. Finn, a former Stormtrooper indoctrinated by the First Order, knows Han Solo as "the Resistance General" and a "war hero." Meanwhile, Rey, a scavenger, mechanic, and self-taught pilot who lives on a planet notorious for being a haven for outlaws, knows Han as "the smuggler" and the Falcon as "the ship that made the Kessel run in 14 parsecs" (Han corrects: "12"). The two of them, starstruck and in awe, are like young fans who have heard of Han Solo and probably watched the original trilogy but never had an encounter not mediated by an older fan.

While older fans might have gravitated toward the trope of an underdog protagonist who is part of a chosen prophecy, Gen Z has different opinions about messianic leaders and tends to prefer ordinary characters who are part of a larger collective. Rey embodies that trope, as evident in how *Awakens* emphasizes her status as an abandoned child who learned to survive, instead of calling attention to her gender and capabilities. Her desire to find her family and the hope of them returning overshadows any obligation she feels toward the Resistance or any greater good. The focus on her status and desire for a family indicates changing ideas of gender representation, heroism, and belonging.

Abrams's casting choices is one of the more obvious ways that *Awakens* attends to Gen Z and reflects their values. Since the beginning, *Star Wars* was critiqued for the lack of diversity; Carl Sagan commented on it on the *Tonight Show with Johnny Carson* in 1978, when he said, "They're all white. The skin of all humans in *Star Wars* is, oddly enough, like this [looking at his own hands]." The backlash against Abrams's casting choices, especially casting John Boyega, confirms this problem.

During their first encounter in the movie, Rey asks Finn if he's with the Resistance, and he says, "Yes, I'm with the Resistance; this is what we look like. Some of us, others look different." Finn subtly comments about race in the *Star Wars* universe and responds to the backlash that arose after the first trailer, where older fans objected to having a Black actor play a Stormtrooper. The comment simultaneously critiques *Star Wars* for its whiteness while gesturing to the general discourse about race and representation. As Robert Daniels states, "While Abrams might have hoped to address the diversity issues of Star Wars' past through Finn, in practice, the results are disappointing. Through casting a Black actor, Abrams thought Finn's Blackness would be apparent. But Blackness is deeper than skin color. It's activism. In that regard, Finn isn't Black. Not to those in the world of Star Wars" (2020). Although Abrams raises his audiences' hopes by casting Boyega and Isaac, their race and individuality are erased for the sake of homogenous unity.

Despite the outcry against Abrams's casting choices and accusations of being politically correct, the cast for *Awakens* remains primarily white. There are gestures toward diversity with casting choices, but that diversity is only skin deep; the movie "never acknowledged Finn's race enough for the hardships that Boyega faced, or the macro view of the world he navigated, to cross over in a meaningful way" (Daniels 2020). The story was centered around the white female protagonist and the white male antagonist, while the characters of color were covered in CGI or rendered to the periphery. This is symptomatic of an "insidious trend: the white female leads bolstered by an ensemble of color" (Salem 2020). It is a gesture toward inclusion by having a white woman replace a white man without engaging more meaningfully with the politics of race and gender.

One of Gen Z's defining characteristics is its political engagement and activism. The proliferation of social media introduced them to new ideas, conversations, and multiple perspectives that a fan of *The Empire Strikes Back*, for example, would not have had access to. Key to that is their exposure to a (paradoxically) unmediated reality through raw footage: social media eliminates the distance created through narrative. Doing so prevents the recipients from mentally dissociating themselves and forcing them to witness acts of discrimination, state-sponsored violence, and systemic racism upfront. Gen Z's exposure to injustices has mobilized them into taking a stand and organizing. This experience is neatly captured in the beginning, when the First Order attacks the village of Tuanul in search of the map with Luke's location. The Stormtroopers round up the villagers at the center and mercilessly shoot anyone who resists; before they retreat, Captain Phasma orders them to kill everyone. As she does, the camera cuts to the villagers' faces, and we can see the fear in their eyes. With streaks of blood on his helmet, Finn stands with the other Stormtroopers but cannot, or will not, fire his weapon after seeing the villagers. Witnessing the consequences of the First Order forces him to recognize the humanity of the villagers and thus unravels all the narrative the First Order has indoctrinated in him; it was the exposure to violence that radicalized Finn and led him to defect to the Resistance.

The film also engages with Gen Z's activism through the politics of the villains of the movie. Rather than the simplistic morality seen in the earlier films, the villains in *Awakens* are more complicated and representative. Armitage Hux

(Domnhall Gleeson) is a zealous military general committed to the First Order regime without being spiritually invested in the Dark Side. Hux's ardor and Nazi aesthetics are representative of the threat of neo-Nazis that Gen Z faces now. Similarly, Kylo Ren (Adam Driver) represents extreme right-wing identity politics that romanticize a previous era. Unlike Anakin in the prequels or Darth Vader in the original movies, Kylo Ren was not seduced by the Dark Side out of anger or a desire for revenge but chose the Dark Side (the later movies suggest that parental neglect may be at the root of it, but that is not fully explored in *Awakens*). Kylo Ren yearns for a perceived golden age that he tries to attain by emulating Darth Vader and forges an identity that distances him from his true heritage (Han, Leia, Luke, Anakin) to an imagined one. Both Kylo Ren and Hux represent the dangers of clinging to a romanticized past, a threat that is particular to Gen Z.

Awakens as a movie has a Janus-like ethos: on the one hand, it is ensnared in nostalgia, while on the other hand, it is future facing; and the tension between the past and the present allows the movie to bridge the cultural gap between generations. When Han finds his Millennium Falcon, he walks in with Chewbacca, blaster in hand, saying, "Chewie, we're home." His comment is a metatheatrical welcome to the audience, serving as a homecoming for older fans and introducing newer ones. Han—both as a metonymic icon himself and through the symbols associated with him—satiates the nostalgia of older fans by connecting the movie to its predecessors through subtle allusions without alienating newer fans. We see as much when Rey calls the Falcon "garbage" (an allusion to when Luke calls it a "hunk of junk" in *Hope* and Leia refers to it as a "bucket of bolts" in *Empire*) . . . or when C-3PO interrupts Han and Leia's reunion, similarly to how he interrupted their first kiss in *Empire*. Later in the movie, when Finn asks Han what they should do with Captain Phasma, Han replies, "Is there a garbage chute? Trash compactor?" with a glint of mischief in his eyes (in *Hope*, Han, Leia, and Luke accidentally end up in a trash compactor when attempting to escape the Death Star).

But while the movie welcomes its heritage, it is also moving forward. Two murders bookend the movie; in the first act, Kylo Ren kills Lor San Tekka (Max von Sydow) out of frustration at being reminded of his past. In the final act, he kills his father, Han Solo, before he can move forward. The murder of two iconic Boomer/Gen Xers signals the end of an era and the start of a new one. The death of Han especially is a way for the movie (and the franchise) to relieve itself of the burden of its own legacy before it can start a new chapter. Similarly, in the scene where Rey finds Anakin's lightsaber, Maz gently tells her, "Dear child, the belonging you seek is not behind you." It is a forward-facing parallel to Han's earlier comment, "Chewie, we're home," to signal that this is not a movie for those who grew up with *Star Wars*; it is one for those who are coming into it now.

Dina Alqassar

See also: *Indiana Jones and the Raiders of the Lost Ark*; *Star Wars: A New Hope*; *Star Wars: Return of the Jedi*

Further Reading

Brown, Jeffrey A. 2018. "#wheresRey: Feminism, Protest, and Merchandising Sexism in *Star Wars: The Force Awakens*." *Feminist Media Studies* 18 (3): 335–348.

Daniels, Robert. 2020, June 3. "John Boyega Is Doing What *Star Wars* Wouldn't." Polygon. https://www.polygon.com/2020/6/3/21278460/star-wars-john-boyega-black-lives-matter-finn-force-awakens-rise-of-skywalker.

Eberl, Jason, and Kevin Decker. 2016. "Star Wars: The Force Awakens." *Philosophy Now* 115 (January): 48–50.

Foster, Alan Dean. 2015. *The Force Awakens (Star Wars)*. New York: Del Rey.

Golding, Dan. 2019. Star Wars *After Lucas*. Minneapolis: University of Minnesota Press.

Green, Mary, Scott Huver, Mia Mcniece, Kara Warner, and Alynda Wheat. 2016. "*Star Wars*' New Heroine: A Star Awakens." *People* 85 (1): 62–65.

Gutiérrez, Peter. 2016. "The Cultural Ubiquity of *Star Wars*." *Screen Education*, no. 82 (Winter): 58–65.

hooks, bell. 2008. *Reel to Real: Race, Class, and Sex at the Movies*. New York: Routledge.

Saiman, Chaim. 2017, December 27. "Why *The Last Jedi* Is More 'Spiritual' than 'Religious.'" *The Atlantic*. https://www.theatlantic.com/entertainment/archive/2017/12/why-the-last-jedi-is-more-spiritual-than-religious/549146.

Salem, Merryana. 2020, May 28. "The White Feminist Lead and Her Posse of Colour." Kill Your Darlings. https://www.killyourdarlings.com.au/article/the-white-feminist-lead-and-her-posse-of-colour.

Wonder Woman

Release Date:	2017
Director:	Patty Jenkins
Box Office:	$412,815,408 (Domestic)
Main Cast:	Diana Prince/Wonder Woman, played by Gal Gadot
	Steve Trevor, played by Chris Pine
	Sir Patrick/Ares, played by David Thewlis

Gal Gadot's Wonder Woman was a scene-stealing sensation in the character's live-action, big-screen debut in *Batman v Superman: Dawn of Justice* (2016), the second installment of the DC Extended Universe (DCEU), after the *Man of Steel* (2013). Fans of Wonder Woman in any of her previous incarnations would have to wait a bit longer before she finally had the lead in a superhero film of her own, in part because, some would argue, of the critical and commercial failure of the first and only previous superhero film with a female lead, *Supergirl* (1984). But unlike Supergirl, Wonder Woman has long been a hit with fans, whether in comic books since 1941, animated series such as *Super Friends* (1973–1985) or *Justice League* (2001–2004), or the live-action series *Wonder Woman* (1975–1979). Directed by Patty Jenkins, with Gal Gadot reprising her previous role but this time as the lead in the film, *Wonder Woman* was a global sensation and an overall critical success. A second installment of her story (*Wonder Woman: 1984*) was released three years later, in 2020, and a third film has already received the green light to proceed with development.

The film opens in the present day with Diana Prince, now curator for the Department of Antiquities at the Louvre Museum, receiving a package from Wayne Enterprises that contains the photographic plate that had caused her so much trouble in the previous film. This functions as her Proustian madeleine, taking her and the audience on a journey to her past that lasts up until the very end of the film where it shifts back to the frame story at the Louvre. But first, viewers are taken on a journey to her past and to her homeland, the hidden island of Themyscira, home to the warrior Amazon women. We learn from her mother, Hippolyta, how the Amazons were created by the gods of Olympus to protect humanity, which had been threatened with destruction by a jealous Ares. Zeus gives the women the "god-killer" to fight Ares, and while initially we are led to believe it is a special sword, it turns out that Diana herself should be the holder of that title. The rebellious Diana, the only child on Themyscira, finally gets her mother's approval to be trained militarily, and it is during a mock battle that one of her superpowers is revealed, the ability to harness and deploy power through her bracelets. This may also have been the cause of the rift that develops in the sky, allowing first an airplane and then a pursing German battleship to slip through from the human world, bringing with them the news and the horrors of World War I.

A battle with the Germans ensues in which several Amazon women lose their lives, but they defeat the soldiers and save the pilot, who although dressed in a German uniform, is actually an American spy working on behalf of the Allies. Diana not only saves him but decides to return to the world of men in order to battle Ares, the god of war, whom she believes is behind the chaos. By the time the two arrive by boat to London, the audience has already been introduced to several of Diana's superhero weapons—her bracelets of submission, the lariat of truth, the god-killer sword, and her impenetrable shield. We have also been privy to some beefcake shots of the pilot, Steve Trevor, who on several occasions reminds Diana, who is unfamiliar with the male of the species, that he is an above-average specimen. It becomes clear to the audience that this film is going to be employing light sexual innuendo and sexual tension as part of its character and plot development, in line with the winning combinations of adventure and romance used so successfully in the Indiana Jones (1981–2022?) or the Mummy (1999–2008) franchises.

Trevor had previously stolen Dr. Poison's notebook, and he was on his way to bring it to British HQ when he crashed in the sea near Themyscira. Here we learn of another of Diana's talents, her knowledge of almost every language that has existed, as she is able to recognize and translate the coded diary, a combination of "Ottoman and Sumerian." It is revealed that Dr. Poison, who is one of Wonder Woman's archenemies in the comic book series, is about to develop the ultimate poison that will wipe out the Allied forces and lead to a German victory, despite the impending armistice that, once signed, is meant to end the war. Although forbidden to go to Belgium to prevent the Germans from deploying the gas, Trevor, with the financial help of Sir Patrick Morgan, is able to gather his ragtag team of fellow adventurers, which consists of the Moroccan spy Sameer, Scottish marksman Charlie, and Native American smuggler Chief Napi, along with, of course, Wonder Woman. In Belgium, the film takes a more serious turn, where the horrific impact of war on civilian populations is seen firsthand. The audience experiences this afresh through Diana's naïve gaze, as she is shocked by the cruelty humans are able to inflict on one another. She stays true to her Amazonian promise to protect humanity and frees the village from German control, and it is in this village, Veld, that the photo seen at the start of the film was taken. It is also where Diana and Steve fall in love, a force that will prove powerful later in the film.

We learn from a phone call with Sir Patrick of a gala that the coconspirators Dr. Poison and General Ludendorff attend, thus combining in one film villains from two different periods of the character's comic history. Upon meeting the general, Diana initially believes he is Ares. She learns the error of her mistake after killing him but, sadly, not before he has launched missiles of gas at Veld, destroying all life in the village. It is revealed that Sir Patrick is actually Ares, and what's more, he is also Diana's half-brother, disclosing that she is Zeus's actual child and thus a half-deity herself. The battle between siblings is fierce, and Diana is weakened by her grief at witnessing Steve blow himself and the plane up while destroying the gas factory. Ares tries to manipulate Diana into killing Dr. Poison, but in the end, Diana chooses to destroy Ares instead out of love for Trevor, who has taught her that all humans have good inside them. The film ends back in the present-day Louvre, with Diana writing a thank-you email to Bruce Wayne, suggesting that, perhaps, they have unfinished business.

While a commercial success and audience pleaser, the film was not without its detractors, a primary one being the way her superhero outfit oversexualized her and created a dubious role model for girls and women alike. Wonder Woman's costume has changed since her earliest depictions in comic books, at times emblazoned with patriotic (American) *WW*s to channel her wartime genesis, at other times coming closer to the Greek warrior attire we see in this film. This film's costume is more in keeping with the focus on her origins story as well as the clearly international audience for which this film was geared. While it did premiere in Los Angeles, it was released globally on June 2, the same day as its North American release.

One of the reasons the film was such a crowd-pleaser was the onscreen chemistry between Wonder Woman and Steve Trevor. One critic said that he was exactly the kind of girlfriend that every superhero needs. Their growing relationship over the course of the film (and—spoiler alert—into the next film, *Wonder Woman: 1984*, despite his having died in this one) allows for an exploration (albeit on a surface level) of many gender issues that were relevant in the early 20th century and, sadly, are still relevant today to a great extent. These include the dismissive attitude toward women's intelligence and physical prowess, double standards in clothing, and general patriarchal attitudes that sexualize or patronize women. Of course, Steve cannot hold these beliefs with Diana outdoing him and the men around them at every turn, whether by translating the diary, breaking through "No Man's Land" to save the village, or defeating the god of war, Ares, in battle. But then we are led to understand that Steve had been a good guy all along, as shown in his trusting and nonsexist attitude toward his secretary, in London.

Wonder Woman herself has long been claimed as a feminist icon and was featured on the first issue of second-wave feminist Gloria Steinem's *Ms.* magazine.

Many popular essays and academic studies have been written about Wonder Woman as a feminist icon, yet many also pay special attention to her physicality and her revealing outfit. Lynda Carter lamented that the Wonder Woman outfit from the 1970s TV show (1975–1979) was marketed as an updated pinup posters for teenage boys all over America. She is a strong, smart, and beautiful female who does not need a man to support or protect her. And while the all-female island of the Amazons has been considered by some to be a kind of feminist utopia, it represents a kind of feminism that is essentializing, identifying her superiority in her in being biologically female. This film seems to strike a balance, not shying away from celebrating Diana's beauty and physical strength but also showing the physical beauty of the male body, in a hot-spring scene of the naked Trevor that is arguably more exploitative than any of Wonder Woman in the film. The final results of Wonder Woman as feminine/feminist role model remain undecided, as her appointment by the UN as "Honorary Ambassador for the Empowerment of Women and Girls" in 2016 was met with protests by UN staff members who stated that the character objectified women and was "not culturally encompassing or sensitive." As a result, Wonder Woman was stripped of her honorary title.

There are many elements of the film that would appeal to a Gen Z and younger Millennial audience (which together constitute "Zillennials"). They have grown up with a steady dose of the supernatural in popular culture (vampires, witches, zombies) to a point where it has become somewhat normalized. Some scholars have suggested that this generational fascination with the supernatural is rooted in the U.S. religious heritage and has led to a blurring between "supernatural" religious narratives and those created by entertainment media. There is a certain fluidity to Wonder Woman's sexuality that also reflects the younger generation's acceptance of this in real life. She comes from an all-female society (with echoes of Sappho's Lesbos), and upon encountering Steve's "above average" male physique (as he keeps reminding her), she is both puzzled and attracted. Younger generations no longer excuse imperial adventuring and Orientalist nation building.

The climate crisis is a major concern for Gen Zers, so Chief Napi's condemnation of environmental destruction would have been well received. But there can also be a feeling of some of this anti-racism and environmentalism being too deliberate at times, a kind of preaching to the choir. While some might think that casting an Israeli in the part challenges Wonder Woman's assumed whiteness (one of several critiques of second-wave feminism and of Hollywood superhero films), Gadot's own roots are Ashkenazi and thus German or Eastern European and not Greek, which are the roots of Amazons. (Similar concerns, among others, have been raised with her recent casting in the role of Cleopatra.) The film does a better job in at least raising contemporary social concerns through direct statements by its characters: Orientalism and racism, by Sameer; the treatment of Native Americans, by Chief Napi; and the horrors of war, including the death of civilians and environmental degradation, by Wonder Woman herself. So this Hollywood film, like the character, is an entertaining, inspiring, and at times uncomfortable mix of the potentials and paradoxes of female superheroes in American society.

Angelica Maria DeAngelis

See also: Batman; The Dark Knight; The Dark Knight Rises; Superman.

Further Reading

Hanley, Tim, and Jonathan Hahn. 2014. *Wonder Woman Unbound: The Curious History of the World's Most Famous Heroine*. Chicago: Chicago Review Press.

Held, Jacob M. 2017. *Wonder Woman and Philosophy: The Amazonian Mystique*. Hoboken, NJ: Wiley.

Marcus, Jaclyn. 2018. "Wonder Woman's Costume as a Site for Feminist Debate." *Imaginations Journal* 9 (2): 55–65.

Robinson, Lillian S. 2004. "Genesis: Departing from Paradise." In *Wonder Women: Feminisms and Superheroes*, by Lillian Robinson, 27–64. Milton Park, UK: Routledge.

Zootopia

Release Date:	2016
Directors:	Byron Howard, Rich Moore, Jared Bush
Box Office:	$1.024 billion
Main Cast:	Judy Hopps, played by Ginnifer Goodwin
	Nick Wilde, played by Jason Bateman
	Chief Bogo, played by Idris Elba
	Mayor Lionheart, played by J. K. Simmons
	Bellwether, played by Jenny Slate
	Gazelle, played by Shakira

2016 was the most profitable year ever for computer-animated films, with six animated films grossing over a half billion dollars, with Disney's *Zootopia* at the top. That year was also a milestone for Disney on several fronts. Disney has from its Mickey Mouse beginnings been quite adept at creating films that appeal to all ages, but *Zootopia*, perhaps more so than ever before, is an animation that is much more than a cartoon. *Zootopia* stands apart from prior animated films as arguably more easily placed in a genre other than animation. Despite its toddler-appealing colorful world of animated animals, *Zootopia* is more of a buddy cop comedy in its own right, an adult neo-noir world full of double entendre, innuendo, and violence. But most significantly, *Zootopia* sets a milestone for Disney as the studio attempts, however successfully, to reckon and amend for its troubling racist past and find its place more comfortably within the era of identity politics and Black Lives Matter (BLM). BLM rose out of 2014–2015 Ferguson riots and protests in response to the killing of a Black by police in the town of Ferguson, Missouri, a community known for its systemic racism manifested by things such as targeting African Americans with unfair ticketing and fines. The movement gained momentum and national attention in 2015 with its protests against the many other police killings of African Americans that year, creating a new generation of activists, Gen Z, who rallied on the streets and online. Disney seems to have been mindful of this political climate in creating *Zootopia*, an allegorical fable strewn with good messages about discrimination that even a child could understand. Though the film's political correctness likely appeals especially to the social justice activists of Gen Z, some viewers have questioned whether the film's message as a whole is an apt metaphor for an illusory postracist, postsexist, polarized American society plagued by disparity and injustice.

The film's protagonists are a rabbit and a fox, reminiscent of anthropomorphic Br'er Rabbit and Br'er Fox in Disney's *Song of the South* (1946), the film Disney seems to wish everyone would forget about due to its idyllic "Zip-a-Dee-Doo-Dah" portrayal of 19th-century American plantation life as racially utopian. *Zootopia*'s rabbit, Judy Hopps, is a self-perceived "woke" bunny who seeks to escape her narrow-minded community of Bunnyburrow to fulfill her dream of becoming a cop in the utopian big city, Zootopia, where both prey and predators live peacefully together. In defiance of the neighborhood bully's southern drawl chiding—"What crazy world are you living in where you think a bunny can be a cop?"—she moves to Zootopia armed with a "fox taser." Like so many American women who still struggle to find their place in a male-dominated world, she becomes the first bunny to be accepted into the police force under a "mammal inclusion initiative." Judy is the first small mammal to be accepted into the exclusively bigger-animal police department. Despite graduating at the top of her class at the police academy, she becomes a meter maid. While issuing a ridiculous number of parking tickets unlawfully, she apprehends Weaselton, a shady predator who has stolen some plant bulbs from a flower shop. The huge water buffalo police chief Bogo reprimands her for not sticking to her demeaning duty but relents to her pleas to allow her to investigate one among a growing number of disappearing mammals. He gives her 48 hours to solve the case, and if she doesn't, she must resign.

Judy starts by profiling Nick Wild, a fox she finds suspicious for no apparent reason. Apparently, foxes, or predators, are synonymous with criminals in her mind, much as Blacks are in the minds of many white American police officers, according to BLM activists. Judy's profiling suspicions turn to empathy when she sees an elephant (Republican?) patron of an ice cream parlor show Nick a "We reserve the right to refuse service to anyone" sign. This emotive scene reminiscent of the Jim Crow era is a far cry from the scene that Disney has removed from its Disney+ streaming version of *Dumbo* (1946) that featured Disney's black crow minstrel-like character named Jim Crow. Judy intervenes, as a white person in the civil rights movement is wont to do, buys Nick a jumbo popsicle, and patronizingly tells him that he's "a really articulate fella," echoing Biden's infamous, implicitly racist gaffe about President Obama. When Judy later realizes that Nick has scammed the ice cream parlor and her, confirming her original profiling expectation of stereotypical Black urban male behavior, she blackmails him for tax evasion in order to recruit him to help her solve the mystery of a missing otter, Mr. Otterton. As in *48 Hrs.* (1982), the buddy cop film starring white Nick Nolte as the cop and Black Eddie Murphy as the hustler, Judy and Nick team up, as in so many buddy-cop interracial duos in film, and solve the case within 48 hours.

As the plot unfolds, the film seems to suggest that not just foxes but all predators in general represent African Americans and that not just bunnies but all prey represent white people. The missing mammals who have begun attacking others all happen to be predators; they have "gone savage." Following a lead from a mobster arctic shrew ironically named Mr. Big—who along with his polar bear thugs are a parody of *The Godfather* (1972)—they interview Manchas, a Latino-voiced, limo driver panther who lives in the Rainforest District. He tells them that Mr. Otterton kept repeating the words "night howler" as he went feral. This tip leads them to discover that Mayor Lionheart has been using wolves to kidnap and secretly quarantine the savage predators to protect the social order. He later confesses that he did "the wrong thing for the right reason." Lionheart is sacked, and Dawn Bellwether, the assistant mayor sheep who helped Judy get her job through affirmative action, becomes Zootopia's leader. Judy, now a hero who has proved to Zootopia that "dumb bunnies" can be capable cops, bumbles over her words at a press conference, explaining that the reason only predators are "reverting back to their primitive savage ways" may be because of "something in their DNA." Judy's statements alienate her from Nick and create panic across Zootopia, disrupting its utopian harmony. Predators picket the insinuations with BLM-like placards, which are countered by shouts such as "Quarantine the predators!" and "Go back to the rain forest!" Nick confronts Judy for her unfortunate word choice, to which she replies, "It's not like a bunny could go savage."

Judy returns to Bunnyburrow dejected, only to discover that the flower bulbs that Duke Weaselton had stolen belong to the psychoactive night howler plant. She deduces correctly that the night howler plant is making predators go feral, so she teams back up with Nick to solve the mystery. They find Weaselton and get him to talk by taking him to Mr. Big in Tundratown, whose thugs threaten him by hanging him over a pit of icy water. The extorted info leads the detective to a secret lab in an abandoned subway car run by sheep chemists with names such as Jesse and Woolter who wear yellow jumpsuits while they make their blue night howler extract. Fans of the critically acclaimed TV series *Breaking Bad* would spot the obvious references to Jesse and Walter, who cook their signature "blue sky" meth in an old RV. One thing leads to another, and the conspiracy is exposed. Assistant Mayor Bellwether, the Machiavellian feminist villain, is behind it all. She is using sheep sharpshooters to target minority predators with pellets of night howler serum. Her thwarted plan was that by drugging predators to make them go savage and by implicating Mayor Lionheart, Bellwether, herself a sheep, could become mayor and solidify her power with the support of the predator-fearing prey majority. Bellwether and her accomplices are arrested, the predators are cured of their savagery, and Nick becomes Judy's partner on the police force.

Zootopia, as a reflection of American society, in all its glory and darkness, may be—as the chicken and egg argument goes—reinforcing the very social ills it portrays. *Zootopia* has an MPAA rating of PG "for some thematic elements, rude humor and action." Presumably, "thematic elements" doesn't refer to the instructive instances of discrimination but to other social ills portrayed, such as extortion, organized crime, kidnapping, torture, and drug-induced violence, among others. This is standard Hollywood content, but in the era of calls by BLM for systemic reform of the police, what kind of message might be conveyed when the protagonist and hero of *Zootopia*, a cute bunny in the police force, produces positive results by unethical means? She tickets unlawfully, recruits Nick by blackmail, and depends on a mafioso to successfully interrogate someone by means of psychological torture. Mr. Big's Vito Corleone–sounding threat of "icing" may seem as innocuous as throwing someone into cold water, but dropping a body into arctic-temperature water is almost certain death. But it works: the end justifies the means. Conceivably, this transgenerational American utilitarianism is what was behind the U.S. military's so-called enhanced interrogation techniques, such as waterboarding of "detainees" at Guantanamo and Abu Ghraib prisons in the War on Terror.

Drug-induced violence is also not a rarity in Hollywood films nor in America, but in *Zootopia*, a movie with which Disney attempts to champion equity and justice among different social identities, we have a possibly race-related motif in the psychoactive night howler. Though the diverse demographics of American meth usage suggest that night howler is not a racial motif in *Zootopia*, its striking parallel with the film *Kill the Messenger* (2014) and crack cocaine usage does. The film is based on the true story of journalist Gary Webb, who investigates the alleged involvement of the government in the inner-city crack epidemic of the 1980s and '90s. Webb claimed that federal agents using Black gangs such as the Crips and Bloods were responsible for flooding predominantly Black South Central Los Angeles with cocaine, feeding conspiracy theories about the government intentionally undermining the African American community, about 10 percent of the population, much as in Zootopia, where "prey outnumber predators 10:1." The minority population "going savage" under the influence of drugs in *Zootopia* may remind Boomers or older viewers of the myth of "Negro cocaine fiends" who informed U.S. drug enforcement policy earlier in the 20th century and even perhaps into the 21st. Viewers of the Netflix documentary *13th* (2016)–a film that helped generate Millennial and Gen Z involvement in the BLM movement–might see Mayor Lionheart's quarantining the night howler–crazed, "savage" minorities as analogous to the ongoing disproportionate incarceration of African Americans for marijuana use. Whether night howler symbolizes meth, crack, pot, or illicit drugs in general, Disney scriptwriters' use of "going savage" to describe minority behavior is particularly troublesome in a parable about stereotypes and racism. The word "savage" alone is loaded. Its connotations of cannibalism and animalistic wildness have long been used to justify the conquest and enslavement of people of color. These connotations suggest that these primitive people need to be controlled and domesticated because of their innate propensity toward violence. In the words of Judy, "For whatever reason, they seem to be reverting back to their primitive ways."

Despite these problematic associations, however coincidental, Disney has indeed come a long way from its earliest sound cartoons, like *Steamboat Willie* (1928), featuring Black minstrel-like Mickey Mouse, and *Cannibal Capers* (1930), featuring Black cannibals. *Zootopia* is an allegory that resonates with a generation of moviegoers who are more acutely aware of issues of inclusion and discrimination. The problem with the allegory, though, is that the metaphors are muddled with inconsistencies that may undermine its central message, which seems to be that we can make the world a better place by overcoming prejudices and never giving up. Judy exemplifies this spirit simplistically by gritty determination, a core value in the American myths of individualism, egalitarianism, and meritocracy. At the beginning of the story, she proclaims resolutely, "Every animal has multitudinous opportunities," which may have been naïve optimism, but by the end of the movie, with the Shakira gazelle singing "Try Everything," she proves that in an unfair world, success is achieved individually. In 2015, under the Obama administration, Black Lives Matter demonstrated against the deaths, through police violence, of many African Americans. Meanwhile, *Zootopia* scriptwriters create Judy, the archetypical white savior, who through the police force, saves the predators from themselves.

Overcoming prejudice necessarily involves doing away with stereotyping, which *Zootopia* is full of not as a matter for scorn but built into the world as a matter of fact. The sole hippie is flea infested with the stereotypical stoner burnout voice Boomers and Gen X would recognize as that of Tommy Chong. And anyone who has seen the *Godfather* would recognize the mobsters in Tundratown as Italian and Catholic. The only animal with a strong American southern accent is a bigoted bully, while others with slight southern accents are nice but still narrow minded. The animals with Latinx accents are sexualized male and female dancers and a limo driver. Animals are also caricatured according to their biological traits. Bunnies have lots of children, the sloth bureaucrats at the DMV are slothful, and the mayor is a powerful lion, for example. Furthermore, due to biological adaptations, animals live in separate communities such as Rainforest District, Tundratown, and Little Rodentia. Zootopia is segregated based on biology. Most confusing is the predator-prey binary. Predators are discriminated against because of their inherent predatory nature. Even though their fangs and claws have been domesticized somehow, predators are still sometimes muzzled and their potential to attack remains, even without night howler.

Perhaps predators are better understood more generally as representing the disenfranchised. Still, allegorizing any class of people as "predatory" by nature is problematic, if not racist. When the Disney+ channel debuted in 2019, some racist content had been clipped out of streaming versions of Disney films. Some racist content remains in streaming films, however, which begin with this disclaimer: "This program includes negative depictions and/or mistreatment of people or cultures. These stereotypes were wrong then and are wrong now."

Perhaps future generations of Americans will see this disclaimer before a Disney+ streaming of *Zootopia*.

Derek Parks

See also: *Frozen*; *Harry Potter and the Chamber of Secrets*; *Toy Story*.

Further Reading

Cramer, Linsay M. 2020. "Whiteness and the Postracial Imaginary in Disney's *Zootopia*." *Howard Journal of Communications* 31 (3): 264–281.

Delehanty, Casey, and Erin Kearns. 2020. "Wait, There's Torture in *Zootopia*? Examining the Prevalence of Torture in Popular Movies." *Perspectives on Politics* 18 (3): 835–850.

Dore, Margherita. 2019. "Revoicing Otherness and Stereotypes via Dialects and Accents in Disney's *Zootopia* and Its Italian Dubbed Version." InTRAlinea. http://www.intralinea.org/specials/article/revoicing_otherness_and_stereotypes.

Hassler-Forest, Dan. 2018. "'Life Isn't Some Cartoon Musical': Neoliberal Identity Politics in *Zootopia* and *Orange Is the New Black*." *Journal of Popular Culture* 51 (2): 356–378.

Sandlin, Jennifer, and Nathan Snaza. 2018. "'It's Called a Hustle, Sweetheart': Black Lives Matter, the Police State, and the Politics of Colonizing Anger in *Zootopia*." *Journal of Popular Culture* 51 (5): 1190–1213.

Seitz, Matt Zoller. 2016, March 4. "Zootopia." RogerEbert.com. https://www.rogerebert.com/reviews/zootopia-2016.

Bibliography

Abbott, Martin L. 1989. "*Tootsie.*" *Teaching Sociology* 17 (1): 135–136.

Abbott, Traci B. 2013. "The Trans/Romance Dilemma in *Transamerica* and Other Films." *Journal of American Culture* 36 (1): 32.

American Cinema video series. 1995. Annenberg Learner/New York Center for Visual History in association with KCET/Los Angeles and the BBC. https://www.learner.org/series/american-cinema.

Anderson, Benedict. 2006. *Imagined Communities. Reflections on the Origins and Spread of Nationalism*. Rev. ed. London: Verso.

Antrim, Taylor. 2010. "Making of *Inception*." *Hollywood Reporter* 416 (55): 50–53.

Aschieris, Jacob. 2020–. *The History of Film*. Apple Podcasts. https://podcasts.apple.com/us/podcast/the-history-of-film/id1519549773.

Asimow, Michael. 2000. "Divorce in the Movies: From the Hays Code to *Kramer vs. Kramer*." *Legal Studies Forum* 14 (221): 1–77.

Audissino, Emilio. 2014. "*Raiders of the Lost Ark* Analysis: The Return of Max Steiner." In *John Williams's Film Music: Jaws, Star Wars, Raiders of the Lost Ark, and the Return of the Classical Hollywood Music Style*, by Emilio Audissino, 161–182. Madison: University of Wisconsin Press.

Audissino, Emilio. 2017. "*Close Encounters of the Third Kind* and *E.T. The Extraterrestrial*: The Bonding Power of Music." In *Film/Music Analysis: A Film Studies Approach*, Emilio Audissino, 191. London: Palgrave Macmillan.

Babb, Valerie. 2020. "The Past Is Never Past: The Call and Response between Marvel's *Black Panther* and Early Black Speculative Fiction." *African American Review* 53, no. 2 (Summer): 95–109.

Baron, Lawrence. 2003. "X-Men as J Men: The Jewish Subtext of a Comic Book Movie." *Shofar: An Interdisciplinary Journal of Jewish Studies* 22 (1): 44.

Bartlett, Myke. 2015. "The Future Is Now." *Screen Education*, no. 79 (Spring): 16–25.

Bassham, Gregory, and Eric Bronson. 2003. *The Lord of the Rings and Philosophy: One Book to Rule Them All*. Chicago: Open Court.

Beck, Bernard. 2009. "Something for the Boys: *Iron Man*, *Transformers*, and *Grand Theft Auto IV*." *Multicultural Perspectives* 11 (1): 27–30.

Beltran, Mary C. 2005. "The New Hollywood Racelessness: Only the Fast, Furious, (and Multiracial) Will Survive." *Cinema Journal* 44 (2): 50–67.

Beltran, Mary C. 2013. "Fast and Bilingual: *Fast & Furious* and the Latinization of Racelessness." *Cinema Journal* 53 (1): 75–96.

Benitez, Jorge, and Matt Wallin. 2011. "Rethinking the Silver Screen: Science, Film, and Art after *Avatar*." *International Journal of Science in Society* 2 (3): 45–54.

Berger, Arthur Asa. 1984. "*Return of the Jedi*: The Rewards of Myth." *Society* 21, no. 4 (May): 71–75.

Bernard, Catherine. 2017. "Christopher Nolan's *Inception*: Spectacular Speculations." *Screen* 58 (2): 229–236.

Bettinson, Gary. 2018. *Superman: The Movie: The 40th Anniversary Interviews*. Bristol, UK: Intellect Books.

Blatty, William Peter. 2019 (1976). "There Is Goodness in *The Exorcist*." *America* 220 (8): 38–41.

Blodgett, Bridget, and Anastasia Salter. 2018. "*Ghostbusters* Is for Boys: Understanding Geek Masculinity's Role in the Alt-Right." *Communication, Culture & Critique* 11 (1): 133–146.

Boddy, William. 1985. "The Studios Move into Prime Time: Hollywood and the Television Industry in the 1950s." *Cinema Journal* 24, no. 4 (Summer): 23–37. https://www.jstor.org/stable/1224894.

Bode, Lisa. 2010. "Transitional Tastes: Teen Girls and Genre in the Critical Reception of *Twilight*." *Continuum: Journal of Media & Cultural Studies* 24 (5): 707–719.

Bowles, Stephen E. 1976. "*The Exorcist* and *Jaws*." *Literature Film Quarterly* 4 (3): 196.

Brabham, Daren C. 2006. "Animated Blackness in *Shrek*." *Rocky Mountain Communication Review* 3 (1): 64–71.

Bradshaw, Peter. 2018, November 15. "*9 to 5* Review: Dolly Parton's Quietly Radical Office Revenge Satire." *The Guardian*. https://www.theguardian.com/film/2018/nov/15/9-to-5-review-dolly-parton.

Brody, Michael. 2012. "Holy Franchise! Batman, Psychic Trauma, and Clinical Cases." In *Seductive Screens: Children's Media—Past, Present, and Future*, by Michael Brody, 33–49. Newcastle upon Tyne, UK: Cambridge Scholars Publishing.

Brooker, Will. 2001. "Readings of Racism: Interpretation, Stereotyping and the Phantom Menace." *Continuum: Journal of Media & Cultural Studies* 15 (1): 1.

Brooker, Will. 2012. *Hunting the Dark Knight: Twenty-First Century Batman*. London: I. B. Tauris.

Brown, Jeffrey A. 1993. "Bullets, Buddies, and Bad Guys." *Journal of Popular Film & Television* 21 (2): 79.

Brown, Jeffrey A. 2018. "#wheresRey: Feminism, Protest, and Merchandising Sexism in *Star Wars: The Force Awakens*." *Feminist Media Studies* 18 (3): 335–348.

Brown, Noel. 2021. "Crossing Boundaries." In *Contemporary Hollywood Animation: Style, Storytelling, Culture and Ideology Since the 1990s*, by Noel Brown, 41–77. Edinburgh, UK: Edinburgh University Press.

Bruckner, Lynee Dickson. 2010. "*Bambi* and *Finding Nemo*: A Sense of Wonder in the Wonderful World of Disney?" In *Framing the World: Explorations in Ecocriticism and Film*, edited by Paula Willoquet-Maricondi, 187–208. Charlottesville, VA: University of Virginia Press.

Brydon, Suzan B. 2009. "Men at the Heart of Mothering: Finding Mother in *Finding Nemo.*" *Journal of Gender Studies* 18 (2): 131–146.

Bucciferro, Claudia. 2016. *The X-Men Films: A Cultural Analysis*. Lanham, MD: Rowman & Littlefield.

Buchanan, Kyle. 2013, June 28. "There Are Even Fewer Female Buddy Comedies Than You Thought." *Vulture Magazine*. https://www.vulture.com/2013/06/female-buddy-comedies-very-rare.html.

Burke, Liam. 2015. *The Comic Book Film Adaptation: Exploring Modern Hollywood's Leading Genre*. Jackson: University Press of Mississippi.

Butler, Tina. 2005, April 2. "The Methods of Madness: *One Flew over the Cuckoo's Nest* and *Awakenings.*" Mongabay. https://news.mongabay.com/2005/04/the-methods-of-madness-one-flew-over-the-cuckoos-nest-and-awakenings.

Callahan, Michael. 2016, January 26. "How *Grease* Beat the Odds and Became the Biggest Movie Musical of the 20th Century." *Vanity Fair*. https://www.vanityfair.com/hollywood/2016/01/grease-movie-musical-john-travolta-olivia-newton-john.

Canby, Vincent. 1978, June 16. "Screen: A Slick Version of 'Grease': Fantasy of the 50's." *New York Times*. https://www.nytimes.com/1978/06/16/archives/screen-a-slick-version-of-greasefantasy-of-the-50s.html.

Canby, Vincent. 1979, December 19. "East Side Story: Review/*Kramer vs. Kramer.*" *New York Times*. https://www.nytimes.com/1979/12/19/archives/screen-kramer-vs-kramereast-side-story.html.

Caperton, Jessica. 2014. "A Gender Role Analysis of *Twilight*." *Kentucky English Bulletin* 64 (1): 66–67.

Caputi, Jane. 2007. "Green Consciousness: Earth-Based Myth and Meaning in *Shrek*." *Ethics & the Environment* 12.

Carpenter, Caroline. 2015. *Guide to* The Hunger Games. Medford, NJ: Plexus Publishing.

Chaplin, Susan. 2017. *The Postmillennial Vampire: Power, Sacrifice and Simulation in* True Blood, Twilight *and Other Contemporary Narratives*. Cham, Switzerland: Springer International Publishing.

Clark, Mark. 2015. Star Wars *FAQ: Everything Left to Know about the Trilogy That Changed the Movies*. Milwaukee, WI: Applause.

Clarke, Amy M., and Marijane Osborn. 2010. *The Twilight Mystique: Critical Essays on the Novels and Films*. Jefferson, NC: McFarland.

Clarke, Gerald. 1990. "*Home Alone* Breaks Away." *Time* 136 (25): 94.

Clasen, Mathias. 2017. *Never Go Swimming Again: Jaws (1975)*. In *Why Horror Seduces*, 104–112. Oxford: Oxford University Press.

Claverie, Ezra. 2019. Storm and the Angels of History: Blackness and Star Image in the *X-Men* Films. *Journal of American Culture*, 42 (1), 55–69.

"Close Encounters of the Third Kind (Movie)." 2018. *Cultural Studies: The UFO Encyclopedia*. Detroit, MI: Omnigraphics.

Cohen, Paula Marentz. 2001. *Silent Film and the Triumph of the American Myth*. Oxford: Oxford University Press.

Collins, Randall. 2004. *Interaction Ritual Chains*. Princeton, NJ: Princeton University Press.

Collis, Clark. 2017. "*Terminator 2: Judgment Day* 3D." *Entertainment Weekly*, no. 1480 (September): 34–35.

Conley, Tom. 2006. *Film Hieroglyphics: Ruptures in Classical Cinema*. Minneapolis: University of Minnesota Press.

Conlon, James. 1990. "Making Love, Not War." *Journal of Popular Film & Television* 18 (1): 18.

Corliss, Richard. 2010. "Whose Mind Is It, Anyway?" *Time* 176 (4): 59–61.

Çöteli, Sami. 2020. "The Concept of Social (In)Justice and Its Portrayals in Todd Phillips's *Joker*." *Communication Today* 11 (2): 36–44.

Cramer, Linsay M. 2020. "Whiteness and the Postracial Imaginary in Disney's *Zootopia*." *Howard Journal of Communications* 31 (3): 264–281.

Crewe, David. 2016. "Excavating Knowledge: *Jurassic Park* in the Classroom," *Screen Education* 83, 14–23.

Crewe, David. 2017. "Cinema Science: *The Fast and the Furious* and the Mechanics of Dangerous Driving." *Screen Education*, no. 87 (October): 32–39.

Crewe, Dave. 2019. "Cinema Science: Playing with Physics in the *Toy Story* Universe." *Education*, no. 96 (August): 38–44.

Cummins, June. 1995. "Romancing the Plot: The Real Beast of Disney's *Beauty and the Beast*." *Children's Literature Association Quarterly* 20 (1): 22–28.

Daniels, Robert. 2020, June 3. "John Boyega is Doing What *Star Wars* Wouldn't." Polygon. https://www.polygon.com/2020/6/3/21278460/star-wars-john-boyega-black-lives-matter-finn-force-awakens-rise-of-skywalker.

Darowski, Joseph J., ed. 2014. *The Ages of the Avengers: Essays on the Earth's Mightiest Heroes in Changing Times*. Jefferson, NC: McFarland.

Darowski, John. 2021. *Adapting Superman: Essays on the Transmedia Man of Steel*. Jefferson, NC: McFarland.

Davé, Shilpa. 2017. "Racial Accents, Hollywood Casting, and Asian American Studies." *Cinema Journal* 56 (3): 142–147.

Davies, Jude. 2005. "'Diversity. America. Leadership. Good over Evil.' Hollywood Multiculturalism and American Imperialism in *Independence Day* and *Three Kings*." *Patterns of Prejudice* 39 (4): 397–415.

Davis, Blair. 2018. *Comic Book Movies. Quick Takes: Movies and Popular Culture*. New Brunswick, NJ: Rutgers University Press.

Davis, Todd F., and Kenneth Womack. 2001. "Narrating the Ship of Dreams." *Journal of Popular Film & Television* 29 (1): 42.

Deamer, David. 2016. "Despicable Me, Despicable Me 2 and Minions." In *Deleuze's Cinema Books: Three Introductions to the Taxonomy of Images*, by David Deamer, 193–195. Edinburgh, UK: Edinburgh University Press.

Degim, Iclal Alev. 2013. "The Ents Will Rise Again: The Representation of Nature in the Film *The Lord of the Rings: The Fellowship of the Ring*." *Journal of Social Studies Research* (January): 91–97.

Delehanty, Casey, and Erin Kearns. 2020. "Wait, There's Torture in *Zootopia*? Examining the Prevalence of Torture in Popular Movies." *Perspectives on Politics* 18 (3): 835–850.

Demetrakas, Johanna, dir. 2018. *Feminists: What Were They Thinking?* Los Gatos, CA: Netflix.

De Semlyen, Nick. 2019. *Wild and Crazy Guys: How the Comedy Mavericks of the '80s Changed Hollywood Forever.* New York: Broadway Books.

D'Heurle, Adma. 1983. "The Image of the Child in Popular American Films." *ETC: A Review of General Semantics* 40 (1): 41–52.

Díaz-Diocaretz, Myriam, and Stefan Herbrechter. 2006. The Matrix *in Theory*. Amsterdam, Netherlands: Rodopi.

Dick, Jeff T. 2003. "Beauty and the Beast (Film)." *Library Journal* 128 (9): 143.

Dixon, John. 1996. "Aliens 'R' Us: A Critique of D4." *Film & History* 26 (1–4): 92–88.

Dodds, Klaus. 2014. "Shaking and Stirring James Bond: Age, Gender, and Resilience in *Skyfall* (2012)." *Journal of Popular Film and Television* 42 (3): 116–130.

Dore, Margherita. 2019. "Revoicing Otherness and Stereotypes via Dialects and Accents in Disney's *Zootopia* and Its Italian Dubbed Version." InTRAlinea. http://www.intralinea.org/specials/article/revoicing_otherness_and_stereotypes.

Dudenhoeffer, Larrie. 2017. *Anatomy of the Superhero Film.* Cham, Switzerland: Palgrave Macmillan.

Duncan, Pansy. 2020. "'Journeys of Adventure among Its Far-Flung Debris': Three Theories of the Blockbuster Explosion Spectacle." *JCMS: Journal of Cinema & Media Studies* 59 (2): 1–22.

Dunn, George A. 2014. Avatar *and Philosophy: Learning to See.* Malden, MA: Wiley-Blackwell.

Durand, Kevin K. J., and Mary K. Leigh. 2011. *Riddle Me This, Batman! Essays on the Universe of the Dark Knight.* Jefferson, NC: McFarland.

"Dustin Hoffman." 2020. *Columbia Electronic Encyclopedia.* 6th ed. New York: Columbia University Press.

Dvorak, Ken. 1996. "*Independence Day*: A Survival Guide for the Next Invasion." *Film & History* 26 (1–4): 90–91.

Dwyer, Michael D. 2015. *Back to the Fifties: Nostalgia, Hollywood Film and Popular Music of the Seventies and Eighties.* Oxford: Oxford University Press.

Eaklor, Vicki. 2011. "*Jurassic Park*." In *Movies in American History: An Encyclopedia*, 1: edited by Philip C. DiMare, 284–286. Santa Barbara, CA: ABC-CLIO.

Eberl, Jason, and Kevin Decker. 2016. "*Star Wars: The Force Awakens.*" *Philosophy Now* 115 (January): 48–50.

Ebert, Roger. 2012, November 7. "The Best Bond in Years." Rogerebert.com. https://www.rogerebert.com/reviews/skyfall-2012

Edwards, Kim. 2009. "Good Looks and Sex Symbols: The Power of the Gaze and the Displacement of the Erotic in *Twilight*." *Screen Education*, no. 53 (March): 26–32.

Edwards, Kim. 2018. "Coming Full Circle: A Study Guide to *The Lion King*." *Education*, no. 88 (January): 8–15.

Ellis, Kathleen. 2002. "New World, Old Habits: Pa-Triarchal Ideology in *Star Wars: A New Hope*." *Australian Screen Education*, no. 30 (Spring): 135.

Elmwood, Victoria A. 2005. "'Just Some Bum from the Neighborhood': The Resolution of Post–Civil Rights Tension and Heavyweight Public Sphere Discourse in *Rocky* (1976)." *Film and History* 35 (2): 49–59.

Erb, Cynthia. 2014. "A Spiritual Blockbuster: *Avatar*, Environmentalism, and the New Religions." *Journal of Film & Video* 66 (3): 3–17.

Erbland, Kate. 2017, May 16. "*Alien* Revisited: Nearly Four Decades Later, Ripley Is Still the Boundary-Busting Heroine We Deserve." IndieWire. https://www.indiewire.com/2017/05/alien-ripley-heroine-ridley-scott-sigourney-weaver-1201817775.

Erlandson, Karen Thea. 2012. "Teaching Intercultural Awareness with *Star Wars: A New Hope*." *Communication Teacher* 26 (1): 17–21.

Evely, Christine. 2004. "*Shrek*: A Study Guide." *Screen Education*, no. 36 (September): 70–81.

Fattal, Isabel. 2018, January 4. "Why Do Cartoon Villains Speak in Foreign Accents?" *The Atlantic*. https://www.theatlantic.com/education/archive/2018/01/why-do-cartoon-villains-speak-in-foreign-accents/549527.

Fear, David. 2021, October 8. "Daniel Craig Is the Best James Bond—It's Not Even Close." *Rolling Stone*. https://www.rollingstone.com/movies/movie-features/daniel-craig-best-james-bond-1234978.

Feldman, Brian. 2015, June 23. "How Minions Destroyed the Internet." The Awl. https://www.theawl.com/2015/06/how-minions-destroyed-the-internet.

Feldman, Dana. 2019, July 28. "How Netflix Is Changing the Future of Movie Theaters." *Forbes*.

Fiduccia, Christopher. 2021, August 22. "Scarlett Johansson's Lawyer Slams Disney's Misogynistic Response to Lawsuit." ScreenRant. https://screenrant.com/black-widow-scarlett-johansson-lawsuit-misogynistic-disney-response.

Follows, Stephen. 2014, September 22. "What's the Average Budget of a Low or Micro-Budget Film?" Stephen Follows. https://stephenfollows.com/average-budget-low-micro-budget-film.

Fradley, Martin. 2013. "What Do You Believe In? Film Scholarship and the Cultural Politics of the Dark Knight Franchise." *Film Quarterly* 66 (3): 15–27.

Freeman, Hadley. 2016. *Life Moves Pretty Fast: The Lessons We Learned from Eighties Movies (and Why We Don't Learn Them from Movies Anymore)*. New York: Simon & Schuster.

Gaine, Vincent M. 2016a. "It's Only a Film, Isn't It? Policy Paranoia Thrillers of the War on Terror." In *Cycles, Sequels, Spin-offs, Remakes, and Reboots*, edited by A. A. Klein and R. B. Palmer, 148–165. Austin: University of Texas Press.

Gaine, Vincent M. 2016b. "'Not Now That Strength': Embodiment and Globalisation in Post-9/11 James Bond." In *American Cinema in the Shadow of 9/11*, edited by Terence McSweeney, 127–146. Edinburgh, UK: Edinburgh University Press.

Gates, Philippa. 2004. "Always a Partner in Crime." *Journal of Popular Film & Television* 32 (1): 20–29.

Gavin, Rosemarie. 1996. "*The Lion King* and *Hamlet*: A Homecoming for the Exiled Child." *English Journal* 85, no. 3 (March): 55.
Geertz, Clifford. 1973. *The Interpretation of Cultures: Selected Essays*. New York: Basic Books.
Ghumkhor, Sahar. 2019. "'To Veil the Threat of Terror': Law and the Other's Question in *The Dark Knight Rises*." *Law, Culture & the Humanities* 15 (3): 862–878.
Gierzynski, Anthony. 2013. *Harry Potter and the Millennials: Research Methods and the Politics of the Muggle Generation*. Baltimore, MD: Johns Hopkins University Press.
Gilmore, Brad. 2020. *Back from the Future: A Celebration of the Greatest Time Travel Story Ever Told (*Back to the Future *Time Travel Facts and Trivia)*. Miami, FL: Mango.
Golding, Dan. 2019. Star Wars *After Lucas*. Minneapolis: University of Minnesota Press.
Gooding-Williams, Robert. 1995. "Disney in Africa and the Inner City: On Race and Space in *The Lion King*." *Social Identities* 1 (2): 373.
Gordon, Andrew. 1978. "*Star Wars*: A Myth for Our Time." *Literature Film Quarterly* 6 (4): 314.
Gottlieb, Carl. 2005. *The Jaws Log*. New York: Newmarket.
Grabarek, Daryl. 2018. "The Real Story: *Pirates of the Caribbean*." *School Library Journal* 64 (5): 56.
Green, Mary, Scott Huver, Mia Mcniece, Kara Warner, and Alynda Wheat. 2016. "*Star Wars*' New Heroine: A Star Awakens." *People* 85 (1): 62–65.
Grindon, Leger. 1996. "Body and Soul: The Structure of Meaning in the Boxing Film Genre." *Cinema Journal* 35 (4): 54–69.
Gutiérrez, Peter. 2015. "Safety in Numbers." *Screen Education*, no. 79 (Spring): 38–45.
Gutiérrez, Peter. 2016. "The Cultural Ubiquity of *Star Wars*." *Screen Education*, no. 82 (Winter): 58–65.
Hagley, Annika, and Michael Harrison. 2014. "Fighting the Battles We Never Could: 'The Avengers' and Post–September 11 American Political Identities." *PS: Political Science and Politics* 47 (1): 120–124.
Hall, Lucia K. B. 2000. "Toy Stories for Humanists?" *Humanist* 60 (2): 38.
Hall, Stefan, and Silvia Pasquini. 2020, July 23. "Can There Be a Fairy-Tale Ending for Hollywood after COVID-19?" World Economic Forum. https://www.weforum.org/agenda/2020/07/impact-coronavirus-covid-19-hollywood-global-film-industry-movie-theatres.
Hancock, Will. 2013. "*The Dark Knight Rises* to Face America's New Fears." *Kentucky English Bulletin* 63 (1): 47–48.
Hanley, Tim, and Jonathan Hahn. 2014. *Wonder Woman Unbound: The Curious History of the World's Most Famous Heroine*. Chicago: Chicago Review Press.
Haridy, Rich. 2019, October 8. "Netflix vs. Cinema: How a Disruptive Streaming Service Declared War on Hollywood." New Atlas. https://newatlas.com/home-entertainment/netflix-disruptive-streaming-hollywood-cinema-exhibition-war.

Hasian, Marouf, Jr. 2014. "*Skyfall*, James Bond's Resurrection, and 21st-Century Anglo-American Imperial Nostalgia." *Communication Quarterly* 62, no. 5.

Hassler-Forest, Dan. 2018. "'Life Isn't Some Cartoon Musical': Neoliberal Identity Politics in *Zootopia* and *Orange Is the New Black*." *Journal of Popular Culture* 51 (2): 356–378.

Heit, Jamey. 2020. "True Love in *Frozen*." In *Disney and Philosophy: Truth, Trust and a Little Bit of Pixie Dust*, edited by Richard B. Davis, 185–192. Hoboken, NJ: Wiley.

Held, Jacob M. 2017. *Wonder Woman and Philosophy: The Amazonian Mystique*. Hoboken, NJ: Wiley.

Hiatt, Brian. 2010. "Leo Faces His Demons. (Cover Story)." *Rolling Stone*, no. 1110 (August): 46–86.

Higgins, Bill. 2019. "Hoffman Cross-Dressed for Success in 1982's *Tootsie*." *Hollywood Reporter* 425 (14): 64.

Higgs, Sam. 2017. "*Finding Nemo* in the Three-Act Structure." *Screen Education* 85, 90–97.

Hoad, Phil. 2017, April 11. "Interview Michael Douglas: How We Made *One Flew over the Cuckoo's Nest*." *The Guardian*. https://www.theguardian.com/film/2017/apr/11/michael-douglas-and-louise-fletcher-how-we-made-one-flew-over-the-cuckoos-nest-interview.

Hoerl, Kristen. 2018. "Good Citizens, Ambivalent Activists, and Macho Militants in *Forrest Gump* and the '60s." In *The Bad Sixties: Hollywood Memories of the Counterculture, Antiwar, and Black Power Movements*, by Kristen Hoerl, 93–122. Jackson: University Press of Mississippi.

Holland, Jesse J., ed. 2021. *Black Panther: Tales of Wakanda*. London: Titan Books.

Holmlund, Chris. 2010. "Sigourney Weaver: Woman Warrior, Working Girl." In *The Star Decades: Acting for America: Movie Stars of the 1980s*, edited by Robert Eberwein, 139–159. New Brunswick, NJ: Rutgers University Press.

Holtmeier, Matthew. 2010. "Post-Pandoran Depression or Na'vi Sympathy: *Avatar*, Affect, and Audience Reception." *Journal for the Study of Religion, Nature & Culture* 4 (4): 414–424.

hooks, bell. 2008. *Reel to Real: Race, Class, and Sex at the Movies*. New York: Routledge.

Hungerford, Kristen. 2010. "The Male 'White' House of Hollywood: A Feminist Critique of What It Means to Be Presidential." *Ohio Communication Journal* 48 (October): 55–75.

Hurley, James S. 2001. "*Titanic* Allegories: The Blockbuster as Art Film." *Strategies: Journal of Theory, Culture & Politics* 14 (1): 91.

Hurwitz, Matt. 2017. "A Track from Hell: Vocal-Rich Sound Design for *The Exorcist*." *Mix* 41 (8): 28–30.

Ilinskaya, Svetlana, and Douglas Robinson. 2018. "#MeToo and the Estrangement of Beauty-and-the-Beast Narratives." *Social Research* 85 (2): 375–405.

Ip, John. 2011. "*The Dark Knight*'s War on Terrorism." *Ohio State Journal of Criminal Law* 9 (1): 209–229.

Irwin, William. 2012. *The Avengers and Philosophy: Earth's Mightiest Thinkers*. Hoboken, NJ: Wiley.

Isaki, Bianca. 2009. "Anarchist Feelings: *The Dark Knight* (2008), A Love Story." In *Conference Papers—Western Political Science Association*, 1. Sacramento, CA: Western Political Science Association.

"James Cameron Says *Terminator 2* as 'Timely as It Ever Was.'" 2017. *TechLife News*, no. 303 (August): 162–165.

Jankiewicz, Patrick. 2015. *Just When You Thought It Was Safe: A Jaws Companion*. Albany, GA: BearManor Media.

Jenkins, Tricia, and Tom Secker. 2021. *Superheroes, Movies, and the State: How the US Government Shapes Cinematic Universes*. Lawrence: University Press of Kansas.

Jeong, Seung-hoon. 2020. "Global Agency between Bond and Bourne: *Skyfall* and James Bond in Comparison to the Jason Bourne Film Series." In *The Cultural Life of James Bond: Specters of 007*, edited by Jaap Verheul, 207–226. Amsterdam, Netherlands: Amsterdam University Press.

Johnson, David. 2012. Inception *and Philosophy: Because It's Never Just a Dream*. Hoboken, NJ: Wiley.

Johnson, Jordan L., and Kristen Hoerl. 2020. "Suppressing Black Power through Black Panther's Neocolonial Allegory." *Review of Communication* 20 (3): 269–277.

Jolin, Dan. 2019. "*Terminator 2: Judgment Day.*" *Empire* (September): 46–47.

Jürgens, Anna-Sophie. 2020. "The Pathology of Joker's Dance: The Origins of Arthur Fleck's Body Aesthetics in Todd Phillips's 2019 *Joker* Film." *Dance Chronicle* 43 (3): 321–337.

Kaur, Harmeet. 2019, November 3. "In Protests around the World, One Image Stands Out: The Joker." CNN. https://www.cnn.com/2019/11/03/world/joker-global-protests-trnd/index.html.

Keen, Richard, Monica L. McCoy, and Elizabeth Powell. 2012. "Rooting for the Bad Guy: Psychological Perspectives." *Studies in Popular Culture* 34 (2): 129–148.

Kendrick, James. 2014. *Darkness in the Bliss-Out: A Reconsideration of the Films of Steven Spielberg*. New York: Bloomsbury Academic.

Kermode, Mark. 2020. *The Exorcist*. BFI Film Classics. London: British Film Institute.

Kimball, A. Samuel. 2001. "Not Begetting the Future: Technological Autochthony, Sexual Reproduction, and the Mythic Structure of *The Matrix*." *Journal of Popular Culture* 35 (3): 175.

King, C. Richard, and David J. Leonard. 2006. "Racing *The Matrix*: Variations on White Supremacy in Responses to the Film Trilogy." *Cultural Studies /Critical Methodologies* 6 (3): 354–369.

Klassen, Chris. 2012. "*Avatar*, Dark Green Religion, and the Technological Construction of Nature." *Cultural Studies Review* 18 (2): 74–88.

Kleinfield, N. R. 1983, September 26. "American Way of Life Altered by Fuel Crisis." *New York Times*.

Knaus, Christopher. 2005. "More White Supremacy? The Lord of the Rings as Pro-American Imperialism." *Multicultural Perspectives* 7 (4): 54–58.

Knee, Adam. 2010. "Harrison Ford: A Well-Tempered Machismo." In *The Star Decades: Acting for America: Movie Stars of the 1980s*, edited by

Robert T. Eberwein, 160–179. New Brunswick, NJ: Rutgers University Press.

Koh, Wilson. 2009. "Everything Old Is Good Again: Myth and Nostalgia in *Spider-Man*." *Continuum: Journal of Media & Cultural Studies* 23 (5): 735–747.

Kramer, Peter. 1998. "Women First: *Titanic* (1997), Action-Adventure Films and Hollywood's Female Audience." *Historical Journal of Film, Radio & Television* 18 (4): 599.

Kripal, Jeffrey. 2015. *Mutants and Mystics: Science Fiction, Superhero Comics, and the Paranormal*. Chicago: University of Chicago Press.

Kushner, Jordan. 2016, February 24. "A Brief History of Sound in Cinema." *Popular Mechanics*. https://www.popularmechanics.com/culture/movies/a19566/a-brief-history-of-sound-in-cinema.

Labrecque, Jeff. 2014. "1984 *Ghostbusters*. (Cover Story)." *Entertainment Weekly*, no. 1337–1338 (November): 50.

Laird, Raymond J. 2014. "J. R. R. Tolkien: Theologian in Disguise? Small Is Powerful: A Guiding Principle of *The Lord of the Rings*." *Evangelical Review of Theology* 38 (1): 81–90.

Laist, Randy. 2020a. *Excavating Indiana Jones: Essays on the Films and Franchise*. Jefferson, NC: McFarland.

Laist, Randy. 2020b. "Heads A-Poppin': The Ambiguous Drama of Seeing in *Raiders of the Lost Ark*." *Journal of Popular Film & Television* 48 (3): 155–162.

Lambe, Jennifer. 2019. "Memory Politics: Psychiatric Critique, Cultural Protest and *One Flew over the Cuckoo's Nest*." *Literature and Medicine* 37, no. 2 (Fall 2019): 298–324.

Lane, Anthony, and Richard Brody. 2019. "No Laughing Matter." *New Yorker* 95 (30): 65–67.

Lash, Jolie. 2021. "James Cameron Reveals How a Sting Song and Ecstasy Inspired Teenage John Connor in *Terminator 2*." *Entertainment Weekly* (July). https://ew.com/movies/james-cameron-sting-song-ecstasy-john-connor-terminator-2.

Lauer, Emily, and Balaka Basu. 2019. *The Harry Potter Generation: Essays on Growing Up with the Series*. Jefferson, NC: McFarland.

Lavery, David. 2001. "From Cinespace to Cyberspace." *Journal of Popular Film & Television* 28 (4): 150.

Law, Michelle. 2014. "Sisters Doin' It for Themselves: *Frozen* and the Evolution of the Disney Heroine." *Screen Education* 74: 16–25.

"Lucas, George W. Jr." 2018. *The Columbia Encyclopedia*. New York: Columbia University Press.

Lyden, John C. 2003. *Film as Religion: Myths, Morals, and Rituals*. New York: New York University Press.

Marcus, Jaclyn. 2018. "Wonder Woman's Costume as a Site for Feminist Debate." *Imaginations Journal* 9 (2): 55–65.

Markman, Ken. 2005. "Movies, Myths, and Messages: How Entertainment Is Creating a Global Brand Culture." *Licensing Journal* 25, no. 6 (June/July): 27–30.

Masters, Kim. 2012. "*Titanic*'s Rough Seas: 'Glub, Glub, Glub.'" *Hollywood Reporter* 418 (13): 36–39.

McAllister, Matt. 2020. Ghostbusters*: The Inside Story*. New York: Hero Collector.

McCreadie, Marsha. 1977. "*One Flew over the Cuckoo's Nest*: Some Reasons for One Happy Adaptation." *Literature Film Quarterly* 5, no. 2 (Spring 1977): 125–131.

McFarlane, Brian. 2006. "*The Matrix*: Cult Classic or Computerized Con?" *Screen Education*, no. 41 (January): 105–109.

McGraw, Peter, and Joel Warner. 2014. *The Humor Code: A Global Search for What Makes Things Funny*. New York: Simon & Schuster.

McIntosh, William D., John D. Murray, Rebecca M. Murray, and Sunita Manian. 2006. "Sexual Humor in Hollywood Films: Influences of Social and Economic Threat on the Desirability of Male and Female Characters." *Mass Communication & Society* 9 (2): 239–254.

McKittrick, Christopher. 2019, June 21 (updated). "How Movies Went from Black and White to Color." Liveabout. https://www.liveabout.com/how-movies-went-from-black-white-to-color-4153390.

McMullen, Wayne. 1996. "Gender and the American Dream in *Kramer vs. Kramer*." *Women's Studies Communication* 19 (1): 29–54.

McSweeney, Terence. 2018. *Avengers Assemble!: Critical Perspectives on the Marvel Cinematic Universe*. London: WallFlower Press.

McSweeney, Terence. 2020. *The Contemporary Superhero Film: Projections of Power and Identity*. New York: WallFlower Press.

Meinel, Dietmar. 2016. *Pixar's America: The Re-Animation of American Myths and Symbols*. Cham, Switzerland: Palgrave Macmillan.

Meyer, David S. 1992. "*Star Wars*, Star Wars, and American Political Culture." *Journal of Popular Culture* 26 (2): 99–115.

Meyer, Michaela D. E. 2003. "Utilizing Mythic Criticism in Contemporary Narrative Culture: Examining the 'Present-Absence' of Shadow Archetypes in *Spider-Man*." *Communication Quarterly* 51 (4): 518–529.

Michaud, Nicolas, and George A. Dunn, eds. 2012. *The Hunger Games and Philosophy: A Critique of Pure Treason*. Hoboken, NJ: Wiley.

Michaud, Nicolas, and Jessica Watkins. 2014. Jurassic Park *and Philosophy: The Truth Is Terrifying*. Chicago: Open Court.

Militz, Thane A., and Simon Foale. 2017. "The 'Nemo Effect': Perception and Reality of *Finding Nemo*'s Impact on Marine Aquarium Fisheries." *Fish and Fisheries* 18 (3): 596–606.

Miller, Laura. 2010, June 7. "Fresh Hell: What's Behind the Boom in Dystopian Fiction for Young Readers?" *New Yorker*. https://www.newyorker.com/magazine/2010/06/14/fresh-hell-laura-miller.

Mintz, Steven, Randy Roberts, and David Welky, eds. 2016. *America's Hollywood, Hollywood's America: Understanding History through Film*. 5th ed. Hoboken, NJ: Wiley.

Mirrlees, Tanner. 2017. "Transforming *Transformers* into Militainment: Interrogating the DoD-Hollywood Complex." *American Journal of Economics & Sociology* 76 (2): 405–434.

Modleski, Tania. 2007. "Misogynist Films: Teaching *Top Gun*." *Cinema Journal* 47 (1): 101–105.

Molstad, Stephen. 2016. *The Complete* Independence Day *Omnibus*. London: Titan Books.

Morgan, Alun. 2010. "*The Lord of the Rings*: A Mythos Applicable in Unsustainable Times?" *Environmental Education Research* 16 (3–4): 383–399.

Morris, Kathleen. 1999, July 19. "This Phantom Is a Menace to Toymakers." *BusinessWeek*, no. 3638, p. 42.

Morton, John. 1996. "Simba's Revolution: Revisiting History and Class in *The Lion King*." *Social Identities* 2 (2): 311–317.

Mueller, Annie. 2020, March 28 (updated). "Why Movies Cost So Much to Make." Investopedia. https://www.investopedia.com/financial-edge/0611/why-movies-cost-so-much-to-make.aspx.

Mulvey, Laura. 2018. "Introduction: 1970s Feminist Film Theory and the Obsolescent Object." In *Feminisms: Diversity, Difference and Multiplicity in Contemporary Film Cultures*, by Anna Backman Rogers and Laura Mulvey, 17–26. Amsterdam, Netherlands: Amsterdam University Press.

Murray, Jonathan. 2016. "'I've Been Inspecting You, Mister Bond': Crisis, Catharsis, and Calculation in Daniel Craig's Twenty-First-Century 007." *Cinéaste* 41 (2): 4–11.

Murtha, Tara. 2015, December 18. "Why *9 to 5* Is Still Radical Today." *Rolling Stone*.

Nashawaty, Chris. 2011. "How Does *Top Gun* Fly Today?" *Entertainment Weekly*, no. 1170 (September): 62.

Nathan, Judith Raizy. 2017. "Disrupting the *Forrest Gump* Effect: Countering Suggestibility in the Social Studies Classroom through the Use of Actual Footage." EdD diss., Hofstra University.

Nelson, Elissa. 2013. "Beneath the Surface and the Excess: An Examination of Critical and Aesthetic Attacks on Films of the 1980s." *Journal of Popular Culture* 46 (5): 1029–1050.

Nesbitt, Jennifer. 2016. "Deactivating Feminism: Sigourney Weaver, James Cameron, and *Avatar*." *Film & History* 46 (1): 21–32.

Newell, Jay, Charles T. Salmon, and Susan Chang. 2006. "The Hidden History of Product Placement." *Journal of Broadcasting & Electronic Media* 50 (4): 575–594.

Nguyen, Viet Thanh. 2015. *The Sympathizer*. New York: Grove Atlantic. Kindle.

Ní Fhlainn, Sorcha. 2010. *The Worlds of* Back to the Future*: Critical Essays on the Films*. Jefferson, NC: McFarland.

O'Connell, Mark. 2017. *The Close Encounters Man: How One Man Made the World Believe in UFOs*. New York: Dey St./William Morrow.

Ødemark, John. 2015. "*Avatar* in the Amazon: Narratives of Cultural Conversion and Environmental Salvation between Cultural Theory and Popular Culture." *Culture Unbound: Journal of Current Cultural Research* 7 (May): 455–478.

Parker, Richard D. 2005. "The Armed Forces Need Another *Top Gun*." *U.S. Naval Institute Proceedings* 131 (12): 58.

Patterson, Diana, ed. 2009. *Harry Potter's World-Wide Influence*. Newcastle upon Tyne, UK: Cambridge Scholars Publisher.

Patton, Craig D. 2012. "From Depp to Breadth: Teaching World History with *Pirates of the Caribbean*." *World History Connected* 9 (1): 13.

Pauly, Rebecca M. 1989. "Beauty and the Beast: From Fable to Film." *Literature Film Quarterly* 17 (2): 84.

Pautz, Michelle C., and Jennifer Lumpkin. 2020. "The Influence of Film on Attitudes about the American Dream: Audiences and *Forrest Gump* and Idiocracy." *Public Voices* 16 (2): 42–65.

Peaslee, Robert Moses, and Robert G. Weiner. 2015. *The Joker: A Serious Study of the Clown Prince of Crime*. Jackson: University Press of Mississippi.

Pimenta, Sherline, and Ravi Poovaiah. 2010. "On Defining Visual Narratives." *Design Thoughts* (August): 25–46. http://www.idc.iitb.ac.in/resources/dt-aug-2010/On%20Defining%20Visual%20Narratives.pdf.

Purse, Lisa. 2005. "The New Spatial Dynamics of the Bullet-Time Effect." In *Spectacle of the Real: From Hollywood to "Reality" TV and Beyond*, edited by Geoff King, 151–160. Bristol, UK: Intellect Books.

Quirk, Antonia. 2002. *Jaws* (BFI Modern Classics). London: British Film Institute.

Richards, Sarah. 2020, December 17. "The Netflix Effect: The Movie Industry and New Data." University of Virginia-Darden, *Ideas to Action*. https://ideas.darden.virginia.edu/movie-industry-and-new-data.

Richardson, Niall. 2004. "The Gospel According to *Spider-Man*." *Journal of Popular Culture* 37 (4): 694–703.

Rinzler, J. W. 2019. *The Making of* Alien. London: Titan Books.

Robb, Brian J. 2012. *A Brief Guide to* Star Wars: *The Unauthorised Inside Story*. London: Perseus Books.

Robbins, Jeff. 2010. "Missing the Big Picture: Studies of TV's Effects Should Consider How HDTV Is Different." *New Atlantis* (Spring): 118–122.

Roberts, Lewis. 2014. "'Happier Than Ever to Be Exactly What He Was': Reflections on Shrek, Fiona and the Magic Mirrors of Commodity Culture." *Children's Literature in Education* 45 (1): 1–16.

Robertson, Dane. 2020, August 18. "How Christopher Nolan Changed Superhero Movies (for the Better)." The Latch. https://thelatch.com.au/christopher-nolan.

Robinson, Ashley Sufflé. 2018. "We Are Iron Man: Tony Stark, *Iron Man*, and American Identity in the Marvel Cinematic Universe's Phase One Films." *Journal of Popular Culture* 51 (4): 824–844.

Robinson, Lillian S. 2004. "Genesis: Departing from Paradise." In *Wonder Women: Feminisms and Superheroes*, by Lillian Robinson, 27–64. Milton Park, UK: Routledge.

Rogoff, Irit. 1998. "Studying Visual Culture." In *The Visual Culture Reader*, 2nd ed., edited by Nicholas Mirzoeff, 24–36. Milton Park, UK: Routledge.

Ross, Deborah. 2004. "Escape from Wonderland: Disney and the Female Imagination." *Marvels & Tales* 18 (1): 53–66.

Rudloff, Maja. 2016. "(Post)feminist Paradoxes: The Sensibilities of Gender Representation in Disney's *Frozen*." *Outskirts* 35: 1–20.

Ruiz-Casares, Mónica, and Cécile Rousseau. 2010. "Between Freedom and Fear: Children's Views on *Home Alone*." *British Journal of Social Work* 40 (8): 2560–2577.

Rushing, Janice Hocker, and Thomas S. Frentz. 2000. "Singing over the Bones: James Cameron's *Titanic*." *Critical Studies in Media Communication* 17 (1): 1.

Russell, Patrick Kent. 2016. "Christopher Nolan's *The Dark Knight Trilogy* as a Noir View of American Social Tensions." *Interdisciplinary Humanities* 33 (1): 171–186.

Ruud, Jay. 1991. "*Back to the Future* as Quintessential Comedy." *Literature Film Quarterly* 19 (2): 127.

Ryu, Jenna. 2020, December 19. "*9 to 5* Turns 40: The Feel-Good 1980 Comedy Covers a Depressing Reality Even in 2020." *Knox News*. https://www.knoxnews.com/story/entertainment/2020/12/19/9-to-5-turns-40-themes-sexism-misogyny-more-relatable-than-ever/3972607001.

Saiman, Chaim. 2017, December 27. "Why *The Last Jedi* Is More 'Spiritual' than 'Religious.'" *The Atlantic*. https://www.theatlantic.com/entertainment/archive/2017/12/why-the-last-jedi-is-more-spiritual-than-religious/549146.

Salem, Merryana. 2020, May 28. "The White Feminist Lead and Her Posse of Colour." Kill Your Darlings. https://www.killyourdarlings.com.au/article/the-white-feminist-lead-and-her-posse-of-colour.

Sandlin, Jennifer, and Nathan Snaza. 2018. "'It's Called a Hustle, Sweetheart': Black Lives Matter, the Police State, and the Politics of Colonizing Anger in *Zootopia*." *Journal of Popular Culture* 51 (5): 1190–1213.

Sanford, Jonathan J. 2012. Spider-Man *and Philosophy: The Web of Inquiry*. Hoboken, NJ: Wiley.

Sarris, Andrew. 1962–1963. "Notes on the Auteur Theory in 1962." *Film Culture* 27 (Winter): 1–8.

Schimmelpfennig, Annette. 2017. "Capitalism and Schizophrenia in Gotham City: The Fragile Masculinities of Christopher Nolan's *The Dark Knight* Trilogy." *Gender Forum*, no. 62 (April): 3–20.

Schulman, Michael. 2016, March 29. "How Meryl Streep Battled Dustin Hoffman, Retooled Her Role, and Won Her First Oscar." *Vanity Fair*. https://www.vanityfair.com/hollywood/2016/03/meryl-streep-kramer-vs-kramer-oscar.

Scott, Ellen. 2014. "Agony and Avoidance: Pixar, Deniability, and the Adult Spectator." *Journal of Popular Film & Television* 42 (3): 150–162.

Scott, Steven D. 2001. "'Like a Box of Chocolates': *Forrest Gump* and Postmodernism." *Literature Film Quarterly* 29 (1): 23.

Seitz, Matt Zoller. 2016, March 4. "Zootopia." RogerEbert.com. https://www.rogerebert.com/reviews/zootopia-2016.

Sergi, Gianluca. 2020, December 17. "Streaming Wars: How Threatening Are They Really to the Film Industry?" The Conversation. https://theconversation.com/streaming-wars-how-threatening-are-they-really-to-the-film-industry-151649.

Seth, Par Radhika. 2019, March 25. "Netflix vs. Hollywood: The Fight to Define the Future of Film." *Vogue*. https://www.vogue.fr/fashion-culture/article/netflix-vs-hollywood-the-fight-to-define-the-future-of-film.

Shaheen, Jack. 2014. *Reel Bad Arabs: How Hollywood Vilifies a People*. Northampton, MA: Olive Branch Press.

Sharman, Russell Leigh. 2020. *Moving Pictures: An Introduction to Cinema*. Fayetteville: University of Arkansas.

Shaw, Deborah. 2019, August 29. "Can Cinema Survive in a Golden Age of Serial TV?" The Conversation. https://theconversation.com/can-cinema-survive-in-a-golden-age-of-serial-tv-122234.

Shay, Don. 1985. *Making* Ghostbusters. New York: Zoetrope.

Simmons, David. 2017. *American Horror Fiction and Class: From Poe to Twilight*. London: Palgrave Macmillan UK.

Smith, James. 2016. "How Safe Do You Feel?: James Bond, *Skyfall*, and the Politics of the Secret Agent in an Age of Ubiquitous Threat." *College Literature* 43 (1): 145–172.

Smith, Stacy L., Marc Choueiti, and Katherine Pieper, with assistance from Ariana Case and Justin Marsden. 2016. "Inequality in 800 Popular Films: Examining Portrayals of Gender, Race/Ethnicity, LGBT, and Disability from 2007–2015." *Media, Diversity, & Social Change Initiative* (September). https://annenberg.usc.edu/sites/default/files/2017/04/10/MDSCI_Inequality_in_800_Films_FINAL.pdf.

Smith, Donna Marie. 2015. "*John Hughes: A Life in Film*." *Library Journal* 140 (6): 95.

Sperb, Jason. 2016. *Flickers of Film: Nostalgia in the Time of Digital Cinema*. New Brunswick, NJ: Rutgers University Press.

Spielberg, Steven, and Melissa Mathison. 2002. *E.T.: The Extra-Terrestrial from Concept to Classic: The Illustrated Story*. New York: Newmarket Press.

Stephens, Mitchell. 1998. *The Rise of the Image, the Fall of the Word*. Oxford: Oxford University Press.

Sterba, Wendy. 2015. "Avenging American Arrogance: Joss Whedon's Filmic Post-9/11 Superheroes in *The Avengers* (2012)." *Revue Francaise D'Etudes Americaines* 4 (145): 21–30.

Streiff, Madeline, and Lauren Dundes. 2017. "Frozen in Time: How Disney Gender-Stereotypes Its Most Powerful Princess." *Social Sciences* 6 (2), 38.

Sturm, Brian. 2000. "The 'Storylistening' Trance Experience." *Journal of American Folklore* 113 (449): 289–304.

Szumskyj, Benjamin. 2008. *American Exorcist: Critical Essays on William Peter Blatty*. Jefferson, NC: McFarland.

"A Tarnished Silver Screen." 2021, March 27. *The Economist*, p. 77.

Taylor, Chris. 2014. *How* Star Wars *Conquered the Universe: The Past, Present, and Future of a Multibillion Dollar Franchise*. London: Head of Zeus.

Taylor, Ella. 2000. "Cyberreality Bites. Boys, Toys and Girl Trouble in 1999's Top Ten." *Nation* 270 (13): 30–34.

Telotte, J. P. 1992. "*The Terminator, Terminator 2*, & the Exposed Body." *Journal of Popular Film & Television* 20 (2): 26.
Telotte, J. P. 2008. *The Mouse Machine: Disney and Technology*. Urbana: University of Illinois Press.
Thompson, Kristin. 2007. *The Frodo Franchise:* The Lord of the Rings *and Modern Hollywood*. Berkeley: University of California Press.
Tietze, Tad. 2020. "Populist Panic at the Movies." *Modern Age* 62 (2): 31–36.
Torry, Robert. 1991. "Politics and Parousia in *Close Encounters of the Third Kind*." *Literature Film Quarterly* 19 (3): 188.
Travers, Peter. 2008. "Superhero Smackdown." *Rolling Stone*, no. 1052 (May): 73–76.
Tye, Larry. 2012. *Superman: The High-Flying History of America's Most Enduring Hero*. New York: Random House.
Ugwu, Reggie. 2020, September 9 (updated). "The Hashtag That Changed the Oscars: An Oral History." *New York Times*. https://www.nytimes.com/2020/02/06/movies/oscarssowhite-history.html.
Verheul, Jaap, ed. 2020. *The Cultural Life of James Bond: Specters of 007*. Amsterdam, Netherlands: Amsterdam University Press.
Wallace, Daniel. 2015. Ghostbusters: *The Ultimate Visual History*. Los Angeles: Insight Editions.
Wang, Jennifer Hyland. 2000. "'A Struggle of Contending Stories': Race, Gender, and Politic Memory in *Forrest Gump*." *Cinema Journal* 39 (3): 92–115.
Ward, Annalee R. 1996. "*The Lion King*'s Mythic Narrative." *Journal of Popular Film & Television* 23 (4): 171.
Whalley, Jim. 2010. *Saturday Night Live, Hollywood Comedy, and American Culture: From Chevy Chase to Tina Fey*. New York: Palgrave Macmillan.
White, Mark D. 2013. *Superman and Philosophy: What Would the Man of Steel Do?* Malden, MA: Wiley-Blackwell.
Whited, Lana A., ed. 2002. *Ivory Tower and* Harry Potter: *Perspectives on a Literary Phenomenon*. Columbia: University of Missouri Press.
The Wiley-Blackwell History of American Film. 2011. 4 vols., edited by Cynthia Lucia, Roy Grundmann, and Art Simon. Hoboken, NJ: Wiley.
Wilkinson, Amy. 2015. "*Home Alone* 25 Years Later." *Entertainment Weekly*, no. 1389 (November): 44–45.
Willis, Sharon. 1997. "Combative Femininity: *Thelma and Louise* and *Terminator 2*." In *High Contrast: Race & Gender in Contemporary Hollywood Films*, by Sharon Willis, 98–128. Durham, NC: Duke University Press.
Wittenberg, David. 2008. "Oedipus Multiplex, or, the Subject as a Time Travel Film: Two Readings of *Back to the Future*." *Discourse: Journal for Theoretical Studies in Media & Culture* 28 (2–3): 51–77.
Wojtas, Paweł. 2019. "Taking a Leap in the Dark: The Ethics of Batman." *European Journal of American Culture* 38 (2): 169–184.
Wooden, Shannon R., and Ken Gillam. 2014. *Pixar's Boy Stories: Masculinity in a Postmodern Age*. Lanham, MD: Rowman & Littlefield.

Wu, Helena. 2018. "The Travelling of *Ten Years*: Imagined Spectatorships and Readerships of Hong Kong's Local." *International Journal of Postcolonial Studies* 20 (8): 1121–1136.

Yockey, Matt. 2014. *Batman*. Detroit, MI: Wayne State University Press.

Zeenat, Afrin. 2017. "'You Are All Wrapped Up in Layers': Pastiche, Paradox, and *Shrek*." *Studies in American Culture* 40 (1): 109–123.

Zipin, Dina. 2021, June 30 (updated). "Movie vs. TV Industry: Which Is Most Profitable?" Investopedia. https://www.investopedia.com/articles/investing/091615/movie-vs-tv-industry-which-most-profitable.asp.

About the Editor and Contributors

EDITOR

BENJAMIN CRACE, PhD, is an assistant professor at the American University of Kuwait. His research is both intercultural and interdisciplinary, exploring T. S. Eliot, Coptic Orthodoxy, Pentecostalism, and apocalypticism. In terms of visual culture, his contributions include entries for ABC-CLIO's *Dystopian States of America: Apocalyptic Visions and Warnings in Literature and Film*, and an analysis of the film *Hillbilly Elegy* through the lens of an Appalachian apocalyptic poetic for *The New Americanist*.

CONTRIBUTORS

DINA ALQASSAR is a PhD student in early modern and Renaissance studies at the University of Massachusetts–Amherst. Her research explores the intersections of religious lyric, embodiment, and sexuality in early 17th-century lyric through the lenses of queer theory and philology. She has a particular interest in the ways in which the lines between the sacred and the profane are blurred in the works of John Milton and his contemporaries.

ANGELICA MARIA DEANGELIS, PhD, is an assistant professor at the American University of Kuwait whose research focuses on the intersection of literature, cinema, and popular culture, especially in North Africa or the North African global diaspora. She has taught film studies at UC Santa Barbara and studied gender and popular culture as a fellow in two National Endowment for the Humanities Summer Institutes. Her publications on cinema include a philosophical approach to French and Algerian cinema on migration, and an exploration of gender and Islam in a feature film adaptation of Andalusian folktales.

KATHERINE HENNESSEY, PhD, is an assistant professor of English at the American University of Kuwait and in 2020–2021 was a research fellow with the National Endowment for the Humanities. Her research explores the intersections of literature, theater, and film, especially in Ireland and the Middle East. She takes a particular interest in theatrical and cinematic adaptations of Shakespeare, and she has also worked as a filmmaker, directing and producing the short film *Shakespeare in Yemen,* which premiered at the Signature Theatre in New York City in 2018.

JOSH MOBLEY, PhD, is a lecturer in the Great Texts program at Baylor University. He is a theologian working in the Christian tradition and is particularly interested in how Christians think about the relation of God to creation and culture. He lives with his family and their pet rabbit in central Texas.

DEREK PARKS has taught English to refugees and university students in Jordan, Syria, and Kuwait. His particular interests include displacement and education, rhetoric, media ecologies, and multimodal critical discourse analysis. He currently teaches writing at the American University of Kuwait.

Index

Page numbers in **bold** indicate the location of main entries.

Abrams, J.J., 276
Academy Award. *See* Oscars
Adamson, Andrew, 205
Afghanistan War, 55, 202, 233
Alcohol, 42, 64, 85, 107, 112, 115, 162
Alien, **53–57**, 131, 173, 219
Allen, Karen, 73
Allen, Tim, 165
Allers, Roger, 145
American: consumerism, 7, 35, 112, 165; dream, xvii, 27, 34, 36, 38, 44, 58, 69, 95, 112, 119, 121, 131, 138, 172, 175, 200, 211, 266, 274; exceptionalism, 27, 36–37, 103, 158, 177, 197; individualism, xv, 6, 32–33, 36–37, 44, 47–48, 78, 154, 159, 168, 201, 209, 248, 276, 287; Judeo-Christian heritage, 41, 42–43, 76, 218; militarism, 103, 202, 235, 261; secularism/secularization, xviii, 40, 43–44, 46, 49, 50, 62, 135, 201, 277
American Graffiti, 59, 70–71, 77
Andrews, Julie, 245
Anti-Semitism, 67–68, 215
Apocalypse, 55, 131, 138, 155, 218, 233, 258
Ashton, John, 122
Astin, Sean, 194
Atomic. *See* Nuclear
Attenborough, Richard, 141
Australia, 69, 70, 174, 180–182
Auteur theory, 28–31, 35, 92
Avatar, 156, 160, **169–173**, 180, 192, 205, 231
The Avengers, 193, 213, 221, 228, **231–236**, 239
Avildsen, John G., 92
Aykroyd, Dan, 122, 129

Baby Boomers, **52–108**; time frame and definition, xvi–xvii, 36–37
Back to the Future, xvii, **109–113**, 125, 129, 161
Baker, Kenny, 97, 148, 214
Bale, Christian, 173, 240
Bardem, Javier, 270
Barrymore, Drew, 61
Basinger, Kim, 113
Bateman, Jason, 284
Bates, Kathy, 156
Batman, 91, **113–117**, 177, 244
Bay, Michael, 217
Beauty and the Beast, **117–122**, 209, 233, 254, 257
Bell, Kristen, 253
Benson, Robby, 117
Benton, Robert, 80
Berry, Halle, 225
Beverly Hills Cop, **122–125**, 209
Binge watching, 12
Black Panther, 103, 125, 148, 193, 228, **236–240**
Blair, Linda, 65
Blockbuster, xvi–xvii, 35–36
Bloom, Orlando, 194, 202
Boseman, Chadwick, 236
Boyega, John, 276
Brand, Russell, 245
Brest, Martin, 122
Brewster, Jordana, 177, 250
Bridges, Jeff, 190
Broderick, Matthew, 145
Brooks, Albert, 181
Buck, Chris, 253
Buddhism, 45, 150, 180, 201, 216

Burton, Tim, 113
Burtstyn, Ellen, 65, 88
Bush, Jared, 284

Caine, Michael, 173, 240, 264
Calame, Niketa, 145
Cameron, James, 29, 153, 156, 169
Candy, John, 133
Capitalism, xvii, 15–25, 28, 33, 37, 53, 57, 103, 142, 144, 168, 172, 235, 246
Carrell, Steve, 245
Channing, Stockard, 69
Chicago, xvi, 113, 134, 136
Chong, Marcus, 198
Christianity: Bible, 41, 200; Catholicism, 41–43, 59, 62, 65, 115, 194, 288; Evangelicalism, 41–43; Jesus Christ, 6, 41, 62, 68, 72, 98, 103, 120–121, 193, 201, 207
Christie, Gwendoline, 276
CIA, 232, 237, 239
Civil rights, 45, 64, 91, 95, 238–239, 285
Clement, Jemaine, 245
Close Encounters of the Third Kind, **57–61**, 64, 76, 77, 80, 138, 141, 145, 218, 221
Coffin, Pierre, 245
Cohen, Rob, 177
Cold War, xiv, 31, 34, 55, 63, 70, 72, 99, 102–103, 109, 114, 141, 144, 147, 153, 156, 161, 194, 232–234, 245, 271, 273–274
Coleman, Dabney, 84, 105
Colin, Margaret, 138
Collins, Randall: interaction ritual model, 10–12
Columbus, Chris, 133, 185
Communism, 151, 214
Conroy, Frances, 266
Coogler, Ryan, 236
Coppola, Francis Ford, 17, 18, 22, 29, 102
Cosgrove, Miranda, 245
Cotillard, Marion, 240, 262
Cowboys. *See* The Western
Craig, Daniel, 270
Cruise, Tom, 161, 222
Culkin, Macaulay, 133
Cullen, Brett, 266

Dafoe, Willem, 181, 210
Daniels, Anthony, 97, 148, 214

The Dark Knight, 104, 117, **173–177**, 240, 242, 244, 265, 269, 275, 284
The Dark Knight Rises, 104, 117, 173, 177, **240–244**, 265, 269, 275, 284
De Niro, Robert, 92, 266
DeGeneres, Ellen, 181
Dench, Judi, 270
Depp, Johnny, 202
Dern, Laura, 141
Despicable Me, **245–250**
DeVito, Danny, 88
Diaz, Cameron, 205
DiCaprio, Leonardo, 156, 262
Diesel, Vin, 177, 250
Dillon, Melinda, 57
Disney, 35, 66, 71, 99, 117–121, 145–148, 167–168, 190, 202, 206, 209, 231–232, 235, 254, 256–257, 284–288
Disney, Walt, 66
Donner, Richard, 100
Dourif, Brad, 88
Downey, Robert, Jr., 190, 231
Dreyfuss, Richard, 57, 70, 76
Driver, Adam, 276
Drugs, 124, 127; cocaine, 287; Just Say "No" campaign, 84; marijuana, 85, 183, 210, 287; meth, 286–287
Duhamel, Josh, 217
Dunst, Kirsten, 210, 222

Eckhart, Aaron, 173
Economics, 4–6, 16–17, 19–20, 28, 30, 31, 35–36, 67, 79, 93–94, 183–184
Edwards, Anthony, 161
Elba, Idris, 284
Elliott, Denholm, 73
Emmerich, Roland, 138
E.T.: The Extra-Terrestrial, **61–65**, 76, 80, 137, 141, 218, 221
Evans, Chris, 231
The Exorcist, **65–69**, 133

Fast and Furious 7, 180, **250–253**
The Fast and the Furious, **177–181**, 253
Favreau, Jon, 190
FBI, 155, 178, 180, 198, 252
Feminism, 36, 86, 283; feminists, 86, 282; key texts, 107; patriarchy, 7, 40–41, 82, 84, 87, 99, 105–106, 118, 120–122, 149, 224–225, 238, 256–257, 282; Second

Wave, 36, 55, 82, 86–87, 99, 106–107, 283–284
Field, Sally, 125
Fiennes, Ralph, 270
Finding Nemo, 36, 122, **181–184**, 249
Fishburne, Laurence, 198
Fisher, Carrie, 96–97, 148
Fisher, Elsie, 245
Fletcher, Louise, 88
Fonda, Jane, 81, 84–87
Ford, Harrison, 73, 96, 148, 276
Forman, Miloš, 88
Forrest Gump, 112, **125–129**, 166, 168
Fox, Megan, 217
Fox, Michael J., 109
Franco, James, 210
Freeman, Martin, 236
Freeman, Morgan, 174, 240
Freeman, Paul, 73
Freudian, 68, 150, 167, 244
Friedkin, William M., 65
Frozen, 37, 249, **253–257**, 288
Furlong, Edward, 153

Gad, Josh, 253
Gadot, Gal, 280
Gaier, Dana, 245
Garr, Teri, 104
Geertz, Clifford, 3
Gender: identity, 36, 63, 104, 107, 125, 228, 261, 277–278; relations and roles, 82–83, 87, 155, 191, 224, 248, 256–257, 283
Generation X, 109–168; time frame and definition, xvii, 37
Generation Z, 231–289; time frame and definition, xvii
Ghostbusters, 69, 107, **129–133**
Gibson, Tyrese, 217, 253
Gleeson, Domhnall, 276
Globalization, xiii, 141, 200, 214
Glover, Crispin, 109
Goff, Jonathan, 253
Goldblum, Jeff, 138, 141
Goodwin, Ginnifer, 284
Gordon-Levitt, Joseph, 240, 262
Gould, Alexander, 181
Grease, 37, **69–73**, 100
Greatest Generation, 58, 65, 73, 79, 97, 98, 103, 107, 124, 138–139, 150, 226, 232, 234; time frame and definition, xvi–xvii

Greene, Ashely, 221
Gregg, Clark, 231
Grint, Rupert, 185
Guinness, Alec, 96, 150
Gulf War. *See* Iraq War
Gurira, Danai, 236
Gyllenhaal, Maggie, 173

Hackman, Gene, 88, 100
Hamill, Mark, 96, 148, 276
Hamilton, Linda, 153
Hanks, Tom, 125–126, 165–166
Happy Days, 70–71, 86, 92
Hardwicke, Catherine, 221
Hardy, Tom, 240
Harrelson, Woody, 257
Harris, Naomie, 270
Harris, Richard, 185
Harris, Rosemary, 210
Harry Potter and the Chamber of Secret, 37, 133, 137, **185–189**, 258, 261
Harry Potter and the Philosopher's Stone, 37, 133, 137, **185–189**, 258, 261, 288
Hathaway, Anne, 240
Heard, John, 133
Hemsworth, Chris, 231
Henry, Justin, 80
Hiddleston, Tom, 231
Higgins, Colin, 84
Hinduism, 44, 56, 59, 235
Hirsch, Judd, 138
Hoffman, Dustin, 80, 101, 104
Hollywood: history and periods, 30–38; studio system, 12, 15–17, 20, 31–35, 87, 144
The Holocaust, 115, 207, 226
Home Alone, xvi, **133–137**, 185
Howard, Ron, 70,
Howard, Terrence, 190
Hudson, Ernie, 129
Hunger Games, 18, 225, **257–262**
Hurt, John, 53
Hussein, Saddam, 119
Hutcherson, Josh, 257

Inception, **262–265**
Independence Day, 95, 125, **138–141**, 145, 164, 197
Indiana Jones and Raiders of the Lost Ark, 60, 64, **73–76**, 80, 100, 153, 192, 197, 279
Iraq War, 119, 129, 139, 147, 214, 232–233

Iron Man, 164, **190–193**, 211, 213, 221, 231, 236, 239
Irons, Jeremy, 145
Isaac, Oscar, 276
Islam, 44, 65, 189, 215

Jackman, Hugh, 225
Jackson, Peter, 194
Jackson, Samuel L., 192, 213, 231
Janssen, Famke, 225
Jaws, xvi, xvii, 35–37, 57, 60, 61, 64, 65, 69, **76–80**, 137, 145
Jenkins, Patty, 280
Jenson, Vicky, 205
Johansson, Scarlett, 20, 231
John, Olivia Newton, 69
Johnson, Dwayne, 250
Joker, 91, 103, 117, 177, 244, **266–270**
Jones, James Earl, 99, 145
Jordan, Michael B., 236
Judaism, 41, 43, 76, 103, 115, 139, 209, 218, 228
Jung, Carl, 102
Jurassic Park, 35, 60, 61, 64, 76, 80, **141–145**, 166

Keaton, Michael, 113
Kelly, Moira, 145
Kendrick, Anna, 221
Kennedy, John F. *See* Presidents (U.S.)
Kennedy, Kathleen, 61
Kidder, Margot, 100
Kilmer, Val, 161
Kinnear, Rory, 270
Kleiser, Randal, 69
Knightly, Keira, 202
Korean War, 90
Kramer vs. Kramer, **80–84**, 104, 106

LaBeouf, Shia, 217
Lane, Nathan, 145
Lang, Stephen, 169
Lange, Jessica, 104
Lansbury, Angela, 88, 117
Las Vegas, 191
Lasseter, John, 165
Lauter, Taylor, 221
Lawrence, Jennifer, 257
Ledger, Heath, 173
Lee, Jennifer, 253
The Lion King, 122, **145–148**, 249, 257

Lithgow, John, 205
Lloyd, Christopher, 109
Lloyd, Jake, 213
London, 174, 186, 237, 250, 272, 281, 282
The Lord of the Rings: The Fellowship of the Ring, 189, **194–198**, 205, 221, 228
Los Angeles, xvi, 104, 156, 180, 223, 282, 287
Lucas, George, 96, 102, 152, 213

MacNaughton, Robert, 61
Maguire, Toby, 210
Main, Roderick, 40, 45
Maron, Marc, 266
Marquand, Richard, 148
The Matrix, 39, 197, **198–202**, 208, 209, 216, 221
Mayhew, Peter (Chewbacca), 96, 148, 279
McDonnell, Mary, 138
McGillis, Kelly, 161
McGregor, Ewan, 213
McKellen, Ian, 194, 225
Mendes, Sam, 270
Menzel, Idina, 253
Meredith, Burgess, 92
Middle East, 74, 110
Millennials, 169–229; time frame and definition, xvii, 37
Miller, Jason, 65
Minkoff, Rob, 145
Moore, Joel David, 169
Moore, Rich, 284
Moral Majority, 43, 72–73, 224–225
Morris, John, 165
Mortensen, Viggo, 194
Moss, Carrie-Anne, 198
Murphy, Cillian, 262
Murphy, Eddie, 122, 205, 285
Murray, Bill, 104, 129
Music, 47–48, 70–72, 86, 89, 127–129, 149, 165, 206, 214, 232, 246, 254
Myers, Mike, 205

NASA, 56, 63, 139, 232, 246
Native Americans, 33, 36, 59–60, 90–91, 94, 152, 170–171, 222–223, 281, 283
Nazis, 35, 61, 67–68, 70, 73–75, 97, 102–103, 115, 124, 151, 207, 214, 222, 232–234, 259, 279
Neeson, Liam, 213, 242
Neill, Sam, 141

New Age movement, 40, 43–48, 216
Newton-John, Olivia, 69
New York, xv, 66, 77–78, 104, 113, 127, 130–131, 156, 180, 211–213, 225–227, 232, 235
Nicholson, Jack, 88, 113
9/11 (September 11 attacks), 147, 172, 177, 189, 194, 196, 200, 205, 210, 212, 219, 225, 232–235, 240, 243, 270, 274–275
9 to 5, **84–88**
Nolan, Christopher, 240, 262, 274
Nuclear: energy, 232, 242–243; family, 106, 146, 167, 211, 252; weapons, 44, 99, 130, 132, 139–141, 144, 151, 154–156, 232–233, 235, 272–273
Nyong'o, Lupita, 236, 276

Obama, Michelle, 238
O'Hara, Catherine, 133
O'Hara, Paige, 117
Oil Crisis of 1973, 67, 72, 79, 94
Oldman, Gary, 174, 240
One Flew Over the Cuckoo's Nest, 37, **88–91**, 113, 117
Orbach, Jerry, 117
Orientalism, 276, 283
Oscars, 20, 59, 69, 80–82, 89, 91–92, 100, 104, 122, 125, 128, 144, 153, 157, 186, 205, 236, 270
Ouija board, 67

Page, Elliot, 262
Paltrow, Gwyneth, 190
Pantoliano, Joe, 198
Paranormal, 48–49
Paris, 131, 134–137
Parton, Dolly, 84
Patrick, Robert, 153
Pattinson, Robert, 221
Paxton, Bill, 156
Percy, Walker, xv–xvi
Pesci, Joe, 133
Pfeiffer, Michelle, 73
Philips, Todd, 266
Phoenix, Joaquin, 266
Pine, Chris, 280
Pirates of the Caribbean: The Curse of the Black Pearl, 197, **202–205**
Plato, 39–40, 50
Pollack, Sydney, 104

Portman, Natalie, 213
Presidents (U.S.): Biden, Joseph, 285; Bush, George, Sr., 141; Carter, Jimmy, 41, 55; Clinton, Bill, 214; Eisenhower, Dwight, 76, 103; Nixon, Richard, 128; Obama, Barack, 188, 285, 288; Reagan, Ronald, 63, 72, 84, 90, 110, 151, 217
Presley, Elvis, 127
Pryce, Jonathan, 202
Pullman, Bill, 138

Racism, 35, 140, 146, 261, 278, 283–284, 287
Radcliffe, Daniel, 185
Raimi, Sam, 210
Ramis, Harold, 129
Rating System, 42–43, 54, 66, 69, 77, 104, 152, 260, 286
Ratzenberger, John, 165
Reeve, Christopher, 100
Reeves, Keanu, 198
Reinhold, Judge, 122
Reitman, Ivan, 129
Renaud, Chris, 245
Renner, Jeremy, 231
Rhys-Davies, John, 73, 195
Ribisi, Giovanni, 169
Rocky, 15, 29, 36, 37, 60, **92–95**
Rodriguez, Michelle, 171, 177, 250
Rogoff, Irit. *See* Visual culture
Romjin, Rebecca, 225
Ross, Gary, 257
Ruffalo, Mark, 231
Rush, Geoffrey, 202
Russell, Kurt, 117, 250
Russo, Anthony, 231
Russo, Joe, 231

Sabella, Ernie, 145
Saldana, Zoe, 169, 202
Sampson, Will, 88
San Francisco, 88, 238
Saturday Night Fever, 69, 71
Saturday Night Live, 122, 206
Scheider, Roy, 76
Schwarzenegger, Arnold, 3, 153
Scientism, xviii, 59
Scott, Ridley, 53, 219
Scott, Tony, 161
Serkis, Andy, 194, 276

Sexuality, 82, 86, 104, 107, 121, 130, 147, 220, 227, 228, 283
Shakira, 284
Shaw, Robert, 76
Shawn, Wallace, 165
Shire, Talia, 92
Shrek, 36, 168, **205–209**, 249
Silent Generation, 135, 137, 226; time frame and definition, xvi–xvii
Simmons, J.K., 210, 284
Singer, Bryan, 225
Sinise, Gary, 125
Skerritt, Tom, 53, 161
Skyfall, **270–275**
Slate, Jenny, 284
Smith, Will, 138
Smoking, xv, 4, 7, 70, 84, 85, 89, 122, 140
Socialization, xvii, 3–13, 204
Soviet. *See* USSR
Space race: moon landing, 56, 246; shuttle program, 56, 63, 96
Spider-Man, **210–213**, 228
Spielberg, Steven, 29, 57, 61, 73, 76, 102, 141, 144, 218
Spirituality, xviii, 40–50, 59, 172, 201, 204, 215–216, 276–277
Stallone, Sylvester, 29, 92, 101
Stanton, Andrew, 181
Star Wars: A New Hope, 57, 60, 64, 76, 77, **96–100**, 112, 141, 148–153, 167, 214, 216, 217, 276, 279
Star Wars: Episode 1—The Phantom Menace, 100, 153, **213–217**
Star Wars: Return of the Jedi, 3–6, 76, 99, 100, 112, 141, **148–153**, 192, 213, 214, 216, 217, 279
Star Wars: The Force Awakens, 100, 153, 217, **276–280**
Statham, Jason, 250
Stephens, Mitchell, 12
Stern, Daniel, 133
Stewart, Kristen, 221
Stewart, Patrick, 225
Stiers, David Ogden, 117
Streaming services, 19–20
Streep, Meryl, 80
Sturm, Brian: story-listening model, 8–9
Suburban, 58, 64, 134, 136–137, 183–184, 245
Superman, **100–104**, 113, 200, 201, 232, 244, 284
Sutherland, Donald, 257
Sydow, Max von, 65

Tahir, Faran, 190
Tarantino, Quentin, 29, 30
Technology, 8, 10–12, 17, 19, 28, 31, 56, 134, 142, 144, 155, 174, 204, 233–235, 265, 271–272
Television, xvii, 15–25, 31, 64, 68, 70, 77, 96, 138, 265
Terminator 2: Judgment Day, 57, 95, **153–156**, 160, 173
Thewlis, David, 280
Thomas, Henry, 61
Thomas, Jonathan T., 145
Thompson, Lea, 109
Titanic, **156–160**, 169, 173, 264, 265
Tomlin, Lily, 84
Tootsie, 83, **104–108**, 133
Top Gun, 141, **161–164**, 172
Toy Story, 36, 122, 129, **165–168**, 184, 249, 257, 288
Transformers, **217–221**
Travolta, John, 69
Trousdale, Gary, 117
Truffaut, François, 57
Turturro, John, 217
Twain, Mark, xiv
Twilight, **221–225**

UFO, 57–61
The Ugly American, xiv, xv
Unkrich, Lee, 181
USSR, 55–56, 96–97, 109, 111, 151, 154, 157, 161–162

Vallé, Jacques, 58
Verbinski, Gore, 202
Vietnam War, 18, 22, 36, 56, 58, 64, 66, 70, 72, 76, 79, 86–87, 90, 94–96, 127–129, 139, 162–164, 202, 276
Virgin Mary, 63, 118–120
Visual culture, 28–30, 38

Wachowski, Lana, 198
Wachowski, Lily, 198
Walker, Paul, 177, 250
Wallace, Dee, 61
Wan, James, 250

War on Terror, 189, 233–235, 240, 243, 271, 274, 287
Washington, D.C., 27, 34, 66, 127
Watanabe, Ken, 262
Watergate, 72, 94–95
Watson, Emma, 185
Weathers, Carl, 60, 92
Weaver, Sigourney, 53, 169
Weaving, Hugo, 198
The Western, 30, 33, 73–75, 96–97, 99, 116, 125, 133, 164–168, 201, 202, 204
Whedon, Joss, 231
Whigham, Shea, 266
Whishaw, Ben, 270
White, Richard, 117
Williams, Billy Dee, 113, 150
Williams, Cindy, 70
Williamson, Mykelti, 125
Wilson, Thomas F., 109
Winfrey, Oprah, 238
Winkler, Henry, 70, 92
Winslet, Kate, 156
Wise, Kirk, 117
Wonder Woman, 87, 100, 104, 244, **280–284**
Working classes: blue collar, 55, 119, 124, 136, 256; white collar, 56
World War I, 281–283
World War II, 67–68, 73, 77, 79–80, 96–99, 102–103, 107, 114, 139, 150, 194, 227, 232, 234
World War III, 151, 154, 156, 163
Worthington, Sam, 169
Wright, Robin, 125
Wuhl, Robert, 113

X-Men, 100, 102, 103, 197, **225–229**

Young, Burt, 92
Yune, Rick, 177

Zane, Billy, 156
Zemeckis, Robert, 109, 125
Zootopia, 37, 73, 122, 184, **284–289**